FREE SPEECH AND THE POLITICS OF IDENTITY

FREE SPEECH AND THE POLITICS OF IDENTITY

DAVID A. J. RICHARDS

Edwin D. Webb Professor of Law
New York University

OXFORD
UNIVERSITY PRESS

OXFORD

UNIVERSITY PRESS

Great Clarendon Street, Oxford OX2 6DP

Oxford University Press is a department of the University of Oxford.
It furthers the University's objective of excellence in research, scholarship,
and education by publishing worldwide in

Oxford New York

Athens Auckland Bangkok Bogotá Buenos Aires Calcutta
Cape Town Chennai Dar es Salaam Delhi Florence Hong Kong Istanbul
Karachi Kuala Lumpur Madrid Melbourne Mexico City Mumbai
Nairobi Paris São Paulo Singapore Taipei Tokyo Toronto Warsaw
and associated companies in Berlin Ibadan

Oxford is a registered trade mark of Oxford University Press
in the UK and in certain other countries

Published in the United States
by Oxford University Press Inc., New York

© David A. J. Richards 1999

The moral rights of the author have been asserted

Database right Oxford University Press (maker)

First published 1999

British Library Cataloguing in Publication Data

Data available

Library of Congress Cataloging in Publication Data
Richards, David A. J.
Free speech and the politics of identity / David A. J. Richards
p. cm.
Includes bibliographical references.
1. Freedom of speech. 2. Identity. 3. Discrimination. I. Title.
K3254.R53 1999 342'.0853—dc21 99–047143

ISBN 0–19–829886–2

1 3 5 7 9 10 8 6 4 2

Typeset by Hope Services (Abingdon) Ltd.
Printed in Great Britain
on acid-free paper by
T. J. International Ltd.
Padstow, Cornwall

For Donald Levy

Acknowledgements

This book was researched and written during a sabbatical leave taken from the New York University School of Law during the academic year 1997–8 and summer of 1998, and revised for publication during the summer of 1999. Work during both the sabbatical leave and the associated summers was made possible by generous research grants from the New York University School of Law Filomen D'Agostino and Max E. Greenberg Faculty Research Fund. I am grateful as well to my colleagues and to my dean, John Sexton, for forging an academic culture of learning at the School of Law hospitable to scholarly work.

My thinking about the issue of this book has been stimulated over the years by conversations with my colleagues Anthony Amsterdam, Jerome Bruner, Peggy Davis, Norman Dorsen, Ronald Dworkin, Thomas Nagel, Burt Neuborne, and Lawrence Sager; and my understanding of comparative public law deepened by conversations with Stephen Holmes and by teaching several seminars with my colleague and friend Thomas M. Franck; my understanding of German constitutional law, in particular, was advanced by co-teaching one of these seminars with Visiting Professor at the School of Law, Dr Georg Nolte of the Max-Planck-Institute für ausländisches öffentliches Recht und Völkerrecht, Heidelberg, Germany. My thought about the issues of this book also much profited from discussions with the distinguished participants (both academics and constitutional judges) at the conference on constitutional jurisprudence, sponsored by the N.Y.U. School of Law, held at La Pietra, Florence, in the summer of 1998; I am grateful to all the participants and, in particular, to the chairs of the conference, my colleagues Ronald Dworkin, Thomas Nagel, and Lawrence Sager, and to my colleague Christopher Eisgruber, who planned the conference. Finally, I acknowledge with pleasure how much I have learned from recent conversations with Carol Gilligan in connection with a seminar we have co-taught (with Jerome Bruner) on gender issues in culture and law.

My work in revising the manuscript was greatly assisted by the anonymous readers (all four of them) of the work for Oxford University Press. It was their comments that clarified for me both the character of the argument of political theory I was making and the ways in which the argument would be advanced by addressing its interpretive and critical implications for the law of free speech and anti-discrimination as a topic of both comparative law (including the emerging law of the European Union) and public international law. I am grateful to all these readers for the stimulus of their comments, and to John Louth, my editor at Oxford University Press, for engaging such excellent readers and for his support of this project.

Work on revising the manuscript was enormously helped by the inspired excellence of the research assistance of Yuval Merin, a graduate student at the New York University School of Law. My secretary, Lynn Gilbert, also ably assisted me in preparing the work for publication.

I am grateful as well for the love and support of my sister and friend, Diane Rita Richards, and for the sustaining and creative love of Donald Levy.

David A. J. Richards

New York
June 1999

Contents

Table of Legislation   xi

Table of Cases   xiii

Chapter 1: Introduction and Methodology   1

Chapter 2: Free Speech and the Argument for Toleration   16

Utilitarian Models of Free Speech   16
Perfectionist Models of Free Speech   17
The Argument from Democracy   18
The Toleration Model of Free Speech   22

**Chapter 3: The Argument for Toleration and the Theory of
Structural Injustice**   36

Racism as a Constitutional Evil   36
The Constitutional Evil of Sexism   59
The Constitutional Evil of Homophobia   76
The Rationalization of Structural Injustice   105

Chapter 4: Free Speech as a Remedy for Structural Injustice: Racism   126

The American Perspective   127
Perspectives Under National and Regional Law in the Shadow of Weimar   150
German and French Law   161
European Court of Human Rights   165
Canadian Law   167
British and Israeli Law   171
The Perspective of Public International Law   176

**Chapter 5: Free Speech as a Remedy for Structural Injustice: Sexism
and Homophobia**   181

Obscenity Laws   182
Blasphemy Laws   209

**Chapter 6: The Scope and Limits of Free Speech and the Promise of
Comparative Public Law**   229

The Limits of the Principle of Free Speech   230
The Scope of the Principle of Free Speech   239
The Promise of Comparative Public Law   248

Bibliography   235

Index   275

Table of Legislation

Austrian Law no. 148, 1992 162
Basic Law of the Federal Republic of Germany.....................................1, 3, 30, 156
Canada, Criminal Code, sections 163, 181 and 319(2)...........167–8, 170, 199–200
Canadian Charter of Rights and Freedoms 1–2, 167
Convention on the Elimination of all Forms of Racial Discrimination
   of 1966 ....4–5, 80, 176, 213
European Convention on Human Rights 1, 3, 30, 87, 161, 165, 218
France, Article 24, of the French Law on the Press (since 1990) 162
Germany, Criminal Code, Articles 130, 185, and 194(1) 161
International Convenant on Civil and Political Rights.............................4–5, 212
Israel, Basic Law: The Knesset sec. 7(a), *amended* in Basic Law: The Knesset
   Amend. No. 9, 1155 Sefer Hahukim [S.H.] 196 (1985).................................175
Israel, Denial of Holocaust (Prohibition Law) 5746–1986......................162, 176
Israel, Knesset Election Law, 1969 sec. 63, 23 L.S.I.110 (consolidated
   version), *amended* in 1155 S.H. 196 (1985)...175
Israel, Penal Code Amendment Law (No. 2), 1986..175
South Africa Constitution (1996) 1, 3–4
Swiss Penal Code, Article 261 162
U.K. Public Order Act 1986, sections 17–28..4, 171
United States, Alien and Sedition Act of 1798 25
United States, Civil Rights Act of 1964 ....67–8, 75
United States, Federal Election Campaign Act 1971..230
United States Constitution 1, 9, 82–3, 89–90
United States, Religious Freedom Restoration Act of 1993, S. Rep. 111,
   103d Cong., 1st sess. 14 (1993) 90

Table of Cases

Canada

Attis v. *Board of School Trustees*, 1 Can. SCR 825 (1996) 170
Canada (Human Rights Commission) v. *Taylor*, 3 Can. SCR 892 (1990) 3
M v. *H.*, 1999 Can. Sup. Ct. Lexis 28 (20 May 1999)....................................227
R. v. *Andrews*, 3 Can. SCR 870 (1990) 3
R. v. *Butler*, 1 Can. SCR 452 (1992)..199–200
R. v. *Keegstra*, 3 Can. SCR 697 (1990)...............2–3, 167–8, 170, 177–8, 200, 205
R. v. *Mara*, 148 DLR 4th 75 (1997) 199
R. v. *Zundel*, 2 Can. SCR 731 (1992) 3, 170

England

R. v. *Chief Metropolitan Stipendiary Magistrate, ex parte Choudhury*
[1990] 3 WLR 986..215
R. v. *Birdwood*, Court of Appeal (Criminal Division), 11 April 1995,
LEXIS transcript no. 172
R. v. *Britton* [1967] 2 QB 51 172
Whitehouse v. *Lemon* [1979] AC 617 214–17

European Convention on Human Rights

Castells v. *Spain* (1992) 14 EHRR 445 (Ct.) 171
Dudgeon v. *The United Kingdom* (1992) 4 EHRR 149 (Ct.) 87, 227
Jersild v. *Denmark* (1995) 19 EHRR 1 (Ct.) 3, 171, 239
Otto-Preminger-Institut v. *Austria* (1995) 19 EHRR 34 (Ct.) 165, 210, 215
Choudhury v. *The United Kingdom*, Application No. 17439/1990,
12 *Hum. Rt. LJ* 172 (Comm.)..215
Gay News v. *United Kingdom* (1983) 5 EHRR 123
(Comm.)..214–17, 223–4, 226

Germany

Abortion I Case (1975) 39 BVerfGE 1..32
Abortion II Case (1993) 88 BVerfGE 203 32
Historical Fabrication Case (1994) 90 BVerfGE 1 ....3, 161
Holocaust Denial Case (1994) 90 BVerfGE 241 ....3, 161
Lebach Case (1973) 35 BVerfGE 202..230

Mephisto Case (1971) 30 BVerfGE 173...30
Princess Soraya Case (1973) 34 BVerfGE 269..32
Schleyer Kidnapping Case (1977) 46 BVerfGE 160 32
Street Theatre Case (1984) 67 BVerfGE 213 30

Hungary

Decision No. 30/1992(V.18) AB, Constitutional Court of the
Republic of Hungary 5

Israel

Meir Kahane v. *The Broadcasting Authority* 41(3) PD 225 (1987) 171, 239

United States

Abington School Dist. v. *Schempp*, 374 US 203 (1963)....................................91, 184
Abrams v. *United States*, 250 US 616 (1919)..16, 27, 196
American Booksellers Ass'n v. *Hudnut*, 771 F 2d 323 (7th Cir. 1985)
aff'd, 475 US 1001 (1986) 199
Austin v. *Michigan Chamber of Commerce*, 494 US 652 (1990) 231
Baker v. *Carr*, 369 US 186 (1962) 232
Beauharnais v. *Illinois*, 343 US 250 (1952) 134, 204
Bond v. *Floyd*, 385 US 116 (1966) 17
Bowers v. *Hardwick*, 478 US 186 (1986)...........36, 60, 81, 87–8, 98–100, 114, 227
Brandenburg v. *Ohio*, 395 US 444 (1969)..................................26, 134, 149, 196
Brown v. *Board of Education*, 347 US 483 (1954) 36–7, 40–1, 56, 69, 147
Brown v. *Louisiana*, 383 US 131 (1966) 197
Buckley v. *Valeo*, 424 US 1 (1976) 19–20, 230–1, 234–8
Burstyn v. *Wilson*, 343 US 495 (1952) 209
Califano v. *Goldfarb*, 430 US 199 (1977)...75
Chaplinsky v. *New Hampshire*, 315 US 568 (1942) 29, 172
Church of the Lukumi Babalu Ave, Inc. v. *City of Hialeah*, 508 US 520 (1993)......90
City of Boerne v. *P. F. Flores*, 117 S. Ct. 2157 (1997) 90
Collin v. *Smith*, 578 F 2d 1197 (1978), *cert. den.*,
439 US 916 (1978)..26, 134, 149
Committee for the First Amendment v. *John Campbell*, 962 F 2d 1516
(10th Cir. 1992) 224
Cox Broadcasting Corp. v. *Cohn*, 420 US 469 (1975)..230
Cox v. *Louisiana*, 379 US 536 (1965) 196–7
Craig v. *Boren*, 429 US 190 (1976)...............................36, 40, 60, 71, 76, 97–8
Cruzan v. *Director, Missouri Dept. of Health*, 496 US 261 (1990) 81

Cummins v. *Campbell*, 44 F 3d 847 (10th Cir. 1994) 224

Debs v. *United States*, 249 US 211 (1919) 27

De Jonge v. *Oregon*, 299 US 353 (1937) 196

Dennis v. *United States*, 341 US 494 (1951) 196

Dred Scott v. *Sanford*, 19 How. 393 (1857) 151

Edwards v. *Aguillard*, 482 US 578 (1987) 91

Edwards v. *South Carolina*, 372 US 229 (1963) 144, 172, 196

Eisenstadt v. *Baird*, 405 US 438 (1972) 97

Employment Division, Dept. of Human Resources v. *Smith*,
   494 US 872 (1990) 89–91

Engel v. *Vitale*, 370 US 421 (1962) 91, 184

Epperson v. *Arkansas*, 393 US 97 (1968) 91, 184

FEC v. *National Right to Work Committee*, 459 US 197 (1982) 231

FEC v. *Massachusetts Citizens for Life*, 479 US 238 (1986) 231

Feiner v. *New York*, 340 US 315 (1951) 144, 172

First National Bank of Boston v. *Bellotti*, 435 US 765 (1978) 231, 234

Fiske v. *Kansas*, 274 US 380 (1927) 196

Florida Star v. *B.J.F.*, 491 US 524 (1989) 230

Frontiero v. *Richardson*, 411 US 677 (1973) 36, 40, 60, 71, 97–8

Geduldig v. *Aiello*, 417 US 484 (1974) 75

General Electric Co. v. *Gilbert*, 429 US 125 (1976) 75

Gertz v. *Robert Welch, Inc.*, 318 US 323 (1974) 26

Gillette v. *United States*, 401 US 437 (1970) 184

Gitlow v. *New York*, 268 US 652 (1925) 16, 49, 186

Gooding v. *Wilson*, 405 US 518 (1972) 26, 29, 172

Griswold v. *Connecticut*, 381 US 479 (1965) 81, 83, 87, 97

Harper v. *Virginia Board of Elections*, 383 US 663 (1966) 232

Herndon v. *Lowry*, 301 US 242 (1937) 196

Hurley v. *Irish-American Gay, Lesbian and Bisexual Group of Boston (GLIB)*,
   115 S Ct. 2338 (1995) 239, 242

Hustler Magazine v. *Falwell*, 485 US 46 (1988) 30

International Union et al. v. *Johnson Controls, Inc.*, 499 US 187 (1991) 75

Jones v. *Alfred H. Mayer Co.*, 392 US 409 (1968) 73

Katzenbach v. *Morgan*, 384 US 641 (1966) 90

Kramer v. *Union Free School District No. 15*, 395 US 621 (1969) 232

Lee v. *Weisman*, 505 US 577 (1992) 91

Lochner v. *New York*, 198 US 45 (1905) 234

Loving v. *Virginia*, 388 US 1 (1967) 56, 101

McCollum v. *Board of Education*, 333 US 203 (1948) 184

McLaughlin v. *Florida*, 379 US 184 (1964) 56

Memoirs v. *Massachusetts*, 383 US 413 (1966) 198

Michael M. v. *Superior Court*, 450 US 464 (1981) 60, 75

Miller v. *California*, 413 US 15 (1973) 26, 198

Mississippi University for Women v. *Hogan*, 458 US 718 (1982) 185
Nashville Gas Co. v. *Satty*, 434 US 136 (1977)...75
New York Times Co. v. *Sullivan*, 376 US 254 (1964) 28, 196, 231, 236
Noto v. *United States*, 367 US 290 (1961)...196
Ollman v. *Evans*, 750 F 2d 970 (DC Cir. 1984) 20
Oregon v. *Mitchell*, 400 US 112 (1970)..90
Pace v. *Alabama*, 106 US 583 (1863)..42, 48–9, 56
Palmore v. *Sidoti*, 466 US 429 (1984) 40
Paris Adult Theatre I v. *Slaton*, 413 US 49 (1973)...198
People v. *Liberta*, 64 NY 2d 152, 474 NE 2d 567 (NY Ct. App. 1984).............118
Planned Parenthood of Southeastern Pennsylvania v. *Casey*,
     112 S Ct. 2791 (1992)...60, 81
Plessy v. *Ferguson*, 163 US 537 (1896)..42, 48–55
R.A.V. v. *City of St. Paul*, 505 US 377 (1992)...134, 148
Red Lion Broadcasting Co. v. *FCC*, 395 US 367 (1969) 232
Redrup v. *New York*, 386 US 767 (1967) 198
Reed v. *Reed*, 404 US 71 (1971) 60, 69, 75, 98
Reynolds v. *Sims*, 377 US 533 (1964) 232
Roe v. *Wade*, 410 US 113 (1973) 60, 81, 87
Romer v. *Evans*, 116 S. Ct. 1620 (1996) 36–7, 93, 124, 228
Rostker v. *Goldberg*, 453 US 57 (1981) 60
Roth v. *United States, Alberts* v. *California*, 354 US 476 (1957)..........................197
Runyon v. *McCrary*, 427 US 160 (1976) 73
Scales v. *United States*, 367 US 203 (1961)..196
Sherbert v. *Verner*, 374 US 398 (1963)..89
Shuttlesworth v. *Birmingham*, 394 US 147 (1969)...197
South Carolina v. *Katzenbach*, 383 US 301 (1956)..90
Stanton v. *Stanton*, 421 US 7 (1975)..75, 98
Street v. *New York*, 394 US 576 (1969)..197
Sullivan v. *Little Hunting Park, Inc.*, 396 US 229 (1969) 73
Sweatt v. *Painter*, 339 US 629 (1950) 60, 186
Torcaso v. *Watkins*, 367 US 488 (1960) 90, 184
United States RR Retirement Bd. v. *Fritz*, 449 US 166 (1980)................................40
United States v. *Ballard*, 322 US 78 (1944)..90, 94, 184
United States v. *Seeger*, 380 US 163 (1965) 90, 184
United States v. *Virginia*, 116 S. Ct. 2264 (1996)...............................36, 60, 186
Vacco v. *Quill*, 117 S. Ct. 2293 (1997) 81
Virginia Pharmacy Board v. *Virginia Consumer Council*, 425 US 748 (1976).........26
Wallace v. *Jaffree*, 472 US 38 (1985)..91
Watts v. *United States*, 394 US 705 (1969) 17
Weinberger v. *Weisenfeld*, 420 US 636 (1975) 75
Welsh v. *United States*, 398 US 333 (1970) 90, 184
Wengler v. *Druggists Mutual Insurance Co.*, 446 US 142 (1980) 75–6, 98

Whitney v. *California*, 274 US 357 (1927) 196
Williamson v. *Lee Optical*, 348 US 483 (1965) 40
Wisconsin v. *Yoder*, 406 US 205 (1972) 89
Yates v. *United States*, 354 US 298 (1957) 196
Zorach v. *Clauson*, 343 US 306 (1952) 184

'But where is the philosophy or statesmanship which assumes that you can quiet the disturbing element in our society which has disturbed us for more than half a century, which has been the only serious danger that has threatened our institutions—I say, where is the philosophy or statesmanship based on the assumption that we are to quit talking about it, and that the public mind is all at once to cease being agitated by it . . . I ask you if it is not a false philosophy? Is it not a false statesmanship that undertakes to build up a system or policy upon the basis of caring nothing about *the very thing that every body does care the most about?*—a thing which all experience has shown we care a very great deal about?'

Abraham Lincoln, in Robert W. Johannsen (ed.), *The Lincoln–Douglas Debates* (Oxford University Press, New York, 1965), at 315.

1

Introduction and Methodology

The theory of free speech is a natural subject of interdisciplinary and comparative study for both political philosophers and lawyers. First, it has a highly abstract component, in which issues of general normative philosophy are at stake (for example, competing arguments of utilitarian or perfectionist teleological consequentialism versus those of deontological natural rights); secondly, it has a historical and contextual component, in which free speech is embedded in a historically evolving tradition of constitutional thought, including both political and legal arguments made over time about its proper meaning. The balance between these two components (political theory and interpretive history) takes a different form in various legal systems, all of which are committed in some form to free speech. Nations with written constitutions and judicial review (the United States, Canada, Germany, South Africa, and the nations governed by the European Convention on Human Rights) give a different institutional expression to abstract normative argument from a nation like Britain, in which free speech is a principle of common law in light of which supreme parliamentary law is interpreted;[1] and those nations with long traditions of judicial review under written constitutions with highly abstract language (like the United States) refer more often to both abstract arguments of political theory and the long history of their interpretive experience than nations (such as Germany) with relatively recent post-Second World War written constitutions (with U.S.-style judicial review) in which guarantees have been drafted in somewhat more specific terms[2] and against the historical background of the political horrors wrought by fascism. The two components of the study of free speech will accordingly interact in different ways depending on such distinctions. Nations, all of whom acknowledge free speech as a basic human and constitutionally protected right, correspondingly give different weights to these components, consequently diverging and sometimes converging in the scope and limits accorded free speech as a basic constitutional value.

---

[1] For a good treatment of this question, with specific focus on the British law of free speech, see Eric Barendt, *Freedom of Speech* (Clarendon Press, Oxford, 1985). In addition to its own common law of free speech, Great Britain is a signatory to the European Convention on Human Rights and, to the extent required by the Convention, is governed by its written guarantees and interpretive institutions. See, in general, Mark W. Janis and Richard S. Kay, *European Human Rights Law* (University of Connecticut Law School Foundation Press, Hartford, Conn., 1990).

[2] e.g. Art. 5 of the German Basic Law textually distinguishes freedom of speech and of the press (in Art. 5(1)) from freedom of art, research, and teaching (in Art. 5(2)), imposing specific textual limitations on the former (in Art. 5(3)), but no such limitations on the latter. See Selected Provisions of the Basic Law in Donald P. Kommers, *The Constitutional Jurisprudence of the Federal Republic of Germany* (2nd edn., Duke University Press, Durham, NC, 1997), at 507–8. In contrast, Art. 10 of the European Convention on Human Rights provides a general guarantee of the right to freedom of expression (in Art. 10(1)), subject to general restrictions applicable to this right in general (in Art. 10(2)). See Janis and Kay, *European Human Rights Law*, n. 1 above, p. xx.

This work addresses both components of the theory of free speech from an American constitutional perspective on the role political theory should play in the interpretation and critical evaluation of these issues. In the course of my argument, I will thus state and criticize several general normative theories of free speech (namely, utilitarian and perfectionist consequentalism and the argument from democracy), and then present a third view (free speech as toleration), and discuss its substantial merits both as political theory and an account of America's historically continuous interpretive experience. I bring the force of my argument into sharper focus in the form of a defence of three of American constitutionalism's quite distinctive views (namely, that the principle of free speech renders group libel laws problematic, and related constitutional scepticism about laws condemning obscene materials and blasphemy) and a criticism of another American view (namely, that the principle of free speech forbids reasonable regulations of the funding of political campaigns).

My account is thus by no means defensive of all current American judicially enforceable views of principles of free speech, but it is concerned to defend certain of them both against the different views taken in other nations (committed as well to principles of free speech) and, in particular, against recent American doubts expressed usually from the political left. These doubts take the following form. There is a tension between American principles of free speech (as currently understood) and principles condemning the political expression of irrational prejudice (racism, sexism, and homophobia). In particular, current constitutional scepticism about laws protecting groups from communicative insults to their group identity illegitimately advances irrational prejudice for reasons of free speech that are without merit.[3] Indeed, in one form of the argument, the very integrity of principles of anti-discrimination is said to require the constitutionality of group libel laws, because these principles themselves condemn, for example, state-sponsored apartheid as a form of constitutionally unjust group libel.[4]

The constitutional defence of such laws in other nations takes a strikingly similar form. For example, such nations with written constitutions and judicial review appeal, in defence of such laws, to the structure of limitation clauses that balance the right of free speech against other important rights (including the right against unjust discrimination). The general limitation clause in section 1 of the Canadian Charter thus stipulates that the rights and freedoms contained therein (including free speech) are guaranteed 'subject only to such reasonable limits prescribed by law as can be demonstrably justified in a free and democratic society';[5] in the leading case, *R. v. Keegstra*, the Supreme Court of Canada found a criminal statute, prohibiting hate

---

[3] See, for a useful compendium of such recent arguments, Mari J. Matsuda, Charles R. Lawrence III, Richard Delgado, and Kimberlè Williams Crenshaw, *Words That Wound: Critical Race Theory, Assaultive Speech, and the First Amendment* (Westview Press, Boulder, Conn., 1993); see also David S. Allen and Robert Jensen (eds.), *Freeing the First Amendment: Critical Perspectives on Freedom of Expression* (New York University Press, New York, 1995).

[4] See Charles R. Lawrence III, 'If He Hollers Let Him Go: Regulating Racist Speech on Campus', in Matsuda *et al.*, *Words That Wound*, n. 3 above, at 53–88.

[5] S. 1, Canadian Charter of Rights and Freedoms.

speech against groups subject to unjust prejudice, to be such a reasonable limit in advancing equal respect for such groups.[6] The German Basic Law similarly stipulates that the rights of free speech and press 'are limited by the provisions of the general laws, the provisions of law for the protection of youth, and by the right to inviolability of personal honour';[7] the German Constitutional Court found the prohibition of a public meeting to hear a revisionist historian deny the Holocaust ever happened to be justified as reasonably protecting the honour of a group from demonstrably false facts.[8] Similarly, the wording of the limitation clauses attached to the different rights contained in the European Convention on the Protection of Human Rights and Fundamental Freedoms follow a basic formula: '[s]ubject to such formalities, conditions, restrictions or penalties as are prescribed by law and are necessary in a democratic society, in the interests of national security, territorial integrity or public safety, for the prevention of disorder or crime, for the protection of health or morals, for the protection of the reputation or rights of others, for preventing the disclosure of information received in confidence, or for maintaining the authority and impartiality of the judiciary';[9] the European Commission of Human Rights has appealed to this limitation in upholding constraints on hate speech applied to the speakers themselves[10] (their application to reporters of such speech has called, however, in the view of the European Court of Human Rights, for a different result[11]). The 1996 Constitution of South Africa similarly provides that 'rights in the Bill of Rights may be limited only in terms of law of general application to the extent that the limitation is reasonable and justifiable in an open and democratic society based on human dignity, equality

---

[6] *R.* v. *Keegstra,* 3 Can. SCR 697 (1990). See also *R.* v. *Andrews,* 3 Can. SCR 870 (1990) (criminal statute, forbidding hate speech, constitutional); *Canada (Human Rights Commission)* v. *Taylor,* 3 Can. SCR 892 (1990) (federal human rights legislation, prohibiting telephonic messages likely to expose a person or group to hatred, held constitutional). But see *R.* v. *Zundel,* 2 Can. SCR 731 (1992) (criminal statute forbidding publication of false news found unconstitutionally vague as applied to Holocaust denial).

[7] S. 5(2), Selected Provisions of the Basic Law, in Kommers, n. 2 above, at 508.

[8] See *Holocaust Denial Case* (1994) 90 BVerfGE 241, translated in *ibid.,* at 382–7. But see *Historical Fabrication* case (1994) 90 BVerfGE 1 (historical claim that Germany not responsible for the Second World War was, as interpretive opinion, constitutionally protected, and thus could not listed among books not to be distributed to youth or generally advertised), discussed at *ibid.,* 387–8. For discussion of cases of this sort under German constitutional law, see Rainer Hoffman, 'Incitement to National and Racial Hatred: The Legal Situation in Germany', in Sandra Coliver (ed.), *Striking a Balance: Hate Speech, Freedom of Expression and Non-discrimination* (Article 19, International Centre Against Censorship, London, and Human Rights Centre, University of Essex, 1992), at 159–70.

[9] Art. 10(2) (qualifying guarantee of freedom of expression in Art. 10(1)), European Convention, reprinted in Janis and Kay, n. 1 above, at p. xx.

[10] See, for discussion of four pertinent cases, Danilo Turk and Louis Joinet, 'The Right to Freedom of Opinion and Expression', in Sandra Coliver (ed.), *Striking a Balance: Hate Speech, Freedom of Expression and Non-discrimination* (Article IX, London, 1992), 35–54 at 46–8; see also Stephanie Farrior, 'Molding the Matrix: The Historical and Theoretical Foundations of International Law Concerning Hate Speech', 14 *Berkeley J. of International Law* 3, 65–8 (1996).

[11] See the decision of the European Court of Human Rights in *Jersild* v. *Denmark* (1995) 19 EHRR 1 (Ct.) (1994) (criminal prosecution of journalist, who conducted a television interview of group who made derogatory remarks about immigrants and ethnic groups, for aiding and abetting dissemination of racist remarks, held unconstitutional); for commentary, see Lene Johannessen, 'Denmark: Racist Snakes in the Danish Paradise', in Coliver (ed.), n. 10 above, 140–3; see also Farrior, n. 10 above, 68–72.

and freedom';[12] constitutionally protected hate speech, not otherwise expressly deemed unprotected,[13] might arguably be subject to limitation on such grounds.[14]

Constitutional democracies without written constitutions justify such laws in a similar way. Great Britain's current hate speech law, the Public Order Act,[15] has been justified as striking a reasonable balance between the right of free speech and the right of minority groups to be free of unjust prejudice,[16] a view followed by New Zealand in adopting its comparable criminal legislation.[17] Israel, as a response to the growing importance of the racist appeals of Rabbi Meir Kahane in its politics, strengthened its laws against hate speech in order to make what was taken to be the reasonable educational statement about the reasonable balance in a constitutional democracy between the right of free speech and the right to be free from unjust discrimination.[18]

The putative constitutional legitimacy of these laws has been importantly influenced by developments in public international law in the wake of the Second World War, most notably the UN Convention on the Elimination of all Forms of Racial Discrimination of 1966, entering into force in 1969.[19] Inspired by anti-Semitic incidents in several parts of the world in 1959 and 1960,[20] the Convention goes further than the International Covenant on Civil and Political Rights, which states that 'any

---

[12] S. 36(1), 1996 Constitution, reprinted in Dennis Davis, Halton Cheadle, and Nicholas Haysom, *Fundamental Rights in the Constitution* (Juta and Co., Kenwyn, 1997), at 303.

[13] The general constitutional protection of free speech in s. 16(1) does not, under s. 16(2), extend, *inter alia*, to 'advocacy of hatred that is based on race, ethnicity, gender or religion, and that constitutes incitement to cause harm', reprinted at *ibid.*, 111.

[14] For commentary, see Davis *et al.*, n. 12 above, at 119–20. For the prior use of hate speech laws in South Africa, see Gilbert J. Marcus, 'Racial Hostility: The South African Experience', in Coliver (ed.), n. 10 above, at 208–22; for critical explorations of whether such laws have a legitimate policy role to play in the new South Africa, see Lene Johannessen, 'Should Censorship of Racist Publications Have a Place in the New South Africa?', in *ibid.*, 223–37; Eric Neisser, 'Hate Speech in the New South Africa: Constitutional Considerations for a Land Recovering from Decades of Racial Repression', 3 *DCLJ of Int'l L. & Prac.* 335 (1994).

[15] See Public Order Act, 1986, ss. 17–28 (U.K.).

[16] See, for illuminating discussion and criticism, Eric Barendt, *Freedom of Speech* (Oxford, Clarendon Press, 1985), at 161–7; Anthony Lester and Geoffrey Bindman, *Race and Law in Great Britain* (Harvard University Press, Cambridge, Mass., 1972), at 343–81; Kenneth Lasson, 'Racism in Great Britain: Drawing the Line on Free Speech', 7 *Boston College Third World LJ* 161 (1987); W. J. Wolffe, 'Values in Conflict: Incitement to Racial Hatred and the Public Order Act 1986', [1987] *Public Law*, 85; Stephen J. Roth, 'Curbing Racial Incitement in Britain: Four Times Tried—Still Without Success' (1992) 22 *Israel Yearbook on Human Rights*, 193–228.

[17] See William C. Hodge, 'Incitement to Racial Hatred in New Zealand', 30 *Int'l & Comparative Law Quarterly* 918 (1981).

[18] See Eliezer Lederman and Mala Tabory, 'Criminalization of Racial Incitement in Israel', 24 *Stanford J of International Law* 55 (1988); Mala Tabory, 'Legislation against Incitement to Racism in Israel', (1987) 17 *Israel Yearbook on Human Rights* 270–99; David Kretzmer, 'Racial Incitement in Israel' (1992) 22 *Israel Yearbook on Human Rights* 243–59. See, for an illuminating general study, Raphael Cohen-Almagor, *The Boundaries of Liberty and Tolerance: The Struggle Against Kahanism in Israel* (University Press of Florida, Gainesville, Flo., 1994).

[19] See, in general, Natan Lerner, *The U.N. Convention on the Elimination of all Forms of Racial Discrimination* (Sijthoff & Noordhoff International Publishers, Alphen aan den Rijn, 1980); Natan Lerner, *Group Rights and Discrimination in International Law* (Martinus Nijhoff Publishers, Dordrecht, 1991).

[20] See Lerner, n. 19 above, 1.

advocacy of national, racial or religious hatred that constitutes incitement to discrimination, hostility or violence shall be prohibited by law'.[21] Article 4 of the Convention confers more expansive authority in the following terms:

States Parties condemn all propaganda and all organizations which are based on ideas or theories of superiority of one race or group of persons of one colour or ethnic origin, or which attempt to justify or promote racial hatred and discrimination in any form, and undertake to adopt immediate and positive measures designed to eradicate all incitement to, or acts of, such discrimination, and to this end, with due regard to the principles embodied in the Universal Declaration of Human Rights and the rights expressly set forth in Article 5 of this Convention, *inter alia*:

(a) Shall declare an offence punishable by law all dissemination of ideas based on racial superiority or hatred, incitement to racial discrimination, as well as all acts of violence or incitement to such acts against any race or group of other persons of another colour or ethnic origin, and also the provision of any assistance to racist activities, including the financing thereof;

(b) Shall declare illegal and prohibit organizations, and also organized and all other propaganda activities, which promote and incite racial discrimination, and shall recognize participation in such organizations or activities as an offence punishable by law;

(c) Shall not permit public authorities or public institutions, national or local, to promote or incite racial discrimination.[22]

To offer only one recent example of the impact of the Convention on the constitutional interpretation of hate speech laws, the Hungarian Constitutional Court in 1992 upheld the constitutionality of a criminal law against hate speech (though disallowing a related law against offensive speech), appealing, *inter alia*, to the international obligations incumbent on Hungary under the Convention.[23] The United States ratified the Convention in 1994, after signing it in 1966, but with substantial reservations to leave unaffected present United States law regarding hate speech.[24] Most other nations, in contrast, frame their constitutional discussions within the terms of the Convention, underwriting its putative normative claims that policies to realize the right against unjust discrimination reasonably require hate speech laws.

[21] See *ibid.*, 52–3. See, for pertinent commentary on the requirements of these and other international conventions, Louis Henkin, 'Group Defamation and International Law', in Monroe H. Freedman and Eric M. Freedman (eds.), *Group Defamation and Freedom of Speech: The Relationship Between Language and Violence* (Greenwood Press, Westport, Conn., 1995), at 123–34.

[22] See Lerner, n. 19 above, 43.

[23] See Decision No. 30/1992(V.18) AB, Constitutional Court of the Republic Hungary, in (1995) 2 East European Case Reporter of Constitutional Law, at 8–26; for commentary, see Andras Sajo, 'Hate Speech for Hostile Hungarians' (1994) 3 *East European Constitutional Law* 82–7.

[24] On these points, see Louis Henkin, 'US Ratification of the Human Rights Conventions: The Ghost of Senator Bricker' (1995) 89 *AJIL* 341; Henry J. Richardson, III, '"Failed States", Self-Determination, and Preventive Diplomacy: Colonialist Nostalgia and Democratic Expectations', 10 *Temp. Int'l Comp. LJ* 1, at 23 (1996); David Sloss, 'The Domestication of International Human Rights: Non-Self-Executing Declarations and Human Rights Treaties', 24 *Yale J. Int'l L.* 129, at 139 n. 35 (1999).

Responses to these claims in the United States usually argue from the perspective of defensible principles of free speech.[25] I agree with many of these arguments, and will support many of them in the work that follows. But such arguments can only be appreciated in their full and proper force if they are integrated structurally with a larger understanding of their important place and role in the understanding of anti-discrimination principles themselves. The interest of the recent doubts about the current state of the American law of free speech is that they argue, like the related legal developments in other nations and under public international law, from the perspective of better advancing the right against unjust discrimination. We should not underestimate the dimensions that this challenge represents in the United States to a reasonable interpretive consensus that had been painfully achieved through the experience of the common grounds in the struggle for respect for civil liberties and against racism, a consensus brilliantly stated as a precious doctrinal legacy to posterity by Harry Kalven, Jr.[26] If the challenge is to be met, it must be met in the terms of the consensus it challenges, which is as much an interpretive issue of principle about the evil of racism (and sexism and homophobia) as an issue of free speech. The argument of this book arises as much from a concern about compromising principles of anti-discrimination as principles of free speech. Much of the recent American critical literature, like the related national and international discourse about striking a balance between the right of free speech and the right against unjust discrimination, assume that both the understanding and implementation of these rights can reasonably be treated as separate questions. But the questions, if I am right, are structurally connected. To see this, we must interrogate both the state of current free speech theory and the theory of anti-discrimination. This book does both.

The problem in free speech theory arises, I believe, from the uncritical allegiance of recent academic free speech theory to the argument from democracy.[27] On this view, both the purposes and scope of free speech must be understood as in service of political democracy. It is from this vantage point that neither restrictions on group libel nor those on campaign expenditures are regarded as raising free speech issues. The inference runs as follows: free speech advances democracy; group libel or campaign finance laws advance democracy; therefore, group libel and campaign finance laws do not raise free speech issues. Now, it must be obvious that much of the argument here rides on what counts as democracy, a contestable concept if there ever was one; for example, the argument for democracy can, depending on your view of democracy, be as plausibly used against as for the constitutionality of campaign

---

[25] See, for a compendium of such arguments, Henry Louis Gates, Jr., Anthony P. Griffin, Donald E. Lively, Robert C. Post, William B. Rubenstein, and Nadine Strossen, *Speaking of Race, Speaking of Sex: Hate Speech, Civil Rights, and Civil Liberties* (New York University Press: New York, 1994).

[26] See Harry Kalven, Jr., *The Negro and the First Amendment* (University of Chicago Press, Chicago, Ill., 1965).

[27] For two recent notable examples, see Cass R. Sunstein, *Democracy and the Problem of Free Speech* (Free Press, New York, 1993); Owen M. Fiss, *The Irony of Free Speech: Liberalism Divided* (Harvard University Press, Cambridge, Mass., 1996); Owen M. Fiss, *Liberalism Divided: Freedom of Speech and the Many Uses of State Power* (Westview Press, Boulder, Colo., 1996).

finance laws. In order to understand the implications of the theory for free speech, much will turn on how richly or thinly the concept is parsed. One area of ongoing controversy (free speech) is thus analysed in terms of another area (democracy) that is even more controversial, a feature of the argument from democracy that does not bode well for its critical power as an account of the legitimate role principles of free speech must play in limiting the scope of democratic politics. Where a good theory of free speech would underscore the tension between free speech and democracy, this theory eliminates the tension without any sense of loss. If the argument from democracy is as inadequate an account of free speech as I shall argue it is, we will have to take seriously, in a way the argument from democracy does not, the independent values served by free speech, against which the legitimacy of democratic politics must be assessed.

To do so, we (both lawyers and citizens) must address basic issues of political theory about the legitimate powers of just government, which encompasses both principles of free speech and of anti-discrimination. This book is very much an essay in political theory, one which integrates, in a common conception, both these principles, now universally acknowledged as normatively appealing. If my argument of political theory is correct, the right of free speech and the right against unjust discrimination cannot be normatively separated. It adds reasonable force, however, to such an argument of political theory when its force can be illustrated by historical experience, in particular, cumulative American historical experience about the important role free speech has played in addressing the most fundamental injustices of American constitutional democracy, including the structural injustice underlying American racism, sexism, and homophobia The relevance of the American example is to examine concretely the implications of taking a certain view (rooted in political theory) of the relationship between the values of free speech and anti-discrimination, showing that certain consequences, otherwise anticipated from the American view (for example, frustrating protection of the right against unjust discrimination), do not take place. It cannot be without some weight that the road not taken by most nations is now the road decidedly taken, after considerable debate and discussion, by one great constitutional people without the consequences often uncritically associated with such a position. There was nothing either inevitable or arbitrary in America's taking a view of this matter that 'stands virtually in splendid isolation'.[28] It represents a reasonable choice, one that needs to be studied both in its own terms and for whatever light it may cast on a problem faced by all peoples who define legitimate government in terms of respect for basic human rights under the rule of law. My project is thus to investigate, as central to the proper understanding of the value and weight of free speech, its connections to the theory of anti-discrimination. Just as we interrogate a theory of free speech that drains it of its critical normative power, we question as well an associated theory of our principles of anti-discrimination that fails to

---

[28] See Stephen J. Roth, 'The Laws of Six Countries: An Analytical Comparison', in Louis Greenspan and Cyril Levitt (eds.), *Under the Shadow of Weimar: Democracy, Law, and Racial Incitement in Six Countries* (Praeger, Westport, Conn., 1993), 177–211 at 192.

address both the nature and appropriate remedies for the underlying constitutional evil, what I shall call the structural injustice of moral slavery. I argue, building on my earlier studies of this matter,[29] that such structural injustice involves two features: first, the abridgment of the basic human rights of a group of persons; and secondly, its unjustly circular rationalization in terms of dehumanizing stereotypes sustained by such abridgement. Our constitutional principles of anti-discrimination condemn the expression through law of prejudices arising from such structural injustice.

I link the questions of free speech and anti-discrimination both in the way I explain the constitutional evil of discriminatory prejudice and address, on that basis, the question of remedy. The evil of discriminatory prejudice is its insult to identity on constitutionally inadequate, suspect grounds. In particular, such prejudices enforce dehumanizing stereotypes of race (racism), gender (sexism), or gendered sexuality (homophobia) as the stigmatized terms of one's identity as an African-American, woman, and/or gay or lesbian. I argue that the construction of such structural injustice crucially turns on the abridgement of basic human rights to the stigmatized group, in particular, basic human rights of conscience, speech, intimate life, and work. The abridgement of rights of conscience and speech plays an especially pivotal role eliminating the voices and views that most reasonably might protest the unjust terms of identity imposed on them. On this view, abridgement of free speech is an important feature of the background structure of discriminatory prejudice.

It is in terms of this background that I argue we must understand the affirmative role guarantees of human rights in general and rights of conscience and speech in particular play as constitutionally reasonable remedies for such an evil (namely, stereotypical dehumanization). Group libel, obscenity, and blasphemy laws are, from this perspective, constitutionally problematic because they enlist the state at exactly the wrong point, enforcing majoritarian judgements of stereotypical harm in ways that replicate and do not deconstruct the underlying cultural evil. In each area (racism, sexism, homophobia), I argue that the stereotypical evils in question can only be responsibly addressed in the domain of conviction by the voice and outlook of protesting individuals who self-organize in their own terms to protest such evils in what I call the politics of identity. I understand such politics broadly to include not only political action and protest of the conventional sort, but the manifold forms of cultural politics that include forging new cultural narratives that more responsibly do justice to the lives and experience of persons who have suffered from and struggled against structural injustice. It is only such cultural politics, conducted on the responsible terms of principle required by the principle of free speech, that can, in my judgement, reasonably remedy the immense cultural evils inflicted by patterns of structural injustice. In this domain (as opposed to others I will discuss), the interposition of state judgments keyed to alleged group harms from speech not only fails responsibly

---

[29] See, for my earlier studies of this question, David A. J. Richards, *Conscience and the Constitution: History, Theory, and Law of the Reconstruction Amendments* (Princeton University Press, Princeton, NJ, 1993); *Women, Gays, and the Constitution: The Grounds for Feminism and Gay Rights in Culture and Law* (University of Chicago Press, Chicago, Ill., 1998).

to address the evil, but worsens it in ways I describe in each of the main areas of structural injustice (racism, sexism, homophobia) I propose to discuss.

The interest of this account of the principle of free speech is, in contrast to others, its linkage of the principle to protest against the terms of structural injustice. Free speech, on the account I offer of it, is based on the inalienable right to conscience also protected by the religion clauses of the First Amendment of the United States Constitution, and takes on special force in making space for conscientious convictions that protest fundamental injustice, including protest of constitutional institutions themselves. A theory of this sort has a certain reasonable scope and force, but it applies only within its own terms. It thus addresses and condemns blatant forms of state censorship in the domain of conviction, but it does not apply to or limit reasonable state concerns for evils outside this domain. For example, it does not, as I shall argue, condemn reasonable legislative attempts to regulate expenditures in political campaigns in order to advance constitutionally legitimate goals of political equality. It is one of the unacceptable consequences of the uncritical dominance of the argument for democracy in thought about free speech that the constitutionality of such legislation has been assessed in terms of it. Usually, such assessment has been fatal to such legislation on the ground that it unconstitutionally interposes the state in the constitutionally protected area of political speech; more recently, forms of the same argument have been urged (somewhat paradoxically) in support of the constitutionality of such legislation. We need to transcend the terms in which this important issue has been unfortunately cast. The argument I offer here gives a way of thinking about this issue in a way that suggests current American judicial treatment of this and related matters, as an issue of free speech principle, is uncritically wrong.

As I earlier observed, the theory of free speech has both an abstract component of political theory and a historical and contextual component, in which free speech is embedded in a historically evolving tradition of constitutional thought. An American constitutional perspective on free speech brings these components into relationship in a historically evolving tradition of constitutional interpretation of a written constitution enduring over 200 years, including both political and legal arguments made over time about its proper meaning. Contemporary American constitutional interpretation ascribes meaning to written texts that are often highly abstract (for example, 'freedom of speech' in the First Amendment) reflecting and revising background historical understandings of Lockean political theory of the conditions on legitimate government, including respect for the inalienable human right of conscience and other basic rights. The interpretation of such abstract texts draws upon not only the background history and political theory at the time of their ratification but the interpretive practice (of both judicial and political argument) of those texts, including significant amendments thereto, over time. The Constitution of 1787, as amended by the Bill of Rights of 1791, largely imposed guarantees of basic human rights (including the Bill of Rights) only on the federal government, leaving state power to constitutional scrutiny largely under applicable state constitutional guarantees of human rights.[30] In the wake of the Civil War, various principles of the Reconstruction Amendments extended national guarantees of basic human rights to both the states and national governments.[31] But the understanding of what those basic rights were and how they should be understood, even after the Reconstruction Amendments, has changed over time, sometimes quite dramatically. A good theory of constitutional interpretation must integrate all these elements (text, history, political theory, interpretive practice), including an informative understanding of how and why basic constitutional principles have been differently contextualized over time. Presumably, a theory of constitutional interpretation will be a better one to the extent that it both explains more of the interpretive domain (including the relations among basic constitutional values) and also, when there is intractable interpretive conflict, affords reasonable normative criteria in terms of which such conflicts may be assessed. Any good constitutional theory must thus be both explanatory and normative.

The motivation for the theory of free speech here proposed is better to meet such criteria than competitor theories both as a theory of free speech and of the structural connections of free speech to other constitutional principles of values. I have elsewhere argued that free speech, on the theory I shall offer of it, offers unifying principles, based on the argument for toleration, that explain and integrate basic constitutional rights of conscience, speech, and intimate life.[32] I extend that argument here to elaborate the argument for toleration, central to my understanding of free speech, to explain as well the structural injustice of moral slavery condemned by various principles of the Reconstruction Amendments. A constitutional theory surely better meets appropriate methodological criteria of adequacy when it both illuminates the structure of each constitutional value (for example, free speech, or religious liberty, or equal protection) and, at the same time, explains how each such value structurally relates to underlying common conceptions and principles.

An argument of political theory, of the sort offered in this work, must be assessed in its own terms, which, if reasonably compelling, call for both the interpretation and normative criticism of law in its terms. I try to show that some (though not all) distinctive interpretive practices of current American public law can be best understood as working out a defensible political theory of constitutional government; I criticize American interpretive practices when (as in the area of campaign financing) they fail reasonably to meet the normative criteria of such political theory. If my argument of political theory, *qua* political theory, is correct, its implications cannot reasonably be limited to the boundaries of the United States.

The natural focus for exploring such implications must be the constitutionality of group libel and related laws, precisely because American interpretive views (grounded, as I argue, in sound political theory) so markedly deviate from interpre-

---

[30] See, for fuller discussion of this and related points, David A. J. Richards, *Foundations of American Constitutionalism* (Oxford University Press, New York, 1989).

[31] See, for fuller discussion of this and related points, *ibid.*

[32] See David A. J. Richards, *Toleration and the Constitution* (Oxford University Press, New York, 1986).

tive views elsewhere, both national, regional, and international. Group libel and related laws are such an illuminating subject for such inquiry because they implicate two of the fundamental human rights (the right of free speech and the right against unjust discrimination) now universally acknowledged as normatively compelling. A common justification for the constitutionality of hate speech laws is, as we have seen, that such laws reasonably balance these two basic human rights. If my argument of political theory is correct, this rationale rests on the undefended and indefensible view that these rights can be reasonably separated, and then traded off against one another. My political theory aims to show that the common normative grounds for these two rights structurally connect them and that, for this reason, the alleged trade-off of free speech against anti-discrimination frustrates the protection of both rights. To this extent, legal systems that institutionalize this trade-off as the ground for hate speech laws incoherently frustrate both the right of free speech and the right against unjust discrimination. If such laws are to be defended, they must be reasonably defended in a different, less incoherent way.

Any reasonable exploration of this matter, of the sort I will later investigate, must take seriously the common ground universally acknowledged as the motivation for such laws, namely, European and international revulsion in the wake of the Second World War at the racist politics of Hitler's Germany (including both the Holocaust and its murderous imperialistic wars[33]) and the policy (in which the United States played an important role) of forging constitutional institutions nationally, regionally, and internationally that would entrench a system of enforceable basic human rights that would appreciably remove the motives and opportunities of such racist politics. The question of the constitutional legitimacy of hate speech laws has thus been framed as one set of legal practices, among others, that are thought to be necessary in the fundamental constitutional reconstruction and rethinking from the politics that made Hitler's successes possible to a politics of respect for human rights. Thinking of this sort proceeds along the following lines: free speech under Weimar constitutionalism made Hitler possible, therefore laws directed against Hitler's genre of speech must reasonably be forbidden.[34] No one could reasonably argue that sound arguments of political theory require basic principles like free speech and anti-discrimination to apply in the same way in all circumstances, and it is one reasonable way to square American with other national, regional, and international views of the constitutionality of group libel to point to such contextual differences, whatever they

[33] On the connection between these two aims of German fascism and its longstanding roots in European racist imperialism, see Sven Lindqvist, *Exterminate All the Brutes* (Joan Tate trans., The New Press, New York, 1996); on the dimensions of the European problem, see Mark Mazower, *Dark Continent: Europe's Twentieth Century* (Knopf, New York, 1999).

[34] See, for an important statement and critical exploration of this way of thinking, as the background for the constitutional legitimacy of hate speech laws, Louis Greenspan and Cyril Levitt (eds.), *Under the Shadow of Weimar: Democracy, Law, and Racial Incitement in Six Countries* (Praeger, Westport, Conn., 1993); see also Monroe H. Freedman and Eric M. Freedman, *Group Defamation and Freedom of Speech: The Relationship Between Language and Violence* (Greenwood Press, Westport, Conn., 1995).

are or may be.[35] Such differences may plausibly be supposed to include reasonable concern for a history of political evils (like political racism) and the need for constitutional rules of transition that responsibly address such evils, both retrospectively (the punishment of crimes against humanity) and prospectively (banning anti-democratic political parties).[36] Along these lines, it may be argued that the role that free speech historically played in the understanding and remedy of American racism, sexism, and homophobia should be contrasted with the putatively quite different role free speech played under Weimar constitutionalism, and, on the basis of such contextual differences, different interpretive views in America as opposed to most other nations both explained and justified. On the other hand, on critical examination from the perspective of the kind of political theory here offered, the now conventional appeal to the flaws of Weimar constitutionalism, as the rationale for hate speech laws, may be fundamentally flawed, and, for that reason, the alleged urgency of such laws (to combat unjust discrimination) debunked as re-enforcing, not combating, the pervasive cultural patterns of European and world-wide structural injustice.

The larger importance of the project of this work may be its utility in raising and analysing issues of this sort, introducing a fruitful critical methodology for exploring both interpretive and normative analysis of such issues of comparative constitutionalism. In the wake of the Second World War and the new national and international institutions to which it gave rise, it is now historically possible reasonably to take up again the agenda of late eighteenth-century comparative constitutionalism; and this work is conceived very much in that spirit. By offering, as it does, a political theory of both the right of free speech and the right against unjust discrimination, yet one suitably contextualized to historical experience, it explains how and why the universal problems of constitutional government as we enter the second millennium crucially arise from the growing recognition of the depth and pervasiveness of heretofore largely unexamined patterns of structural injustice, including the ravages wrought on humankind by European imperialism and racism, of which Hitler may be regarded as the demonic culmination.[37] We need both to understand the normative implications of this great shift in political and constitutional institutions, including both how far we have come and how far we have yet to go. We need a comparative constitutionalism not only of free speech but of anti-discrimination; we need to explore, as I shall later discuss, racism as both an American and European problem, for example, how and why the racist politics of the American South after its defeat in the American Civil War so strikingly resembles the anti-Semitic politics of Hitler in the wake of Germany's defeat in the First World War. The many self-conscious connections between such developments and the resistance to them (the resistance being much

---

[35] See Theodor Meron, 'The Meaning and Reach of the International Convention on the Elimination of All Forms of Racial Discrimination', 79 *American J. of Int'l Law* 283, 298–9 (1985).

[36] See, for discussion of these and related points in the construction of German constitutionalism in the wake of the Second World War, Robert G. Moeller (ed.), *West Germany under Construction: Politics, Society, and Culture in the Adenauer Era* (University of Michigan Press, Ann Arbor, Mich., 1997).

[37] See, for exploration of these themes, Lindqvist, n. 33 above; Mazower, n. 33 above.

more successful in America and Britain than in continental Europe), must be explored and understood; and we need as well a comparative theory of racism (as well as of sexism and homophobia) that addresses these evils in the political life of all peoples, including the people of Africa as well as Asia.[38] In this way, we may come to see the struggle against such evils as one calling upon the best experience and learning of all peoples in a common conversation about the construction of a constitutionalism (national, regional, and international) that better protects the basic human rights of all persons.

Constitutional theory, as I understand and practise it in this work, is a universal discourse of political theory about the terms of legitimate government, a discourse increasingly preoccupied with the protection of both the basic human right of free speech and the right against unjust discrimination. American constitutional jurisprudence was, after all, born in a founding more deliberatively based on such universal discourse (of political philosophy, political science, and history) than the comparable founding of any other constitutional people;[39] it must re-engage its discourse, in the spirit of its astonishing founding, now leavened by the interpretive experience of two centuries (including seminal constitutional struggles over slavery and racism), with the constitutional discourse of humankind, exploring the common problems of entrenched structural injustice that plague all nations and peoples. My aim, applying normative political theory to American interpretive experience, is to advance such discourse by defending, on that basis, a position on how the basic rights of free speech and against unjust discrimination should be understand, one that both answers internal critics of the American view and challenges the conventional understanding of their relationship in most other nations. Drawing on such experience, for example, one may reasonably question, as incoherent if not self-defeating, a conventional national, regional, and international understanding that claims to condemn racism but does not condemn blatant forms of religious intolerance. To the extent this challenge has the reasonable force which I believe it does have, it will be because it suggests how profound and still largely unrecognized the problem of structural injustice is among all nations and peoples. The very plausibility in most nations of the compromise of free speech principles, which I criticize in this work, suggests the dimensions of the problem. It is the gravamen of my argument, drawing on the long and chequered American experience with these issues, to offer good reasons for thinking there may be such a problem, arising not from too much but too little reasonable constitutional concern with the understanding and remedy of structural injustice, a matter that should be the central concern of constitutional theory as a universal discourse of the political theory of legitimate government that reasonably enjoys universal appeal in the wake of the political atrocities of the twentieth century.

---

[38] On Africa, see Kwame Anthony Appiah, *In My Father's House: Africa in the Philosophy of Culture* (Oxford University Press, New York, 1992); on Asia, see Amy L. Chua, 'Markets, Democracy, and Ethnicity: Toward a New Paradigm for Law and Development', 108 *Yale LJ* 1 (1998).

[39] See, on this point, Richards, n. 30 above.

If the ambition of constitutional theory is so general, why the priority accorded free speech? Certainly, in the long perspective of American constitutional history, free speech only began to enjoy serious federal judicial enforcement in the twentieth century and, even then, largely after the Second World War. Such increasingly aggressive judicial enforcement itself requires interpretive explication both as a commentary on our contemporary sense of basic constitutional principles and our sense of normative deficits in our constitutional tradition with consequences we self-consciously want not to repeat. A historically self-conscious theory of American constitutional interpretation must thus address earlier interpretive mistakes, examining with care the larger consequences of such mistakes for related constitutional principles. For example, as we shall see, the failure to extend respect for basic rights of free speech to abolitionist advocacy in the *antebellum* period, on terms of principle, uncritically enforced the hold of both American slavery and racism on the American public mind at the intolerable sacrifice of basic constitutional values of respect for universal human rights, sowing the seeds of the Second American Revolution, the Civil War.[40] The value we place on free speech is and must be informed by an interpretive mistake of such tragic dimensions, which cannot be of interest only to Americans but must engage the reasonable attention of any people that frames its constitutional identity in terms of respect for basic human rights. No constitutional tradition, including that of the United States, can be regarded as uniformly progressive or enlightened. Indeed, a theory of basic constitutional values of human rights will surely be a better critical guide to the extent that it helps us understand today how disastrous mistaken interpretations of human rights have been in the American constitutional tradition, how self-blinding they have been in our betrayals of the most fundamental principles of constitutional government.

I focus here on free speech because the growing federal judicial protection of its principle in the twentieth century has, in my judgement, been the interpretive model that has guided and framed the American interpretation of related constitutional principles (including principles of religious liberty, constitutional privacy, and equal protection). The answer to, why the priority of free speech?, is thus importantly set by contemporary American self-understanding of the legitimate agenda of judicially enforceable constitutional principles. It is a datum of our interpretive practices that the judicial protection of free speech has played such a role as a model for the protection of related constitutional principles, and it is therefore a reasonable interpretive demand on constitutional theory that it explain, why the constitutional priority accorded speech?

Of course, any interpretive practice may be challenged, and it is not an acceptable answer to appeal, positivistically, to a practice as self-validating. It is at this point that the historical and contextual component of a theory of free speech must engage with its abstract component of political theory. The question, why speech?, is a free standing question of normative political theory that engages philosophical interest in polit-

---

[40] See, on this point, Richards, *Conscience*, n. 29 above, 15, 21, 109, 110, 116–18, 121, 134, 136–7, 144.

ical justice whether or not those claims of justice are embodied in constitutional law. But if those claims are embodied in constitutional law, as they are under American constitutionalism, such normative political theory plays a crucial role in our interpretive understanding of the normative basis, if there is one, for the priority accorded free speech in historically evolving American interpretive practice.

If there is such a normative priority, such priority may be usefully harnessed in the deeper interpretive understanding not only of the principle of free speech but in the role judicial protection of that principle has played in the elaboration of related constitutional principles (like those condemning structural injustice). The argument of this book will proceed along these lines. The argument for toleration will be offered and defended against competitor political theories (including the argument from democracy) as the best theory of the priority of free speech (Chapter 2). The interpretive and critical power of the argument for toleration will then be illustrated by its elaboration to explain as well the principles that condemn structural injustice (anti-Semitism, racism, sexism, and homophobia) (Chapter 3). The most important thesis of this work is, as I earlier indicated, its attempt structurally to integrate understanding of both the right of free speech and the right against unjust discrimination in a common normative conception; to deal with this matter adequately, I must explain at some length how each of the main forms of unjust discrimination (extreme religious intolerance, racism, sexism, and homophobia), usually treated in isolation both from one another and from the theory of free speech, must be reasonably understood, in light of the political theory I offer, as resting on common normative grounds that crucially appeal, for their sense, to the abridgement of basic rights, most prominently, freedom of conscience and speech. This structural connection, once stated and defended at length, is then further explored in the context of the great constitutional issues that are the focus of the argument of this book (Chapters 4–6). In light of the argument for toleration and the theory of structural injustice, constitutional scepticism of group libel laws will be explained and justified, and other modes of attacking these evils defended (including, where reasonable, affirmative action); in this light, American views will be both defended and critically compared to other national, regional, and international views (Chapter 4). Similarly, constitutional scepticism of laws condemning obscenity and blasphemy will be similarly defended, and attempts to press the analogy of group libel in the defence of such laws (on the alleged grounds of protecting against unjust discrimination women as well as gays and lesbians, or protecting religious identity) criticized (Chapter 5). Finally, I turn to the relationship of the principle of free speech to the regulation of democratic campaign financing, focusing, in particular, on American constitutional scepticism, on such grounds, of campaign finance restrictions; I criticize this American view from the perspective of the theory of free speech offered in this work and conclude with some general observations about the promise of comparative public law as a normative discourse, grounded in a political theory of respect for the basic human right of free speech and the right against unjust discrimination (Chapter 6).

2

Free Speech and the Argument for Toleration

Why, among the important constitutionally protected interests that we have, does American public law identify and weight our interest in free speech as one calling for the high level of constitutional protection it does? I address this question from the perspective of normative political theory. On the basis of a criticism of several alternative views, I defend a more defensible view, one based on the argument for toleration.

Utilitarian models for free speech take a wide variety of forms, such as John Stuart Mill's classically complex and nuanced arguments in *On Liberty*[1] to Oliver Wendell Holmes's crude appeal to the amoral deliverances of Social Darwinian competition in his dissent in *Abrams* v. *United States*.[2] The abstract structure of these arguments is that protection of free speech is justified because over all (its tendency to advance truth, and the like) it promotes the greatest net balance of pleasure over pain among all sentient beings. But such arguments will not justify principles of free speech of the sort that American constitutional law now requires. The net aggregate of pleasure over pain is often advanced, not frustrated, by the restriction of speech. Large populist majorities often relish (hedonically speaking) the repression of outcast dissenters; the numbers and pains of dissenters are by comparison small; and there is often no offsetting future net aggregate of pain over pleasure to make up the difference. Holmes's more sceptical and less humane utilitarian vision may therefore reflect a sounder balancing of the competing utilitarian consequences than Mill's. For Holmes, free-speech values should protect only those 'puny anonymities'[3] unlikely to harm anyone and from whom something might be learned; it would not protect a more politically effective speaker (like the challenge of a Eugene Debs to American involvement in the First World War, or comparable dissenters to the Vietnam War later) whose threat to existing institutions and policies was clear and whose benefit to those institutions and policies was unclear.[4] But that approach is decidedly not the

---

[1] See John Stuart Mill, *On Liberty* (ed. Alburey Castell, Appleton-Century-Crofts, New York, 1947), chs. 2–3.

[2] 250 US 616 (1919).   [3] *Ibid.*, at 629.

[4] This interpretation of Holmes's views on free speech is not inconsistent with the rather more expansive language of his dissent in *Gitlow* v. *New York*, 268 US 652 (1925) ('[i]f in the long run the beliefs expressed in proletarian dictatorship are destined to be accepted by the dominant forces of the community, the only meaning of free speech is that they should be given their chance and have their way') if that language is to be contextually understood in terms of the protection of a political group of fringe left-wing socialists whom Holmes regarded as, in contrast to Debs, politically impotent.

current approach to free-speech protection in American constitutional law, and rightly so.[5] The credible critical challenge to American war policies in both cases was precisely the dissenting speech most worthy of protection. Otherwise, free-speech protection would be extended only to the incredible fatuities of the lunatic fringe.

PERFECTIONIST MODELS OF FREE SPEECH

For reasons already suggested, John Stuart Mill's liberal theory of free speech and private life seems to many more normatively powerful than the utilitarian grounds he urges in support of it. In particular, nothing in the structure of utilitarian argument (which gives equal weight to all pleasures and pains) can reasonably explain the normative priority Mill, like most liberals, accords speech. Mill's conclusions seem sounder than his normative premises, which suggests that his premises should be reformulated in some way more likely to lead to supporting his conclusions.[6]

One appealing solution along these lines is to retain the teleological character of utilitarianism as a kind of moral theory, but to revise the conception of what is aggregated. Utilitarianism is a form of teleological moral theory: right conduct is defined as the aggregate of goods or evils, where goods are understood as pleasures and evils as pains. Such a proposed alternative form of teleological moral theory is perfectionism: right conduct is defined as the aggregate of goods or evils, but goods are now defined as human excellences and evils as human degradations. The liberal normative appeal of such a conception is better to understand the kind of normative weight Mill accords speech as a higher pleasure, thus entitled, in his conception, to a greater utilitarian weight over lower pleasures.[7] Such a conception hardly coheres well with what many, including Mill, claimed to find normatively appealing in utilitarianism as a moral theory: its equal weighting of pleasures or pains as such (whatever their sources).[8] If, from this perspective, 'everybody to count for one, nobody for more than one',[9] presumably the pleasure of speech for one should be no greater than that of a good meal for another (at least hedonically understood); and there seems no natural way to accord speech the kind of priority over other values that liberal political theories, including Mill's, mean to accord it.

Perfectionism, however, has no difficulties in claiming that certain activities are more excellent or worthy than others. It precisely resists what it takes to be the philistinism of utilitarian normative theory, insisting that certain activities (involving our higher human faculties, like speech) are more valuable and thus more worthy to be pursued, whether they yield aggregate pleasure or not overall. We have then a

---

[5] See, e.g., *Bond* v. *Floyd*, 385 US 116 (1966) (speech of Julian Bond protesting Vietnam War held constitutionally protected); *Watts* v. *United States*, 394 US 705 (1969) (anti-draft speech, including threats to kill President Johnson, held constitutionally protected).

[6] See, e.g., C. L. Ten, *Mill on Liberty* (Clarendon Press, Oxford, 1980).

[7] See John Stuart Mill, *Utilitarianism* (ed. Oskar Piest, Library of Liberal Arts, Indianapolis, Ind., 1957), ch. 2.

[8] See *ibid.*, at 76–8.   [9] See *ibid.*, at 76.

teleological normative theory that can give us the normative priority of free speech that we are looking for, one that better explains and justifies Mill's liberal principles of free speech and personal autonomy.

The problem, however, is that any form of perfectionism, understood as an ultimate foundation of normative theory, takes as its starting point interpretations of excellences in living that threaten to be highly personal or even sectarian, imposing controversial values in violation of the liberal imperative of equal concern and respect. To this extent, perfectionism is an insecure basis for a liberal political theory. On perfectionist grounds alone, there seems little way to choose between more liberal interpretations of such premises (as by Haksar[10] and Raz[11]) and illiberal interpretations (Finnis[12] and George[13]). Finnis thus condemns as moral evils abortion, contraception, and consensual homosexuality not in terms of reasonable arguments accessible to all, but sectarian arguments internal to a certain version of Catholic moral theology.[14] If Finnis is wrong about the reasonable force of his arguments for those outside his religious tradition (as he clearly is), how can we be sure that any perfectionist litany of foundationally ultimate perfectionist goods and evils is not similarly either confused or question-begging in ways that threaten the most basic values of the liberal state? If we want to do better justice to Mill's liberalism, we must seek elsewhere for a more secure foundation for the priority of free speech in constitutional democracy.

THE ARGUMENT FROM DEMOCRACY

In light of the controversies among substantive normative political theories already discussed, one appealing move is to look away from substantive political theory entirely and seek salvation in democratic political processes. The political process model of free speech conceives the core function of such speech to be the protection of the democratic political process from the abusive censorship of political debate by the transient majority which has democratically achieved political power.[15] In the form of this view offered by John Hart Ely, the appeal of the theory is its forthright response to the democratic objection to judicial review.[16] On this model, judicial review on free speech grounds does not fall foul of the democratic objection to judicial review; judicial review here protects the integrity of democracy itself from the ille-

---

[10] See Vinit Haksar, *Equality, Liberty, and Perfectionism* (Oxford University Press, Oxford, 1979).

[11] See Joseph Raz, *The Morality of Freedom* (Clarendon Press, Oxford, 1986).

[12] See John Finnis, *Natural Law and Natural Rights* (Clarendon Press, Oxford, 1980).

[13] See Robert P. George, *Making Men Moral: Civil Liberties and Public Morality* (Clarendon Press, Oxford, 1993).

[14] See, on this and related points, David A. J. Richards, 'Kantian Ethics and the Harm Principle: A Reply to John Finnis', 87 *Colum. L Rev.* 547 (1987); David A. J. Richards, 'Perfectionist Moral Theory', the Criminal Law, and the Liberal State', 13 *Criminal Justice Ethics* 93 (1994).

[15] See, for an early influential statement of the view, Alexander Meiklejohn, *Political Freedom* (Oxford University Press, New York, 1965).

[16] See John Hart Ely, *Democracy and Distrust: A Theory of Judicial Review* (Harvard University Press, Cambridge, Mass., 1980), esp. ch. 4.

gitimate attempt of a transient majority to entrench its own power by manipulating the agenda of political debate in its own favour. The judiciary does not, on Ely's view, illegitimately impose on democratic majorities a substantive value, but legitimately insists upon and monitors a view of democratic procedural fairness.

The very coherence of this approach to free speech protection requires a background conception of democratic legitimacy, i.e., forms of political power that democratic majorities may and may not legitimately exercise. But the idea of democracy is essentially contestable; views differ about what is and what is not essential to a well-functioning democracy, or, conversely, what counts as democratic 'pathology' for purposes of determining the legitimate scope of free speech.[17] For example, recent proponents of the argument from democracy (Cass Sunstein[18] and Owen Fiss[19]) claim that it shows, among other things, that regulations of campaign financing should not raise free speech issues, on the ground that such regulations better ensure a well-functioning and properly responsive political democracy.[20] I agree that such regulations should not be regarded as violating free speech principles, but fail to see how such a result can be forthrightly squared with the argument from democracy. Indeed, it was the very force of the argument from democracy in the thinking of the Supreme Court that led them, I believe, to take the view that Sunstein, Fiss, and I criticize in *Buckley* v. *Valeo*,[21] namely, that restrictions on campaign expenditures violate free speech. Within the framework of the argument from democracy, the Court's reasoning is at least as plausible as its democratic critics, indeed perhaps more so. On one plausible interpretation, the argument from democracy construes political speech to be core protected speech, in particular, protected from infringement by politicians trying to self-entrench their political power. But restrictions on campaign expenditures can plausibly be regarded as falling in this domain: attempts to interfere with resources closely related to political speech in ways that favour the political interests of politicians in retaining or gaining power. It was an uncritical commitment to the argument from democracy that led the Court to the position in *Buckley* now so widely criticized, assimilating, as it did, regulation of campaign expenditures to a constitutionally problematic self-entrenchment of political power by skewing political dialogue. The ostensibly democratic argument to the contrary emphasizes quite rightly, in support of such legislation, reasonable substantive values of political equality,[22] but fails to engage the barriers that the argument from democracy itself puts in the way of pursuing such a goal in the domain identified by the argument as the core of

---

[17] For a range of perspectives on the democratic pathologies that free speech should remedy, see, e.g., Vincent Blasi, 'The Pathological Perspective and the First Amendment', 85 *Colum. L Rev.* 449 (1985); Owen M. Fiss, *Liberalism Divided: Freedom of Speech and the Many Uses of State Power* (Westview Press, Boulder, Colo., 1996), 9–16.

[18] See Cass R. Sunstein, *Democracy and the Problem of Free Speech* (Free Press, New York, 1993).

[19] See Owen M. Fiss, *The Irony of Free Speech; Liberalism Divided* (Harvard University Press, Cambridge, Mass., 1996).

[20] See Sunstein, n. 18 above, 93–101; Fiss, *The Irony of Free Speech*, n. 19 above, 11; n. 17 above, 28–9.

[21] 424 US 1 (1976).

[22] See, e.g., Sunstein, n. 18 above, at 94–101.

protected free speech. At this point, the preferred conception of democracy is no longer procedural in Ely's sense at all, but substantive in a way that suggests independent substantive principles against which the legitimacy of democracy is being tested. The whole point of the argument from democracy, as a way of avoiding substantive political theory, is now idle. Substantive political theory is now doing all the work, albeit through a glass darkly. We must, indeed, forthrightly engage in such normative political theory, which makes possible an alternative understanding of why *Buckley* was wrongly decided but which also contests, as we shall see, the suggestion of some of these proponents of the argument from democracy that group libel and related laws should not be constitutionally problematic.[23] The debate, however, will now be conducted in terms of better and worse arguments of substantive political theory, not in terms of a question-begging appeal to the procedures of democracy (for development of this point, see Chapter 6).

The point may be generalized as an objection to the argument from democracy as a theory of free speech. The legitimate scope of democratic debate may be interpreted either broadly or narrowly. The narrow interpretation limits such debate to the issues directly in controversy in political campaigns among the main contenders for majoritarian political power;[24] the broader interpretation construes such debate as extending to any possible public issue, including the very legitimacy of political power in general and democracy in particular.[25] Neither of these interpretations provides a secure and convincing basis for the priority of speech as a constitutionally protected interest. The narrow interpretation trivializes free speech by restricting its scope to consensus politics; it thus excludes from protection precisely the dissenting discourse outside the political mainstream often most crucial to critical examination of central issues of justice and the common good. The broader interpretation seems itself to compromise democratic legitimacy by protecting attacks on the very foundations of such legitimacy, including attacks on free speech itself. If such attacks should be protected, as current American law indeed requires,[26] it seems rather strained to justify such protection on the ground that it invariably advances democracy when the speech it allows may sometimes self-consciously aim to subvert it. We value such speech intrinsically, certainly not because it always advances democratically determined policies and aims.

This latter point suggests that we value democracy or, to be more precise, democratic constitutionalism to the extent that it respects independent substantive values

---

[23] Fiss, e.g., regards regulation of hate speech and pornography as resting on the same grounds as regulation of campaign financing: see Fiss, n. 19 above, 11; for Sunstein on the legitimacy of anti-pornography laws, see Sunstein, n. 18 above, at 210–26.

[24] See Robert Bork, 'Neutral Principles and Some First Amendment Problems', 47 *Indiana LJ* 1 (1971). As a federal judge, Bork later offered a more expansive interpretation of this requirement, see *Ollman* v. *Evans*, 750 F 2d 970, 995 ff. (DC Cir. 1984).

[25] See Alexander Meiklejohn, 'The First Amendment Is an Absolute' [1961] *Supreme Court Review* 245.

[26] For pertinent discussion, see David A. J. Richards, *Toleration and the Constitution* (Oxford University Press, New York, 1986), 178–87.

of free speech; and those values cannot themselves be plausibly understood in terms of perfecting the majoritarian political process. C. Edwin Baker has recently put this point in terms of a substantive value of equal respect for the moral self-determination of all persons, and assesses the legitimacy of democracy, to the extent that it is legitimate, as a political process that realizes that independent value;[27] and Kent Greenawalt had advanced a similar argument in terms of the remarkable American constitutional commitment to principles of religious liberty and the important place of free speech in giving proper expression to these principles[28]. To the extent that free speech must give expression to the communicative interests of liberty of conscience, the limitation of protection of free speech to politics is clearly inadequate. As Greenawalt puts the point:

Once freedom of religious ideas is acknowledged, distinguishing protected speech from unprotected speech, say about science or personal morality, becomes almost absurd.[29]

From the perspective of Baker and Greenawalt, constitutionally legitimate political power must respect substantive spheres of moral independence like liberty of conscience (including all matters of fact and value fundamental to the exercise of conscience); the right of free speech, through which persons exercise their constructive powers of moral independence, must correlatively extend to all such matters. The limitation of free speech protection to politics is, on this view, illegitimate because it allows forms of censorship that deprive persons of the inalienable liberties essential to the moral self-government of a free people. Many of these liberties are not, in their nature, political. The limitation of free speech protection to the political is therefore illegitimate because it fails the ultimate test of rights-based constitutional legitimacy, the equal protection of the basic rights of free persons.

Baker and Greenawalt suggest (in my view quite rightly) a larger research project about the principles of democratic constitutionalism. Those principles cannot, as a matter either of sound interpretation of American constitutional tradition or of defensible democratic political theory, be understood on the political process model of perfecting the majoritarian political process, i.e., rendering the political process more truly majoritarian (and therefore democratic). As an interpretive matter, the constitutional tradition regards all forms of political power (including the power of democratic majorities) as corruptible; it subjects such power to a system of institutional constraints (including judicial review) designed to harness such power to the legitimate ends of government, namely, respect for human rights and the use of power to advance the public good.[30] A perfected political majoritarianism, often hostile to respect for both human rights and the public good when involving minorities,

---

[27] See, in general, C. Edwin Baker, *Human Liberty and Freedom of Speech* (Oxford University Press: New York, 1989), esp. ch. 3.

[28] Kent Greenawalt, *Speech, Crime, and the Uses of Language* (Oxford University Press, New York, 1989), 177–9.

[29] *Ibid.*, 178.

[30] See, for extensive development and exploration of this theme in American constitutionalism, David A. J. Richards, *Foundations of American Constitutionalism* (Oxford University Press, New York, 1989).

cannot be the measure of constitutional legitimacy. As a matter of democratic political theory, political process models usually rest on a form of preference utilitarianism.
Such utilitarianism not only has already mentioned defects as an account of current
American law; it has independently been subjected to searching contemporary criticism as an inadequate normative theory of equality. Part of this criticism has been
that its theory of equality fails to give adequate expression to the place of respect for
human rights in the normative idea of treating persons as equals.[31] We need an alternative view of democratic constitutionalism that better captures, both as a matter of
sound interpretation and of defensible political theory, the ways in which constitutional principles subject the exercise of political power to scrutiny and constraint.

THE TOLERATION MODEL OF FREE SPEECH

We need to return to substantive normative political theory but of a non-teleological,
deontological sort, one that better captures the normative structure of constitutional
argument in terms of a set of principles that recognize basic human rights to be
accorded all persons as equals, prior to the legitimate pursuit of other political goals
and purposes. I want here to sketch such an alternative view, explain its roots in
American constitutional thought, and consider some of its distinctive consequences
for the understanding of the place and role of free speech in American constitutional
law. In later chapters, I will further develop this theory both to explicate some related
constitutional evils (anti-Semitism, racism, sexism, and homophobia) and to explain
and defend, in light of that analysis, some distinctive features of the American public
law of free speech, and to criticize some others.

The theories of religious liberty and free speech are natural starting points for an
alternative research project for constitutionalism because the American doctrines of
religious liberty and free speech are pivotal constructive components of the kind of
reasonable public argument in terms of which exercises of political power must be justified if they are to be constitutionally legitimate. Constitutional argument has in the
United States a dignity and weight distinctive from ordinary political argument
because it addresses the fundamental question of what lends legitimacy to any exercise of political power. It was fundamental to this constitutional project from its
inception not only that all forms of political power were corruptible, but that they
had been and were corruptible in a distinctive way. Corruptible political power had
deprived persons of the capacity to know, understand, and make effective claim to
their basic human rights by entrenching sectarian views as the measure of what could
count either as a legitimate conviction or of expression of such conviction. As a consequence, political power had been distorted from its proper role in the pursuit of the
justice of equal rights and advancing the interests of all alike in pursuit of the public

---

[31] The now classic contemporary treatment of this point is John Rawls, *A Theory of Justice* (Harvard
University Press, Cambridge, Mass., 1971).

good.[32] The argument for religious toleration was, for leading American constitutionalists like Thomas Jefferson and James Madison,[33] a model for both the corruptibility of political power (subverting the inalienable right to conscience) and its constitutional remedy (namely, depriving the state of any power to enforce or endorse sectarian religious belief, unless in service of a compelling secular purpose reasonably accessible to all as based on general goods irrespective of other philosophical or religious disagreements). In effect, the exercise of political power for religious ends had entrenched a sectarian conception of religious truth as the measure of all reasonable inquiry about religious matters; it thus had deprived persons of their inalienable human rights reasonably to exercise their own moral powers about such matters. Such exercises of political power entrenched a kind of self-perpetuating political irrationalism that deprived people of reasonable government; political power was exercised in ways that neither respected people's right to reasonable self-government in their own moral and religious life, nor subjected its own power to reasonable criticism in terms of equal justice and the public good. Arguments of constitutional principle have the weight that they do precisely because they subject such corruptions of political power to appropriate constraint in service of the reasonable justification of political power in terms of respect for rights and the use of political power to advance justice and the public good.

The principle of free speech plays the central role it does among constitutional principles and structures because it deprives the state of power over speech based on self-entrenching judgements of the worth or value of the range of speech that protects the inalienable right to conscience, i.e., sincere convictions about matters of fact and value in which a free people reasonably has a higher-order interest. That interest is nothing less than the free exercise of the moral powers of their reason through which persons give enduring value to their lives and communities.[34] Speech in the relevant sense must be free from certain forms of state control both to ensure that censorious state judgements are not the measure of reasonable discussion in society at large and to allow the broadest possible exercise of the reasonable powers of a free people consistent with both respect for their human rights and their rights as citizens to hold political power accountable in terms of its respect for such rights and the public good. If constitutional argument depends for its dignity and weight on subjecting political power to such independent tests of reasonable justification, free speech is the foundation for the practicability of such justification; it ensures a constitutional space for the kind of reasonable public argument against which, on grounds of constitutional legitimacy, all forms of political power must be subject to open debate and criticism. It would, of course, doom the entire project to emptiness and triviality if the state's majoritarian judgements of the worth or value of speech were the procrustean measure to which all such discourse must be fitted.

[32] See, for a general development of this theme, Richards, n. 30 above.
[33] For further discussion, see Richards, n. 26 above, 111–16.
[34] See, in general, David A. J. Richards, *A Theory of Reasons for Action* (Clarendon Press, Oxford, 1971).

The nerve of this argument is implicit in the way James Madison argued that the principle of free speech is an elaboration of the argument for liberty of conscience as an inalienable human right.[35] The argument for religious toleration was, as I earlier suggested, that the state may have no power over religion because enforceable state judgements about the worth or value of particular religious beliefs fail to respect the right of persons reasonably to make such judgements for themselves. The idea is not that the state is always mistaken in judging certain religious views to be false or noxious; rather, judgements of that sort cannot, in principle, be made by a state committed to respect for the right of people reasonably to exercise their own judgement in these matters. In his seminal formulation of the Virginia Bill for Religious Freedom, Jefferson put the point thus:

to restrain the profession or propagation of principles on supposition of their ill tendency is a dangerous falacy [*sic*], which at once destroys all religious liberty, because he [the civil magistrate] being of course judge of that tendency will make his opinions the rule of judgment, and approve or condemn the sentiments of others only as they shall square with or differ from his own.[36]

In effect, abridgement of religious liberty could not be justified on sectarian grounds but could only be justified on independent grounds of preventing harm to secular general goods like life, liberty, and property. As Jefferson put the point, 'it is time enough for the rightful purposes of civil government for its officers to interfere when principles break out into overt acts against peace and good order'; the normal means for rebuttal of noxious belief, consistent with respect for the right of conscience, is 'free argument and debate'.[37] As he wrote elsewhere: 'it does me no injury for my neighbor to say there are twenty gods, or no god. It neither picks my pocket nor breaks my leg.'[38] The limitation of the exercise of state power to the protection of general goods expresses respect for the diverse ways that people may interpret and weight life, liberty, and property consistent with the independent exercise of their moral powers.

Madison saw that the same argument justified a special protection for speech because the state was inclined to make and enforce the same kinds of illegitimate judgements about the worth of the speech through which we express, develop, and revise conscientiously held beliefs. Accordingly, the principle of free speech took the form of a prohibition against the enforcement of state judgements about the truth or worth of what is said (thus anticipating the contemporary free speech doctrine forbidding content-based restrictions on speech[39]). The criterion for the limitation of speech was the same as Jefferson's criterion for the abridgement of religious liberty;

[35] See Richards, n. 30 above, 173–82.

[36] Julian P. Boyd (ed.), *The Papers of Thomas Jefferson, 1777–1779* (Princeton University Press, Princeton, NJ, 1950), ii, 546.

[37] *Ibid.*, 546.

[38] Thomas Jefferson, *Notes on the State of Virginia* (ed. William Peden, University of North Carolina Press, Chapel Hill, NC, 1955).

[39] See Richards, n. 26 above, chs. 6–7.

speech may be constitutionally limited only 'when principles break out into overt acts' inflicting secular harms (a criterion anticipating the highly demanding contemporary American requirements for satisfaction of the 'clear and present danger' test, namely, the danger of some imminent, non-rebuttable, and very grave secular harm[40]).

Madison's expansive view of protection derives from a deontological contractualist conception of political legitimacy; state power is only acceptable when it acts in ways that no person, understood to have basic higher-order interests in rational and reasonable self-government, could reasonably reject.[41] From this perspective, conscience is an inalienable human right constitutionally immune from political power because, consistent with this contractualist conception, it is the right that enables persons, on terms of equal respect, to be the sovereign moral critics of values, including political values like the legitimacy of government. Constitutionally guaranteed respect for this right ensures that free and equal persons are the ultimate judges of whether the government respects their rights and pursues the public good in a way that justifies obedience and, if so, on what terms and to what extent. The scope of free speech protection, thus understood, must in its nature be much more expansive than the actual cases when political power is illegitimate, or, more extremely, when revolution might be justified. The point of free speech is not that revolution, on grounds of rights-based political illegitimacy, is often justified, but that the deliberative question of ultimate political legitimacy must, consistent with respect for the inalienable right to conscience, be always vividly addressed to the public mind of a free people if they are to be the ultimate free and equal sovereigns in matters of judgement about those questions of political justice in terms of which political power must be searchingly tested and held accountable. Persons could not reasonably reject this constitutional principle because it ensures the only reasonable basis for holding political power accountable to the basic requirements of its own legitimacy. But the protections of speech—which are also protections of conscience—cannot be limited to religious speech narrowly understood (as Jefferson, for example, supposed[42]). Madison's objection to the prosecutions brought by the federal government under the Alien and Sedition Act of 1798[43] was that they sought to enforce a suspect judgement of the worth of speech (notably, speech critical of the government) that improperly allowed the government's own beliefs about the legitimate scope of political criticism to settle the issue of what people might and should find reasonable. This was, of course, the same abuse of state power Jefferson noted in religious persecution. If anything, the temptations to such abuse would be as at least as great in the case of speech expressly

---

[40] See *ibid.*, 178–87.

[41] See T. M. Scanlon, 'Contractualism and Utilitarianism' in Amartya Sen and Bernard Williams (eds.), *Utilitarianism and Beyond* (Cambridge University Press, Cambridge, 1982), 103–28.

[42] For Jefferson's quite restrictive conception of the scope of free speech (in contrast to his expansive protection of religious liberty), see Leonard W. Levy, *Jefferson and Civil Liberties: The Darker Side* (Quadrangle, New York, 1973), 42–69.

[43] See James Madison, 'Report on the Virginia Resolutions', in Jonathan Elliot (ed.), *Debates on the Federal Constitution* (Printed for the editor, Washington, DC, 1836), iv, 546–80.

critical of the state. Accordingly, speech should enjoy at least a comparable kind of protection.[44] Nothing in Madison's argument, however, endorses, as Sunstein quite mistakenly supposes,[45] the argument from democracy as the measure or limit of free speech. Madison's defence of free speech is, as we have seen, rooted in the argument for toleration, which extends the protection of free speech as broadly as the underlying right to conscience and threats thereto. These included, as Madison made clear, seditious libel laws, not because such laws were political, but because they so politically threatened the moral integrity of the underlying right of conscience. What Madison clearly takes to be the underlying grounds for an expansive protection of speech (moral independence of conviction), extending to blatant political threats (like seditious libel laws), has been quite erased by Sunstein, means inverted into ends, doing interpretive justice neither to American Madisonian history nor political theory.

The scope of such Madisonian protection is clearly responsive to an evolving public understanding of the extent of reasonable conscientious debate about values; as the scope of reasonable application of the idea of protected conscience widens, so must the scope of free speech, an issue we must explore in much greater depth in following chapters. Anticipating that discussion, however, we may note, in a preliminary way (to be further explained in light of discussion to follow), some of the ways in which, in general, this perspective may explain a range of interpretive developments. Such background shifts may thus explain the expanding class of expressions to which the American judiciary now applies the guarantees of free speech and free press. For example, subversive advocacy[46] and group libel[47] are now fully protected; and much that was traditionally excluded from free speech protection—fighting words,[48] defamation of individuals,[49] obscene materials,[50] advertising[51]—is now more fully protected. Madison himself expanded the scope of the argument from free conscience to protect public criticism both of religion and of the state; and the modern judiciary has further expanded the argument to protect expressions of dissent from suppression by majorities essentially motivated by hostility to such dissent, rather than by the desire to combat clear and present dangers of secular harms. As Madison clearly saw, the pattern of intolerance familiar in unjust religious persecution occurs as well in the censorship of speech; and the modern United States Supreme Court has correctly understood that the same protections fundamental to our Jeffersonian conception of religious liberty apply, as a matter of principle, to free speech.

[44] For a recent important historical study of the background of early American journalism that was the context of Madison's argument, see Jeffery A. Smith, *Printers and Press Freedom: The Ideology of Early American Journalism* (Oxford University Press, New York, 1988).
[45] See, e.g., Sunstein, n. 18 above, at pp. xvi–xx, 18–23.
[46] See *Brandenburg* v. *Ohio*, 395 US 444 (1969).
[47] See *Collin* v. *Smith*, 578 F 2d 1197 (1978), cert. den., 439 US 916 (1978).
[48] See *Gooding* v. *Wilson*, 405 US 518 (1972).
[49] See *Gertz* v. *Robert Welch, Inc.*, 418 US 323 (1974). For an illuminating recent commentary on this development in American constitutional law, see Anthony Lewis, *Make No Law: The Sullivan Case and the First Amendment* (Random House, New York, 1991).
[50] See *Miller* v. *California*, 413 US 15 (1973).
[51] See *Virginia Pharmacy Board* v. *Virginia Consumer Council*, 425 US 748 (1976).

The theory quite cogently explains, for example, something that both the utilitarian and political process models have difficulty in explaining, namely, the inclusion of subversive advocacy in free speech protection. From a utilitarian perspective, as Holmes himself clearly saw, speech advocating the subversion of constitutional institutions, at least when made by a socialist political leader of the eloquence and effectiveness of Eugene Debs,[52] is sufficiently dangerous to warrant suppression on utilitarian grounds ('puny anonymities' are quite another matter[53]). And from the political process perspective, as earlier suggested, why should speech itself subversive of democracy be protected at all? But from the perspective of the toleration model here proposed, subversive advocacy, precisely because it makes substantive claims that go to the very legitimacy of constitutional government, is at the very core of free speech protection. Such advocacy conscientiously addresses the public conscience of the community in terms of putative failures to so respect rights and the public good that disobedience, indeed revolution, is justified. From the perspective of a conception of free speech rooted in respect for freedom of conscience about ultimate issues of value like justice and the right to rebel, that is the speech most worthy of protection. It raises the questions of public conscience central to a free society; the constitutional guarantee of the moral independence of such speech and speakers from state majoritarian censorship ensures that the legitimacy of state power is subject to searching and impartial testing in terms of its respect for universal human rights and the public interest. It is very much the point of such robust protection of free speech that, precisely because of such protection, the claims of subversive advocates thus protected will be tested by the deliberative judgement of a people empowered by their freedom responsibly to assess such claims. Often they will reject such claims as false and unjustified; sometimes, they will accept them. The meaning of free speech is the impartial moral independence of the testing.

The theory of free speech proposed here straightforwardly explains, in a way in which other views do not, both the constitutional identity and weight accorded the constitutional protection of speech, including our grounds for scepticism about certain state abridgments of speech. The speech protected is coextensive not with all speech, or with speech as such, but with the independent communication of willing speakers and audiences sincerely engaged in the critical discussion and rebuttal central to the conscientious formation, revision, and evaluation of values in living against the background of the threats to such moral independence identified by the argument for toleration. The constitutional priority accorded free speech, thus understood, is given weight in terms of a deontological contractualist political theory of equal respect for persons. The theory thus explains, in a way utilitarianism cannot, the weight accorded our interest in speech as opposed to our other interests, and explains, in a way perfectionism cannot, the egalitarian basis of this interest in the role conscience plays in the higher-order moral interests of all persons. It also explains, in

---

[52] See *Debs* v. *United States*, 249 US 211 (1919).
[53] See Holmes, J., dissenting, in *Abrams* v. *United States*, 250 US 624 at 629 (1919).

a way the argument from democracy cannot, how and why this interest extends beyond the political narrowly or broadly construed to include our moral interests as persons.

On the other hand, the theory suggests reasonable limits on the scope of protection of free speech. For example, some communications do not serve such independent conscientious expression and rebuttal about critical values. Some may bypass reflective capacities (subliminal advertising); others do not express or appeal to sincere evaluative convictions but make knowingly false statements of fact (fraud and knowing or reckless defamation of individuals[54]) that manipulatively distort and certainly do not respect rational autonomy as the basis of reasonable persuasion;[55] and still others state true but private facts in which there is no ground for a reasonable interest from the perspective of the critical expression and discussion of general values. Because of the fundamental structural importance of the protection of the right to conscience to political legitimacy, the line between protected and unprotected speech should be drawn in the way that gives the broadest reasonable protection to moral independence in the expression and discussion of values; speech should be regarded as unprotected only on a strong showing of no reasonable ground for protection on this basis. In such cases of unprotected speech, the state may, consistently with the principle of free speech, pursue legitimate secular interests such as protection from consumer fraud and protection of individual reputation and privacy, harms to individuals not subject to rebuttal in public debate in the way in which disagreements over values are. It is therefore not an objection to a theory of free speech grounded in the communicative independence of our rational powers that the theory fails to accommodate such legitimate regulatory interests; the theory, properly understood, gives them proper weight.[56] In general, free speech has the priority we accord it against a background of reasonable state regulations (including fair time, place, and manner regulations[57]) that afford a supportive framework of communicative dialogue of reasonable persuasion among free, rational, and equal persons and a constitutionally reasonable pursuit of legitimate state interests without prejudice to free speech.

Correspondingly, our scepticism about state power over speech is rooted not in a general suspicion of the state as such, but in a desire to avoid specific evils that our constitutional tradition identifies in historically familiar patterns of persecutory state

[54] By reckless defamation, I mean not mere negligence in stating a false fact, but subjective awareness that a fact stated is likely to be false. On my view, both knowledge of the falsity of one's statements of fact or awareness of their likely falsity remove such statements from the core of free speech protection, since in both cases the statements are not the sincere expression of conviction. In contrast to *New York Times Co. v. Sullivan*, 376 US 254 (1964) and subsequent cases, my view does not turn on the speech being about public officials or figures, and would tend wholly to immunize conscientious public speech from abridgement by libel actions of any kind.

[55] On this point, see David A. Strauss, 'Persuasion, Autonomy, and Freedom of Expression', 91 *Colum. L Rev.* 334 (1991).

[56] For somewhat fuller development of this theme, see Richards, n. 26 above, ch. 7; Richards, n. 30 above, 195–201.

[57] For somewhat fuller development of this point, see Richards, n. 26 above, 173, 194, 217, 220, 225.

intolerance of moral and political criticism. This explains the background principle of toleration that prohibits the state's enforcement of its own judgements about the critical worth of public speech rooted in conviction. Laws condemned by this principle include not only seditious-libel laws that prohibit either express or implied criticism of the government. This principle condemns as well state prohibitions of speech motivated by the offence taken by groups of citizens at the critical advocacy of values of other groups; such prohibitions improperly substitute state enforcement of general views believed to be true for the play of the critical moral powers of free and equal people engaged in responsible discourse. It is this reason of principle, as I shall further argue in later chapters, that may explain and justify why group libel laws (laws making it a criminal and/or civil wrong to engage in defamation of racial, ethnic, or religious groups) are currently constitutionally suspect in the United States.[58]

The reason is this. The principle of free speech, properly understood, discriminates among kinds of interests that may enjoy weight in the balance of political argument about free speech (for example, consumer protection or reputational integrity or privacy), and disentitles certain other interests to any weight whatsoever. These latter interests include offence taken at the exercise of the right of conscience itself, i.e., arguments for the repression of conscientious speech based on offence taken at the general evaluative merits of what is said, in effect, a kind of general 'ideological fighting words'.[59] A free speech balancing consequentialism predicated on giving weight to such interests (triggered by offence of this sort) may be radically misconceived. Whatever a clear and present danger may reasonably mean, it cannot, consistently with respect for the right to conscience, mean this. This conception of 'harms' (sufficient to justify state action) in this case is defined by the objection that offended people take to the conscientious advocacy of certain general views, and the enforceable state judgements are based on this sense of offence. At bottom, the offence taken at a form of conscience (viewed as corrupt) is taken to be sufficient to abridge the exercise of conscience. Such a ground for repressive state action is, in principle, unacceptable, for the same reason that the equal moral independence of conscience is, in principle, immune from state power. The state can, consistently with respect for conscience, no more proscribe conscientious moral convictions on such a basis than it can religious or political convictions. Disagreements about issues of conscience (including the corruption of conscience) must, in a free society, be resolved through the free exercise of conscience in debate that appeals to persuasion through free public reason. Conscience can only be free in this way if a putative error in conscience is not sufficient for state censorship in the domain of conscientious conviction and expression.

[58] The constitutionality of such laws (directed at general normative claims) must be distinguished from the question of laws directed against *ad hominem* insulting epithets of a sort contextually highly likely to lead to violence, so-called 'fighting words'. See *Chaplinsky* v. *New Hampshire*, 315 US 568 (1942). However, constitutional protection of offensive public speech, making general claims, may require that the latter laws be narrowly construed. See, e.g., *Gooding* v. *Wilson*, 405 US 518 (1972).

[59] See Harry Kalven, Jr., *A Worthy Tradition: Freedom of Speech in America* (Harper & Row, New York, 1988), at 95.

If this argument is based on a proper understanding of the right to conscience as an inalienable human right, it will clarify its force and weight to contrast its American interpretation of these matters with the ostensibly rights-based forms of constitutionalism that take a different view of the constitutionality of group libel, indeed that accept group libel as itself a protection of rights. German constitutionalism is usefully illustrative. This constitutional system, like many others,[60] justifies the prohibition of group libel in rights-based terms of another right defined either as 'the right to inviolability of personal honour'[61] or a general guarantee that '[t]he dignity of man shall be inviolable'.[62] This general framework of free speech analysis in Germany is older than the current German constitutional order. Its current sense is, however, framed by a distinctive feature of current German constitutionalism, its commitment to militant democracy; on this view, democracy must be protected against groups and persons that would subvert its general constitutional principles.[63] As I earlier suggested, some rights (like those of individual reputation and of privacy) may reasonably be legally protected to the extent that they do not conflict with the right of free speech. But these rights in their nature fall in spheres (wilfully false statement of facts about individuals or statement of private facts in which there is no reasonable public interest) that do not trench upon the core interests of free speech, the conscientious discussion and criticism of public matters of fact and value by people free of improperly censorious state judgements about the worth or value of such discussion. But the German rights of honour or dignity are not similarly so limited.[64] Rather, the state may prohibit conscientious expression of general evaluative views essentially on the ground that persons experience such expression as disrespectful.[65] In effect, the scope of pub-

---

[60] See, e.g., Art. 10, European Convention for the Protection of Human Rights, in Mark W. Janis and Richard S. Kay, *European Human Rights Law* (University of Connecticut Law School Foundation Press, Hartford, Conn., 1990), at p. xx, and further discussion of this point in Chap. 1, above.

[61] See Art. 5(2) of the Basic Law of the Federal Republic of Germany, which sets limits on the scope of protection of the rights of free speech and press under Art. 5(1).

[62] See Art. 1(1), of *ibid.*, which sets general limits on otherwise absolute rights like the right of art and science, research, and teaching under Art. 5(3). For an example of judicial balancing of this sort, see the *Mephisto Case* (1971), 30 BVerfGE 173, translated into English in Donald P. Kommers, *The Constitutional Jurisprudence of the Federal Republic of Germany* (2nd edn., Duke University Press, Durham, NC, and London, 1997), 301–4, 427–30.

[63] See Art. 5(3) (obligation of loyalty of university teachers to the constitution); Art. 9(2) (prohibition of associations directed against the constitutional order); Art. 18 (abuse of rights like free speech can lead to forfeiture of such rights); Art. 20(4) (in the absence of any available alternative, all Germans given right of resistance against anyone attempting to overthrow the constitutional order); Art. 21(2) (on the basis of a finding of the Constitutional Court, unconstitutionality of political parties directed against the basic democratic order), Basic Law of the Federal Republic of Germany. For associated legal developments, see Eric Stein, 'History Against Free Speech: The New German Law Against the "Auschwitz"—and Other—"Lies" ', 85 *Mich. L Rev.* 277 (1986).

[64] The problem is not limited to group libel alone; German constitutional law, like that of other European countries, permits its individual libel laws to encompass disparaging value statements about public figures. See, for a case illustrative of this approach, the *Street Theatre Case* (1984), 67 BVerfGE 213, reprinted in Kommers, n. 62 above, at 431–5. For the contrasting American approach, see *Hustler Magazine* v. *Falwell*, 485 US 46 (1988).

[65] It would be a closer case if group libel laws were limited to knowingly false statements of facts about groups, statements that therefore do not express conviction and are not therefore sincere expressions of

lic debate is to be circumscribed to the measure of ideological inoffensiveness to important persons and groups in society (as those persons and groups are defined by the state).

People do often identify themselves with some larger group with which they associate their self-respect; and they take a lively interest in how they take such groups, and thus themselves, to be represented and discussed in the public culture of their societies, and sometimes experience reasonable indignation at such discussions as forms of heresy or blasphemy or group libel challenging their essential values in living, indeed the very core of their identities. Such indignation cannot, however, count as a harm sufficient to limit free speech protection, as it would be if such indignation gave rise to a right of sufficient force (as it does under German law) to limit the scope of application of the right of free speech. The German constitutional theory wrongly counts the occasion of such indignation as a secular evil from which free people may, like threats to physical integrity, be protected. In fact, a proper understanding of free speech as toleration regards such occasions as precisely the kinds of spiritual challenge to public discussion and debate that the tradition of free speech should protect and encourage. Otherwise, the essential public rights and responsibilities of a free and democratic people (indeed, the core of their inalienable rights) are illegitimately transferred to others, who protect citizens from even hearing speech they might find offensive. A people, thus protected, may privately gain in peace of mind, but such privatization deprives a free people of the inalienable public liberties and responsibilities of citizenship that alone dignify them as a people worthy of freedom (reasonably confronting the central issues of public conscience of their age and culture). For this reason, such indignation should, consistent with the values of free speech, express itself not in censorship but in creative forms of voluntary organization to rebut such arguments in the usual way. As we have seen, the principle of free speech is grounded in scepticism about the corruptibility of political power in the domain of the conscientious expression of public values; state judgements about the worth or value of speech in this domain fail to allow proper scope to the reasonable debate of morally independent and free persons about public matters of fact and value. Such reasonable scepticism extends as well to state abridgements of speech ostensibly grounded in protecting groups from disrespectful speech. The point is not that such speech is not sometimes disrespectful of groups and persons or that conscience is not sometimes corrupt; but that the prohibition of such speech by the state makes the state the improper enforcer of that respect as the arbiter of what counts as a good or bad conscience in a domain of public debate where enforcement of this kind contemptuously usurps the sovereign right of persons to be the ultimate critics of value in living.

conscience. In my judgement, the constitutionally relevant difference between such a more circumscribed form of group libel action and an individual libel action would be that the former is embedded in general debate about values that can be rebutted in the usual way; in contrast, individual libel is targeted at an individual as such, and can only be adequately rebutted by the forms of legal actions through which persons uphold their reputation. For this reason, even a more circumscribed form of group libel action would violate the principle of free speech, a point to be further elaborated in Chap. 4 below. I am indebted for this clarification of my thinking to Thomas Franck.

Respect for liberty of conscience requires of us the minimal civic courage of overcoming the fear of hearing views we detest and disallowing such fears of freedom as the basis of state censorship. Such a risk, if it is a risk, is reasonably borne if we, as free people, both understand and value the foundational role in a just polity of the sovereign public reason about issues of conscience it makes available to all on fair terms.

The interposition of the state in these matters enlists state power in the support and legitimation of what counts as a group identity and the proper respect owed that identity as the measure of what can count as reasonable public debate about such matters. But the state's judgements in this domain are no more impartially reasonable than they are in the area of religion or politics; the state here enforces inevitably crude majoritarian stereotypes of group identity on a par with similarly illegitimate enforceable state judgements about true religion and good politics. The relationship between individual and group identity must, in a free society, be open to the fullest range of reasonable discussion and debate on terms that allow persons to question, debate, and renegotiate their evaluative understanding of value in living on their own terms, including the relationship between their sense of themselves as individuals and as self-identified members of various groups. Perhaps the relationship between individual and group identity will be more reasonably contestable in a society as ethnically diverse and ideologically pluralistic as the United States than it is in more homogeneous societies; but even in more homogeneous societies, the terms of individual and group identity must, in those that are free societies, be open to broad and robust discussion and debate to allow the fullest range of public intelligence and imagination reasonably to be available to all on terms that respect moral autonomy and individuality. Otherwise, essential issues of public debate about value in living—the very terms of one's moral integrity—will be truncated to the measure of unreflective and often oppressive majoritarian stereotypes.

Much serious discussion of public values could, in virtue of the German rights of honour or dignity, give rise to state protection of persons who take offence at such discussion. The general structure of German constitutional argument imposes a duty on the state to protect rights.[66] In effect, the legitimacy of state power turns, like the comparable American Lockean constitutional theory,[67] on the way in which the state organizes and protects the basic rights of its people, including their basic rights of conscience, life, personal security, and the like. To this extent, the German constitutional theory is normatively appealing on grounds of its commitment to the protection of human rights. But the interpretation of this theory to include protection from offensive discussion rests on an inadequate understanding of the weight of free speech

---

[66] For judicial elaboration on this point, see the *Princess Soraya Case* (1973), 34 BVerfGE 269, translated in Kommers, n. 62 above, 124–8; the *Abortion I Case* (1975), 39 BVerfGE 1, translated in *ibid.*, at 336–46; the *Abortion II Case*, 88 BVerfGE 203, translated in *ibid.*, 349–55; the *Schleyer Kidnapping Case* (1977), 46 BVerfGE 160, in *ibid.*, at 356–7.

[67] See, in general, Richards, n. 30 above.

in such an overall theory of constitutional legitimacy.[68] This interpretation does not take seriously the nature of the right of free speech in question, precisely because respect for this right requires a principled scepticism about abuses of state power in a certain domain. In short, the concern of free speech is not protection by the state, but from the state, empowering free exercise of the inalienable right of conscience on terms of equal respect. In the area of free speech, however, the German interpretation of this theory of the state as the positivistic source and protector of rights here subverts such protection by its legitimation of an improper state role, an illiberal moral paternalism in the domain of conscience directed at protecting people from offence to their convictions, in effect, from challenge and debate. Such 'protection', if carried to its logical extreme, might massage the complacencies of a public opinion that concurs on bromides and symbolic gestures of group solidarity; it does not empower people responsibly to understand, claim, and enforce their human rights as free and reasonable people.

There is a larger point worth making here, associated with the relationship of this view of free speech to the idea of defensive democracy. The protection of human rights, if it means anything, cannot be limited in its scope to those who, in the view of the state, support and do not subvert the constitutional order. A constitutional order, ostensibly grounded in the protection of human rights, must extend human rights to all subject to its political power. German constitutionalism undoubtedly espouses this general constitutional theory, and surely self-consciously means to transcend more traditional German national ideologies constructed around rights-sceptical polarities of friends and enemies[69] often founded on retaining the purity of the nation's allegedly constitutive ethnic homogeneity.[70] But the German constitutional ideology of defensive democracy is in tension with its more fundamental commitment to inalienable human rights; indeed, its terms suggest the return of the repressed, the older ideology of friends and enemies that it surely means constructively to transcend. Correlatively, its limitation of the right to free speech (by rights of honour or dignity) is unjustifiable for the same reason. The protection of the right to conscience, as an inalienable human right, must extend to all persons within the scope of its principle, namely, those who conscientiously express views on matters of

---

[68] On the kind of balancing between the right of free speech and rights protected by private law to which the German approach has led, see the illuminating discussion in Peter E. Quint, 'Free Speech and Private Law in German Constitutional Theory' (1989) 48 *MLR* 247.

[69] For a clear statement and defence of such a German national ideology, see Carl Schmitt, *The Concept of the Political* (trans. George Schwab, Rutgers University Press, New Brunswick, NJ, 1976). For an illuminating account of Schmitt's life and work, including his complicity with the Nazi regime, see Joseph W. Bendersky, *Carl Schmitt: Theorist for the Reich* (Princeton University Press, Princeton, NJ, 1983). Schmitt's complicity with the Nazis places him, like Heidegger, among the leading German intellectuals of their period now very much under critical scrutiny in Germany and elsewhere as part of a tradition that the new German constitutional order very much wants to repudiate. On Heidegger, see Victor Farias, *Heidegger and Nazism* (Temple University Press, Philadelphia, Penn., 1989). It would be paradoxical indeed if German constitutional doctrines like defensive democracy were, as I suggest, very much in unconscious thrall to such a now repudiated tradition.

[70] For a development of this idea as central to the modern idea of political democracy, see Carl Schmitt, *The Crisis of Parliamentary Democracy* (trans. Ellen Kennedy, MIT Press, Cambridge, Mass., 1985), at 9.

public value and fact. Respect is owed them as persons who originate views and claims and who have the right to authenticate themselves by speaking conscientiously in their own voice and their own terms. The principle of free speech requires that each person is guaranteed the greatest equal liberty to exercise this right in its proper domain consistent with a like liberty for all. It subverts the principled moral force of this right to truncate its protection in terms of some range of views that are politically or morally mainstream and others that are not. This makes ideological conformity, not respect for the human rights of all persons (whatever their convictions), the measure of membership in the constitutional community. As I earlier argued, respect for a right like free speech enjoys its greatest moral force when it extends its protection even to subversive advocates who challenge its authority; the same point applies here to group libel. Respect for the moral sovereignty of dissenters from mainstream views makes the best statement that could be made about the constitutive inner morality of a constitutional community based on respect for human rights.

There is legitimate political power enough to deal with those dissenters who would move beyond dissent to overt acts that threaten the rights of others (for further discussion, see Chapter 4, below). Most dissenters do not do so, and many non-dissenters will threaten such acts. The principle of free speech insists that the mere offence taken at dissenting views cannot be the measure of a clear and present danger sufficient to justify the abridgement of speech. Jefferson's earlier cited point about religious liberty applies here as well: 'he [the civil magistrate] being of course judge of that tendency will make his opinions the rule of judgment', thus falsely and mischievously conflating ideological dissidence with overt acts that violate rights.

The issue of constitutional principle may be more abstractly stated. The principle of free speech arises from a historical scepticism, rooted in rights-based political theory, about the uses of state power to curtail the free exercise of public opinion by the use of its coercive power to criminalize heresy or blasphemy or seditious libel and the like. In each case, criminal prohibitions of thought and speech were based on state judgements about the worth or value of thought and speech (on the ground of a putative corruption of conscience); such judgements both unreasonably limited the scope of thought and discussion to the measure of the dominant political orthodoxy and correlatively deprived persons of their inalienable rights reasonably to think and discuss public matters as free people. The principle of free speech, based on rights-based scepticism about such enforceable political judgements, must extend to all such judgements, including those based on the offence taken by persons to conscientious views expressed by other persons. Such constitutional concern must apply not only to group libel prosecutions but prohibitions analogously based on disrespectful thoughts and speech.

I have so far offered reasons for scepticism about group libel laws largely based on what I take to be the best theory of the principle of free speech. But these arguments will not have reasonable force unless integrated into a constitutional understanding of the evils that such laws are meant to combat. I hope to show that the argument for toleration gives us reasons not only for valuing a strong principle of free speech, but for questioning group libel and related laws as an appropriate remedy for the constitutional evil of discrimination. To do so, we must first elaborate with some care the ways in which the argument for toleration enables us to understand this evil in various domains (anti-Semitism, racism, sexism, and homophobia). On that basis, we may then deepen our understanding of the constitutional grounds for scepticism of the role group libel and related laws are alleged legitimately to play in combating this evil in its various contemporary manifestations.

3

The Argument for Toleration and the Theory of Structural Injustice

The right against unjust discrimination (that condemns the expression through public law of the evils of anti-Semitism, racism, sexism, and homophobia) is now as constitutionally fundamental as the right of free speech, and we need now to consider how this basic right is to be understood. I offer a theory of this right in terms of a normative conception of structural injustice that draws upon and elaborates elements of the argument for toleration already proposed. Using an approach that combines interpretive history and normative political theory, I begin with anti-Semitism and racism, and then turn to sexism and homophobia. In later chapters, I use and elaborate this theory to address a range of free speech issues.

RACISM AS A CONSTITUTIONAL EVIL

The struggle for racial justice enjoys a central role in American interpretive understanding of the Reconstruction Amendments both in terms of the hermeneutic background of those Amendments in the antebellum abolitionist movement and in terms of the successful African-American struggle, after their ratification, to rectify the crudely racist interpretation they had irresponsibly been given by the judiciary.[1] The success of that later struggle culminated in *Brown* v. *Board of Education*[2] and the reasonable national consensus that accepts the legitimacy of that opinion as a fixed point in contemporary discussions of judicially enforceable constitutional principles. Contemporary constitutional theories are importantly defined and valued in terms of the account they give of the legitimacy of *Brown* and its progeny (including, as we shall see, judicial expansion of its principle to include gender[3] and, most recently, sexual orientation[4]). Some such constitutional theories focus on the political powerlessness of African-Americans, supposing judicial intervention to be appropriate to the extent it rectifies such powerlessness, suitably interpreted;[5] others associate the

---

[1] I discuss both these matters at length in David A. J. Richards, *Conscience and the Constitution: History, Theory, and Law of the Reconstruction Amendments* (Princeton University Press, Princeton, NJ, 1993); *Women, Gays, and the Constitution: The Grounds for Feminism and Gay Rights in Culture and Law* (University of Chicago Press, Chicago, Ill., 1998); and *Identity and the Case for Gay Rights: Race, Gender, Religion as Analogies* (University of Chicago Press, Chicago, Ill., in press).

[2] *Brown* v. *Board of Education*, 347 US 483 (1954).

[3] See, e.g., *Frontiero* v. *Richardson*, 411 US 677 (1973); *Craig* v. *Boren*, 429 US 190 (1976); *United States* v. *Virginia*, 116 S Ct. 2264 (1996).

[4] See *Romer* v. *Evans*, 116 S Ct. 1620 (1996); but cf. *Bowers* v. *Hardwick*, 478 US 186 (1986).

[5] See, e.g., Bruce Ackerman, 'Beyond *Carolene Products*', 98 *Harv. L Rev.* 713 (1985); John Hart Ely, *Democracy and Distrust: A Theory of Judicial Review* (Harvard University Press, Cambridge, Mass., 1980).

constitutional defect with the basis of the disadvantage (namely, an immutable and salient personal characteristic).[6] Presumably, any plausible elaboration of the principle of *Brown*, as understood by such theories, would require plausible analogies to be made to either the political powerlessness of African-Americans or to personal characteristics that, like race, are immutable and conspicuously salient.

The theory of political powerlessness might, on at least one interpretation of it,[7] raise much more serious questions about the analogy of gender to race than of race to sexual orientation in view of the majority political power of women in contrast to the minority status of gays and lesbians; but, on the interpretation of political power in terms of relative wealth and media access, the analogy might disfavour judicial protection of gays and lesbians as well.[8] However, it is the theory of immutability and salience (a solider analogy between race and gender) that raises the sharpest critical questions about the analogy of principle between race and sexual orientation.[9] It is the pressure of this theory of the analogy that motivates much of the interest of some gay activists in three studies, in the early 1990s, one in neuroanatomy, and two in behavioural genetics, that claimed to suggest significant links between sexual orientation and biology.[10] On this view of the causal story of homosexual sexual orientation, the alleged biology of sexual orientation conveniently is a proxy for the immutability of race, and thus a ground for pursuing the constitutional analogy of race and sexual orientation as a basis for a larger reasonable constitutional concern against unjust forms of discrimination.

If this, however, were the alleged short-term strategic price we must pay to secure protection for gay rights, it is, in my view, a price not worth paying. My objection is not to the reasonable pursuit of scientific research on sexual orientation within ethical parameters about the nature and uses of such research.[11] But it is not a reasonable interpretation of any of these studies that they have found a biological cause of homosexuality; none of them makes any such claim, nor are even their limited findings free from scientific doubt.[12] There is reasonable evidence that sexual orientation is for many a largely settled and irreversible erotic preference long before the age of

[6] See, e.g., Michael J. Perry, 'Modern Equal Protection: A Conceptualization and Appraisal', 79 *Colum. L Rev.* 1023 (1979).

[7] See John Hart Ely, *Democracy and Distrust: A Theory of Judicial Review* (Harvard University Press, Cambridge, Mass., 1980); but cf. Bruce Ackerman, 'Beyond *Carolene Products*'. 98 *Harv. L Rev.* 713 (1985).

[8] For Justice Scalia's appeal to this ground for scepticism about the judicial protection of gays and lesbians, see his dissent in *Romer* v. *Evans*, 116 S Ct. at 1637.

[9] See Perry, n. 6 above, 1066–7.

[10] See Simon LeVay, 'A Difference in Hypothalamic Structure Between Heterosexual and Homosexual Men', *Science*, 30 Aug. 1991; J. Michael Bailey and Richard C. Pillard, 'A Genetic Study of Male Sexual Orientation', 48 *Archives Gen. Psychiatry* 1089 (1991); Dean H. Hamer *et al.*, 'A Linkage between DNA Markers on the X Chromosome and Male Sexual Orientation', *Science*, 16 July 1993.

[11] See, for an illuminating and balanced recent study of this issue, Timothy F. Murphy, *Gay Science: The Ethics of Sexual Orientation Research* (Columbia University Press, New York, 1997).

[12] For a review of the criticisms which these studies have received, see Janet Halley, 'Sexual Orientation and the Politics of Biology: A Critique of the Argument from Immutability', 46 *Stan. L Rev.* 503 (1994), at 529–46.

responsibility,[13] but this fact, if it is fact, may more often be true of gay men than lesbians[14] and does not require, to the extent it is true, a biological explanation. Language acquisition may be a useful analogy here; it is certainly made possible by our biological heritage, but also clearly turns on early social experience, after which it remains a fixed and fundamental orientation of our attitude to the world,[15] as immutably profound a feature of our humanity as anything else.[16] In any event, a fact of this sort, even if it were biologically explicable, is not a fact like race or gender but a complex system of psychological propensities (thoughts, fantasies, desires, vulnerabilities, deeply rooted in our imaginative lives as persons) that may be ethically interpreted and developed by the subject in quite different ways against different contextual backgrounds and, in light of those interpretations, acted on in correspondingly very different ways, and sometimes not acted on at all. Indeed, for these very reasons, nothing in the alleged immutability of sexual orientation (were it a fact and even a biologically explicable fact) makes it socially transparent in the way that race and gender are usually conspicuous, as the very real debates about outing in the gay and lesbian community make quite clear.[17]

My objection to the biological story (as a way of invoking the racial analogy in support of gay rights) arises both from what the story omits and what it distorts in the central normative case for gay rights. It thus omits what motivates the rights-based case for the emancipation of gay and lesbian people, namely, a normative analysis of the injustice imposed on the interpretive moral complexity of the relationship between sexual orientation and action in the life of the subject in terms of an ethically responsible choice of one's identity as, significantly, that of a gay or lesbian person. From this perspective, the possible concealment or repression or failure to develop one's sexual preference, as gay or lesbian, is not a reasonable condition of political respect if sexual preference is integral to the authenticity of moral personality and the prejudice against it as unreasonable as racism and sexism. In fact, as more fully argued below, sexual preference is central to self-authenticating claims to lesbian and gay

[13] On irreversibility, see Wainwright Churchill, *Homosexual Behaviour Among Males* (Hawthorn, New York, 1967), at 283–91; Michael Ruse, *Homosexuality* (Basil Blackwell, Oxford, 1988), at 59–62. On the early age of its formation, see John Money and Anke A. Ehrhardt, *Man & Woman, Boy & Girl* (Johns Hopkins University Press, Baltimore, Md., 1972), at 153–201; C. A. Tripp, *The Homosexual Matrix* (McGraw-Hill, New York, 1975), at 251; Donald J. West, *Homosexuality* (Aldine, Chicago, Ill., 1968), at 266. One study hypothesizes that gender identity and sexual object choice coincide with the development of language, between the age of 18 to 24 months. John Money, J. G. Hampson, and J. L. Hampson, 'An Evidence of Some Basic Sexual Concepts: The Evidence of Human Hermaphroditism', 97 *Bull. Johns Hopkins Hosp.* 301, 308–10 (1955); for elaboration of this linguistic analogy, see John Money, *Gay, Straight, and In-Between: The Sexology of Erotic Orientation* (Oxford University Press, New York, 1988), at 11–12, 54, 71, 74, 76, 80, 129–30; cf. Alan P. Bell, Martin S. Weinberg, and Sue K. Hammersmith, *Sexual Preference* (Simon & Schuster, New York, 1978). For a recent judicious review of the scientific literature, see Richard Green, *Sexual Science and the Law* (Harvard University Press, Cambridge, Mass., 1992), at 62–86; on irreversibility of orientation, see Murphy, n. 11 above, at 185, 190.

[14] See Murphy, n. 11 above, at 184.

[15] For development of this analogy, see Money, n. 13 above, at 11–12, 54, 71, 74, 76, 80, 129–30.

[16] Cf., on this point, *ibid.*, at 74.

[17] See, e.g., Larry Gross, *Contested Closets: The Politics and Ethics of Outing* (University of Minnesota Press, Minneapolis, Minn., 1993).

personal and ethical identity, and the prejudice against such claims is politically unreasonable in the same way racism and sexism are unreasonable. The sacrifice of moral authenticity is not a demand any person could reasonably be asked to accept as the price for freedom from irrational prejudice; and homosexual persons can no more be reasonably asked to make such a crippling sacrifice of self than any other person.

But the real threat of the biological story is not only what it omits, but what it distorts or may distort in the case for gay rights. The biological story falsely and malignly reduces to crude physical terms what is essentially a principled argument for the just and ethical emancipation of the moral powers of conscience of gay and lesbian persons in terms that subvert its emancipatory potential. Biological reductionism was central to the unjust cultural subjugation of African-Americans and women as a separate species,[18] and has historically wreaked comparable havoc on early advocates of gay and lesbian rights by confirming, rather than challenging, the unjust cultural stereotypes of an inferiority rooted in nature (for example, gay men as a congenitally abnormal male who is a female 'third sex'[19]). Otto Weininger, for example, on this basis combined advocacy of gay rights with grotesque misogyny, racism, and anti-Semitism.[20] The repetition of the terms of one's subjugation is not needed, but an empowering critical perspective on the cultural terms of one's degradation (including its continuities with evils like racism, sexism, and anti-Semitism) and on corresponding political, ethical, and intellectual responsibilities to exercise our active moral powers of criticism and reconstruction of that culture on terms of justice.[21] Lesbians and gays need responsibly to insist on and to demand personal and moral identity as lesbian and gay persons, and to resist those unjust and objectifying stereotypes that have stripped them of their powers of moral personality.

In fact, such an emphasis on legitimate claims to ethical identity, as the background of a cultural orthodoxy that unjustly represses such claims, suggests an alternative way of thinking about the larger fabric of constitutional principles that condemns, as suspect, related evils like racism and sexism. We may have as much reason to question constitutional theories of suspectness, appealing to powerlessness or immutability and salience, in the areas of race or gender as we do in the area of sexual orientation. Maintaining the integrity of the case for gay rights, by resisting the biological model, may have as much to teach us about gay rights as it does about related injustices.

A plausible general theory of suspect classification analysis must unify, on grounds of principle, the claims to such analysis of African-Americans, women, and lesbians and gays. Political powerlessness cannot do so. Lack of political power—measured

---

[18] See Stephen J. Gould, *The Mismeasure of Man* (W. W. Norton, New York, 1981); Carol Tavris, *The Mismeasure of Woman* (Simon & Schuster, New York, 1992).

[19] For discussion of this development and its malign consequences, see David A. J. Richards, *Women, Gays, and the Constitution: The Grounds for Feminism and Gay Rights in Culture and Law* (University of Chicago Press, Chicago, Ill., 1998), at 305–6, 313, 314, 317, 322–3, 332–6, 369.

[20] See, for discussion, *ibid.*, at 332–6, 433, 461, 465.

[21] See, in general, *ibid.*

either by some statistical norm[22] or by a principle of fair representation[23]—does not capture the plane of ethical discourse of suspect classification analysis as it has been developed in authoritative case law. An analysis based on political powerlessness wrongly suggests that the gains in political solidarity of groups subjected to deep racial, sexist, or religious prejudice (in virtue of resistance to such prejudice) disentitle them from constitutional protection,[24] as if the often meager political gains of blacks, women, and gays and lesbians (when measured against their claims of justice) are the measure of constitutional justice.[25] This analysis preposterously denies constitutional protection to women because they are a statistical majority of voters.[26] This approach also proves too much: it extends protection to any political group, though subject to no history of rights-denying prejudice, solely because it has not been as politically successful as it might have been (e.g., dentists).[27] Procedural models of suspect classification analysis suppress the underlying substantive rights-based normative judgements central to how equal protection should be and has been interpreted. Such models neither explanatorily fit the case law nor afford a sound normative model with which to criticize the case law.

Suspect classification analysis focuses on the political expression of irrational prejudices of a certain sort: namely, those rooted in a history and culture of unjust exclusion of a certain group from participation in the political community required by their basic rights of conscience, speech, association, and work. The fundamental wrong of racism and sexism has been the intolerant exclusion of blacks and women from the rights of public culture, exiling them to cultural marginality in supposedly morally inferior realms and unjustly stigmatizing identity on such grounds. Such unjust cultural marginalization and stigmatization also victimize homosexuals, and its rectification entitles sexual orientation to be recognized as a suspect classification.

Analysis of this sort suggests why immutability and salience do not coherently explain even the historical paradigm of suspect classification of race, and therefore cannot normatively define the terms of principle reasonably applicable to other claims to suspect classification analysis. The principle of *Brown* v. *Board of Education*[28] itself cannot reasonably be understood in terms of the abstract ethical ideal that state benefits and burdens should never turn on an immutable and salient characteristic as

---

[22] See Ackerman, n. 5 above.   [23] See Ely, n. 5 above.

[24] Ackerman likewise makes this erroneous suggestion, n. 5 above, at 718, 740–6.

[25] Racial classifications, e.g., remain as suspect as they have ever been irrespective of the political advances of African-Americans. See, e.g., *Palmore* v. *Sidoti*, 466 US 429, 434 (1984) (awarding custody of child on grounds of race of adoptive father held unconstitutional).

[26] The Supreme Court has expressly regarded gender as a suspect classification irrespective of the status of women as a political majority. See, e.g., *Frontiero* v. *Richardson*, 411 US 677, 686 n.17 (1973); cf. *Craig* v. *Boren*, 429 US 190, 204 (1976) (holding that gender classification is not substantially related to traffic laws). But cf. Ely, n. 5 above, at 164–70 (asserting that women should be denied constitutional protection because they constitute a majority of voters and are non-insular).

[27] The Supreme Court has declined to regard the mere fact of the greater political success of one interest group over another as relevant to according closer scrutiny to legislation favourable to one group over another. See, e.g., *United States RR Retirement Bd.* v. *Fritz*, 449 US 166, 174–6 (1980); cf. *Williamson* v. *Lee Optical*, 348 US 483, 488 (1965).

[28] 347 US 483 (1954).

such. There is no such ethical ideal.[29] It is not a reasonable objection that a distribution of goods may be owed to persons on the basis of an immutable and salient characteristic if justice requires or allows such a characteristic to be given such weight. Disabled persons are born with disabilities that often cannot be changed; nonetheless, resources are appropriately accorded them because of their disabilities to accord them some fair approximation to the opportunities of non-disabled persons.

The example is not an isolated one; its principle pervades the justice of rewards and fair distribution more generally. For example, we reward certain athletic achievements very highly and do not finely calibrate the components of our rewards attributable to acts of self-disciplined will from those based on natural endowments. Achievement itself suffices to elicit reward even though some significant part of it turns on immutable physical endowments that some have and others lack. Or, we allocate scarce places in institutions of higher learning on the basis of an immutable factor such as geographic distribution, an educational policy we properly regard as sensible and not unfair. The point can be reasonably generalized to include that part of the theory of distributive justice concerned with maintaining both an economic and social minimum and some structure of differential rewards to elicit better performance for the public good. The idea of a just minimum turns on certain facts about levels of subsistence, not on acts of will; we would not regard such a minimum as any the less justly due if the human sciences showed us that some significant component of it turned on immutable factors. Differential rewards perform the role of incentives for the kind of performance required by modern industrial market economies; the human sciences may show us that immutable factors such an genetic endowment play some significant role in such performance. Nonetheless, we would not regard it as unjust to reward such performance so long as the incentives worked out with the consequences specified by the theory of distributive justice. Our conclusion, from a wide range of diverse examples, must be that immutability and salience do not identify an ethical ideal that could be a reasonable basis for suspect classification analysis.

In particular, race is a suspect classification, not on such grounds (which would include much that we regard as just), but when it expresses a background structural injustice of a certain sort that sustains a rights-denying culture of irrational political prejudice. Persons are not regarded as victimized by this prejudice because they are physically unable to change or mask the trait defining the class, but because the prejudice itself assigns intrinsically unreasonable weight to and burdens on identifications that define one's moral personality. Race in America is culturally defined by the 'one-drop' rule under which quite small proportions of black genes suffice to be regarded as black, including persons who are for all visibly salient purposes non-black.[30] Persons who are black by this definition could pass as white; most, including some

---

[29] For a similar analysis, see Ronald Dworkin, *Law's Empire* (Harvard University Press, Cambridge, Mass., 1986), at 381–99.

[30] See generally F. James Davis, *Who Is Black?: One Nation's Definition* (Pennsylvania State University Press, University Park, Pennsylvania, 1991).

historically important African-American leaders, chose not to do so.[31] Choosing to pass as white would cut them off from intimately personal relationships to family and community that nurture and sustain self-respect and personal integrity;[32] the price of avoiding racial prejudice is an unreasonable sacrifice of basic resources of personal and ethical identity that they will not accept. In effect, one is to avoid injustice by a silencing of one's moral powers to protest injustice, degrading moral integrity into silent complicity with evil. The same terms of cultural degradation apply to all victims of racism whether visibly or non-visibly black, the demand of supine acceptance of an identity unjustly devalued.

Racial prejudice is an invidious political evil because it is directed against significant aspects of a person's cultural and moral identity on irrationalist grounds of subjugation because of that identity. The point is not that its irrationalist object is some brute fact that cannot be changed, but that it is directed at important aspects of moral personality: in particular, 'the way people think, feel, and believe, not how they look'—the identifications that make them 'members of the black ethnic community'.[33] Racial prejudice, thus analysed, shares common features with certain forms of religious intolerance. In particular, racism and anti-Semitism share a common irrationalist fear: *invisible blackness* or the *secret Jew*, persons who can pass as white or Christian but who are allegedly tainted by some fundamental incapacity fully to identify themselves as authentically a member of the majoritarian race or religion.[34] Such incapacity is ascribed to persons on the basis of 'perceived attitudes and social participation rather than on . . . appearance or lineage'.[35] On this basis, any dissent from the dominant racist or anti-Semitic orthodoxy, let alone sympathetic association with the stigmatized minority, is interpreted as evidence of being a member of the defective minority, thus imposing a reign of intellectual terror on any morally independent criticism of racial or religious intolerance and encouraging a stigmatized minority to accept the legitimacy of subordination.[36] The structural resemblance of racism to a form of religious intolerance is an important feature of its American historical background and is fundamental to a sound interpretation of the suspectness of race under American constitutional law.

The interpretive status of race, as the paradigm interpretive case of a suspect classification under the American constitutional law of the Equal Protection Clause, arose against the background of the interdependent institutions of American slavery and racism and the persistence of racism, supported by its judicial legitimation in cases like *Plessy* v. *Ferguson*[37] and *Pace* v. *Alabama*[38] long after the formal abolition of

---

[31] F. James Davis, n. 30 above, at 7, 56–7, 77–8, 178–9.   [32] *Ibid.*, at 56–7.

[33] *Ibid.*, at 179.   [34] *Ibid.*, at 55–6, 145.   [35] *Ibid.*, at 145.

[36] For exploration of this phenomenon, in the form of Jewish anti-Semitism, see, e.g., Sander L. Gilman, *Jewish Self-Hatred: Anti-Semitism and the Hidden Language of the Jews* (Johns Hopkins University Press, Baltimore, Mld., 1986); Michael Lerner, *The Socialism of Fools: Anti-Semitism on the Left* (Tikkun Books, Oakland, Cal., 1992).

[37] 163 US 537 (1896) (state segregation by race held constitutional).

[38] *Pace* v. *Alabama*, 106 US 583 (1863) (stronger penalties for interracial, as opposed to intraracial, sexual relations not racially discriminatory).

slavery. Racist institutions, like race-based slavery and its legacy of American apartheid,[39] evolved from an unjust and constitutionally illegitimate religious intolerance against the culture of African-Americans held in slavery. Racist prejudice was thus, in its origins, an instance of religious discrimination. This discrimination later developed, in ideological support of the institutions of American slavery, into a systematically unjust cultural intolerance of African-Americans as an ethnic group, reflected in their degradation from the status of bearers of human rights such as the basic rights of conscience, speech, intimate association, and work.[40] Race is constitutionally suspect when and to the extent that public law expresses such unjust racial prejudice, reflecting the unjust cultural degradation of a class of persons from their status as bearers of basic human rights.[41] The evil of such prejudice is its systematic degradation of identifications at the heart of free moral personality, including powers to protest injustice in the name and voice of one's human rights.

African-American self-understanding of American racism was deepened and energized by the scholarship and activism of W. E. B. Du Bois in exactly these terms. His historical studies challenged the dominant, often racist orthodoxy of the age,[42] and his 1903 *The Souls of Black Folk*[43] offered a pathbreaking interpretive study of African-American culture and the struggle for ethical self-consciousness under circumstances of racial oppression:[44]

a world which yields him [a black person] no true self-consciousness, but only lets him see himself through the revelation of the other world. It is a peculiar sensation, this double-consciousness, this sense of always looking at one's self through the eyes of others, of measuring one's soul by the tape of a world that looks on in amused contempt and pity. One ever feels his two-ness,—an American, a Negro; two souls, two thoughts, two unreconciled strivings, two warring ideals in one dark body, whose dogged strength alone keeps it from being torn asunder.[45]

The struggle for justice was thus a struggle for self-respecting identity on terms of justice that would transform both:

[39] For a recent important study of the persistence of this injustice, see Douglas S. Massey and Nancy A. Denton, *American Apartheid: Segregation and the Making of the Underclass* (Harvard University Press, Cambridge, Mass., 1993).

[40] I develop this argument at greater length in David A. J. Richards, *Conscience and the Constitution: History, Theory, and Law of the Reconstruction Amendments* (Princeton University Press, Princeton, NJ, 1993), at 80–9, 150–70; see also, in general, Richards, n. 19 above.

[41] For further development of this argument, see Richards, n. 40 above, at 170–7.

[42] See W. E. B. Du Bois, 'The Suppression of the African Slave-Trade', in *W. E. B. Du Bois* (ed. Nathan Huggins, 1896, Library of America, New York, 1986), 3–356; *Black Reconstruction in America, 1860–1880* (1935, Atheneum, New York, 1969).

[43] See W. E. B. Du Bois, 'The Souls of Black Folk', in *W. E. B. Du Bois*, n. 42 above, 359–586.

[44] See, in general, David Levering Lewis, *W. E. B. Du Bois: Biography of a Race, 1868–1919* (Henry Holt, New York, 1993); Eric J. Sundquist, *To Wake the Nations: Race in the Making of American Literature* (Harvard University Press, Belknap Press, Cambridge, Mass., 1993), 457–625; for a more critical, less rights-based reading of Du Bois's theory and practice, see Adolph L. Reed, Jr., *W. E. B. Du Bois and American Political Thought: Fabianism and the Color Line* (Oxford University Press, New York, 1997).

[45] See W. E. B. Du Bois, n. 43 above, at 364–5.

The history of the American Negro is the history of this strife,—this longing to attain self-conscious manhood, to merge his double self into a better and truer self. In this merging he wishes neither of the older selves to be lost. He would not Africanize America, for America has too much to teach the world and Africa. He would not bleach his Negro soul in a flood of white Americanism, for he knows that Negro blood has a message for the world. He simply wishes to make it possible for a man to be both a Negro and an American, without being cursed and spit upon by his fellows, without having the doors of Opportunity closed roughly in his face.[46]

I describe Du Bois's theory in terms of a normative struggle for redefining identity as a way of making the best sense of his remarkable insights both against the retrospective background of the tradition of abolitionist dissent he both reflects and elaborates and the prospective development of this struggle in the movements for civil liberties that include African-Americans, women, and, most recently, gays and lesbians.[47] Du Bois is a towering figure in the history of both the theory and practice of these movements because he speaks so powerfully from within the experience of the ethical struggle for voice and reasonable discourse, as claims of basic human rights, against a cultural tradition that both promised and betrayed its guarantees of basic human rights as minimal constitutional conditions of legitimate exercises of state power. The extraordinary importance of African-American dissent to American constitutionalism has been not only its demands that these basic rights be extended on fair terms to all persons, but its analysis of the ways in which structural injustice (denying a class of persons their very status as bearers of human rights) has been unjustly rationalized in terms of a question-begging entrenchment of such injustice. The most illuminating way to come to terms with the ethical enormity of this structural injustice and the role of claims for identity in protesting it is to start with the inalienable human right which, more than any other, models both the significance and weight of what an inalienable human right is, the right to conscience.

The normative value placed on conscience, as an inalienable human right, was seminally articulated by Locke and Bayle in stating the argument for toleration as a constitutive principle of justice in politics.[48] Constraints of principle must be placed on the power of the state to enforce sectarian religious views because the enforcement of such views on society at large entrenched, as the measure of legitimate convictions in matters of conscience, irrationalist intolerance; such intolerance was unjustly rationalized both by limiting standards of debate and speakers to the sectarian measure that supported dominant political and moral authority. The rights-based evil of such intolerance was the inadequate ground on which it abridged the inalienable right to conscience, the free exercise of the moral powers of rationality and reasonableness in terms of which persons define personal and ethical meaning in living. While this

---

[46] See W. E. B. Du Bois, n. 43 above, at 365.

[47] See, for further exploration of this retrospective and prospective background, Richards, *Conscience and the Constitution* and *Women, Gays, and the Constitution*, both n. 1 above.

[48] For full discussion of the terms and scope of their argument and its implications for American constitutionalism, see David A. J. Richards, *Toleration and the Constitution* (Oxford University Press, New York, 1986), at 85–281.

human right, like others, may be abridged on compelling secular grounds of protecting public goods reasonably acknowledged as such by all persons (irrespective of other philosophical or evaluative disagreements), the self-entrenching of a sectarian view could not suffice.[49]

The argument for toleration was a judgement of and response to such abuses of political epistemology (political enforcement at large of a sectarian view). The legitimation of religious persecution by both Catholics and Protestants (drawing authority from Augustine, among others) had rendered a politically entrenched view of religious and moral truth the measure of permissible ethics and religion, including the epistemic standards of inquiry and debate about religious and moral truth. By the late seventeenth century (when Locke and Bayle wrote), there was good reason to believe that politically entrenched views of religious and moral truth (resting on the Bible and associated interpretive practices) assumed essentially contestable interpretations of a complex historical interaction between pagan, Jewish, and Christian cultures in the early Christian era.[50]

The Renaissance rediscovery of pagan culture and learning reopened the question of how the Christian synthesis of pagan philosophical and Jewish ethical and religious culture was to be understood. Among other things, the development of critical historiography and techniques of textual interpretation had undeniable implications for reasonable Bible interpretation.[51] The Protestant Reformation both assumed and further encouraged these new modes of inquiry, and encouraged as well the appeal to experiment and experience, methodologies associated with the rise of modern science. These new approaches to thought and inquiry had made possible the recognition that there was a gap between the politically enforceable conceptions of religious and moral truth and the kinds of reasonable inquiries that the new approaches made available. The argument for toleration arose from the recognition of this disjunction between the reigning political epistemology and the new epistemic methodologies.

The crux of the problem was that unjustly entrenched political conceptions of truth have made themselves the measure both of the standards of reasonable inquiry and of who could count as a reasonable inquirer after truth. But, in light of the new modes of inquiry now available, such political entrenchment of religious truth was often seen to rest not only on the degradation of reasonable standards of inquiry, but on the self-fulfilling degradation of the capacity of persons to conduct such inquiries. In order to rectify these evils, the argument for toleration forbade, as a matter of principle, the enforcement by the statement of any such conception of religious truth. The scope of legitimate political concern must, as we have seen, rest on the pursuit of general ends such as life and basic rights and liberties (for example, the right to conscience). The pursuit of such goods was consistent with the full range of ends free people might rationally and reasonably pursue.

---

[49] See *ibid.*, at 244–7.   [50] See *ibid.*, at 25–7, 84–98, 105, 125.
[51] See *ibid.*, at 125–6.

A prominent feature of the argument for toleration was its claim that religious persecution corrupted conscience itself (both Bayle and Locke, religious Christians, thus argued that religious persecution has corrupted ethics and, for this reason, what they took to be Christianity's elevated and simple ethical core of a universal brotherhood of free people). Such corruption, a kind of self-induced blindness to the evils one inflicts, is a consequence of the political enforcement at large of a conception of religious truth that immunizes itself from independent criticism in terms of reasonable standards of thought and deliberation. In effect, the conception of religious truth, though perhaps having once been importantly shaped by more ultimate considerations of reason, ceases to be held or to be understood and defended *on the basis of reason.*

A tradition, which thus loses a sense of its reasonable foundations, stagnates and depends increasingly for allegiance on question-begging appeals to orthodox conceptions of truth and the violent repression of any exercise of free speech in dissent from such conceptions as a kind of disloyal moral treason. The politics of loyalty (based on the repression of free speech and the reasonable discourse it makes possible) rapidly degenerates, as it did in the antebellum South's repression of any criticism of slavery, into a politics that takes pride in widely held community values solely because they are community values. Standards of discussion and inquiry become increasingly parochial and insular; they serve only a polemical role in the defence of the existing community values and are indeed increasingly hostile to any more impartial reasonable assessment in light of such independent standards.[52]

Such politics tends to forms of irrationalism in order to protect its now essentially polemical project. Opposing views relevant to reasonable public argument are suppressed, facts distorted or misstated, values disconnected from ethical reasoning, indeed deliberation in politics denigrated in favour of violence against dissent and the æsthetic glorification of violence. Paradoxically, the more the tradition becomes seriously vulnerable to independent reasonable criticism (indeed, increasingly in rational need of such criticism), the more it is likely to generate forms of political irrationalism (including scapegoating of outcast dissenters) in order to secure allegiance. This paradox of intolerance (the internal need for criticism generating repression of dissent) works its irrationalist havoc through its war on the inalienable rights to conscience and speech, in particular, constructing a group of scapegoats on the basis of the unjust repression of this central human right.

The history of religious persecution amply illustrates these truths; and as the American antebellum abolitionist advocates of the argument for toleration clearly saw,[53] no aspect of that history more clearly so than Christian anti-Semitism. The development of the worst ravages of medieval anti-Semitism (totally baseless and irrational beliefs about ritual crucifixions and cannibalism of Christians by Jews) was associated with growing internal doubts about the reasonableness of certain Catholic

[52] See John Hope Franklin, *The Militant South, 1800–1861* (Harvard University Press, Belknap Press, Cambridge, Mass., 1956); cf. W. J. Cash, *The Mind of the South* (Vintage Books, New York, 1941).

[53] See Richards, *Conscience and the Constitution*, n. 1 above, 59–63, 67–9.

religious beliefs and practices (for example, transubstantiation) and the resolution of such doubts by the forms of irrationalist politics associated with anti-Semitism (centring on fantasies of ritual eating of human flesh that expressed the underlying worries about transubstantiation[54]). The politics of such anti-Semitism illustrates the paradox of intolerance, which explains the force of the example for abolitionists. Precisely when the dominant religious tradition gave rise to the most reasonable internal doubts, these doubts were displaced from reasonable discussion and debate into blatant political irrationalism against one of the more conspicuous, vulnerable, and innocent groups of dissenters. It did not escape the abolitionists, who were critics of American slavery, that such irrationalism against Jews was made possible by the long history of Christian Europe's restrictions on Jews (including access to influential occupations, intercourse with Christians, living quarters, and the like) rationalized, as it was, by Augustine, among others, in the quite explicit terms of slavery: 'The Jew is the slave of the Christian.'[55]

The argument for toleration was importantly developed and elaborated as an internal criticism of cultural traditions, so corrupted by construction of cultural identity on terms of injustice that the tradition no longer served reasonable ethical values. Locke and Bayle, for example, forged the argument for toleration as an internal criticism of their own identity as Christians, identifying the unjust abridgement of the right to conscience as corrupting what they took to be the ethical core of true Christianity and calling for the reconstruction of Christian identity on terms of justice. The American abolitionist elaboration of the argument, to condemn both American slavery and racism,[56] was an internal criticism of their own identities as both Christians and Americans, calling for a reconstruction of Christian and American identity on terms of justice. In particular, abolitionist moral and constitutional thought condemned the corruption of American constitutional guarantees of universal human rights by the structural injustice of slavery and racism.[57] American slavery and racism, like anti-Semitism, rested on the structural justice of the abridgement of the basic human rights of a group of persons (including, prominently, protesting rights of conscience and speech) on speciously circular grounds of alleged incapacity to be bearers of human rights that, in fact, rested on their unjust dehumanization.

For the abolitionists, consistent with the argument for toleration, slavery and discrimination were forms of religious, social, economic, and political persecution motivated by a politically entrenched conception of black incapacity. That conception enforced its own vision of truth (repressing rights of conscience and speech) against both the standards of reasonable inquiry and the reasonable capacities of both blacks and whites that might challenge the conception. A conception of political unity,

---

[54] For fuller discussion, see *ibid.*, at 68–9.

[55] Cited in Gavin I. Langmuir, *History, Religion, and Antisemitism* (University of California Press, Berkeley and Los Angeles, Cal., 1990), 294.

[56] See, for further discussion, Richards, *Conscience and the Constitution*, n. 1 above, at 73–89.

[57] On abolitionist constitutional theory, see *ibid.*, at 89–107.

subject to reasonable doubt about its basis and merits, had unreasonably resolved its doubts, consistent with the paradox of intolerance, in the irrationalist racist certitudes of group solidarity on the basis of unjust group subjugation.

Black Americans were the scapegoats of southern self-doubt in the same way that European Jews had been victims of Christian doubt. Frederick Douglass, the leading black abolitionist, stated the abolitionist analysis with a classical clarity:

Ignorance and depravity, and the inability to rise from degradation to civilization and respectability, are the most usual allegations against the oppressed. The evils most fostered by slavery and oppression are precisely those which slaveholders and oppressors would transfer from their system to the inherent character of their victims. Thus the very crimes of slavery become slavery's best defence. By making the enslaved a character fit only for slavery, they excuse themselves for refusing to make the slave a freeman.[58]

In his classic account of African-American double consciousness, Du Bois calls for a reconstruction of African-American identity on terms of justice that would address injustices in the construction of both black ethnic and American identity. Douglas addresses both; he insists, as Martin Luther King was also later to claim,[59] on holding Americans to their constitutional promises of guarantees of the universal human rights of all persons;[60] but he also addresses, like other ex-slaves such as Sojourner Truth and Harriet Jacobs,[61] the unjust terms of the construction of African-American identity. As Du Bois clearly saw, the questions could not be separated: the injustice of American racism (including its rights-denying construction of African-American identity as subhuman) was made possible by the unjust construction of American identity as, contradictorily, both rights-based and, in light of structural injustices like slavery and racism, rights-denying. African-American claims for identity on terms of justice thus moved along both parameters, and no aspect of their struggle more profoundly addressed this problem than their demand to speak and be heard in the ethically transformative exercise of their free moral powers of conscience in protest of the terms of their subjugation.

The force of such rights-based claims for identity is well illustrated by the ultimately successful African-American struggle, under the leadership of the legal redress committee of the NAACP (in which Charles Houston and Thurgood Marshall played central roles), to secure the judicial repudiation of *Plessy* and *Pace*.[62] Black

[58] 'The Claims of the Negro Ethnologically Considered', in Philip S. Foner (ed.), *The Life and Writings of Frederick Douglass* (International Publishers, New York, 1975), ii, 295.
[59] For a good general study, see Taylor Branch, *Parting the Waters: Martin Luther King and the Civil Rights Movement, 1954–63* (Papermac, London, 1990).
[60] On the various forms of abolitionist constitutional theory, see Richards, *Conscience and the Constitution*, n. 1 above, at 89–107.
[61] See, for further discussion, Richards, *Women, Gays, and the Constitution*, n. 1 above, at 115–24.
[62] See Mark V. Tushnet, *The NAACP's Legal Strategy against Segregated Education, 1925–1950* (University of North Carolina Press, Chapel Hill, NC, 1967) and *Making Civil Rights Law: Thurgood Marshall and the Supreme Court, 1956–1961* (Oxford University Press, New York, 1994); Genna Rae McNeil, *Groundwork: Charles Hamilton Houston and the Struggle for Civil Rights* (University of Pennsylvania Press, Philadelphia, Penn., 1983); Jack Greenberg, *Crusaders in the Courts: How a Dedicated Band of Lawyers Fought for the Civil Rights Revolution* (Basic Books, New York, 1994).

Americans in the South and elsewhere asserted and were finally accorded some measure of national protection by the Supreme Court (reversing early decisions to the contrary[63]) in the exercise of their first amendment free speech rights of protest, criticism, and advocacy.[64] On this basis, Martin Luther King brilliantly used and elaborated the right of conscience and free speech to protest American racism very much in the spirit of the strategy of Garrisonian non-violence in the antebellum period;[65] he thus appealed, as he did in his classic 'Letter from Birmingham City Jail',[66] for the need for 'non-violent direct action . . . to create such a [moral] crisis and establish such creative tension that a community that has constantly refused to negotiate is forced to confront the issue'.[67] Like Garrisonian radical abolitionists in the antebellum period, King demanded his basic human rights of conscience and speech to engage in reasonable public discourse about basic issues of justice, including criticism of the racist orthodoxy 'that degrades human personality' and is therefore 'unjust'.[68]

No aspect of that criticism was more profound than the attack on the foundations of American racism, as it had been legitimated in *Plessy* and *Pace*. The foundations of that racism lay in eighteenth-century thought. The eighteenth century comparative science of human nature, developed by Montesquieu and Hume, had seen human nature as more or less constant subject to modification from the environment, history, institutional development, and the like. Both had discussed race differences from this perspective. Montesquieu's position was one of ironic scepticism.[69] Hume, however, departed from the model of a uniform human nature to suggest significant, constitutionally based race differences inferred from comparative cultural achievements.[70] The Humean suggestion of separate races had an anti-theological significance; it was thus condemned, notably by James Beattie,[71] as one aspect of a larger repudiation of a Christian ethics of equality based on the biblical idea of one divine creation of humans. Hume's suggestion was later developed in the nineteenth century into polygenetic theories of human origins by the American ethnologists and others,[72] who

[63] See *Gitlow* v. *New York*, 268 US 652 (1925) (First Amendment held applicable to states under Fourteenth Amendment).

[64] See, in general, Harry Kalven, Jr., *The Negro and the First Amendment* (University of Chicago Press, Chicago, Ill., 1965).

[65] For further discussion, see, in general, Richards, *Conscience and the Constitution*, n. 1 above, ch. 3.

[66] See Martin Luther King, 'Letter from Birmingham City Jail', in *A Testament of Hope: The Essential Writings of Martin Luther King, Jr.* (ed. James Melvin Washington, 1963, Harper & Row, New York, 1986), 289–302.

[67] *Ibid.*, 291.   [68] *Ibid.*, 293.

[69] For further discussion, see Richards, *Conscience and the Constitution*, n. 1 above, 74.

[70] See David Hume, 'Of National Characters', in David Hume, *Essays Moral Political and Literary* (Liberty Classics, Indianapolis, Ind., 1987), 208 n. 10.

[71] See James Beattie, *An Essay on the Nature and Immutability of Truth* (Garland Publishing, Inc., New York, 1983), 479–84. See also James Beattie, *Elements of Moral Science* (Scholars' Facsimiles & Reprints, Delmar, NY, 1976), 183–223.

[72] See William Stanton, *The Leopard's Spots: Scientific Attitudes toward Race in America, 1815–59* (University of Chicago Press, Chicago, Ill., 1960); George M. Fredrickson, *The Black Image in the White Mind: The Debate on Afro-American Character and Destiny, 1817–1914* (Wesleyan University Press, Middletown, Conn., 1971); Thomas F. Gossett, *Race: The History of an Idea in America* (Schocken Books, New York, 1965).

thought of their theories as part of the battle of progressive science against reactionary religion.

In the nineteenth century, this artificially drawn contrast was hardened into one between certain approaches to the human sciences and nearly anything else. These approaches, very much under the influence of models of explanation drawn from the physical sciences, assumed that good explanations in the human sciences must be crudely reductive to some physical measure, like brain capacity or cephalic indices. There was little attention to, let alone understanding of, culture as an independent explanatory variable, and thus no concern with the interpretive dimension of human personality in general and of our moral powers in particular. To the extent that culture was attended to at all, cultural transmission was thought of in Lamarckian terms[73] (even Du Bois may have accepted such a view[74]). The efforts and resulting achievements of one generation were, as it were, wired into the physical natures of the offspring of that generation. As a result, any cultural advantage that one people might have had was not only peculiarly its own (not necessarily transmissible to other peoples), but a matter of rational pride for all those born into such a people. The cultural advances in question were never accidents of time and circumstances, but products of the achieving will, with each generation playing its part in further acts of progressive will building on the achievements of past generation.

These views failed to appreciate what culture is, let alone its explanatory weight in the human sciences. They confused culture with acts of will, failing to understand the nature of cultural formation and transmission, the role of contingency and good luck in cultural progress, and the complete impropriety of taking credit for such advances just by virtue of being born into such a culture. This whole way of thinking naturally created ethical space for explanations in terms of superior and inferior races as a proxy for the comparison between the remarkable scientific advances in Western culture in the nineteenth century in contrast to the putative lack of comparable advances nearly everywhere else.[75] If the least such progress appeared to be in African cultures, such peoples must be inferior; and if Egyptian culture clearly had been for some long period advanced and had an important impact on progressive cultures like that of ancient Greece, then Egyptians could not be black.[76]

It was assumptions of these sorts that explain why the Supreme Court in *Plessy* could be so ethically blind, in the same way as pro-slavery thinkers had been blind, to the ignoble and unjust contempt that its legitimation of the further cultural degradation of blacks inflicted on black Americans.[77] For the *Plessy* Court, race was not morally arbitrary, but a physical fact crucially connected with other physical facts of rational incapacity for which blacks, being from a non-progressive culture, must be

---

[73] See George W. Stocking, Jr., *Race, Culture, and Evolution: Essays in the History of Anthropology* (The Free Press, New York, 1968), 47–8, 124, 234–69.

[74] See Reed, n. 44 above, 39, 58.   [75] *Ibid.*, 234–69.

[76] See, e.g., Stanton, n. 72 above, 50.

[77] On the roots of *Plessy* in the dominant racist social science of the nineteenth century, see Charles A. Lofgren, *The Plessy Case* (Oxford University Press, New York, 1987).

ethically responsible. In contrast, white Americans, taking rational ethical pride in their willed success in sustaining a progressive culture, should take the same pride in their race, and might reasonably protect their achievements from those of another race who were culpably non-progressive by nature. Race, a physical fact supposed to be causally connected to other physical facts, had been transformed into a trait of character. The highly moralistic mind of nineteenth-century America had no problem, once having bought the idea of such transformation, in protecting people of good moral character from those who were culpably of unworthy character.

Abolitionist thought had taken the moral insularity of pro-slavery defences as an example of the corruption of conscience so common in the history of religious persecution;[78] and modern racism both in America and Europe comparably exemplified one of human nature's more artfully self-deceiving evasions of the moral responsibilities of liberal political culture—illustrated, in *Plessy*, by the way in which the culture's respect for science had been manipulated to serve racist ends. Fundamental public criticism of this view of the human sciences must, by its nature as a form of public reason bearing on constitutional values, reshape constitutional argument.

The pivotal figure in such criticism was a German Jew and immigrant to the United States, Franz Boas, who fundamentally criticized the racial explanations characteristic of both European and American physical anthropology in the late nineteenth century.[79] Boas argued that comparative anthropological study did not sustain the explanatory weight placed on race in the human sciences. In fact, there was more significant variability within races than there was between races.[80] Indeed, many of the human features, supposed to be unchangeably physical (like the cephalic index), were reponsive to cultural change; Boas had thus shown that the physical traits of recent immigrants to the United States had changed in response to acculturation.[81]

The crucial factor, heretofore missing from the human sciences, was culture; Boas made this point to Du Bois on a visit to Atlanta University, a visit which 'had an impact of lasting importance'[82] for Du Bois's interest in black culture and its sources. Cultural formation and transmission could not be understood in terms of the reductive physical models that had heretofore dominated scientific and popular thinking. In particular, Lamarckian explanation—having been discredited by Mendelian

---

[78] See, for fuller discussion, Richards, *Conscience and the Constitution*, n. 1 above, 80–9.

[79] See Franz Boas, *The Mind of Primitive Man* (rev. edn., 1911; Greenwood Press, Westport, Conn., 1983); George W. Stocking, Jr. (ed.), *A Franz Boas Reader: The Shaping of American Anthropology, 1883–1911* (University of Chicago Press, Chicago, Ill., 1974). For commentary, see Stocking, n. 73 above; Carl N. Degler, *In Search of Human Nature: The Decline and Revival of Darwinism in American Social Thought* (Oxford University Press, New York, 1991), 61–83. For a useful recent comparative study of comparable such developments in the United States and Britain, see Elazar Barkan, *The Retreat of Scientific Racism: Changing Concepts of Race in Britain and the United States Between the World Wars* (Cambridge University Press, Cambridge, 1992).

[80] See Franz Boas, 'Race', in Edwin R. A. Seligman (ed.), *Encyclopædia of the Social Sciences* (Macmillan, New York, 1937), vii, 25–36; *id.*, n. 79 above, 45–59, 179. For commentary, see Stocking, n. 73 above, 192–4.

[81] See Franz Boas, 'Changes in Immigrant Body Form', in Stocking (ed.), *A Franz Boas Reader*, n. 79 above, 202–14; *id.*, n. 79 above, 94–6. For commentary, see Stocking, n. 73 above, 175–80.

[82] See Lewis, n. 44 above, 352; see also *ibid.*, 414, 462.

genetics in favour of random genetic mutation—was not the modality of cultural transmission, which was not physical at all but irreducibly cultural. One generation born into a progressive culture could take no more credit for an accident of birth than a generation could be reasonably blamed for birth into a less progressive culture. In fact, cultures advance often through accident and good luck and through cultural diffusion of technologies from other cultures. Such diffusion has been an important fact in the history of all human cultures at some point in their histories. No people has been through all points in its history the vehicle of the cultural progress of humankind, nor can any people reasonably suppose itself the unique vehicle of all such progress in the future.[83]

Boas's general contributions to the human sciences were powerfully elaborated in the area of race by his students Otto Klineberg[84] and Ruth Benedict.[85] They argued that the explanatory role of race in the human sciences was, if anything, even less important than the judicious Boas might have been willing to grant[86] (Boas's student, Margaret Mead, suggested much the same might be true to some significant extent of gender[87]).

But the most important study of the American race problem was not by an American but by the Swedish social scientist, Gunnar Myrdal. His monumental *An American Dilemma*[88] brought the new approach to culture powerfully to bear on the plight of American blacks who, from the perspective of the human sciences, now were increasingly well understood as victims of a historically entrenched unjust cultural construction of racism. In effect, the advances in morally independent critical standards of thought and analysis in the human sciences had enabled social scientists to make the same sort of argument that abolitionist theorists of race, like Lydia Maria Child[89] and, as we earlier saw, Frederick Douglass, had made earlier largely on ethical grounds.

Previously, the human sciences had been claimed on the side of race differences against regressive religion and ethics; now, however, developments in the human sciences had cleared away as so much rationalizing self-deception the false dichotomy between science and ethics and revealed the ethically regressive uses to which even science may be put by politically entrenched epistemologies concerned to preserve the politics of race. Such political epistemologies, a modernist expression of essentially sectarian conceptions of religious and moral truth, cannot legitimately be the basis of political enforcement on society at large. Rather, legitimate political power must be

[83] See, in general, Boas, n. 79 above. For commentary, see, in general, Stocking, n. 73 above.

[84] See Otto Klineberg, *Race Differences* (Harper & Brothers, New York, 1935).

[85] See Ruth Benedict, *Race: Science and Politics* (The Viking Press, New York, 1945).

[86] See, e.g., Franz Boas, 'Human Faculty as Determined by Race', in Stocking (ed.), n. 79 above, 231, 234, 242; Boas, *Mind of Primitive Man*, n. 79 above, 230–1.

[87] See Degler, n. 79 above, 73, 133–7.

[88] See Gunnar Myrdal, *An American Dilemma: The Negro Problem and Modern Democracy* (1944, Pantheon Books, New York, 1972), 2 vols. For commentary, see David W. Southern, *Gunnar Myrdal and Black–White Relations: The Use and Abuse of an American Dilemma, 1944–1969* (Louisiana State University Press, Baton Rouge, La, 1987).

[89] See Richards, *Conscience and the Constitution*, n. 1 above, 82–5.

based on impartial standards of reasonable discussion and debate not hostage to entrenched political orthodoxies. An old ethical point—that of the argument for toleration already used by the abolitionists against slavery and racism—was articulated yet again, now used in the service of an articulate argument of public reason against the force that American racism had been permitted to enjoy in the mistaken interpretation of equal protection in cases like *Plessy*. Such cultural criticism made possible public understanding of the naturalization of injustice that supported American racism, namely, the grounds for abridgement of basic human rights rested on a stereotypical dehumanization of African-Americans (as non-bearers of human rights) that reflected not nature, but a viciously circular cultural injustice reflecting the abridgement of such rights. Such naturalization of injustice pivotally rationalized racism.

This point of public reason was much highlighted in the American public mind by the comparable kind of racism that had flourished in Europe in the relevantly same period in the form of modern anti-Semitism. As I have elsewhere argued,[90] during this period both American racism and European anti-Semitism evolved into particularly virulent political pathologies under the impact of the respective emancipations of American blacks from slavery and European Jews from various civil disabilities keyed to their religious background. In both cases, the respective emancipations were not carried through by consistent enforcement of guarantees of basic rights (in the United States, in despite of clear constitutional guarantees to that effect).

The characteristic nineteenth-century struggles for national identity led, in consequence, to rather stark examples of the paradox of intolerance in which the exclusion of race-defined cultural minorities from the political community of equal rights became itself the irrationalist basis of national unity. Strikingly similar racist theorists evolved in Europe to sustain anti-Semitism (Houston Chamberlain[91]) and in America to sustain a comparable racism against the supposedly non-Aryan (Madison Grant[92]). American constitutional institutions were, as a consequence, misinterpreted, but nonetheless increasingly were the vehicle of organized black protest and dissent, including the forms of protest we have already mentioned. Certainly, American institutions did not collapse on the scale of the German declension into atavistic totalitarianism and the genocide of five million European Jews.[93] In both cases, however, the underlying irrationalist racist dynamic was strikingly similar: emancipation, inadequate protection of basic rights, a devastating and humiliating defeat which took the excluded minority as an irrationalist scapegoat.

Boas's important criticism of the role of race in the human sciences had, of course, been motivated as much by his own experience of European anti-Semitism as by American racism; Boas as much forged his own self-respecting identity as a Jew

[90] See *ibid.*, n. 1 above, 156–60.
[91] See Houston Stewart Chamberlain, *The Foundations of the Nineteenth Century* (trans. John Lees, John Lane, London, 1911), 2 vols.
[92] See Madison Grant, *The Passing of the Great Race or The Racial Basis of European History* (Charles Scribner's Sons, New York, 1919).
[93] See Raul Hilberg, *The Destruction of the European Jews* (Holmes & Meier, New York, 1985), iii, 1201–20.

against anti-Semitism as Frederick Douglass or Du Bois defined theirs as African-Americans against American racism. The subsequent elaboration of his arguments by Klineberg, Benedict, and Myrdal had further raised the standards of public reason to expose both the intellectual and ethical fallacies of racism both in America and Europe. In light of such criticism, the constitutional attack in the United States on the analytical foundations of *Plessy* began well before the Second World War in the litigation strategy undertaken by the NAACP to question and subvert the racist principle of separate but equal in the area of public segregated education.

But the Second World War itself, not unlike the Civil War, played an important role in stimulating the development of much more enlightened public attitudes on racial questions than had prevailed theretofore. Not only did the distinguished military service of African-Americans in both wars call for recognition of full citizenship; but the allied victory in the Second World War raised corresponding questions about the state of American constitutionalism prior to the war not unlike those raised by the Reconstruction Amendments about antebellum American constitutionalism. The United States successfully fought that war in Europe against a nation that, like the American South in the Civil War, defined its world historic mission in self-consciously racist terms. The political ravages of such racism—both in the unspeakable moral horrors of the Holocaust of five million innocent European Jews and in the brutalities the Second World War inflicted on so many others—naturally called for a moral interpretation of that war, again like the Civil War, in terms of the defence of the political culture of universal human rights against its racist antagonists. In the wake of the Second World War and its central role in the allied victory and in European reconstruction, the United States took up a central position on the world stage as an advocate of universal human rights. America was thus naturally pressed critically to examine not only at home but abroad as well practices like state-sponsored racial segregation in light of the best interpretation of American ideals of human rights in contemporary circumstances.[94]

The Second World War played, as it were, a role in American moral and political thought of a kind of Third American Revolution (the Civil War being the second such revolution[95]). American ideals of revolutionary constitutionalism were tested against the aggression on human rights of a nation, Nazi Germany, that attacked everything the American constitutional tradition valued in the idea and constitutional institutions of respect for universal human rights.[96] The self-conscious American defence of human rights against the totalitarian ambitions of Nazi Germany required Americans, after the war, to ask whether their own constitutionalism was indeed adequate to their ambitions.

[94] See Mary L. Dudziak, 'Desegregation as a Cold War Imperative', 41 *Stan. L Rev.* 41 (1988); Fredrickson, n. 72 above, 330.
[95] I develop this thought at length in Richards, *Conscience and the Constitution*, n. 1 above.
[96] See, in general, Hannah Arendt, *The Origins of Totalitarianism* (Harcourt Brace Jovanovich, New York, 1973).

In fact, the painful truth was what Du Bois and Boas and others had long argued, namely, that America had betrayed the revolutionary constitutionalism of its Reconstruction Amendments in ways and with consequences strikingly similar to the ways in which Germany had betrayed the promise of universal emancipation. Americans did not, however, have to reconstruct their constitutionalism in order to do justice to this sense of grievous mistake. Unlike the question that faced the nation in the wake of the Civil War, the problem was not one of a basic flaw in the very design of American constitutionalism. Rather, the issue was corrigible interpretive mistake. The judiciary had failed to understand and give effect to the moral ambitions fundamental to the Reconstruction Amendments themselves, namely, that the American political community should be a moral community committed to abstract values of human rights available on fair terms of public reason to all persons, not a community based on race.

The focus for such testing of American interpretive practice was, naturally, *Plessy* v. *Ferguson*, in which the Supreme Court had accepted the exclusion of black Americans from the American community of equal rights. But the intellectual and ethical foundations of *Plessy*, to the extent it ever had such foundations, had collapsed under the weight of the criticism we have already discussed at some length. The idea of natural race differences had been thoroughly discredited as itself the product of a long American history of the unjust cultural construction of racism in precisely the same way that European anti-Semitism had been discredited. The Supreme Court, which in 1896 in *Plessy* could rationalize itself as merely following nature or history, faced in the early 1950s a wholly different space for moral choice, which Boasian cultural studies and African-American activism had opened up.

Thurgood Marshall in his argument to the Supreme Court for the NAACP morally dramatized this choice in terms of the blue-eyed innocent African-American child indistinguishable in all reasonable respects from other children playing with them and living near them except for the role the Supreme Court would play in legitimating a constructed difference (segregated education) which enforced, in fact, an irrationalist prejudice with a long history behind it of unjust subjugation.[97] The Supreme Court was compelled to face, on behalf of American culture more generally, a stark moral choice *either* to give effect to a culture of dehumanization, *or* to refuse any longer to be complicitous with such rights-denying evil. Moral responsibility for one's complicity with evil could not be evaded. In effect, Marshall, as an African-American, stood before the Court in the full voice of his moral personality as a free person, and asked the Court either to accept its responsibility for degrading him as subhuman or to refuse any longer to degrade any person. State-sponsored racial segregation, once uncritically accepted as a reasonable expression of natural race differences, now was construed as itself an unjust construction of an irrationalist dehumanization that excluded citizens from their equal rights as members of the political

[97] See Anthony G. Amsterdam, 'Thurgood Marshall's Image of the Blue-Eyed Child in *Brown*', 68 *NYU L Rev.* 226 (1993).

community, and, as such, unconstitutional. In 1954 in *Brown* v. *Board of Education*[98] the Supreme Court of the United States articulated this deliberative interpretive judgement for the nation by unanimously striking down state-sponsored racial segregation as a violation of the Equal Protection Clause of the Fourteenth Amendment.

In 1967 in *Loving* v. *Virginia*,[99] a similarly unanimous Supreme Court struck down as unconstitutional state anti-miscegenation laws. Repeating, as it had in *Brown*, that the dominant interpretive judgements of the Reconstruction Congress could not be dispositive on the exercise by the judiciary of its independent interpretive responsibilities, the Court rejected the equal application theory of *Pace* v. *Alabama*. The Equal Protection Clause condemned all state-sponsored sources of invidious racial discrimination and, the Court held, anti-miscegenation laws were one such source. Indeed, the only basis for such laws was the constitutionally forbidden aim of white supremacy.

Anti-miscegenation laws had come to bear this interpretation as a consequence of the Court's endorsement of the cultural theory of the rights-denying construction of racism first suggested by Lydia Maria Child in 1833[100] and importantly elaborated by Ida Wells-Barnett in 1892.[101] Child had examined and condemned both American slavery and racism in light of the argument for toleration: basic human rights of the person were abridged on wholly inadequate sectarian grounds that Child, like other radical abolitionists, expressly analogized to religious persecution. Anti-miscegenation laws violated the basic human right of intimate association on such inadequate grounds, thus dehumanizing a whole class of persons as sub-human animals unworthy of the forms of equal respect accorded rights-bearing persons. Ida Wells-Barnett, elaborating the role of the rights-denying sexual dehumanization of African-Americans under slavery made clear earlier by Harriet Jacobs,[102] analysed Southern racism after emancipation as resting on a similar basis sustained, in part, by anti-miscegenation laws. The point of such laws was, Wells showed, not only to condemn all interracial marriages (the focus of Child's analysis), but the legitimacy of all sexual relations (marital and otherwise) between white women and black men; illicit relations between white men and black women were, in contrast, if not legal, socially acceptable. The asymmetry rested on the enforcement at large (through anti-miscegenation and related laws and practices, including lynching) of a sectarian sexual and romantic idealized mythology of white women and a corresponding devaluation (indeed, dehumanization) of black women and men as sexually animalistic; illicit sexual relations of white men with black women were consistent with this political epistemology, and thus were tolerable; both licit and illicit consensual

---

[98] *Brown* v. *Board of Education*, 347 US 483 (1954).
[99] 388 US 1 (1967); cf. *McLaughlin* v. *Florida*, 379 US 184 (1964).
[100] For citations and commentary, see Richards, *Conscience and the Constitution*, n. 1 above, 80–9.
[101] For citations and commentary, see Richards, *Women, Gays, and the Constitution*, n. 1 above, 182–90.
[102] For citations and commentary, see Richards, *Women, Gays, and the Constitution*, n. 1 above, 117–24.

relations of black men with white women were not, and thus were ideologically transformed into violent rapes requiring lynching.

W. E. B. Du Bois, a life-long feminist like Frederick Douglass, condemned in related terms the role the idealized image of women (as either virgin or prostitute) played in sustaining not only racism, but a sexism that unjustly treated all women:

> The world wants healthy babies and intelligent workers. Today we refuse to allow the combination and force thousands of intelligent workers to go childless at a horrible expenditure of moral force, or we damn them if they break our idiotic conventions. Only at the sacrifice of intelligence and the chance to do their best work can the majority of modern women bear children. This is the damnation of women.
>
> All womanhood is hampered today because the world on which it is emerging is a world that tries to worship both virgins and mothers and in the end despises motherhoood and despoils virgins.
>
> The future woman must have a life work and economic independence. She must have knowledge. She must have the right of motherhood at her discretion. The present mincing horror at free womenhood must pass if we are ever to be rid of the bestiality of free manhood; not by guarding the weak in weakness do we gain strength, but by making weakness free and strong.
>
> The world must choose the free women or the white wraith of the prostitute. Today it wavers between the prostitute and the nun.[103]

American racism, on this analysis, rested on a culturally constructed and sustained racialized sexual mythology of gender (white virgin versus black prostitute); and anti-miscegenation laws were unconstitutional because of the central role they played unjustly in sustaining this sectarian ideology. Both Harriet Jacobs and Ida Wells-Barnett had analysed this injustice from the perspective of black women who had experienced its indignities at first hand.

James Baldwin, one of the greatest American writers of his generation and a black homosexual, brought the same experienced sense of indignity to bear on his later explorations of American sexual racism.[104] When he travelled in the South, Baldwin wrote 'about my unbelieving shock when I realized that I was being groped by one of the most powerful men in one of the states I visited'.[105] He wrote searingly of his indignation from his experience as a black man, and what he learned of the way racism fulfilled men's 'enormous need to debase other men':[106]

> To be a slave means that one's manhood is engaged in a dubious battle indeed, and this stony fact is not altered by whatever devotion some masters and some slaves may have arrived at in relation to each other. In the case of American slavery, the black man's right to his women, as well as to his children, was simply taken from him and whatever bastards the white man begat on the bodies of black women took their condition from the condition of their mothers: blacks were not the only stallions on the slave-breeding farms! And one of the many results of this

---

[103] See W. E. B. Du Bois, 'The Damnation of Women' (1920), in *W. E. B. Du Bois*, n. 42 above, 952–3. On the specifically racist use of such an unjust idealization, see *ibid.*, 958: 'one thing I shall never forgive, neither in this world nor the world to come: its wanton and continued and persistent insulting of the black womanhood which it sought and seeks to prostitute to its lust'.

[104] See, in general, David Leeming, *James Baldwin* (Knopf, New York, 1994).

[105] See James Baldwin, *No Name in the Street* (Dell, New York, 1972), 61.   [106] *Ibid.*, 63.

loveless, money-making conspiracy was that, in giving the masters every conceivable sexual and commercial license, it also emasculated them of any human responsibility—to their women, to their children, to their wives, to themselves. The results of this blasphemy resound in this country, on every private and public level, until this hour. When the man grabbed my cock, I didn't think of him as a faggot, which, indeed, if having a wife and children, house, cars, and a respectable and powerful standing in that community, mean anything, he wasn't: I watched his eyes, thinking with great sorrow, *The unexamined life is not worth living.*[107]

Baldwin made clear the general role that sexual dehumanization played in American racism as such: the mythological reduction of both black women and men to their sexuality on terms that fundamentally denied their moral personalities and their human rights to respect for conscience, speech, work, and, of course, intimate life, including their right to love on terms of respect (a right, for Baldwin, owed all persons, heterosexual or homosexual, male or female, white or non-white).[108]

Obviously, African-American rights-based protest of the terms of their unjust subordination (the politics of identity) led, on grounds of principle, to protest of related forms of structural injustice, as the anti-sexist arguments of Jacobs, Well-Barnett, and Du Bois and the anti-homophobic arguments of Baldwin make quite clear. To challenge the unjust terms of the structural injustice of American racism was, as Du Bois made clear, to demand one's ethnic and American identity be recognized and acknowledged in a new way, namely, on terms of justice that extended as well to related forms of structural injustice. The moral empowerment of making claims to one's basic human rights in one domain generalizes, on grounds of rights-based principle, to empowering claims to revise the terms of all identities marred by such structural injustice. Such protest, based on the self-respecting sense of one's humanity as a bearer of human rights, calls for often profound criticism of the cultural forms that have sustained such injustice, including not only political protest but the creation of new cultural forms that make imaginative space for moral and human protest affirming a self-respecting sense of the creative and critical powers expressive of one's sense of one's human rights.[109] Under the pressure of such criticism, as we have seen, a matter that had been supposed to be a fundamentally important physical difference comes reasonably to be regarded as a profoundly unjust construction of difference in service of an indefensible conception of national identity. If there is nothing in the traditional American importance attached to race but culture, then we have ethically responsible choices to make about addressing and rectifying the history and culture that have sustained such choices. The African-American struggle is a rights-based narrative of choices made to identify and protest injustice, exposing to the American public mind its ugly nescience and complacency in the face of fundamental injustice

---

[107] See James Baldwin, *No Name in the Street*, 62–3.

[108] For Baldwin's frankest first-person treatment of these issues, see James Baldwin, 'Here Be Dragons', in James Baldwin, *The Price of the Ticket: Collected Non-fiction, 1948–1985* (St. Martin's, New York, 1985), 677–90; for a much more elliptical, self-hating treatment, see James Baldwin, 'The Male Prison', *ibid.*, 101–5.

[109] See, for example, George Hutchinson, *The Harlem Renaissance in Black and White* (Harvard University Press, Cambridge, Mass., 1995).

rationalized as in the nature of things. Nothing in this dynamic of self-respecting claims to an identity based on justice corresponds to the terms of immutability and salience in which much constitutional theory claims to address this matter. Indeed, it gets it quite perversely wrong, repeating the way of regarding the problem (as a physical fact) that it should protest. The protest is not to giving weight to immutable and salient facts as such, but to the imposition of a cultural identity of dehumanizing self-contempt resting, as we have seen, on structural injustice.

I have suggested that the abridgement of the inalienable right to conscience should normatively frame our understanding of such injustice, because, as we have seen, making self-respecting claims on the basis of this right addresses the dehumanizing evil both by affirming what the evil denies and making possible reasonable debate and discourse about the irrationalist basis on which the evil has been sustained. The perspective opens up a new way of understanding not only the structural injustice of racism but the way in which we should interpret that analogy in the understanding of sexism and homophobia.

THE CONSTITUTIONAL EVIL OF SEXISM

The struggle for a strong anti-racist constitutional principle had implicit within it a criticism of the racialized ideal of gender roles in persistent patterns of American racism. The constitutional repudiation of anti-miscegenation laws clearly reflected this criticism. Since the purpose of state-sponsored segregation was importantly to discourage even the possibility of such intimate relations, the unconstitutionality of segregation reflected this critical theme as well. Some of the most important exponents of this criticism had been black women, like Harriet Jacobs and Ida Wells-Barnett, who spoke from within their own moral experience about the indignity this dehumanizing stereotype of black sexuality inflicted on them. The criticism was, in its nature, an assault upon the normative conception of women in suffrage feminism that placed white women on a romantically idealized pedestal of wife and mother allegedly inconsistent with the rights and responsibilities of men.[110] For this reason, Ida Wells-Barnett was at loggerheads with the leading suffrage feminist advocate of this conception, Frances Willard, over Willard's refusal to acknowledge the ugly facts of consensual inter-racial sex underlying the lynching of black men in the South.[111] Activist anti-racist black women, like Wells-Barnett and others, were for good reasons sceptical of a feminism rooted in such an ideology, and would continue to be so for a long period.[112] Only a feminism, itself sceptical of this ideology, would have the

[110] For fuller discussion of this normative conception, see Richards, *Women, Gays, and the Constitution*, n. 1 above, ch. 4.

[111] For fuller discussion, see *ibid.*, 182–90.

[112] See, for a good general study, Paula Giddings, *When and Where I Enter . . . : The Impact of Black Women on Race and Sex in America* (William Morrow, New York, 1984). See also Bell Hooks, *Ain't I a Woman: Black Women and Feminism* (South End Press, Boston, Mass., 1981); *id., Feminist Theory: From Margin to Center* (South End Press, Boston, Mass., 1984).

promise of both advancing anti-racist and anti-sexist principles in an acceptable way and thus engage the moral convictions of black as well as white women.

Second-wave feminism arose on such a basis,[113] and, in the wake of the earlier described successes of the NAACP in securing judicial recognition rendering racial classifications constitutionally highly suspect, gradually persuaded the Supreme Court to regard gender classifications as increasingly suspect.[114] Indeed, a recent case, *United States* v. *Virginia*,[115] suggests that the Supreme Court may be shifting the standard of review accorded to gender to a level of scrutiny much closer to that of race. In striking down the exclusion of women from the Virginia Military Institute, the Court invoked the standard of whether the justification for exclusion was 'exceedingly persuasive',[116] was quite sceptical of the weight accorded to putative gender differences as a rationale for the exclusion,[117] and expressly invoked an important racial case, *Sweatt* v. *Painter*,[118] as a relevant analogy for the unconstitutionality of separate-but-equal in the realm of gender.[119] Consistent also with its views on the unconstitutionality of anti-miscegenation laws, the Court has also struck down laws imposing criminal penalties on the right of reproductive autonomy, laws often not unreasonably thought unjustly to enforce traditional views of gender and sexuality.[120] The Supreme Court declined, however, to extend this principle to consensual adult homosexual relations in *Bowers* v. *Hardwick*.[121]

The constitutional analogy between race and gender must be understood as the elaboration of an interpretive development whose roots lie in abolitionist feminism, a movement of radical antebellum abolitionists who constructed, on what they called the same platform of human rights, common principles to condemn racism and sexism.[122] The principles of that movement were compromised, in increasingly racist and sexist directions, during the struggles of suffrage feminism.[123] Second-wave

---

[113] See, for elaboration of this point, Richards, *Women, Gays, and the Constitution*, n. 1 above, ch. 5.

[114] See, e.g., *Reed* v. *Reed*, 404 US 71 (1971) (mandatory preference for men over women in the appointment of the administrator of a decedent's estate held unconstitutional); *Frontiero* v. *Richardson*, 411 US 677 (1973) (federal law permitting male members of armed forces an automatic dependency allowance, but requiring servicewomen to prove that their husbands were dependent, held unconstitutional); *Craig* v. *Boren*, 429 US 190 (1976) (gender distinction between men and women in drinking age— men at 21, women at 18, held unconstitutional). But cf. *Michael M.* v. *Superior Court*, 450 US 464 (1981) (statutory rape law, holding only men liable for intercourse with female under 18, held constitutional); *Rostker* v. *Goldberg*, 453 US 57 (1981) (Congressional limitation of registration for draft to men held constitutional).

[115] *United States* v. *Virginia*, 116 S Ct. 2264 (1996).   [116] *Ibid.*, at 2274.

[117] *Ibid.*, at 2276, 2280.

[118] *Sweatt* v. *Painter*, 339 US 629 (1950) (establishment of separate law school for blacks held unconstitutional).

[119] *United States* v. *Virginia*, n. 115 above, at 2285, 2286.

[120] See *Griswold* v. *Connecticut*, 381 US 479 (1965) (criminalization of use of contraceptives held unconstitutional); *Roe* v. *Wade*, 410 US 113 (1973) (criminalization of abortion services held unconstitutional); the Supreme Court reaffirmed the central principle of *Roe* in 1992 in *Planned Parenthood of Southeastern Pennsylvania* v. *Casey*, 112 S Ct. 2791 (1992).

[121] See *Bowers* v. *Hardwick*, 478 US 186 (1986).

[122] For elaboration of this background, see Richards, *Women, Gays, and the Constitution*, n. 1 above, ch. 3.

[123] For elaboration of this background, see *ibid.*, ch. 4.

feminism, building on the insights of abolitionist feminism, arose in the wake of the most profound public criticism and action against American racism since antebellum radical abolitionism, and based its anti-sexist principles on the same platform of human rights as the anti-racist principles that increasingly informed both American public opinion and the constitutional interpretation of the Reconstruction Amendments. The development of the principled elaboration of the analogy between race and gender required both a practice and theory of a certain kind of struggle based on an appeal to basic inalienable human rights and a closer scrutiny of traditional grounds for abridgement of such rights in light of the kinds of independent standards of public reason that the argument for toleration requires. Thus the anti-racist and anti-sexist struggles powerfully used and sponsored increasingly muscular rights of conscience, speech, intimate life, and work; both struggles subjected traditional grounds for the abridgement of such rights to a more searching and reasonable public examination. In both cases, such rights empowered traditionally subjugated groups to come to understand and to demand their basic rights of moral personality and to engage increasingly in the reasonable public discourse and debate in their own voice that such rights make possible. Two prominent examples of the development and articulation of second-wave feminism illustrate this approach: the seminal argument of Betty Friedan and the development of anti-sexist principles by women within the anti-racist civil rights movement. Both examples exemplify, consistent with Du Bois's theory of double consciousness, the importance of rights-based claims to identity in understanding the common grounds of anti-racist and anti-sexist principles.

Betty Friedan's 1963 *The Feminine Mystique*[124] struck a responsive chord among American women, more of whom now worked outside the home than before,[125] when she critically addressed both the idealized conception of gender roles and the force it had over women's lives.[126] Citing abolitionist feminist dissatisfaction with the claims of domesticity as the occasion with distinctively feminist claims,[127] Friedan argued that American women in the post-Second World War period experienced a comparable crisis of identity but over contemporary gender roles so impoverished that they 'had no name for the problem troubling them'.[128] Friedan spoke from her own personal experience of an advanced education that went unused in domestic life[129] and of the unjust epistemological power over women's consciousness and lives

[124] See Betty Friedan, *The Feminine Mystique* (originally published, 1963) (Penguin, London, 1982).
[125] For the changes in the 1940s, see William H. Chafe, *The Paradox of Change: American Women in the 20th Century* (Oxford University Press, New York, 1991), 166–72; for the 1950s, see *id.*, at 188–92.
[126] On the importance of Friedan's book, see Chafe, n. 125 above, at 195; Jo Freeman, *The Politics of Women's Liberation: A Case Study of an Emerging Social Movement and Its Relation to the Policy Process* (Longman, New York, 1975), at 27, 53; Judith Hole and Ellen Levine, *Rebirth of Feminism* (Quadrangle, New York, 1971), at 17, 82; Nancy E. McGlen and Karen O'Connor, *Women's Rights: The Struggle for Equality in the Nineteenth and Twentieth Centuries* (Praeger, New York, 1983), at 29; Carl N. Degler, *At Odds: Women and the Family in America from the Revolution to the Present* (Oxford University Press, New York, 1980), at 443.
[127] For discussion of Stanton's dissatisfaction as the motivation for her role in calling the Seneca Falls Convention, see Friedan, n. 124 above, at 81–2.
[128] See *ibid.*, at 10.   [129] See *ibid.*, at 26, 62–3.

of the normative conception of gender roles that had been appealed to as the ground for pathologizing any feminist dissent.[130] A woman's problematic sense of herself, Friedan argued, was not to be dismissed or trivialized as merely psychologically personal and deviant as perceived through the prism of this normative conception when its political force was so demonstrably unjust. Otherwise, injustice would be the measure of the awakening sense of justice that alone might protest it. Friedan's criticisms of the justice of this normative conception, the feminine mystique, questioned not only its substance (making of femininity an end in itself[131] or sex as women's exclusive career[132]), but its sectarian religious force[133] that permitted no reasonable doubts to be raised[134] and fictionalized facts.[135] Indeed, using the very terms of the paradox of intolerance earlier noted, Friedan pointed to the polemical force of the ideology precisely when it was most reasonably open to doubt. She called this:

the basic paradox of the feminine mystique: that it emerged to glorify women's role as housewife at the very moment when the barriers to her full participation in society were lowered, at the very moment when science and education and her own ingenuity made it possible for a woman to be both wife and mother and to take an active part in the world outside the home. The glorification of 'woman's role', then, seems to be in proportion to society's reluctance to treat women as complete human beings; for the less real function that role has, the more it is decorated with meaningless details to conceal its emptiness.[136]

The general terms of the analysis are, of course, familiar from our earlier examination of the argument for toleration and its critical applications to American slavery and racism. What was so striking and original in Friedan's analysis was the way she plausibly applied it both to popular American culture and the uncritical social scientists[137] who supported its cult of women's domesticity in the mid-twentieth century.[138] Friedan self-consciously saw herself quite rightly as in a similar position to leading advocates of abolitionist feminism like Theodore Parker and Elizabeth Stanton against the background of the way suffrage feminism had undercut their rights-based critique of American gender roles and thus re-enforced women's moral slavery.[139] All the terms of the abolitionist feminist analysis of moral slavery were in place in Friedan's critique. The force of the sectarian ideology of gender roles rested on the abridgement of basic human rights to critical mind and speech,[140] associated rights to critical education,[141] fair terms for rights to intimate life,[142] and the right to

[130] See Friedan *Feminine Mystique*, at 37, 107, 139, 169–70. For discussion of Lundberg and Farnham's *Modern Women: The Lost Sex*, a work that took this view, see Richards, *Women, Gays, and the Constitution*, n. 1 above, at 197–8.

[131] See Friedan, n. 124 above, at 38, 40–1.   [132] See *ibid.*, at 228.
[133] See *ibid.*, at 38, 44, 111, 173.   [134] See *ibid.*, at 44.
[135] See *ibid.*, at 53.   [136] See *ibid.*, at 210.
[137] On critical versus uncritical uses of social science, see *ibid.*, at 149.
[138] For social background, see Glenna Matthews, *'Just a Housewife' The Rise and Fall of Domesticity in America* (Oxford University Press, New York, 1987).
[139] See, in general, Friedan, n. 124 above, at 72–90; on Parker, see *ibid.*, at 76; on Stanton, *ibid.*, 81–2; on securing the suffrage and the death of feminism, *ibid.*, 88.
[140] See *ibid.*, at 59, 282–3.   [141] See *ibid.*, 155, 158, 211, 223.
[142] See, e.g., *ibid.*, at 148–9.

creative work.[143] The result was the cultural dehumanization of women[144] in terms of an objectified sexuality[145] or biology.[146] Women's struggle was thus one for personal identity[147] on terms responsive to a morally independent basis to live a life from convictions of conscience, the voice within.[148]

Friedan importantly made reference early in her book[149] to Simone de Beauvoir's pathbreaking *The Second Sex*,[150] which had prominently explored analogies among anti-Semitism, racism, and sexism.[151] The terms of Friedan's analysis were drawn from a tradition, certainly familiar to her, that had recently applied all the terms of analysis used by her to the criticism of American racism; she acknowledged as much when she criticized the application of separate but equal to women's education (which had been struck down by the Supreme Court in 1954 as applied to the education of African-Americans) on the ground that such 'sex-directed education segregated recent generations of able American women as surely as separate-but-equal education segregated able American Negroes from the opportunity to realize their full abilities in the mainstream of American life'.[152] Friedan used the analogy to address a constitutional culture on whom '[t]he black civil rights movement had a very profound effect'.[153] Gunnar Myrdal himself, at the conclusion of his massive 1944 cultural analysis of American racism, had noted that the status of women had been 'the nearest and most natural analogy'[154] for those justifying slavery and racism and might be subject to similar rights-based criticism, as indeed the abolitionist feminists had urged. Friedan's argument assumed the analogy, including the very terms of a personal struggle for moral identity and self-consciousness that Du Bois had brought to the black struggle for a stronger anti-racist constitutional principle of equal protection.

Friedan also assumed and used another critical principle that was central to the stronger anti-racist principle that the Supreme Court had accepted, namely, the Boasian cultural science that had reframed issues from the pseudo-science of race to an unjust culture of racist subjugation. That principle was plausibly applied not only to race but, as Myrdal suggested, to gender as well. Boas had laid the foundations,[155] but his students Margaret Mead[156] and Ruth Benedict[157] had elaborated the point. Indeed, such scepticism may first have been suggested about gender differences by

[143] See *ibid.*, at 289–91.   [144] See *ibid.*, at 244, 251, 264, 265–8.
[145] See *ibid.*, at 72, 228, 233.   [146] See *ibid.*, at 275.
[147] See *ibid.*, at 67–8, 289–91.   [148] See *ibid.*, at 29, 207, 331.   [149] See *ibid.*, at 16.
[150] See Simone de Beauvoir, *The Second Sex* (trans. H. M. Parshley, first published in English, 1953) (Vintage, New York, 1974).
[151] See *ibid.*, at pp. xvi, xx, xxi, 131, 144 (citing Sartre and Myrdal), 335.
[152] See Friedan, n. 124 above, at 158; see also *ibid.*, at 211.
[153] See Freeman, n. 126 above, at 27.
[154] See Gunnar Myrdal, *An American Dilemma* (Harper & Row, New York, 1944), ii, appendix 5, 'A Parallel to the Negro Problem', 1073.
[155] See Rosalind Rosenberg, *Beyond Separate Spheres: Intellectual Roots of Modern Feminism* (Yale University Press, New Haven, Conn., 1982), at 162–9, 177.
[156] See *ibid.*, 213–19, 226–32.   [157] See *ibid.*, at 223–6.

those sceptical of the dominant suffrage feminist ideology of basic differences[158] and then extended to race differences.[159] The greater and earlier political success of the racial case may be due to historical accident (an organized black movement that powerfully used the argument, a divided woman's movement many of whom espoused physical differences), not to the underlying issues of principle.[160] Friedan both acknowledged Mead for having made a form of the argument, and then criticized her for not carrying it far enough.[161] Clearly, the recent success of the argument in the racial area made it much easier to deploy a form of the argument, as a matter of principle, in the criticism of the unjust cultural construction of gender. If *The Feminine Mystique* was about anything, it was about that.

The dimensions of the analogy of principle became explicit in the moral experience of the black and white women who participated in the civil rights movement of the 1960s, as Sara Evans has made clear in her now classic study of this period.[162] Drawing an explicit analogy to the transformative experience of the Grimke sisters as pathbreaking abolitionist feminists,[163] Evans noted how the struggle of black and white women to end racial discrimination led women to develop a heightened consciousness of their own oppression. In the 1950s the civil rights movement had grown in both confidence and sense of vision. Black women played major roles in this effort, from the actions of Rosa Parks and Jo Ann Robinson in starting the Montgomery bus boycott in 1955 to Ella Baker's part in giving birth to the Student Non-Violent Coordinating Committee (SNCC) in 1960.[164] As the civil rights movement became a central topic in American news media, Americans became sensitized to the existence of profound constitutional injustices (including racial segregation and anti-miscegenation laws) that had been rationalized on grounds that denied whole classes of persons any decent respect for their basic human rights. Like their abolitionist feminist ancestors, many women who became active in this movement only came to a realization of the comparable injustices to which they were subjected when they experienced sexism from their own male colleagues in the movement.

One group of women who realized the link between race and sex discimination were young Southern activists who took part in the direct-action civil rights struggle of the Student Non-Violent Coordinating Committee. Both black and white, these women found their moral voice in the protests, including sit-ins, of the civil rights movement; as one white woman later testified, 'To this day I am amazed. I just did it.'[165] For the white women, in particular, such activism constituted a moral revolt, similar in moral force to that of the Grimke sisters, against the idealized conception of white women central to Southern racism: '[i]n the 1830's and again in the 1960s

---

[158] For Jane Addams on physical differences as the ground for women's superiority, see *ibid.*, at p. 41; on scepticism about this ideology, see *ibid.*, at 111, 176–7, 236.

[159] See *ibid.*, at 108, 195, 245.   [160] See *ibid.*, at 245.

[161] See Friedan, n. 124 above, at 129–31.

[162] See Sara Evans, *Personal Politics: The Roots of Women's Liberation in the Civil Rights Movement and the New Left* (Vintage, New York, 1980).

[163] See *ibid.*, at 24, 25–6, 57, 101, 120.   [164] See Chafe, n. 125 above, at 197.

[165] See Evans, n. 162, above, at 38.

the first voices to link racial and sexual oppression were those of Southern white women.'[166] These women, responsive to a Protestant sense of radical personal conscience and ethical responsibility, took as their model black women like Ella Baker whose life realized in practice Anna Cooper's transformative model of '[w]omen in stepping from the pedestal of statue-like inactivity in the domestic shrine, and daring to think and move and speak'.[167] In so doing, these white women spiritually exiled themselves from their own mothers in as radical a way as Angelina and Sarah Grimke's physical exile from the South, an experience, like the Grimkes, 'exceptionally lonely, for it shattered once-supportive ties with family and friends'.[168] Falling back upon personal resources they did not know they had, 'they developed a sense of self that enabled them to recognize the enemy within as well—the image of the "southern lady"'.[169] In contrast to northern students who came and left the South, 'southern white students were in an important sense fighting for their own identities'.[170]

These white dissenting women were struggling with and against the idealized conception of white women's sphere that, as we have seen, enforced the correlative dehumanization of black men and women as sexually animalistic. No action more outraged this ideology than the idea of consensual sexual relations between white women and black men. Not only anti-miscegenation laws but the whole structure of Southern apartheid were rationalized as measures directed against this ultimate mythological evil. The participation of white women in interracial co-operation protesting these and other such laws represented for many of their southern white parents 'a breakdown in the social order';[171] one such father, when his daughter announced 'she wanted to leave school to work in a small-town black community accused her of being a whore and chased her out of the house in a drunken rage, shouting that she was disowned'.[172] Within a movement of anti-racist struggle led by Southern black men and women, such young white women had 'to forge a new sense of themselves, to redefine the meaning of being a woman quite apart from the flawed image they had inherited';[173] their struggle was the one Du Bois had earlier defined as the anti-racist struggle for a new kind of identity and self-consciousness. They self-critically recognized that the struggle for racial equality called for fundamental changes in gender roles, including what they now recognized and condemned as a conspicuously sectarian religiously based moral 'defense of white women's sexual purity in a racist society [that] held them separate from and innocent of the "real world" of politics'.[174]

The catalyst for the development of a rights-based feminism, on the model of abolitionist feminism, was the experience these women encountered of pervasive

---

[166] See *ibid.*, at 25.

[167] See Anna Julia Cooper, *A Voice from the South* (1892, reprinted edited by Mary Helen Washington, Oxford University Press, New York, 1988), 121–2.

[168] See Evans, n. 162 above, at 43.   [169] See *ibid.*, at 43.   [170] See *ibid.*, at 45.

[171] See *ibid.*, at 44.   [172] See *ibid.*, at 44.   [173] See *ibid.*, at 57.

[174] See *ibid.*, at 58.

attitudes of male supremacy within SNCC. Their self-critical development and support of anti-racist principles had required them to question and reject traditional gender roles, regarding 'the term "southern lady" . . . [as] an obscene epithet';[175] they thus asserted their own human rights to conscience, speech, intimate life, and work against a sectarian racist orthodoxy that had traditionally abridged these rights. Now, within SNCC, these hard-fought personal rights were again at hazard; rights of conscience and speech were subordinated in decision making, rights of intimate life compromised by expectations that women would automatically acquiesce when men asked them to sleep with them, rights of work by limiting them to the sphere of housework.[176] More and more of these young women began to talk with one another about their common experiences. Initially, the hope was that simply pointing out the problem in an anonymous memorandum would bring change.[177] Stokely Carmichael's rebuttal, 'The only position for women in SNCC is prone',[178] led them to conclude that they must be assertive in defence of their own rights as they had been—together with men—in the struggle for racial equality.

Increasingly, their moral experience in this rights-based struggle led them to link the two causes directly. In a summation of their thinking addressed to women in the peace and freedom movement, Casey Hayden and Mary King declared in the fall of 1965 that women, like blacks, 'seem to be caught up in a common-law caste system that operates, sometime subtly, forcing them to work around or outside hierarchical structures of power which may exclude them. Women seem to be placed in the same position of assumed subordination in personal situations too. It is a caste system which, at its worst, uses and exploits women.'[179] The identity-transforming struggle for a morally independent exercise of basic rights, which had led them 'to think radically about the personal worth and abilities of people whose role in society had gone unchallenged before',[180] required the same analysis and criticism of 'the racial caste system' and 'the sexual caste system'.[181] Failure to extend the criticism of racial caste to sexual caste reflected, Hayden and White argued, the depth of the injustice of the sexual caste system and the dimensions of the problem of remedy. In particular, they pleaded for open discussion of these issues among women, creating 'a community of support for each other so we can deal with ourselves and others with integrity and can therefore keep working',[182] thus identifying the centrality to rights-based feminism of the praxis of consciousness raising.[183] As the development of the Black Power movement made it increasingly difficult at this time for white and black women to co-operate across racial lines, the white women veterans of the civil rights struggle took such sentiments into the student movement, the anti-war movement, and the like, becoming in the process the cutting edge of second-wave feminism as itself a civil rights movement.[184]

---

[175] See Evans, n. 162 above, at 57.
[176] See *ibid.*, at 83–101.
[177] For the memorandum, see *ibid.*, at 233–5.
[178] See *ibid.*, at 87.
[179] See *ibid.*, at 235.
[180] See *ibid.*, at 236.
[181] See *ibid.*
[182] See *ibid.*, at 237.
[183] See *ibid.*, at 203–4, 214–15.
[184] See *ibid.*, at 156–232.

The emerging feminism both of these women and of Betty Friedan centred feminist discourse, in a way it had not been since the abolitionist feminists, in the criticism, on rights-based grounds, of the normative gender roles that had theretofore, under the impact of suffrage feminism, largely been immunized from such criticism. Rather than idealizing these gender roles as the source of a higher morality, on the model of a Catharine Beecher or Frances Willard,[185] the roles themselves (including their idealization) were now critically examined in the light of morally independent values of human rights. A new centrality was accorded to both the appeal to basic human rights (conscience, free speech, association, and work), and the lack of the kind of compelling secular public justification constitutionally required before such rights might be abridged. Indeed, books like Kate Millett's 1969 *Sexual Politics*[186] and Shulamith Firestone's 1970 *Dialectic of Sex*[187] initiated the serious American study of the cultural depth and polemical power of the traditional sectarian ideology of gender, its fundamental rights-denying injustice, and the extent of imaginative (even utopian) theory and practice of change that might be required to dislodge and subvert this ideology and make space available for women to understand and claim their human rights, as persons, on fair terms.

It was such fundamental criticism of gender roles (already, as we have seen, an ingredient of the stronger anti-racist principle that many black and white women now defended) that made normative space available on which black and white women could reasonably aspire to find common ground.[188] The very terms of rights-based feminism required white women to raise questions about racialized ideals of gender,[189] and suggested as well that the integrity of both the stronger anti-racism and anti-sexism rested on common principles of non-discrimination that should be pursued together.

Certainly, for second-wave feminists, the achievements of the civil rights movement offered both a normatively powerful and relevant model of how to proceed to secure change. Virtually every legislative act, judicial decree, and executive order that applied to race could, in their view, apply to gender as well. Hence it was principled that one of the great legislative achievements of the civil rights movement (the Civil Rights Act of 1964) should, in Title VII, prohibit discrimination in employment on grounds of sex as well as race. Although a conservative opponent of the bill had proposed the additional grounds as a ludicrous attempt to cripple support for the legislation and liberal supporters opposed it for that reason,[190] the leading feminist in the House, Martha Griffiths of Michigan, held off from sponsoring the addition because

---

[185] See, for explorations of their views, Richards, *Women, Gays, and the Constitution*, n. 1 above, 72–8, 144–55.

[186] See Kate Millett, *Sexual Politics* (Avon, New York, 1969).

[187] See Shulamith Firestone, *The Dialectic of Sex: The Case for Feminist Revolution* (originally published, 1970) (Woman's Press, London, 1988).

[188] On this development, see, in general, Giddings, n. 112 above.

[189] See, e.g., Ruth Frankenberg, *The Social Construction of Whiteness: White Women, Race Matters* (University of Minnesota Press, Minneapolis, Minn., 1993).

[190] See Hole and Levine, n. 126 above, at 30–1.

she knew that the conservative's addition would bring 100 votes with it. Determined leadership by the congresswomen supporting the addition and vigorous lobbying by its supporters, including the National Women's Party, used the logic of the connection between race and sex to persuade a majority to support the new language.[191]

The civil rights movement also supplied a model of how to proceed organizationally to implement the changes that the new legislation required. In response to the failure of implementation of the ban on sex discrimination in employment, women in the various states who had served on the various state commissions on the status of women joined with activists like Betty Friedan to form in 1966 the National Organization for Women (NOW), an organization in the civil rights mode that vowed to use lobbying, litigation, and other political means to force the Equal Employment Opportunities Commission (EEOC) to make women's issues as central to its mandate as racial issues. Friedan was elected its first president.[192] Groups like NOW and others[193] took responsibility not only for securing compliance with progress in women's rights already achieved, but for initiating new struggles to secure further victories for gender equality. Second-wave feminism embraced a range of issues and concerns, from abortion rights to equal pay to ERA itself.[194]

The central place of the ERA on the second-wave feminist agenda shows how far it had departed from its predecessors. What had once been a marginal position among feminists now became mainstream. One impact of Title VII of the Civil Rights Act was numerous court rulings invalidating state laws protective of women. Many groups, formerly opposed to ERA because of their support for these laws, had changed their minds.[195] ERA was sent to the states in 1972, where, after a spirited right-wing opposition, it failed in 1982.[196] But the level of support it now enjoyed both among feminists and the nation at large (the Congress and thirty-five states had ratified[197]) suggests the crucial importance in the appeal of contemporary rights-based feminist theory and practice of arguments about the unjust cultural construction of gender and the need to alter such arrangements accordingly. The appeal to differences, which had been accepted as axiomatic and the basis for a higher morality of women by Frances Willard and Jane Addams,[198] was now the basis for rights-based criticism (the differences, being unjustly culturally constructed, could reasonably be criticized and changed in light of justice).

In all of this, the civil rights movement was the impetus both for the new forms of substantive argument women now made and for women organizing themselves into a civil rights movement. It was also indispensable in preparing the constitutional mind of the nation for greater concern for related issues of constitutional justice, and indeed urging the judiciary interpretively to recognize such claims. As we have seen,

---

[191] See Freeman, n. 153 above, at 53–4; McGlen and O'Connor, n. 126 above, at 175–6.

[192] See Hole and Levine, n. 126 above, at 81–95.   [193] See *ibid.*, 95–107.

[194] See Chafe, n. 125 above, 201.   [195] See Freeman, n. 153 above, 212.

[196] See, on this political struggle, Donald G. Mathews and Jane Sherron De Hart, *Sex, Gender, and the Politics of ERA: A State and the Nation* (Oxford University Press, New York, 1990); Jane J. Mansbridge, *Why We Lost the ERA* (University of Chicago Press, Chicago, Ill., 1986).

[197] See *ibid.*, 1.   [198] See Rosenberg, n. 155 above, at 41.

the Supreme Court both responded to and encouraged such claims of a significant analogy between race and gender.

The claim of a rights-based analogy between racism and sexism was in the similar method of structural injustice inflicted in both cases, namely, 'that others have controlled the power to define one's existence'.[199] This structural injustice is marked by two features: first, abridgement of basic human rights to a group of persons; and secondly, the unjust rationalization of such abridgement on the inadequate grounds of dehumanizing stereotypes that reflect a history and culture of such abridgement. I call this injustice moral slavery (such a category of persons is so defined to rationalize its servile status and roles), and believe it can be plausibly argued that its moral condemnation is, properly understood, the abstract normative judgement of the Thirteenth Amendment of the United States Constitution.[200] From the perspective of the constitutional condemnation of such structural injustice, race and gender should be equally suspect as grounds for state action or inaction because blacks and women share a common history of such rights-denying moral degradation that continued with the complicitous support of law long after their formal emancipation and enfranchisement and powerfully and unjustly persists today. The guarantee of equal protection in the Fourteenth Amendment was ratified in 1868, but was held inapplicable to women until 1971[201] and was interpreted until 1954[202] to allow racial segregation. In both cases, the Supreme Court of the United States and the constitutional culture it reflects and shapes acted as powerful agents in the transmission and reinforcement of moral slavery in the domains of gender and race. The betrayal of basic rights expressly guaranteed is functionally often equivalent to the express deprivation of such rights, and may be even less morally excusable or justifiable when such betrayal powerfully reinforces, through the rationalizing power of the paradox of intolerance, the political force of sexism and racism as forms of moral slavery. Racial apartheid in the United States was an instrument of racial subjugation of blacks, isolating them from their basic rights of fair access on equal terms to public culture on specious racist grounds; as such, it gave powerful political legitimacy to the illegitimate force of racism in American public and private life, and thus to a continuing unjust cultural pattern of moral slavery in the domain of race that persists in various illegitimate forms today.[203] The wholesale failure even to acknowledge the evils of the subjugation of women gave powerful constitutional support to the illegitimate force of sexism in American public and private life, and thus to moral slavery in the domain of gender; gender segregation in separate spheres was, as in the case of race, a pivotal institutional mechanism of such degradation; and a still largely unchallenged sexist political epistemology of gender roles, operative in still powerful sectarian religious

---

[199] See William H. Chafe, *Women and Equality: Changing Patterns in American Culture* (Oxford University Press, New York, 1977), at 77; on the similar methods of repression, see *ibid.*, at 58–9, 75–6.

[200] See, for extensive defence of this claim, Richards, *Women, Gays, and the Constitution*, n. 1 above.

[201] See *Reed* v. *Reed*, 404 US 71 (1971).

[202] See *Brown* v. *Board of Education*, 347 US 483 (1954).

[203] See, e.g., Douglas S. Massey and Nancy A. Denton, *American Apartheid: Segregation and the Making of the Underclass* (Harvard University Press, Cambridge, Mass., 1993).

and moral traditions, undercuts the resources of public reason by which such mechanisms might be subjected to criticism and reform. Such silencing of the morally independent critical voice of reason rendered unjustly entrenched patterns of gender hierarchy largely unquestioned and unquestionable.

From the perspective of the theory of moral slavery, the constitutional injury of racism and sexism was the unjust cultural burden of contempt placed on identifications important to moral personality. Du Bois made this point in characterizing the struggle of African-Americans as two souls in one body: the one an African, the other an American identity, and the struggle to reconstruct both identities on terms of rights-based justice central to American revolutionary constitutionalism. Betty Friedan, anticipated by Sarah Grimke,[204] also defined women's struggle on similar grounds as 'a problem of identity',[205] the struggle to reconstruct American culture on terms of justice that would reconcile the identity of oneself as a woman and as a rights-bearing person and equal citizen. In both cases, the struggle for constitutional justice would by its nature reconstruct both personal identity and public (including constitutional) culture. In both cases, the personal and the political would become inextricably intertwined questions of both personal and moral-constitutional identity.

This perspective clarifies the justice of the remarkable interpretive development in American public law in the twentieth century that, on the basis of a radical abolitionist interpretation of the argument for toleration, subjected the cultural construction of racism and later of sexism to increasingly demanding sceptical constitutional principles as suspect.[206] Arguments of toleration and anti-subordination are, on this analysis, not contradictory and, properly understood, not even in tension. Anti-subordination is, on analysis, a structurally more profound form of cultural intolerance along the two dimensions of the argument for toleration: identification of certain basic rights of the moral person and the requirement of a compelling form of reasonably public justification for the abridgement of such basic rights. In particular, moral slavery, as I develop that idea, identifies a structural injustice marked by both its abridgement of such basic rights to a certain class of persons and the unjust enforcement at large of irrationalist stereotypical views whose illegitimate force has traditionally degraded the class of persons from their status as full bearers of human rights. European anti-Semitism (with its associated ideology of Jews as the slaves of Christians) is a case study that, in my approach, classically exemplifies a form of structural injustice along these two dimensions: it is certainly a species of religious intolerance but, in its European forms, a form of unjust subordination as well. Suspect classification analysis, on this view, sceptically condemns the expression through law of the structural injustices underlying such unjust subordination (reflected in the cultural stereotypes of race and gender that express such unjust subordination). Equal

---

[204] On this point, see Richards, *Women, Gays, and the Constitution*, n. 1 above, at 100.

[205] See Friedan, n. 124 above, 68.

[206] For further defence of this claim, see, in general, Richards, *Women, Gays, and the Constitution*, n. 1 above.

protection requires that political power must be reasonably justifiable in terms of equal respect for human rights and the pursuit of public purposes of justice and the common good.[207] Suspect classification analysis enforces this principle by rendering constitutionally suspect grounds for laws that not only lack such public reasons, but war against public reason by illegitimately rationalizing, on inadequate grounds, structural injustice. Laws, whose irrationalist bases thus war on public reason, lack constitutional legitimacy and are, for this reason, subjected to demanding tests of constitutional scepticism. The unconstitutionality of state-sponsored racial segregation and anti-miscegenation laws show the force of this constitutional scepticism in the area of race; and the comparable developments in the sphere of gender reflect a comparable scepticism (both in protecting basic rights, including aspects of the right to reproductive autonomy, and in subjecting gender classifications to a constitutional scrutiny increasingly close to that accorded to race). All these interpretive developments are systematically clarified and organized by the insights afforded by the theory and practice of rights-dissent of the terms of one's moral slavery.

In particular, the recent interpretive heightening of the standard of review for gender closer to that for race is supported by the theory of moral slavery. Much of the US Supreme Court's work, heightening the level of scrutiny for gender, is well explained by the theory of moral slavery, the terms of which, including various analogies between the abridgement of the rights of blacks and women, were quite self-consciously invoked in Justice Brennan's important opinion in *Frontiero* v. *Richardson*.[208] Further, Justice Brennan's scepticism about the enforcement of gender stereotypes through public law in *Craig* v. *Boren* also is well explained by this theory.[209] On the view taken by the theory of moral slavery, the proper interpretation of gender, as a suspect classification, must be contextually sensitive to the rights-denying cultural background of appeals to gender in the illegitimate service of the moral slavery of women as non-bearers of human rights. In particular, such illegitimate appeals to gender have culturally centred in unjust moral paternalism; a public and private culture, unjustly based on the exclusion of women from central rights of conscience, speech, association, and work, illegitimately dehumanized its victims in terms of a nature in love with and only capable of their servile dependency, and on that basis paternalistically moralized their dependency. Accordingly, the constitutional scrutiny of both express and implied gender-based classifications must be sceptical of those gender distinctions that rest on the unjust cultural ascription to women of stereotypes of dependency, passivity, or lack of autonomous judgemental and other capacities linked to the traditional cultural forms that illegitimately rationalized their subjugation. In particular, those stereotypes must be suspect that enforce a sexist political epistemology of servile gender roles based on deprivation of rights of

[207] For the classic statement of equal protection as a form of public reasonableness, see Joseph Tussman and Jacobus ten Broek, 'The Equal Protection of the Laws', 37 *Calif. L Rev.* 341 (1949); cf. Jacobus ten Broek, *Equal under Law* (Collier, New York, 1969).

[208] See, for further discussion, Richards, *Women, Gays, and the Constitution*, n. 1 above, at 257–8.

[209] For discussion, see *ibid.*, at 258–60.

conscience, speech, association, and work, i.e., a conception of women's natural sphere defined by, for, and in terms of the sexual and other interests of men untested in terms of public reasons expressive of the dignity of women's free moral powers of conscience, speech, association and work, and reasonably acceptable to them in such terms. In the abolitionist feminist terms of analysis,[210] indulging such gender stereotypes through law distorts public understanding and acknowledgement of the principles of ethical responsibility incumbent on all persons, as such, and, for this reason, flouts constitutional principles of equal citizenship. On this normative view, it should be irrelevant to the constitutional analysis of the suspectness of gender distinctions of such sorts that they reflect gender-linked statistical probabilities. Otherwise, the fact of the longstanding enforcement of an unjust sexist orthodoxy, to which its victims have accommodated themselves as best they can, would undercut the legitimacy of constitutional scrutiny where it is, in fact, exigently needed on grounds of justice.

In addition, the anti-racist and anti-sexist practice of abolitionist feminism was as integral to these interpretive developments as was their theory. Rights-based arguments against moral slavery, whether by African-Americans or women, took the form of originating claims of basic human rights in one's own voice that, sceptical as they were of traditionally dominant orthodoxies of race or gender (the mythologizing pedestal being common to both), morally transformed personal identity in the way the civil rights movement transformed both racial and gender identity; second-wave feminism as a civil rights movement, if anything, reinforced this momentum. To give voice to one's human rights of moral independence, against the background of a subjugating tradition of moral slavery, is to forge a new personal and moral-constitutional identity on the platform of human rights, one that demands, on grounds of principle, not only one's basic rights of moral personality but a private and public culture that no longer gives expression to an unjust tradition of dehumanization and marginalization. The practice of such protest of the terms of one's moral slavery both expresses and elaborates not only new forms of identity but of consciousness and the dissident associations that sustain such consciousness. Consciousness in turn gives rise to the need for new forms of critical theory. Personally, morally, and politically transformative arguments of human rights require a complementary and mutually reinforcing theory and practice.

Such protest of the terms of one's moral slavery must be examined closely as the background to the increasingly suspect character of gender under American public law. Two features of such protest are especially important in this connection: first, its challenge to the conventional terms of the public/private distinction; secondly, its worries about the weight placed on gender stereotypes in the distribution of rights and responsibilities.

With respect to the public/private distinction, the condemnation of moral slavery in the Thirteenth Amendment extends as broadly as the underlying rights-denying evil, including the traditions pivotal in the subjection of women. Moral slavery was

---

[210] For further discussion, see Richards, *Women, Gays, and the Constitution*, at ch. 3.

as much an injury to private as it was to public life; indeed, the attempt to privatize injustice was one of its most insidious and morally corrupting evils (one's slave or one's wife as most intimately oneself).[211] Our constitutional concern under the Thirteenth Amendment should thus extend to both public and private dimensions both of racism[212] and of sexism.[213] This concern includes the uncritical privatization of interspousal violence and resistance, which obfuscates rights-based normative issues of constitutional dimensions.[214]

The ever-increasing level of constitutional scepticism about the enforcement of gender stereotypes through law may reasonably be understood and evaluated against the background of increasing scepticism about the ways in which unjust cultural traditions of gender roles had been and were enforced through law. The very exclusion of women from the traditional understanding of basic human rights (of conscience, speech, intimate association, and work) appealed to an unjustly gendered conception of the person that provided the uncritical benchmark for questions of equality; the abolitionist feminist criticism of this exclusion crucially demanded that the background ideal of moral personality must not assume such unjust culturally constructed differences, but the demands of moral personality reasonably accessible to all.[215] The objection of this rights-based feminism to the trajectory of suffrage feminism was precisely along these lines, namely, the temperance and purity movements unjustly assumed gender differences that failed to subject their claims to an appropriately reasonable standpoint on the demands of moral personality (to which all persons are subject), thus enforcing not only sexism but racism and ethnocentrism as well.[216]

Even the abolitionist feminists, however, appealed to those aspects of women's moral experience that, in their view, better stated and enforced the appropriately demanding normative standpoint of universal justice on issues of race and gender (for example, the appeal to white women's experience as wives and mothers to yield moral

---

[211] See *ibid.*, n. 1 above, 253, 347–8, 367–8.

[212] See *Jones* v. *Alfred H. Mayer Co.*, 392 US 409 (1968) (under the Thirteenth Amendment, Congress has power to forbid racial discrimination in both public and private sales and rentals of property); *Sullivan* v. *Little Hunting Park, Inc.*, 396 US 229 (1969) (Congressional power under the Thirteenth Amendment reaches racial discrimination in leasing by residents' association); *Runyon* v. *McCrary*, 427 US 160 (1976) (Congressional power under the Thirteenth Amendment extends to racial discrimination by private, non-sectarian schools).

[213] For a different argument to the same effect, see Emily Calhoun, 'The Thirteenth and Fourteenth Amendments: Constitutional Authority for Federal Legislation Against Private Sex Discrimination', 61 *Minn. L Rev.* 313 (1977), at 355–8. For the background of such arguments, see Note, 'The "New" Thirteenth Amendment: A Preliminary Analysis', 82 *Harv. L Rev.* 1294 (1969); Note, 'Jones v. Mayer: The Thirteenth Amendment and the Federal Anti-Discrimination Laws', 69 *Colum. L Rev.* 1019 (1969). For a classic background historical study arguing for the pivotal role of the Thirteenth Amendment in the structure of the Reconstruction Amendments, see Jacobus ten Broek, 'Thirteenth Amendment to the Constitution of the United States: Consummation to Abolition and Key to the Fourteenth Amendment', 39 *Calif. L Rev.* 171 (1951).

[214] For an important exploration of this issue along these lines, see Jane Maslow Cohen, 'Regimes of Private Tyranny: What Do They Mean to Morality and for the Criminal Law?', 57 *U Pitt. L Rev.* 757 (1996).

[215] For further discussion, see Richards, *Women, Gays, and the Constitution*, n. 1 above, at ch. 3.

[216] See, for further discussion, *ibid.*, at chs. 3–5.

insight into the indignities inflicted on the intimate lives of African-American men and women[217]). Such ideas of women's distinctive moral experience are often metaphors or tropes calling for interpretation, and lend themselves to quite inconsistent interpretations.[218] Abolitionist feminism suggests an interpretation that enhances appropriate respect for universal human rights. Perhaps, as some contemporary feminists have argued,[219] some such arguments (exploring women's moral experience to enlarge public understanding of the critical demands of universal human rights) may be appropriate in our circumstances as well.[220] Certainly, any reasonable concern for rights-based justice to women, in the related areas of family life and employment opportunities, must not assess such matters in terms of a superficially neutral standard that, in fact, imposes an uncritical masculine standard either of family responsibilities or of competitive success in work that reflects injustice in the conception of the fair distribution of basic rights and opportunities of intimate life and of work.[221]

On the other hand, second-wave feminism arises from scepticism about the abusive use of uncritical conceptions of gender roles to abridge the basic rights of both women and men. We need to be both interpretively charitable and yet appropriately critical of the force of such women-centred arguments in the history of American feminism. On the one hand, such interpretations of women's roles were not only empowering of voice but often rooted in strategic political judgements based on some real concerns (for example, interspousal violence linked to alcohol abuse). On the other hand, such an insular politics, however historically understandable, also often ideologically obfuscated basic issues of human rights in service of re-enforcing uncritical conceptions of gender roles that legitimated sexism as well as racism along various dimensions.[222] In light of this historical experience and our contemporary interpretive concerns for articulating and elaborating common anti-racist and anti-sexist constitutional principles properly contextualized in our circumstances, we must, at least as a matter of constitutional law, set a high standard of scepticism for the enforcement through law of conventional gender roles particularly when such roles are alleged uncritically to reflect the appropriate normative weight to be accorded 'natural' facts like pregnancy or mothering. The tradition of moral slavery, that abolitionist feminism identified and criticized, rationalized its subjugation of

[217] See Richards, *Women, Gays, and the Constitution*, n. 1 above, at 82, 83, 84–5, 282.

[218] e.g., the idea of protecting the home, that had been used by temperance women to advocate constitutional entrenchment of prohibition, was later to be used by women to urge constitutional repeal of prohibition. For recent illuminating discussion of this paradoxical ideological point, see Kenneth D. Rose, *American Women and the Repeal of Prohibition* (New York University Press, New York, 1996), at 63–89.

[219] For an argument along these lines, see Sara Ruddick, *Maternal Thinking: Towards a Politics of Peace* (Beacon Press, Boston, Mass., 1989).

[220] For some sense of the range of views among contemporary feminists on the merits of equality versus difference feminism in contemporary circumstances, see Marianne Hirsch and Evelyn Fox Keller, *Conflicts in Feminism* (Routledge, New York, 1990).

[221] See, for an incisive general argument to this effect, Susan Moller Okin, *Justice, Gender, and the Family* (Basic Books, New York, 1989).

[222] For fuller discussion of this point, see Richards, *Women, Gays, and the Constitution*, n. 1 above, ch. 4.

women in terms of the unjust interpretation accorded to pregnancy. The ground for the abridgement of basic rights of conscience, speech, association, and work was the reduction of women solely to this biological possibility, to which they were consigned on terms that did even acknowledge their basic equal rights of moral personality, in terms of which they might rationally and reasonably decide (against a background of equal justice and fair opportunity in public and private life) what weight, if any, this biological possibility, among manifold other such possibilities, should and would play in their conception of a good and ethical life. Against this unjust background, any interpretation given pregnancy, as a basis for the differential treatment, must be sceptically scrutinized to ensure that it does not unjustly impose an uncritical conception of gender roles that enforces, rather than contests the traditional moral slavery of women.[223]

It is in light of these concerns that we may reasonably understand and evaluate the judicial elaboration of anti-sexist principles to condemn public legitimation of the way traditional gender roles defined domesticity, including entitlements to women as such. A number of these cases involved benefits keyed to the understanding of domesticity in terms of a gendered dichotomy between ideal worker and caretaking spouse: a statutory preference for males to be administrators of decedents' estates;[224] a policy that servicemen, but not servicewomen, had the automatic right to claim their spouses as dependents for purposes of eligibility for housing and medical benefits;[225] a policy allowing mothers, but not fathers, to claim suvivors' benefits to care for the decedent's children;[226] and policies that automatically awarded suvivors' benefits to women but not men.[227] In all these cases, the gender distinctions were struck down as unconstitutional; a programme designed to help women marginalized by traditional gender roles would have to be drafted as a programme to help caregivers, not as a programme to help women as such. Moreover, in these and other cases, the condemnation extends to gender stereotypy as such, whether immediately harmful to women or to men.[228] These cases reflect a principled interpretation and condemnation of sexism in terms of

---

[223] For an opinion that failed to observe the appropriate level of sceptical scrutiny about these issues, see *Michael M.* v. *Superior Court*, 450 US 464 (1981). But see Frances Olsen, 'Statutory Rape: A Feminist Critique of Rights Analysis', 63 *Tex. L Rev.* 387 (1984). For related opinions that also fail to observe the appropriate level of scrutiny, see *Geduldig* v. *Aiello*, 417 US 484 (1974) (exclusion of pregnancy from California's disability insurance system held constitutional); *General Electric Co.* v. *Gilbert*, 429 US 125 (1976) (holding that Title VII of the Civil Rights Act of 1964 did not bar exclusions of pregnancies from private disability plans); but see *Nashville Gas Co.* v. *Satty*, 434 US 136 (1977) (*Gilbert* distinguished in case where pregnant employees were not only required to take pregnancy leave and denied sick pay while on leave, but also lost all accumulated job seniority when they returned to work). The *Gilbert* holding was overturned by Congress when it amended Title VII in 1978: see 92 Stat. 2076. For a recent decision that gives proper weight to the relevant considerations, see *International Union et al.* v. *Johnson Controls, Inc.*, 499 US 187 (1991) (violation of Title VII for an employer to preclude women from holding certain jobs because of a fear that those jobs would endanger the health of a foetus).

[224] *Reed* v. *Reed*, 404 US 71 (1971).   [225] *Frontiero* v. *Richardson*, 411 US 677 (1973).

[226] *Weinberger* v. *Weisenfeld*, 420 US 636 (1975).

[227] *Califano* v. *Goldfarb*, 430 US 199 (1977); *Wengler* v. *Druggists Mutual Insurance Co.*, 446 US 142 (1980).

[228] For cases that protect women, see *Reed* v. *Reed*, 404 US 71 (1971) (right to administer estates); *Frontiero* v. *Richardson*, 411 US 677 (1973) (dependency allowances to servicewomen); *Stanton* v. *Stanton*,

the unjust construction of gender roles by the enforcement of such roles through law on both women and men. If the mythological idealization of women's roles was the price exacted to obfuscate this injustice, we must address this ideological problem in terms of the common grounds of basic human rights reasonably available to all persons. An insistence on functional categories, in terms of which the rights and responsibilities of both men and women may be understood and evaluated, corresponds to this critical imperative of justice. That men as well as women may benefit from such assessment confirms its justice, in particular, that it addresses the ideological problem posed by the rights-denying structural injustice of sexism.

The injustice is not based in biological sex or biology at all (any more than racism is rooted in biology), but in a cultural tradition that has defined and enforced gender and its significance in ways that have divided men and women from their common humanity by appeal to stereotypes that reflect structural injustice. Sexism as much distorts the life of women as it does that of men in the same way, as Du Bois observed, racism as much deforms the image of African-Americans as it does the image of white America. It is for this reason, as we have seen, that rights-based constitutional protest of the terms of one's moral slavery transforms not only one's own identity, as an African-American or a woman, but the identity of America (as white, or as masculine). The theory and practice of such protest includes challenge to the cultural weight of race and gender as ethical dichotomies. Such challenge to the weight of gender reasonably includes critical appeal to principles of justice that affirm the common rights and responsibilities of all. Only principles of this sort correspond critically to addressing the depth of the structural injustice.

Understanding the constitutional evil of sexism in this way not only illuminates authoritative case law, but also suggests the role that the analogy of gender might play in addressing constitutional issues relating to sexual orientation.

THE CONSTITUTIONAL EVIL OF HOMOPHOBIA

Sexism, as a constitutional evil, informs in several related ways a reasonable understanding of the case for gay rights. First, the issues of identity, so important in understanding the suspectness of gender, illuminate issues of identity of the case for gay rights. Secondly, the grounds for scepticism about state purposes, developed in areas of gender (both protecting basic rights and in constitutional suspicion about traditional grounds for abridging such rights), apply, as a matter of principle, to related areas in the case of sexual orientation. Indeed, several of the familiar ways in which the constitutional evils of racism and sexism were constructed (namely, the distortion of the public/private distinction, segregation, anti-miscegenation) reasonably inform understanding of the constitutional evil of homophobia.

421 US 7 (1975) (child support for education). For cases that protect men, see *Wengler* v. *Druggists Mutual Insurance Co.*, 446 US 142 (1980) (widower's right to death benefits); *Craig* v. *Boren*, 429 US 190 (1976) (age of drinking for men).

As we have seen, sexism has achieved the status it has, as a constitutional evil, because of the unjust burdens thus placed on pivotal identifications of moral personality, in particular, those associated with gender identity. Gender identity has been accorded this constitutional status because rights-based protest to the structural injustice of sexism has been to the terms unjustly imposed on such identity. The terms of such injustice included imposing on gender a script that not only excluded women as such from the status of bearers of basic human rights of conscience, speech, association, and work, but did so on grounds of depersonalizing stereotypes that, in a vicious circle, reflected such dehumanization. The consequence of such injustice was to impose a natural hierarchy keyed to gender on human consciousness and life and to make of any deviation from such hierarchy, literally, an unnatural and inhuman act.[229] The rights-based protest of the terms of such injustice has thus, crucially, attacked such naturalization of injustice. Indeed, such protest, made on the grounds of the basic human rights the injustice structurally denied, demanded exactly the scope of self-defining personal and ethical choice of identity, on rational and reasonable terms, that self-originating claims based on human rights call for. Sexism is the profound constitutional evil that it is now acknowledged to be because it submerged and silenced the freedom and reason of a deliberative autonomous choice of a good and ethical life of half the human race. Gender identity is so pivotal a feature of this constitutional development because its very terms (as a form of identity) make the appropriate normative space for raising the questions that addressing the evil of sexism requires of us, namely, that persons afflicted by this injustice be guaranteed the respect for basic human rights that allows them not only to contest the traditional naturalization of such injustice, but the normative resources to acknowledge the range of rational and reasonable choice of gender identity, as an identity, available to them, as a free and equal rational persons endowed with basic human rights.

The operative point is not that gender, any more than race, is immutable and salient, for, as we have seen, many other things about us are both and yet raise no comparable issues of structural injustice. The point is, rather, that gender, like race, is freighted with an impersonal script whose cultural power draws its force from a naturalization of injustice, denying any space for coming to understand and claim the basic human rights that rationally and reasonably contest the naturalized terms of such injustice. Such an impersonal script accords gender a totalizing force in the shape of human lives, marked by a gender-based dichotomy in the choices and opportunities that define the personal and ethical meaning and value of human lives. The burdens thus placed on gender identity (namely, insistence on rigid conformity to the impersonal script) raise such profound issues of structural injustice, like the comparable burdens placed on racial identity, because the cultural imposition of the impersonal script derives its totalizing force precisely from the abridgment of the basic human rights of conscience, speech, intimate life, and work that might rationally and

[229] See, e.g., Horace Bushnell, *Women's Suffrage: The Reform against Nature* (Charles Scribner and Co., New York, 1869).

reasonably contest the script. In particular, the abridgement of conscience, as in the area of race, takes on such pivotal importance in understanding the unjust political force of sexism because such denial of the free exercise of the rational and reasonable powers of conscience to a class of persons makes possible the enforcement of a tightly scripted gender against either the persons or the kinds of arguments that might rationally and reasonably contest it. Literally, thoughts, feelings, arguments, and critical debate—the resources of a life lived from an internal sense of rationally and reasonably tested personal and ethical conviction—are made unthinkable.

It is against this background of structural injustice, once we have come to acknowledge and address it as an intolerable constitutional evil, that the terms of gender identity become so important an object of constitutional concern. Gender identity takes on the significance that it now constitutionally has for us because rectifying this injustice crucially calls both for extending basic human rights of conscience, speech, intimate life, and work to persons and arguments that contest the gender orthodoxy, and for sceptical assessment of the enforcement through law of the gender orthodoxy itself (centring, as it does, on gender identity). For these reasons, all the terms of the gender orthodoxy must become contestable and contested, making space, in particular, for the free exercise of rational and reasonable conviction about how and on what terms gender should and will play a role in the shape of a good and ethical life in light of choices and opportunities based on basic human rights of conscience, speech, intimate life, and work fairly available to all. The interpretation of one's gender identity thus becomes possible and thinkable not as an externally imposed natural script or fact of nature to be conformed to, but as an intensely personal matter calling for the responsible exercise of one's moral powers of freedom and reason, consistent with respect for human rights, both in reflecting on one's desires, needs, and talents and in critically independent assessment of and revision of the cultural terms of gender as a force in the shape of one's life.

One's gender identity becomes, for this reason, so profoundly personal a matter because the issues, traditionally governed by the impersonal script, now are so exquisitely and intimately personal, indeed, for many of us, at what we self-identify as the core of our sense of ourselves as an ethically responsible person and agent. The issues of gender identity now open to deliberative choice and debate—conscience, speech, intimate life, and work—are the questions raised and addressed when we think of ourselves, as all persons do, as responsible for finding personal and ethical meaning in living and thus in life.

There is, of course, no necessary conceptual linkage between gender identity and sexual orientation; one may have a secure sense of one's identity as a man or as a woman and also as either heterosexual or homosexual. The relationship, if any, between gender identity and sexual orientation and practice has differed and differs among human cultures; in ancient Greece, one's identity as a man was consistent with both heterosexuality and homosexuality; indeed, ancient Greek culture not only tolerated, but idealized pederastic male homosexual relations as central elements in Greek pedagogy and artistic and political culture (only passivity in same-sex relations was inconsistent with adult male gender identity).[230] However, in the culture that is of concern to us, the unjust cultural construction and enforcement of an impersonal script of gender orthodoxy has been and continues to be freighted with a rigid script of heterosexuality. The script has importantly been coded in the terms of gender: being gay or lesbian has thus been coded and indeed stigmatized as improperly (or unthinkably or unnaturally) feminine (if gay) or masculine (if lesbian).[231] Such coding raises fundamental issues of justice for homosexuals as well as heterosexuals because its enforcement through law, as compulsory heterosexuality, is an important structural feature of the unjust imposition of the gender orthodoxy itself.[232] One of the ways in which the gender orthodoxy erases questioning of its injustice is by rendering unthinkable and thus unspeakable claims that sexual and intimate relations might be conducted free of the hierarchy in these matters demanded by the gender orthodoxy. The scapegoating of homosexuals, in terms of the gender orthodoxy, historically arose precisely as one way, among others, of domesticating claims for gender equality in terms that could normatively resist arguments that pressed for equality of basic human rights,[233] including equal rights and opportunities in both private and public life. The way ideologically to achieve such a truncated public understanding of gender equality was importantly to render unthinkable serious debate about the structural injustice we call sexism, including its ideologically driven interpretation of the public/private distinction as a male/female distinction. The most important ideological mechanism for such truncation was the development of an idealized stereotype of women's higher moral nature, as wife and mother, a stereotype which usefully rationalized the inapplicability to the assessment of gender roles of basic values of human rights.[234] The scapegoating of homosexuals further re-enforced the stereotype by rendering unthinkable the kinds of relations between men or between women or between men and women that would challenge the stereotype both of rigid gender hierarchy and the public/private ideology that supports it. If the values of sexual

---

[230] Important studies include William Armstrong Percy III, *Pederasty and Pedagogy in Archaic Greece* (University of Illinois Press, Urbana, Ill., 1996); Kenneth J. Dover, *Greek Popular Morality in the Time of Plato and Aristotle* (Basil Blackwell, Oxford, 1974); *id.*, *Greek Homosexuality* (London: Duckworth, 1978); *id.*, 'Greek Homosexuality and Initiation', in K. J. Dover, *The Greeks and Their Legacy* (Blackwell, Oxford, 1988), 115–34; Peter Green, 'Sex and Classical Literature' in Peter Green, *Classical Bearings: Interpreting Ancient History and Culture* (Thames and Hudson, New York, 1989), 130–50; Eva Cantarella, *Bisexuality in the Ancient World* (trans. Cormac O'Cuilleanain, Yale University Press, New Haven, Conn., 1992); David M. Halperin, *One Hundred Years of Homosexuality: And Other Essays on Greek Love* (Routledge, New York, 1990); David M. Halperin, John J. Winkler, and Froma I. Zeitlin (eds.), *Before Sexuality: The Construction of Erotic Experience in the Ancient Greek World* (Princeton University Press, Princeton, NJ, 1990).

[231] See, for the historical background of this linkage, Richards, *Women, Gays, and the Constitution*, n. 1 above, 289–97.

[232] For an important statement of this position, see Adrienne Rich, 'Compulsory Heterosexuality and Lesbian Existence', in Catharine R. Stimpson and Ethel Spector Person, *Women: Sex and Sexuality* (University of Chicago Press, Chicago, Ill., 1980), 62–91.

[233] See Richards, *Women, Gays, and the Constitution*, n. 1 above, 294–7.

[234] See, for elaboration of this ideological development and its malign political consequences, *ibid.*, ch. 4.

intimacy could be realized in same-sex relations, such relations need no longer be structured by the inequality of genders central to the idealizing stereotype of the nature of gender, nor need the relations between men and women either in or outside private life be rigidly defined as essentially romantic and sexual (as the stereotype required). Neither public nor private life could any longer be reasonably confined to the rigid terms of the gender stereotype, which must now itself be impartially assessed in terms of requirements of equal rights and opportunities.

In a culture like ours that thus codes homosexuality in terms of gender stereotypes, the experience of one's identity as a homosexual will raise issues of one's gender identity as well. On the analysis of the constitutional evil of sexism earlier proposed, rights-based protest of the stigmatized terms of one's identity, as gay or lesbian, may plausibly be structured as well in terms of a rights-based protest of the unjust cultural terms of one's gender identity, *viz.*, as a protest of a form or manifestation of sexism. If such protest is of a structural injustice at least as evil as sexism proper, the personal and ethical issues of identity will be at least as profound as those of race or gender. Certainly, abridgement of the rights of conscience, speech, intimate life, and work has been as complete in the case of homosexuals as it has historically been for African-Americans and women, and the grounds for such abridgement arguably rest on dehumanizing stereotypes analogous to those that supported racism and sexism. If so, the issues of identity, for gays and lesbians, work at a level at least as profound as those for racial minorities or women. The struggle here, as elsewhere, must engage personal and ethical resources of thought, feeling, reason, and conviction in the self-defining reconstruction of identity against an impersonal script of naturalized injustice that has reduced the moral complexity of homosexual passion, love, and life to the crude and objectifying measure of a sexist fantasy. The protest of such injustice must extend as broadly and deeply as the injustice itself, critically addressing the yet explored issues of sexism that still popularly sustain such structural injustice. The object of such protest is here, no more than elsewhere, the immutability and salience of the basis for the injustice, but the unjust imposition of an impersonal script of gender and sexuality on grounds that naturalize injustice.

Understood in these terms, the case for gay rights is properly understood, like Du Bois on the case for anti-racism and Friedan on anti-sexism, as a rights-based struggle for personal and ethical identity on terms of justice against objectifying stereotypes rationalized as natural. To make claims in this spirit is not to reflect an identity which is somehow naturally given, but, quite the opposite, to protest the cultural stereotype of naturally given differences that, in a vicious circle, rationalize injustice. Making such protests on such grounds is to forge an identity, as a responsible moral agent, through the deliberative free exercise of one's moral powers of rationality and reasonableness.

The analogy of sexism thus clarifies the identity-based focus of the case for gay rights. But the case for gay rights is incomplete without further examination of the inadequate grounds traditionally supposed to rationalize abridgement of such rights. I have already suggested reasons for thinking that such grounds include a form of sexism. The analogy of sexism affords yet further illumination in terms both of its case for protection of basic rights and its scepticism about traditional grounds for abridgement of such rights. I focus here on two such issues: the right to intimate life, and the construction of the structural injustice of sexism.

In 1965 the Supreme Court in *Griswold* v. *Connecticut*[235] constitutionalized the argument for a basic human right to contraception that had been persistently and eloquently defended and advocated by Margaret Sanger for well over forty years, a decision which Sanger lived to see.[236] The Court extended the right to abortion services in 1973 in *Roe* v. *Wade*[237] (reaffirming its central principle in 1992[238]), and denied its application in 1986 to consensual homosexual sex acts in *Bowers* v. *Hardwick*;[239] a related form of analysis was used, albeit inconclusively, in cases involving the right to die.[240] Three of these cases (contraception, abortion, homosexuality) can be understood on the grounds of a basic right to intimate personal life, one of them (death) involving another basic right (an aspect of the right to life or meaningful life).[241] I focus here on the first three cases.

Sanger's argument for the right to contraception was very much rooted in rights-based feminism.[242] Sanger's opponents certainly made that point very clear. When her then husband, Bill Sanger, was convicted of obscenity for distributing one of his wife's publications, the judge emphasized that the dispute was over woman's role:

> Your crime is not only a violation of the laws of man, but of the law of God as well, in your scheme to prevent motherhood. Too many persons have the idea that it is wrong to have children. Some women are so selfish that they do not want to be bothered with them. If some persons would go around and urge Christian women to bear children, instead of wasting their time on woman suffrage, this city and society would be better off.[243]

Sanger's argument had two prongs, both of which were implicit in the Supreme Court's decisions in *Griswold* and later cases: first, a basic human right to intimate life and the role of the right to contraception as an instance of that right; and secondly, the assessment of whether laws abridging such a fundamental right met the heavy burden of secular justification that was required.

The basis of the fundamental human right to intimate life was, as Lydia Maria Child, Stephen Andrews, and Victoria Woodhull had earlier made clear,[244] as basic

---

[235] See *Griswold* v. *Connecticut*, 381 US 479 (1965).
[236] See Ellen Chesler, *Woman of Valor: Margaret Sanger and the Birth Control Movement in America* (Anchor, New York, 1992), at 11, 230, 376, 467.   [237] See *Roe* v. *Wade*, 410 US 113 (1973).
[238] See *Planned Parenthood of Southeastern Pennsylvania* v. *Casey*, 112 S. Ct. 2791 (1992).
[239] See *Bowers* v. *Hardwick*, 478 US 186 (1986).
[240] See *Cruzan* v. *Director, Missouri Dept. of Health*, 496 US 261 (1990). Justice Rehnquist, writing for a 5–4 majority, accepts that a right to die exists and applies to the case but denies that the state has imposed an unreasonable restriction on the right on the facts of the case. But see *Vacco* v. *Quill*, 117 S Ct. 2293 (1997) (unanimously upholding prohibition on physician assisted suicide).
[241] For further discussion, see David A. J. Richards, *Sex, Drugs, Death, and the Law: An Essay on Human Rights and Overcriminalization* (Rowman and Littlefield, Totowa, NJ, 1982), at 215–70.
[242] For elaboration of this point, see Richards, *Women, Gays, and the Constitution*, n. 1 above, 178–81.
[243] Cited in Chesler, n. 236 above, 127.
[244] For citations and discussion, see Richards, *Women, Gays, and the Constitution*, n. 1 above, ch. 4.

an inalienable right of moral personality (respect for which is central to the argument for toleration) as the right to conscience. Like the right to conscience, it protects intimately personal moral resources (thoughts and beliefs, intellect, emotions, self-image and self-identity) and the way of life that expresses and sustains them in facing and meeting rationally and reasonably the challenge of a life worth living—one touched by enduring personal and ethical value. The right to intimate life centres on protecting these moral resources as they bear on the role of loving and being loved in the tender and caring exfoliation of moral personality, morally finding one's self, as a person, in love for and the love of another moral self.

The human right of intimate life was not only an important right in the argument for toleration central to American constitutionalism, but a right interpretively implicit in the historical traditions of American rights-based constitutionalism. In both of the two great revolutionary moments that framed the trajectory of American constitutionalism (the American Revolution and the Civil War), the right to intimate life was one of the human rights the abridgement of which rendered political power illegitimate and gave rise to the Lockean right to revolution.[245]

At the time of the American Revolution, the background literature on human rights, known to and assumed by the American revolutionaries and founding constitutionalists, included what the influential Scottish philosopher Francis Hutcheson called 'the natural right each one to enter into the matrimonial relation with any one who consents'.[246] Indeed, John Witherspoon, whose lectures Madison heard at Princeton, followed Hutcheson in listing even more abstractly as a basic human and natural right a 'right to associate, if he so incline, with any person or persons, whom he can persuade (not force)—under this is contained the right to marriage'.[247] Accordingly, leading statesmen at the state conventions ratifying the Constitution, both those for and against adoption, assumed that the Constitution could not interfere in the domestic sphere. Alexander Hamilton of New York denied that federal constitutional law did or could 'penetrate the recesses of domestic life, and control, in all respects, the private conduct of individuals'.[248] And Patrick Henry of Virginia spoke of the core of our rights to liberty as the sphere where a person 'enjoys the fruits of his labor, under his own fig-tree, with his wife and children around him, in peace and security'.[249] The arguments of reserved rights both of leading proponents (Hamilton) and opponents (Henry) of adoption of the Constitution thus converged on the private sphere of domestic married life.

---

[245] See, on American revolutionary constitutionalism as framed by these events, Richards, *Foundations of American Constitutionalism* (Oxford University Press, New York, 1989); *Conscience and the Constitution*, n. 1 above.

[246] See Francis Hutcheson, *A System of Moral Philosophy* (1755), 2 vols. in 1 (Augustus M. Kelley, New York, 1968), at 299.

[247] See John Witherspoon, *Lectures of Moral Philosophy* (ed. Jack Scott, Associated University Presses, East Brunswick, NJ, 1982), 123. For further development of this point, see David A. J. Richards, *Toleration and the Constitution* (Oxford University Press, New York, 1986), at 232–3.

[248] See Jonathan Elliot (ed.), *The Debates in the Several State Conventions on the Adoption of the Federal Constitution* (Printed for the editor, Washington, DC, 1836), ii, 269.

[249] See *ibid.*, iii, 54.

At the time of the Civil War, the understanding of marriage as a basic human right took on a new depth and urgency because of the antebellum abolitionist rights-based attack on the peculiar nature of American slavery; such slavery failed to recognize the marriage or family rights of slaves,[250] and indeed inflicted on the black family the moral horror of breaking them up by selling family members separately.[251] One in six slave marriages thus were ended by force or sale.[252] No aspect of American slavery more dramatized its radical evil for abolitionists and Americans more generally than its brutal deprivation of intimate personal life, including undermining the moral authority of parents over children. Slaves, Weld argued, had 'as little control over them [children], as have domestic animals over the disposal of their young'.[253] Slavery, thus understood as an attack on intimate personal life,[254] stripped persons of essential attributes of their humanity.

It is against this historical background (as well as background rights-based political theory) that it is interpretively correct to regard the right to intimate life as one of the unenumerated rights protected both by the Ninth Amendment and the Privileges and Immunities Clause of the Fourteenth Amendment, as Justice Harlan may be regarded as arguing in his concurrence in *Griswold*.[255] The Supreme Court quite properly interpreted the Fourteenth Amendment in particular as protecting this basic human right against unjustified state abridgement, and, as Sanger had urged, regarding the right to use contraceptives as an instance of this right. The right to contraception was, for Sanger, so fundamental a human right for women because it would enable women, perhaps for the first time in human history, reliably to decide whether and when their sexual lives will be reproductive. Respect for this right was an aspect of the more basic right of intimate life in two ways. First, it would enable women to exercise control over their intimate relations with men, deciding whether and when such relations will be reproductive. Secondly, it would secure to women the right to decide whether and when they will form the intimate relationship with a child. Both forms of choice threatened the traditional gender-defined role of women's sexuality as both exclusively and mandatorily procreational and maternally self-sacrificing, and were resisted, as by Bill Sanger's judge, for that reason.

[250] See Kenneth M. Stampp, *The Peculiar Institution* (Vintage, New York, 1956), 198, 340–9; Eugene D. Genovese, *Roll, Jordan, Roll: The World the Slaves Made* (Vintage Books, New York, 1974), 32, 52–3, 125, 451–8.

[251] See Stampp, n. 250 above, 199–207, 204–6, 333, 348–9; Herbert G. Gutman, *The Black Family in Slavery and Freedom, 1750–1925* (Vintage Books, New York, 1976), 146, 318, 349.

[252] See *ibid.*, 318.

[253] See Theodore Weld, *American Slavery as It Is* (1839, Arno Press and The New York Times, New York, 1968), 56.

[254] See Ronald G. Walters, *The Anti-slavery Appeal: American Abolitionism after 1830* (W. W. Norton, New York, 1978), 95–6.

[255] Justice Harlan, in fact, grounds his argument on the Due Process Clause of the Fourteenth Amendment, but the argument is more plausibly understood, as a matter of text, history, and political theory, as based on the Privileges and Immunities Clause of the Fourteenth Amendment for reasons I give in Richards, *Conscience and the Constitution*, n. 1 above, ch. 6. For further elaboration of this interpretation of *Griswold*, see Richards, n. 247 above, at 256–61.

But second, this human right, like other such rights, may only be regulated or limited on terms of public reason not themselves hostage to an entrenched political hierarchy (for example, compulsorily arranged marriages[256]) enforced by the abridgement of such rights. For example, from the perspective of the general abolitionist criticism of slavery and racism, the pro-slavery arguments in support of Southern slavery's treatment of family life were transparently inadequate, not remotely affording adequate public justification for the abridgement of such a fundamental right.

These arguments were in their nature essentially racist:

His natural affection is not strong, and consequently he is cruel to his own offspring, and suffers little by separation from them.[257]

Another striking trait of negro character is lasciviousness. Lust is his strongest passion; and hence, rape is an offence of too frequent occurrence. Fidelity to the marriage relation they do not understand and do not expect, neither in their native country nor in a state of bondage.[258]

The blind moral callousness of Southern pro-slavery thought was nowhere more evident than its treatment of what were in fact agonizing, crushing, and demeaning family separations[259]:

He is also liable to be separated from wife or child—but from native character and temperament, the separation is much less severely felt.[260]

With regard to the separation of husbands and wives, parents and children, . . . Negroes are themselves both perverse and comparatively indifferent about this matter.[261]

The irrationalist racist sexualization of black slaves was evident in the frequent justification of slavery in terms of maintaining the higher standards of sexual purity of Southern white women.[262] Viewed through the polemically distorted prism of such thought, the relation of master and slave was itself justified as an intimate relationship, like that of husband and wife, that should similarly be immunized from outside interference.[263] In this Orwellian world of the distortion of truth by power, the defence of slavery became the defence of freedom.[264] Arguments of these sorts

---

[256] See Werner Sollors, *Beyond Ethnicity: Consent and Descent in American Culture* (Oxford University Press, New York, 1986), 112.

[257] Thomas R. R. Cobb, *An Inquiry into the Law of Negro Slavery in the United States of America* (1858; reprint, Negro Universities Press, New York, 1968), at 39.

[258] See *ibid.*, at 40.

[259] See, in general, Gutman, n. 251 above.

[260] See William Harper, 'Memoir on Slavery', reprinted in Drew Gilpin Faust (ed.), *The Ideology of Slavery: Proslavery Thought in the Antebellum South, 1830–1860* (Louisiana State University Press, Baton Rouge, La., 1981), at 110

[261] See James Henry Hammond, 'Letter to an English Abolitionist', reprinted in *ibid.*, at 191–2.

[262] See, e.g., William Harper, 'Memoir on Slavery', reprinted in Faust (ed.), n. 260 above, at 107, 118–19; James Henry Hammond, 'Letter to an English Abolitionist', reprinted in *ibid.*, at 182–4.

[263] See, e.g., Thomas Roderick Dew, 'Abolition of Negro Slavery', reprinted in Faust (ed.), n. 260 above, at 65; William Harper, 'Memoir on Slavery', *ibid.*, at 100 (citing Dew).

[264] For a good general discussion of such inversions, see Kenneth S. Greenberg, *Masters and Statesman: The Political Culture of American Slavery* (The Johns Hopkins University Press, Baltimore, Md., 1985).

assumed interpretations of facts and values completely hostage to the polemical defence of entrenched political institutions whose stability required the abridgement of basic rights of blacks and of any whites who ventured reasonable criticism of such institutions.

If the antebellum experience of state abridgements of basic rights must inform a reasonable interpretation of the Privileges and Immunities Clause,[265] the protection of intimate personal life must be one among the basic human rights thus worthy of national protection. The remaining question is whether there is any adequate basis for the abridgement of so basic a right, namely, in the case of contraception, the right to decide whether or when one's sexual life will lead to offspring, indeed, to explore one's sexual and emotional life in personal life as an end in itself.

That right can only be justified by a compelling public reason, not on the grounds of reasons that are today sectarian (internal to a moral tradition not based on reasons available and accessible to all). In fact, the only argument that could sustain such laws (namely, the Augustinian[266] and Thomistic[267] view that it is immoral to engage in non-procreative sex) is not today a view of sexuality that can reasonably be enforced on people at large. Many people regard sexual love as an end in itself and the control of reproduction as a reasonable way to regulate when and whether they have children consistent with their own personal and larger ethical interests, that of their children, and of an overpopulated society at large. Even the question of having children at all is today a highly personal matter, certainly no longer governed by the perhaps once compelling secular need to have children for necessary work in a largely agrarian society with high rates of infant and adult mortality.[268] From the perspective of women in particular, as Sanger made so clear, the enforcement of an anti-contraceptive morality on society at large not only harms women's interests (as well as that of an overpopulated society more generally), but impersonally demeans them to a purely reproductive function, depriving them of the rational dignity of deciding as moral agents and persons, perhaps for the first time in human history, whether, when, and on what terms they will have children consistent with their other legitimate aims and ambitions (including the free exercise of all their basic human rights). Enforcement of such a morality expresses a now conspicuously sectarian conception of gender hierarchy in which women's sexuality is defined by mandatory procreative role and responsibility. That conception, the basis of the unjust construction of gender hierarchy, cannot reasonably be the measure of human rights today.[269]

---

[265] For further defence of this position, see Richards, *Conscience and the Constitution*, n. 1 above, ch. 6.

[266] See Augustine, *The City of God* (trans. Henry Bettenson, Penguin, Harmondsworth, 1972), at 577–94.

[267] Thomas Aquinas elaborates Augustine's conception of the exclusive legitimacy of procreative sex in a striking way. Of the emission of semen apart from procreation in marriage, he wrote: '[a]fter the sin of homicide whereby a human nature already in existence is destroyed, this type of sin appears to take next place, for by it the generation of human nature is precluded': Thomas Aquinas, *On the Truth of the Catholic Faith: Summa Contra Gentiles* (trans. Vernon Bourke, Image, New York, 1956), pt. 2, ch. 122(9), 146.

[268] On how personal this decision now is, see, in general, Elaine Tyler May, *Barren in the Promised Land: Childless Americans and the Pursuit of Happiness* (BasicBooks, New York, 1995).

[269] For further discussion of the right to privacy and contraception, see Richards, n. 247 above, 256–61.

Similar considerations explain the grounds for doubt about the putative public, non-sectarian justifications for laws criminalizing abortion and homosexual sexuality. Anti-abortion laws, grounded in the alleged protection of a neutral good like life, unreasonably equate the moral weight of a foetus in the early stages of pregnancy with that of a person and abortion with murder; such laws fail to take seriously the weight that should be accorded to a woman's basic right to reproductive autonomy in making highly personal moral choices central to her most intimate bodily and personal life against the background of the lack of reasonable public consensus that foetal life, as such, can be equated with that of a moral person.[270] There are legitimate interests that society has in giving weight at some point to foetal life as part of making a symbolic statement about the importance of taking the lives of children seriously and caring for them analogous to the symbolic interest society may have in preventing cruelty to animals or in securing humane treatment to the irretrievably comatose to advance humane treatment of persons properly understood. But such interests do not constitutionally justify forbidding abortion as such throughout all stages of pregnancy.[271] Rather, such interests can be accorded their legitimate weight after a reasonable period has been allowed for the proper scope of a woman's exercise of her decision whether or not to have an abortion.

The moral arguments for the prohibition of abortion cluster around certain traditional conceptions of the natural processes of sexuality and gender. Once, however, one takes seriously that foetal life is not a reasonable public value sufficient to outweigh the right of reproductive autonomy, the argument for criminalizing abortion is not a constitutionally reasonable argument for regarding abortion as homicide, but a proxy for complex background assumptions often no longer reasonably believed in the society at large, namely, a now controversial, powerfully sectarian ideology about proper sexuality and gender roles. From this perspective, the prohibitions on abortion encumber what many now reasonably regard as a highly conscientious choice by women regarding their bodies, their sexuality and gender, and the nature and place of pregnancy, birth, and child rearing in their personal and ethical lives. The traditional condemnation of abortion fails, at a deep ethical level, to take seriously the moral independence of women as free and rational persons, lending the force of law, like comparable anti-contraceptive laws, to theological ideas of biological naturalness and gender hierarchy that degrade the constructive moral powers of women themselves to establish the meaning of their sexual and reproductive life histories. The underlying conception appears to be at one with the sexist idea that women's minds and bodies are not their own, but the property of others, namely, men or their masculine God, who may conscript them and their bodies, like cattle on the farm, for the greater good. The abortion choice is thus one of the choices essential to the just moral independence of women, centring their lives in a body image and aspirations expressive of their moral powers. The abortion choice is a just application of the right to

---

[270] For further discussion, see Richards, n. 247 above, 261–9; Ronald Dworkin, *Life's Dominion: An Argument about Abortion, Euthanasia, and Individual Freedom* (Knopf, New York, 1993), 3–178.
[271] See Richards, n. 247 above, 266–7.

intimate life, because the right to the abortion choice protects women from the traditional degradation of their moral powers, reflected in the assumptions underlying anti-abortion laws.

Anti-homosexuality laws have, as I shall later argue, even less semblance of a public justification (like foetal life) that would be acceptably enforced on society at large and brutally abridge the sexual expression of the companionate loving relationships to which homosexuals, like heterosexuals, have an inalienable human right. That right encompasses the free moral powers through which persons forge enduring personal and ethical value in living a complete life. The decision in *Bowers* v. *Hardwick* was, for this reason, an interpretively unprincipled failure properly to elaborate the principle of constitutional privacy in an area of populist prejudice where the protection of that right was exigently required.[272] The European Court of Human Rights properly came to the opposite result in *Dudgeon* v. *the United Kingdom*.[273]

In the background of the laws at issue in all these cases lies a normative view of gender roles. That is quite clear, as I earlier suggested, in the case of *Griswold* v. *Connecticut*, less obviously so in *Roe* v. *Wade* and *Bowers* v. *Hardwick*. On analysis, however, the little weight accorded women's interests and the decisive weight accorded the foetus in anti-abortion laws make sense only against the background of the still powerful traditional conception of mandatory procreational, self-sacrificing, caring, and nurturant gender roles for women; it is its symbolic violation of that normative idea that imaginatively transforms abortion into murder. Similarly, the failure of the majority of the Supreme Court in *Bowers* to accord *any* weight whatsoever to the rights to privacy of homosexuals and decisive weight to incoherently anachronistic traditional moralism reflect, as we shall later see, a still powerful ideology of unnatural gender roles that renders homosexuals constitutionally invisible, voiceless, and marginal.

The gender analogy thus helps us to understand why intimate life now enjoys the status of a constitutionally protected right, and further usefully advances understanding of the role the abridgement of such a fundamental right importantly has played in the unjust construction of structural injustices like sexism and racism. Both the anti-racist and anti-sexist struggles have included significant focus on protecting the right to intimate life on fair terms. Anti-slavery and anti-racist argument, as we have seen, thus identified abridgement of the rights to marry and custody of children as components of the dehumanization of African-Americans as cattle; and the long struggle against anti-miscegenation laws, from Lydia Maria Child[274] to Ida Wells-Barnett,[275] condemned the place of such laws and their enforcement in the unjust construction of a racialized mythology of gender (the sexual purity of white women

---

[272] For further discussion, see Richards, n. 247 above, 269–80; *Foundations of American Constitutionalism* (Oxford University Press, New York, 1989), at 202–47.

[273] See *Dudgeon* v. *United Kingdom* (1982) 4 EHRR 149 (Eur. Ct. HR) (Northern Irish legislation, criminalizing consensual homosexual private acts, held to be inconsistent with Art. 8 (guaranteeing the right of private life) of the European Convention on Human Rights).

[274] For further discussion, see Richards, n. 1 above, at 55–6, 115.

[275] For further discussion, see *ibid.*, at 185–90.

versus the sexual impurity of black women) that legitimated, on the one hand, lynchings for what was often, in fact, consensual interracial sex between white women and black men and, on the other hand, *de facto* tolerance for what were often exploitative, even coercive sexual relations of white men to black women. Comparably, rights-based feminism, as we have seen, regarded unjust abridgement of the right to reproductive autonomy (both anti-contraception and anti-abortion laws) as constructive elements in the dehumanizing objectification of women in terms of compulsory heterosexuality and mandatory procreational roles. Securing constitutional recognition of women's rights to intimate life was thus not only intrinsically valuable on its own terms (as a basic human right extended on fair terms of principle to women), but instrumentally valuable in rectifying one of the cultural supports of the sexist devaluation of women as not bearers of human rights.

Both the anti-racist and anti-sexist concerns for the right of intimate life suggest useful analogies for the case for gay rights that may be brought into play in criticism of not only the legitimacy of *Bowers* v. *Hardwick*, but the populist political outrage at the idea of same-sex marriage.[276] Andrew Koppelman has persuasively explored, in this connection, the analogy of the anti-miscegenation laws.[277] The prohibition of racial intermarriage was to the cultural construction of racism what the prohibition of same-sex marriage is to sexism and homophobia: 'just as miscegenation was threatening because it called into question the distinctive and superior status of being white, homosexuality is threatening because it calls into question the distinctive and superior status of being male.'[278] The condemnation of same-sex intimacies (including same-sex marriage) is, on this view, a crucial aspect of the cultural construction of the dehumanization of homosexuals as a kind of fallen woman.[279]

Finally, the gender, like the racial, analogy suggests the general importance of segregation in sustaining longstanding patterns of structural injustice. The segregation of African-Americans and of women effectively constructed servile roles that walled them off from access to basic rights of conscience, speech, intimate life, and work, unjustly rationalized as in the nature of things. The operative analogy, for the case for gay rights, may be not the servile roles culturally constructed for homosexuals to occupy, but the absence of any such legitimate role (as an intolerable heresy to any acceptable values in living). Such radical illegitimacy suggests that, while the gender analogy clarifies many important features of the case for gay rights, there is another analogy that must also be appealed to and elaborated, the religious analogy.

Thus, the constitutional evil of both sexism and racism can, I have argued, be plausibly understood as an elaboration of the argument for toleration to identify and condemn structural injustice marked by two features: abridgement of basic human rights

---

[276] For further discussion of this point, see Richards, n. 1 above, at 438–53.

[277] See Andrew Koppelman, 'The Miscegenation Analogy: Sodomy Laws as Sex Discrimination', 98 *Yale LJ* 145 (1988).

[278] *Ibid.*, 159–60.

[279] On the close ideological relationship between the condemnation of prostitution and homosexuality, see Richards, *Women, Gays, and the Constitution*, n. 1 above, at 295–7, 300, 310, 329, 370, 433, 443, 447, 461.

of conscience, speech, intimate life, and work of a certain class of persons, and rationalization thereof in terms of dehumanizing stereotypes unjustly derived from the
culture of such abridgement. Rights-based protest of the terms of such injustice both
challenges and transforms identity. The case for gay rights is also based on such structural injustice, and its protests are similarly identity challenging and transforming.
But there is another aspect of the case for gay rights which draws not only on the
account of structural injustice which is, as we have seen, an elaboration of the argument for toleration, but directly on the argument for toleration itself. On this view,
gay and lesbian identity should be understood as an expression of the inalienable right
to conscience, and some contemporary forms of political aggression against gay rights
understood as the expression through public law of constitutionally forbidden religious intolerance.

As I said earlier, the argument for toleration calls for constraints of principle to be
placed on the power of the state to enforce sectarian religious views because the
enforcement of such views on society at large entrenched, as the measure of legitimate
convictions in matters of conscience, irrationalist intolerance; such intolerance was
unjustly rationalized by limiting standards of debate and speakers to the sectarian
measure that supported dominant political authority. The rights-based evil of such
intolerance was its unjust abridgement of the inalienable right to conscience, the free
exercise of the moral powers of rationality and reasonableness in terms of which persons define personal and ethical meaning in living. While this human right, like
others, may be abridged on grounds of secular goods reasonably acknowledged as
such by all persons (irrespective of other philosophical or evaluative disagreements),
a sectarian view is not sufficient.

The argument for toleration underlies and clarifies the place and weight of the
central human rights protected as constitutional rights by the United States
Constitution, as amended, in particular, the rights of conscience and free speech protected by the First Amendment and the right to intimate life protected by the Ninth
and Fourteenth Amendments.[280] The American constitutional tradition of the protection of the right to conscience is a particularly robust one, rooted, as it is, in the
guarantees of religious liberty of the free exercise and anti-establishment clauses of the
First Amendment. Both these clauses protect different aspects of the exercise of the
right to conscience. The Free Exercise Clause thus addresses the exercise of settled
conscientious convictions, condemning as suspect state burdens placed on the exercise of such convictions unsupported by a compelling secular justification;[281] and its

---

[280] See, for an extended statement and defence of this position, Richards, n. 247 above.

[281] See, in general, *ibid.*, 141–6. Free exercise analysis was somewhat narrowly interpreted in
Employment Division, Dept. of Human Resources v. *Smith*, 494 US 872 (1990) (religiously inspired peyote
use not constitutionally exempt from neutral criminal statute criminalizing such use, and thus state permitted to deny employment benefits to persons dismissed from their jobs because of such use). The case,
however, notably acknowledges the continuing authority of leading free exercise cases like *Sherbert* v.
Verner, 374 US 398 (1963) (state unemployment benefits, unavailable to Seventh Day Adventist because
of failure to work on sabbath day, unconstitutionally burdens free exercise rights) and *Wisconsin* v. *Yoder*,
406 US 205 (1972) (state compulsory education law unconstitutionally burdens free exercise rights of

companion Establishment Clause renders suspect state support of sectarian religious views, again unsupported by an independently compelling secular justification, at stages of acquisition or change in conscientious views, for example, contexts of state action that support or encourage the teaching of and/or conversion to such views.[282] The state may not discriminate either against or in favour of sectarian conscience, but must extend equal respect to all forms of conscience.

The constitutional protection of conscientious conviction in this way makes sense against the background of history and political theory which these guarantees reflect. As I noted earlier, both Locke and Bayle, who importantly state the argument for toleration as a constitutive principle of legitimate politics, were concerned to protect the free exercise of moral powers of rationality and reasonableness, in terms of which persons define the personal and ethical meaning of their lives, against sectarian impositions on this basic moral freedom; such impositions had, in their view as believing Christians, corrupted the ethical core of Christianity (simple and elevated imperatives of humane mutual respect and charity) by degrading conscience itself to the measure of sectarian theological dogmas.[283] Both Locke and Bayle, consistently with the dominant Protestant theological ethics of their age, limited the scope of protected conscience (excluding Catholics and atheists[284]); but Locke and Bayle were surely wrong in linking ethical independence to theism in general or Protestant theism in particular, as Jefferson and Madison—the central architects of the religion clauses—acknowledged in extending protected conscience to include Catholics and atheists.[285] By the twentieth century, consistent with an even wider understanding of the diverse sources of reasonable ethical conviction, the scope of conscience includes a wide range of religious and irreligious views protected by both the Free Exercise and Establishment Clauses of the First Amendment.[286]

Amish parents to remove children from school after eighth grade). In *Church of the Lukumi Babalu Aye, Inc.* v. *City of Hialeah*, 508 US 520 (1993), the Supreme Court clarified that *Employment Div.* v. *Smith* in no way limited the availability of free exercise analysis of a state law that non-neutrally targeted a specific religion (in this case, criminalizing animal sacrifice in Santeria religious rituals). The authority of *Smith* was cast in doubt in light of the Religious Freedom Restoration Act of 1993, S. Rep. 111, 103d Cong., 1st sess. 14 (1993); for commentary, see Douglas Laycock, 'Free Exercise and the Religious Freedom Restoration Act', 62 *Ford. L Rev.* 883 (1994). The constitutionality of the Religious Freedom Restoration Act of 1993 was recently assessed by the Supreme Court in light of whether, on grounds of s. 5 of the Fourteenth Amendment, it constitutionally expands or unconstitutionally contracts the constitutional right judicially defined by the Supreme Court in its free exercise jurisprudence, including *Smith*. For relevant case law on this question, see *South Carolina* v. *Katzenbach*, 383 US 301 (1956); *Katzenbach* v. *Morgan*, 384 US 641 (1966); *Oregon* v. *Mitchell*, 400 US 112 (1970). The Act was held unconstitutional. See *City of Boerne* v. *P. F. Flores*, 117 S Ct. 2157 (1997).

[282] See Richards, n. 247 above, 146–62.　　　[283] See, for further argument on this point, *ibid.*, 89–98.

[284] See *ibid.*, 95–8.　　　[285] See *ibid.*, 111–13.

[286] Under the Free Exercise Clause, the Supreme Court has tended, in the interest of reasonably developing the basic value of equality, to expand the constitutional concept of religion to protect conscience as such from coercion or undue burdens. See, e.g., *United States* v. *Ballard*, 322 US 78 (1944) (forbidding any inquiry into the truth or falsity of beliefs in a mail fraud action against the bizarre 'I am' movement of Guy Ballard (alias 'Saint Germain, Jesus, George Washington, and Godfre Ray King')), *Torcaso* v. *Watkins*, 367 US 488 (1960) (declaring unconstitutional a state requirement that state officials must swear belief in God), and *United States* v. *Seeger*, 380 US 163 (1965) and *Welsh* v. *United States*, 398 US 333 (1970)

No small part of the background of this contemporary interpretive attitude lies in American experience, as a people, with the role of often quite religiously heterodox ethical dissent as the motor of some of the most important and enlightened constitutional reform movements in our history. I have in mind the abolitionist movement that structured the nation's normative understanding, in the wake of the Civil War, of both the meaning of that conflict and of the Reconstruction Amendments, and the anti-racist and anti-sexist movements that have cumulatively transformed our understanding of how constitutional guarantees (including the Reconstruction Amendments) should be interpreted.[287] As we have already seen, such dissent protested the unjust enforcement of the dominant pro-slavery or racist or sexist orthodoxy as the sectarian measure of claims and speakers, because such enforcement repressed precisely the claims and speakers who would most reasonably challenge the justice of its views and practices. To subject the dominant orthodoxy to this kind of fundamental ethical criticism, such dissent often questioned the unjust role of established churches in the support of such rights-based evils as slavery or racism or sexism; such dissent was empowered often by conscientious convictions which were, to say the least, religiously highly unorthodox and sometimes not conventionally religious at all.[288] The American tradition of religious liberty, precisely because it made space for ethically independent criticism of politically enforceable religious and moral views, opened the public mind of the nation to the ethical voices and views that addressed its gravest injustices, including the role such injustices played in the corruption of basic constitutional principles and ideals.

It is against this background that we must understand and evaluate what must be the most striking feature of the kind of protest involved in the case for gay rights. It protests a structural injustice of the sort also exemplified by racism and sexism, namely, abridgement of basic human rights of conscience, speech, intimate life, and

(congressional statutory exemption from military service—limited to religiously motivated conscientious objectors to all wars—extended to all who conscientiously object to all wars). But see *Employment Div. Ore. Dept. of Human Res.* v. *Smith*, 494 US 872 (1990) (religiously inspired peyote use not exempt from general prohibition on such drug use and thus may be properly invoked by state to deny unemployment benefits to persons dismissed from their jobs because of such religiously inspired use). And under the Establishment Clause, the Supreme Court has notably insisted that the public education curriculum may not privilege sectarian religious rituals and views over others. See, e.g., *Engel* v. *Vitale*, 370 US 421 (1962) (use of state-composed 'non-denominational' prayer in public schools held violative of anti-establishment clause), *Abington School Dist.* v. *Schempp*, 374 US 203 (1963) (reading of selections from Bible and Lord's Prayer in public schools violative of anti-establishment), *Wallace* v. *Jaffree*, 472 US 38 (1985) (state authorization of one-minute period of silence in public schools 'for meditation or voluntary prayer' held violative of anti-establishment clause); *Lee* v. *Weisman*, 505 US 577 (1992) (non-denominational prayer at high school graduation held violative of anti-establishment); *Epperson* v. *Arkansas*, 393 US 97 (1968) (state statute forbidding teaching of evolution in public schools violative of anti-establishment clause); *Edwards* v. *Aguillard*, 482 US 578 (1987) (state statute requiring balanced treatment of creationist and evolution science held violative of anti-establishment).

[287] See, in general, Richards, *Conscience and the Constitution* and *Women, Gays, and the Constitution*, both n. 1 above.

[288] For specific elaboration and defence of this point, see David A. J. Richards, 'Public Reason and Abolitionist Dissent', 69 *Chicago-Kent L Rev.* 787 (1994); see also, in general, Richards, *Women, Gays, and the Constitution*, n. 1 above.

work, unjustly rationalized in terms of dehumanizing stereotypes resting on such abridgement. But the traditional cultural status of homosexuals was not a servile social status thus rationalized, but no status at all. Homosexuals, on this view, were outside any conception of moral community at all, an exile given expression by the striking normative idea of homosexuality as unspeakable. It was, in Blackstone's words, 'a crime not fit to be named; *peccatum illud horribile, inter christianos non nominandum*'[289]—not mentionable, let alone discussed or assessed. Such total silencing of any reasonable discussion rendered homosexuality into a kind of cultural death, naturally thus understood, and indeed condemned, as a kind of ultimate heresy or treason against essential moral values.[290] The English legal scholar, Tony Honoré, captured this point exactly by his observation about the contemporary status of the homosexual: '[i]t is not primarily a matter of breaking rules but of dissenting attitudes. It resembles political or religious dissent, being an atheist in Catholic Ireland or a dissident in Soviet Russia.'[291]

The case for gay rights thus centrally challenges the cultural terms of the unspeakability of homosexuality, the claim of its exclusion from the scope of religious and non-religious conscience that, on grounds of principle, now ostensibly enjoys constitutional protection. It does so in the two ways familiar from the similar protests to racism and sexism: it demands basic human rights of conscience, speech, intimate life, and work; and it challenges, in terms of its own moral powers of rationality and reasonableness, the sectarian terms of the moral orthodoxy that have traditionally condemned homosexuality. We must shortly assess the merits of both claims, but the important point for present purposes is that its very making of such claims challenges the terms of the peculiar character of the underlying structural injustice. As such, claims of gay and lesbian identity—whether irreligiously, non-religiously, or religiously grounded—are decidedly among the dissident forms of conscience that should fully enjoy protection under the American tradition of religious liberty. This is shown as much by the nature of the claims made as by the character of the political opposition to them.

The case for gay rights rests, of course, on arguments of justice, which must be assessed by the larger society in such terms (as we shall shortly see). But their empowering significance to homosexuals is that they offer them, perhaps for the first time in human history, the responsible personal and ethical choice of a private and public identity of equal dignity with that of heterosexuals. Such a choice of identity has two compelling features for the homosexuals who increasingly make it. First, it integrates one's authentic sexual passions with a compelling interpretation of the personal and moral good of homosexual friendship and love (grounded in the basic human good of love) as the basis of a life well and ethically lived. Secondly, it offers and elaborates arguments of public reason about the injustice and ethical wrong of the condemnation and marginalization of homosexuality as a legitimate way of life (centring on the

[289] William Blackstone, *Commentaries*, iv, 215.
[290] See, on this point, Richards, n. 247 above, 278–9.
[291] See Tony Honoré, *Sex Law* (Duckworth, London, 1978), 89.

unprincipled failure to respect the self-authenticating right of all persons to the humane and basic good of love); such arguments, properly developed, advance understanding not only of claims of justice to homosexuals, but deepen public under-standing of the arguments of principle that explain our condemnation of interlinked injustices like racism, sexism, and homophobia. The identity expresses itself in varied personal and political associations of mutual recognition, support, and respect and in demands for equal justice and for a public culture (including institutional forms) ade-quate to the reasonable elaboration and cultivation of its ethical vision of humane value in public and private life. Both its constructive and critical arguments are, in their nature, ethical arguments of public reason, appealing to the fundamental and broadly shared ethical imperative of treating persons as equals.[292]

The self-understanding, by homosexuals, of gay rights in these terms corresponds to the political opposition to it. Colorado Amendment Two, which the Supreme Court struck down as unconstitutional,[293] expressly made its reactionary point in terms of banning all laws that recognized anti-discrimination claims of gay and les-bian people; its target was specifically the claims to justice that constitute gay and les-bian identity.[294] Its aim is decisively that advocates of gay and lesbian identity should be compelled to abandon their claims to personal and ethical legitimacy and either convert to the true view, or return to the silence of their traditional unspeakability. The political opposition to gay rights agrees with the case for gay rights on one thing: gay and lesbian identity is a choice. Whereas, however, the opposition (on sectarian religious grounds) interprets the choice as moral heresy beyond the pale of acceptable views, its advocates construe the choice as an exercise of legitimate moral freedom long overdue.

Both the advocacy of and opposition to gay rights suggest the distinctively illumi-nating power of the religious analogy in understanding the case for gay rights. The constitutional protection of religion never turned on its putative immutable and salient character (people can and do convert, and can and do conceal religious con-victions), but on the traditional place of religion in the conscientious reasonable for-mation of one's moral identity in public and private life and the need for protection, consistent with the inalienable right to conscience, of persons against state imposi-tions of sectarian religious views. In particular, the identifications central to one's self-respect as a person of conscience are not to be subject to sectarian impositions through public law that unreasonably burden the exercise of one's conscientious con-victions (the free exercise principle) or encourage conversions of such convictions to

---

[292] On the pervasive of this ideal in Western religious and ethical culture, see Richards, n. 247 above, at 69, 71, 78, 93, 123–8, 134, 272–3, 275. For an exploration of the form, content, and force of the crit-ical and constructive aspects of these ethical arguments on behalf of lesbian and gay identity, see *ibid.*, at 269–80; David A. J. Richards, *Sex, Drugs, Death, and the Law* (Rowman and Littlefield, Totowa, NJ, 1982), at 29–83; Richards, 'Unnatural Acts and the Constitutional Right to Privacy: a Moral Theory', 45 *Ford. L Rev.* 1281 (1977); Richards, 'Sexual Autonomy and the Constitutional Right to Privacy: A Case Study in Human Rights and the Unwritten Constitution', 30 *Hastings LJ* 957 (1979).

[293] See *Romer* v. *Evans*, 116 S Ct. 1650 (1966).

[294] For fuller discussion, see Richards, *Women, Gays, and the Constitution*, n. 1 above, ch. 7.

sectarian orthodoxy (the anti-establishment principle). Claims by lesbian and gay persons today have, for both proponents and opponents, exactly the same ethical and constitutional force. For proponents, they are in their nature claims to a self-respecting personal and moral identity in public and private life through which they may reasonably express and realize their ethical convictions of the moral powers of friendship and love in a good, fulfilled, and responsible life protesting against an unjust and now conspicuously sectarian tradition of moral subjugation. For opponents, the political reaction to such claims, reflected in Colorado Amendment Two, is precisely based on sectarian religious objection to the conscientious claims of justice made by and on behalf of lesbian and gay identity as a form of conscience that is entitled to equal respect under fundamental American constitutional guarantees of freedom of conscience. At bottom, for opponents, the point is that the very fact of lesbian and gay identity, in virtue of its conscientious claims to justice, is as unworthy of respect as a traditionally despised religion like Judaism; the practice of that form of heresy may thus be abridged, and certainly persons may be encouraged to convert from its demands or, at least, be supinely and ashamedly silent.

Of course, to state the opposition to gay rights in this way is constitutionally to condemn it, for nothing can be clearer than that, if imposing burdens on gay identity is analogous to anti-Semitism, it is forbidden; '[h]eresy trials are foreign to our Constitution'.[295] There are two ways to resist this conclusion; neither is defensible. First, gay and lesbian identity may be dismissed as not a conscientious view. Secondly, even assuming it is a conscientious view, there are adequate secular grounds for it to be disfavoured and even condemned.

Several ways to limit the scope of protected conscience (excluding gay identity) may be rejected easily. The constitutional protections for liberty of conscience, grounded on equal respect for conscience, have not been and cannot reasonably be limited to established or traditional churches or the dogmas of such churches; the traditional condemnation of homosexuality by traditional American religions cannot be a ground to exclude it from constitutional protection. The American tradition of liberty of conscience has protected, indeed fostered, the many forms of new forms of conscience that arose uniquely in America,[296] including, as we have seen, the claims of conscience expressed through the abolitionist movement that were so sharply critical of established churches.[297] Claims to gay and lesbian identity stand foursquare in this distinguished tradition of new forms of dissenting conscience, and are, as such, fully entitled to constitutional protection on terms of principle. Correlatively, the

[295] *United States* v. *Ballard,* 322 US 78, 86 (1944) (Douglas J, writing for the Court).
[296] See, in general, Sydney E. Ahlstrom, *A Religious History of the American People* (Yale University Press, New Haven, 1972), especially at 491–509 (Shakers, Society of the Public Universal Friend, New Harmony, Oneida Community, Hopedale, Brook Farm, the Mormons), 1019–33 (Science of Health (Christian Science), New Thought, Positive Thinking), 1059–78 (Black Pentecostalism, Father Divine, Sweet Daddy Grace, Nation of Islam, Booker T. Washington, Martin Luther King).
[297] For specific elaboration and defence of this point, see David A. J. Richards, 'Public Reason and Abolitionist Dissent', 69 *Chicago-Kent L Rev.* 787 (1994). See also Richards, *Conscience and the Constitution,* n. 1 above, 58–107.

American tradition of religious liberty cannot be and has not been limited to theistic forms of conscience as such, but embraces all forms of conscience.[298] Nor has the tradition been limited to protect only the conscientious identities in which one has been born, for its guarantees are no less for recent converts and include robust guarantees of state neutrality in circumstances that would lend the state's sectarian encouragement to conversion to one form of belief as opposed to another.[299] All forms of conscientious conviction, whether old or new, theistic or non-theistic, are thus guaranteed equal respect on terms of a constitutional principle that renders issues of conscience morally independent of factionalized political incentives.

It would trivialize such guarantees, indeed render them nugatory, not to extend them precisely when they are most constitutionally needed, namely, to anti-majoritarian claims of conscience that challenge traditional wisdom on non-sectarian grounds of public reason. Otherwise, the mere congruence of sectarian belief among traditional religions (for example, about the alleged unspeakable evil of homosexuality) would be, as it was in antebellum America on the question of slavery,[300] the measure of religious liberty in particular and human and constitutional rights in general. The traditional orthodoxy, to which any form of dissenting conscience takes objection on grounds of public reason, would be permitted to silence as unworthy the newly emancipated voice of such progressive claims of justice. In effect, the culture of degradation that sets the terms of a structural injustice like racism or sexism would, on this view, set the terms of argument on their behalf. It is, however, precisely such claims of justice of dissenting, anti-majoritarian conscience that most require, on grounds of principle, constitutional protection against nescient majorities, who would aggressively and uncritically repress such a group on the ground of its daring to make claims to justice critical of the dominant religio-cultural orthodoxy.

The only remaining ground for excluding gay and lesbian identity from the scope of protected conscience must be to dismiss it as not a conscientious view of the requisite sort, presumably because it is concerned with sex. But there are two difficulties with this view.

First, on the assumption that gay and lesbian identity is about sex or sexual life, that fact would, if anything, bring it closer to central concerns of the human conscience in general and religions in particular. Religions organize the terms of sexual life and its place in the mysteries of birth, love, and death under the aspect of eternity, supplying rituals that endow the cycle of living with a sense of enduring personal and ethical values before the terrors of loneliness, loss, decline, and death. Moreover, the experience of one's sexuality is, from its inception, a mysterious, even awful, force fraught with a sense of ultimate concern with the other, a longing for communion and transcendence in relationship with a beloved though alien other. It is, thus, no accident, in the American rights-based constitutional tradition, that the right to

[298] For further development of this argument, see Richards, *Toleration and the Constitution*, n. 247 above, 67–162.
[299] For fuller discussion, see *ibid.*, 146–62.
[300] For further development of this point, see Richards, n. 297 above.

intimate life is as much a basic human right as the right to conscience; conscience is so personally engaged with the issues of intimate sexual life because both involve the resources of thought, conviction, feeling, and emotion at the heart of the ultimate concerns of moral personality. The claims of gay and lesbian identity address these traditionally religious ultimate concerns, and are no less religious for doing so than more traditional approaches to these questions. Indeed, the significance of gay and lesbian identity, for many contemporary homosexuals, is that it enables them, as responsible moral persons and agents, to make redemptive personal and ethical sense of the human depth of our experience of sexuality on equal terms with heterosexuals. We need no longer acquiesce in the unjust stereotypes of our sexuality as inhuman or unnatural or even a diabolic possession, but responsibly engage in rights-based protest of such stereotypes, reclaiming our sexuality and our moral powers of love and transcendence on terms of equal justice.

Secondly, from the perspective of the case for gay rights, homosexuality is, as Walt Whitman seminally suggested,[301] no more or less exclusively about sex than heterosexuality. We have no difficulty, surely, in understanding the place of heterosexuality in nurturing and sustaining the relationships, more than any other, that are touched with enduring personal and ethical value in living, indeed, that are, if anything is, the personal relationships of mutual transparency, respect, and tender care and concern through which we understand what divine love could mean or reasonably be taken to mean. It does not count against the conscientiousness or even the religiosity of such convictions that opposite-sex intimacies are involved, because our traditions—both secular and religious—afford us the moral vocabulary to interpret them as expressions of love (sometimes even as models of divine love) as well as sensual delight. But the case for gay rights argues that homosexuals, on grounds of structural injustice, have been denied such moral vocabulary, indeed denied any vocabulary (on the grounds of unspeakability); such repression often sustained and was sustained by unjust stereotypes that crudely sexualized homosexuality in ways structurally similar to the unjust sexualization that supported racism and sexism.[302] The appeal to sexual content (as a ground for excluding gay and lesbian identity from protected conscience) fatally begs the question by arguably indulging such prejudice rather than responsibly facing what must be addressed: whether there is an adequate ground for burdening this form of conscientious conviction. Conscientious conviction, it certainly is, as much as any other convictions about the ethical meaning of personal love that are the common sense of our romantic age.

We need, then, to investigate what acceptable secular grounds, if any, exist to burden gay and lesbian identity as conscientious convictions that are, like any other, entitled to equal respect. The question applies not just to the right to conscience, but to the other human rights traditionally denied to gay and lesbian persons, namely, rights

---

[301] For citations and commentary, see Richards, *Women, Gays, and the Constitution*, n. 1 above, at 307, 366, 434.

[302] On this point, see, in general, Elisabeth Young-Bruehl, *The Anatomy of Prejudices* (Harvard University Press, Cambridge, Mass., 1996).

to free speech, intimate life, and work. In all these cases, such basic human rights may only be abridged on grounds of compelling secular grounds of public reason. In fact, as we shall see, there are no acceptable secular grounds for such abridgement in any of these areas, which supports the argument that abridgement of these basic rights to homosexuals is rooted in the same structural injustice as racism and sexism (what I earlier called moral slavery).

To be clear on this point, we need to examine critically the grounds traditionally supposed to rationalize the condemnation of homosexuality. Plato in *The Laws* gave influential expression to the moral condemnation in terms of two arguments: its non-procreative character, and (in its male homosexual forms) its degradation of the passive male partner to the status of a woman.[303] Neither of these two traditional moral reasons for condemning homosexuality can any longer be legitimately and indeed constitutionally imposed on society at large or any other person or group of persons.

One such moral reason (the condemnation of non-procreational sex) can, for example, no longer constitutionally justify laws against the sale to and use of contraceptives by married and unmarried heterosexual couples.[304] The mandatory enforcement at large of the procreational model of sexuality is, in circumstances of overpopulation and declining infant and adult mortality, a sectarian ideal lacking adequate secular basis in the general goods that can alone reasonably justify state power; accordingly, contraceptive-using heterosexuals have the constitutional right to decide when and whether their sexual lives shall be pursued to procreate or as an independent expression of mutual love, affection, and companionship.[305]

And the other moral reason for condemning homosexual sex (the degradation of a man to the passive status of a woman) rests on the sexist premise of the degraded nature of women that has been properly rejected as a reasonable basis for laws or policies on grounds of suspect classification analysis.[306] If we constitutionally accept, as we increasingly do, the suspectness of gender on a par with that of race, we must, in principle, condemn, as a basis for law, any use of stereotypes expressive of the unjust enforcement of gender roles through law. That condemnation extends, as authoritative case law

---

[303] See Plato, *Laws*, Book 8, 835d–842a, in Edith Hamilton and Huntington Cairns (eds.), *The Collected Dialogues of Plato* (Pantheon, New York, 1961), at 1401–2. On the moral condemnation of the passive role in homosexuality in both Greek and early Christian moral thought, see Peter Brown, *The Body and Society: Men, Women, and Sexual Renunciation in Early Christianity* (Columbia University Press, New York, 1988), at 30, 382–3. But, for evidence of Graeco-Roman toleration of long-term homosexual relations even between adults, see John Boswell, *Same-Sex Unions in Premodern Europe* (Villard Books, New York, 1994), at 53–107; I am grateful to Stephen Morris for conversations on this point. Whether these relationships were regarded as marriages may be a very different matter. For criticism of Boswell's argument along this latter line, see Brent D. Shaw, 'A Groom of One's Own?', *The New Republic*, 18 and 25 July 1994, at 33–41.

[304] See *Griswold* v. *Connecticut*, 381 US 479 (1965); *Eisenstadt* v. *Baird*, 405 US 438 (1972).

[305] For further discussion, see Richards, n. 247 above, at 256–61.

[306] See, e.g., *Frontiero* v. *Richardson*, 411 US 677 (1973); *Craig* v. *Boren*, 429 US 190 (1976). On homophobia as rooted in sexism, see Young-Bruehl, n. 302 above, 143, 148–51.

makes clear, to gender stereotypy as such whether immediately harmful to women or to men.[307]

Nonetheless, although each moral ground for the condemnation of homosexuality has been independently rejected as a reasonable justification for coercive laws enforceable on society at large (applicable to both men and women), they unreasonably retain their force when brought into specific relationship to the claims of homosexual men and women for equal justice under constitutional law.[308] These claims are today in their basic nature arguments of principle made by gay men and lesbians for the same respect for their intimate love life and other basic rights, free of unreasonable procreational and sexist requirements, now rather generously accorded to men and women who are heterosexually coupled (including, as we have seen, even the right to abortion against the alleged weight of foetal life). Empirical issues relating to sexuality and gender are now subjected to more impartial critical assessment than they were previously; and the resulting light of public reason about issues of sexuality and gender should be available to all persons on fair terms. However, both the procreational mandates and the unjust gender stereotypy, constitutionally condemned for the benefit of heterosexual men and women, are ferociously applied to homosexual men and women.[309] It bespeaks the continuing political power of the traditional moral subjugation of homosexuals that such a claim of fair treatment (an argument of basic constitutional principle if any argument is) was contemptuously dismissed by a majority of the Supreme Court of the United States (5–4) in 1986 in *Bowers* v. *Hardwick*.[310] No sceptical scrutiny whatsoever was accorded state purposes elsewhere acknowledged as illegitimate. Certainly, no such purpose could be offered of the alleged weight of foetal life that has been rejected as a legitimate ground for criminalization of all forms of abortion; any claim of public health could be addressed, as it would be in comparable cases of heterosexual relations involving the basic constitutional right of intimate life, by constitutionally required alternatives less restrictive

---

[307] For cases which protect women from such harm, see *Reed* v. *Reed*, 404 US 71 (1971) (right to administer estates); *Frontiero* v. *Richardson*, 411 US 677 (1973) (dependency allowances to servicewomen); *Stanton* v. *Stanton*, 421 US 7 (1975) (child support for education). For cases that protect men, see *Wengler* v. *Druggists Mutual Ins. Co.*, 446 US 142 (1980) (widower's right to death benefits); *Craig* v. *Boren*, 429 US 190 (1976) (age of drinking for men).

[308] On the continuities among heterosexual and homosexual forms of intimacy in the modern era, see, in general, John D'Emilio and Estelle B. Freedman, *Intimate Matters: A History of Sexuality in America* (Harper & Row, New York, 1988), 239–360; Anthony Giddens, *The Transformation of Intimacy: Sexuality, Love, and Eroticism in Modern Societies* (Polity, Cambridge, 1992). See also Barbara Ehrenreich, Elizabeth Hess, and Gloria Jacobs, *Remaking Love: The Feminization of Sex* (Anchor, New York, 1986); Anne Snitow, Christine Stansell, and Sharon Thompson (eds.), *Powers of Desire* (Monthly Review Press, New York, 1983); Carole S. Vance (ed.), *Pleasure and Danger: Exploring Female Sexuality* (Routledge & Kegan Paul, Boston, Mass., 1984).

[309] On the unjust gender stereotypy uncritically applied to homosexual men and women, see Susan Moller Okin, 'Sexual Orientation and Gender: Dichotomizing Differences', in David M. Estlund and Martha C. Nussbaum, *Sex, Preference, and Family: Essays on Law and Nature* (Oxford University Press, New York, 1997), at 44–59.

[310] *Bowers* v. *Hardwick*, 478 US 186 (1986).

and more effective than criminalization (including use of prophylactics by those otherwise at threat from transmission of AIDS).[311]

Traditional moral arguments, now clearly reasonably rejected in their application to heterosexuals, were uncritically applied to a group much more exigently in need of constitutional protection on grounds of principle.[312] Reasonable advances in the public understanding of sexuality and gender, now constitutionally available to all heterosexuals, were suspended in favour of an appeal to the sexual mythology of the Middle Ages.[313] It is an indication of the genre of dehumanizing stereotypes at work in *Bowers* v. *Hardwick*, stripping a class of persons (blacks, women, Jews, homosexuals) of moral personality by reducing them to a mythologized sexuality, that the Court focused so obsessionally on one sex act (sodomy); as Leo Bersani perceptively observed about the public discourse (reflected in *Bowers*), it resonates in images (inherited from the nineteenth century) of homosexuals as sexually obsessed prostitutes.[314] The transparently unprincipled character of *Bowers*[315] in such terms thus suggests a larger problem, which connects such treatment of homosexuals with the now familiar structural injustice underlying racism and sexism.

As we have seen, this structural injustice involves two features: the abridgement of the basic human rights of a class of persons on inadequate grounds, and the rationalization of such treatment in terms of dehumanizing stereotypes supported by the denial of such rights. We have now seen that the grounds traditionally supposed to support the condemnation of homosexuality are not, in contemporary circumstances, the compelling secular purposes constitutionally required to justify basic human rights, including conscience, speech, intimate life, and work. The continuing force of such condemnation suggests the continuing power, in the case of homosexuals, of the

---

[311] The argument applies, in any event, only to those forms of sex by gay men likely to transmit the disease; it does not reasonably apply to lesbians, nor does it apply to all forms of sex (including anal sex) by gay men. So, the argument that sex acts as such can be criminalized on this basis is constitutionally over-inclusive inconsistent with the basic right thus abridged. The regulatory point is that even gay men at threat by virtue of their sexual practices can take preventive measures against this threat (by using condoms). For a recent discussion of what further such reasonable preventive measures the gay men at threat might also take, see Gabriel Rotello, *Sexual Ecology: AIDS and the Destiny of Gay Men* (Dutton, New York, 1997).

[312] For further criticism, see Richards, n. 272 above, at 209–47.

[313] Justice Blackmun put the point acidly: 'Like Justice Holmes, I believe that "it is revolting to have no better reason for a rule of law than that so it was laid down in the time of Henry IV. It is still more revolting if the grounds upon which it was laid down have vanished long since, and the rule simply persists from blind imitation of the past" ': *Bowers*, 478 US at 199 (quoting Oliver Wendell Holmes, 'The Path of the Law', 10 *Harv. L Rev.* 457, 469 (1897)).

[314] See Leo Bersani, 'Is the Rectum as a Grave?', in Douglas Crimp, *Cultural Analysis/Cultural Activism* (The MIT Press, Cambridge, Mass., 1988), 197–222, at 211–22.

[315] I develop this argument at greater length in Richards, n. 272 above, ch. 6; and in David A. J. Richards, 'Constitutional Legitimacy and Constitutional Privacy', 61 *NYUL Rev.* 800 (1986). See also Anne D. Goldstein, 'History, Homosexuality, and Political Values: Searching for the Hidden Determinants of *Bowers* v. *Hardwick*', 97 *Yale LJ* 1073 (1988); Nan D. Hunter, 'Life After *Hardwick*', 27 *Harv. Civ Rts.–Civ. Lib. L. Rev.* 531 (1992); Janet E. Halley, 'Reasoning About Sodomy: Act and Identity In and After *Bowers* v. *Hardwick*', 79 *Va. L Rev.* 1721 (1993); Anne B. Goldstein, 'Reasoning About Homosexuality: A Commentary on Janet Halley's "Reasoning About Sodomy: Act and Identity In and After *Bowers* v. *Hardwick*" ', 79 *Va. L Rev.* 1781 (1993); Kendall Thomas, 'The Eclipse of Reason: A Rhetorical Reading of *Bowers* v. *Hardwick*', 79 *Va. L Rev.* 1805 (1993).

pattern of structural injustice of racism and sexism earlier analysed. Indeed, homophobia (as I shall call this structural injustice) today more conspicuously retains its traditional force than either racism and sexism, as we shall shortly see when we note several cases, in addition to *Bowers*, of populist unjust aggression against the basic human rights of gays and lesbians.

To begin with, however, we may and should, on grounds of principle, extend our earlier analysis of moral slavery to the traditional reprobation of homosexuality. Homophobia reflects a cultural tradition of rights-denying moral slavery similar to, and indeed overlapping with, the American tradition of sexist degradation; the root of homophobia is, like sexism, a rigid conception of gender roles and spheres, only here focusing specifically on gender roles in intimate sexual and emotional life.[316] As my earlier analysis of the basis of the Western condemnation of homosexuality suggests, homophobia may be reasonably understood today as a persisting form of residual and quite unjust gender discrimination both in its object (stigmatizing homosexuality as inconsistent with gender identity, as a man or woman) and in its grounds. With respect to the latter, the non-procreative character of homosexual sexuality may be of relatively little concern, but its cultural symbolism of disordered gender roles excites anxieties in a political culture still quite unjustly sexist in its understanding of gender roles; and indeed the condemnation of homosexuality acts as a reactionary re-enforcement of sexism generally. As we earlier saw, the emergence of the modern conception of homosexual identity, as intrinsically effeminate (in gay men) (and later mannish (in lesbians)[317]), accompanied the emergence of modern Western culture after 1700, and was associated with the re-enforcement of the sexist definition of gender roles in terms of which the supposedly greater equality of men and women was interpreted.[318] Male homosexuals as such were thus symbolically understood as 'effeminate members of a third or intermediate gender, who surrender their rights to be treated as dominant males, and are exposed instead to a merited contempt as a species of male whore'[319] (in the more overtly sexist and homophile ancient Greek world only the passive male partner would be thus interpreted[320]). Homosexuals as such—both lesbians and male homosexuals—are, on this persisting

---

[316] See Suzanne Pharr, *Homophobia: A Weapon of Sexism* (Chardon Press, Inverness, Calif., 1988); Sylvia A. Law, 'Homosexuality and the Social Meaning of Gender' [1988] *Wisc. L Rev.* 187; Young-Bruehl, n. 302 above, 35–6, 143–51; Susan Moller Okin, 'Sexual Orientation and Gender: Dichotomizing Differences', n. 309 above.

[317] On the later development of lesbian identity, see Lillian Faderman, *Odd Girls and Twilight Lovers: A History of Lesbian Life in Twentieth-Century America* (Columbia University Press, New York, 1991); Carroll Smith-Rosenberg, *Disorderly Conduct: Visions of Gender in Victorian America* (Knopf, New York, 1985), at 245–97.

[318] See, in general, Randolph Trumbach, 'Gender and the Homosexual Role in Modern Western Culture: The 18th and 19th Centuries Compared', in Dennis Altman *et al.*, *Homosexuality, Which Homosexuality?: International Conference on Gay and Lesbian Studies* (GMP Publishers, London, 1989), at 149–69.

[319] See *ibid.*, at 153.

[320] For a probing recent study, see Eva Cantarella, *Bisexuality in the Ancient World* (trans. Cormac O'Cuilleanain, Yale University Press, New Haven, Conn., 1992); but see also Boswell, n. 303 above, at 53–107.

modern view, in revolt against what many still suppose to be the 'natural' order of gender hierarchy: women or men, as the case may be, undertaking sexual roles improper to their gender (for example, women loving other women (independent of men),[321] and men loving men, or dominance in women, passivity in men). It is plainly unjust to displace such sexist views, no longer publicly justifiable against heterosexual women or men, against a much more culturally marginalized and despised group—symbolic scapegoats of the feeble and cowardly sense of self that seeks self-respect in the unjust degradation of morally innocent people of goodwill.[322] It should also be clearly constitutionally condemned as a form of unjust gender discrimination, perpetuating unjustly rigid and impermeable gender stereotypes (whether of women or men) that enforce their claims by indulging the dehumanization of any gender dissident (as a degraded or fallen woman).[323]

Homosexuals, because they violate these gender roles, are traditionally supposed to be outcasts from the human race as well, and thus incapable and indeed unworthy of being accorded what all persons are, on equal terms, owed, respect for their basic human rights to conscience, speech, intimate life, and work. A way of making this point is to observe that homophobic prejudice, like racism and sexism, unjustly distorts the idea of human rights applicable to both public and private life. The political evil of racism expressed itself in a contemptuous interpretation of black family life (enforced by segregation and anti-miscegenation laws that confined blacks, as a separate species, to an inferior sphere).[324] The political evil of sexism expressed itself in a morally degraded interpretation of private life (to which women, as morally inferior, were confined as, in effect, a different species[325]). In similar fashion, the evil of homophobic prejudice is its degradation of homosexual love to the unspeakably private and secretive not only politically and socially, but intra-psychically in the person whose sexuality is homosexual; the intellectual reign of terror that once aimed to impose racism and anti-Semitism on the larger society and even on these stigmatized minorities themselves today aims to enforce homophobia at large and self-hating homophobia in particular on homosexuals as well. Its vehicle is the denigration of gay and lesbian identity as a devalued form of conscience with which no one, under pain of ascribed membership in such a devalued species, can or should identify. Such

---

[321] For commentary on the sexism of heterosexism, see Adrienne Rich, 'Compulsory Heterosexuality and Lesbian Existence', in Stimpson and Person, n. 232 above, also reprinted in Henry Abelove, Michele Aina Barale, and David M. Halperin (eds.), *The Lesbian and Gay Studies Reader* (Routledge, New York, 1993), at 227–54.

[322] On the anti-feminism of anti-gay sectarian groups, see Didi Herman, *The Antigay Agenda: Orthodox Vision and the Christian Right* (University of Chicago Press, Chicago, Ill., 1997), at 103–10; on their opposition, in general, to the agenda of civil rights in all areas, see *ibid.*, at 111–36, 140.

[323] For important recent arguments along these lines, see Katherine M. Franke, 'The Central Mistake of Sex Discrimination Law: The Dissagregation of Sex from Gender', 144 *U Penn. L Rev.* 1 (1995); Mary Ann C. Case, 'Disaggregating Gender from Sex and Sexual Orientation: The Effeminate Man in the Law and Feminist Jurisprudence', 105 *Yale LJ* 90 (1995).

[324] See *Loving v. Virginia*, 388 US 1 (1967) (anti-miscegenation laws held unconstitutional expression of racial prejudice).

[325] See Lillian Faderman, *Surpassing the Love of Men* (William Morrow, New York, 1981), at 85–6, 157–8, 181, 236.

degradation constructs not, as in the case of gender, merely a morally inferior sphere, but an unspeakably and inhumanly evil sphere, a culturally constructed and imagined diabolic hell to which gays and lesbians must be compulsively exiled on the same irrationalist mythological terms to which societies we condemn as primitive exiled devils and witches and werewolves;[326] homosexuals, self-consciously demonized (as devils) as they are by contemporary sectarian groups, must be kept in the sphere consistent with their inhumanity.[327] Gays and lesbians are thus culturally dehumanized as a non-human or inhuman species whose moral interests in love and friendship and nurturing care are, in their nature, radically discontinuous with anything recognizably human. The culture of such degradation is pervasive and deep, legitimating the uncritically irrationalist outrage at the very idea of gay and lesbian marriage,[328] which unjustly constructs the inhumanity of homosexual identity on the basis of exactly the same kind of viciously circular cultural degradation unjustly imposed on African-Americans through anti-miscegenation laws.[329] Groups, thus marked off as ineligible for the central institutions of intimate life and cultural transmission, are deemed subculturally non-human or inhuman, an alien species incapable of the humane forms of culture that express and sustain our inexhaustibly varied search, as free moral persons, for enduring personal and ethical meaning and value in living.

Both racism and sexism arose in the context of close living relationships between the hegemonic and oppressed groups, drew their potent political power from such allegedly loving relationships, and were rationalized accordingly as protections of intimate personal life. As James Madison saw in his constitutionally seminal elaborations of his theory of faction, factions are most powerful when they are most local and parochial;[330] consistent with this view, racism and sexism are the prepotent forms of faction they are precisely because they culturally arose and were sustained in the most local and personal of intimate relationships as forms of moral paternalism.

Homophobia shares a comparable cultural background of moral slavery. Heterosexuals and homosexuals lived together closely under the moral slavery of homosexuals,[331] but, as heterosexuals have now learned, in different worlds, one hegemonically and polemically assertive, the other resignedly withdrawn into a com-

---

[326] On the imaginative processes that sustain such a sphere, see Alan E. Bernstein, *The Formation of Hell: Death and Retribution in the Ancient and Early Christian Worlds* (Cornell University Press, Ithaca, NY, 1993); Elaine Pagels, *The Origin of Satan* (Random House, New York, 1996).

[327] For the view of public identified gays and lesbians as, from within the perspective of sectarian theology, devils or demonic, see Didi Herman, *The Anti-gay Agenda: Orthodox Vision and the Christian Right* (University of Chicago Press, Chicago, Ill., 1997), at 82–91, 143; for the similar sectarian view taken of Jews and the analogy to scapegoating homosexuals today, see Pagels, n. 326 above, 102–5.

[328] For further development of this argument, see Richards, *Women, Gays, and the Constitution*, n. 1 above, ch. 8.

[329] See, for eloquent development of this point, Andrew Koppelman, 'The Miscegenation Analogy: Sodomy Law as Sex Discrimination', 98 *Yale LJ* 145 (1988). See also Andrew Koppelman, *Anti-discrimination Law and Social Equality* (Yale University Press, New Haven, Conn., 1996), at 146–76.

[330] See Jacob E. Cooke (ed.), *The Federalist* (Wesleyan University Press, Middletown, Conn., 1961), No. 10, at 56–65; for background and commentary, see Richards, n. 272 above, at 32–9.

[331] For a powerful study of this phenomenon in renaissance England, see Alan Bray, *Homosexuality in Renaissance England* (Gay Men's Press, London, 1982).

pulsory and silent servitude mistaken for consent. Homosexuals were not remitted to servile status as blacks and women were under their forms of moral slavery. Their moral slavery was, rather, more hegemonically absolute—servitude to an unjust moral paternalism that, based on crushing their basic rights (to conscience, speech, association, and work), exiled them from any legitimate space in public or private life into the realm of the unspeakable. Homosexuals were thus radically denied the very resources of self-respecting personal and ethical identity as homosexuals; and homophobia thus naturally takes, as its dominant contemporary form, the violent attack on the relatively recent development of conscientious moral claims to such a self-respecting identity either in public or private life;[332] the essentially hegemonic and subjugating force of this prejudice is shown in its insistence that homosexuality remain an unspeakably privatized debasement, tolerable only on terms of a servile, apologetic, and shrunken self-contempt, not on terms of respect for basic human rights (including the inalienable right to conscience) owed all persons, including lesbian and gay persons. The oppression of homosexuals, like that of blacks and women under moral slavery, is thus perversely rationalized as itself a protection of intimate life (family values), when it, in fact, wars on a legitimate form of intimate life. This marks the roots of the prejudice, like other forms of moral slavery, in the most intimately debasing forms of unjust moral paternalism (the totalizing assumption that the community legitimately can and should know and control the very heart and mind of another's most intimate resources of moral personality). Indeed, consistent with our earlier Madisonian observations, homophobia, focusing on gender roles in intimate life, may be regarded as among the most intractable and virulent of factions, manifesting, as it does, an intrapsychic landscape of the gendered meaning of love based on sexist degradation in intimate life itself (as if, the equality traditionally understood to exist among men or among women could never be fertile soil for the garden of love).[333]

The common ground of our concern with racism, sexism, and homophobia is the radical political evil of a political culture, ostensibly committed to toleration on the basis of universal human rights, that unjustly denied a class of persons their inalienable human rights as persons with moral powers on the basis of the structural injustice of moral slavery. Liberal political culture, consistent with respect for this basic right, must extend to all persons the cultural resources that enable them critically to explore, define, express, and revise the identifications central to free moral personality;[334] the

---

[332] For the history of this development in Great Britain, see Jeffrey Weeks, *Sex, Politics, and Society: The Regulation of Sexuality since 1800* (2nd edn., Longman, London, 1989) and *Coming Out: Homosexual Politics in Britain from the Nineteenth Century to the Present* (rev. edn., Quartet Books, London, 1990). For the American development of this movement, see John D'Emilio, *Sexual Politics, Sexual Communities: The Making of a Homosexual Minority in the United States, 1940–1970* (University of Chicago Press, Chicago, Ill., 1983); John D'Emilio and Estelle B. Freedman, *Intimate Matters: A History of Sexuality in America* (Harper & Row, New York, 1988).

[333] Cf. Okin, n. 309 above.

[334] For development of this theme, see Will Kymlicka, *Liberalism, Community, and Culture* (Clarendon Press, Oxford, 1989), at 162–78; Yael Tamir, *Liberal Nationalism* (Princeton University Press, Princeton, NJ, 1993), at 13–56.

constitutional evil, condemned by suspect classification analysis under the Equal
Protection Clause of the Fourteenth Amendment, is the systematic deprivation of this
basic right to a group of persons, unjustly degraded from their status as persons entitled
to respect for the reasonable exercise of their free moral powers in the identifications of
an ethical life based on mutual respect.[335] To deny such a group, already the subject of
a long history and culture of moral slavery, their culture-creating rights is to silence in
them the very voice of their moral freedom, rendering unspoken and unspeakable the
sentiments, experience, and reason that authenticate the moral personality that a political culture of human rights owes each and every person (including their moral powers
to know and claim their basic rights and to protest injustice on such grounds). Sexual
orientation is and should be a fully suspect classification because homosexuals are today
victimized, in the same way claims to basic rights by African-Americans and women are
and have been, by irrational political prejudices rooted in this radical political evil,
denying them the cultural resources of free moral personality.

Racism, sexism, and homophobia share a common background in moral slavery,
which explains both the character and depth of the political evil they represent, in
particular, its imposition of such injustice on the very terms of personal and moral
identity both for the individuals afflicted by such injustice and the society at large.
Both Du Bois and Friedan thus characterized the struggles, respectively, against
racism and sexism in such terms, as a claim of African-Americans and women to forge
a new identity as blacks and as women but also of the role of race and gender in the
constitution of American constitutional identity. By its very rights-based terms, such
protest challenged the terms of moral slavery, whose unjust cultural force politically
required abridgement of basic human rights of conscience and speech; the structural
injustice thus under criticism attacked the very making of such criticism, as in, for
example, the attempt in antebellum America to silence abolitionist dissent; it was not
that such dissent was not conscientious or did not have a perceived basis in justice,
but because it was thus conscientious and perceived by many (including slaveowners)
as just that it was regarded as so dangerous (inciting slave revolts, for example).[336]
Rights-based protests of the cultural terms of homosexuality have a similar character
and have excited a similar repressive response, but one that attacks the very making
of such claims as conscientious. Rights-based protests of racism and sexism both challenged and transformed identity, but identity which at least occupied a familiar if
embattled cultural space in conscientious public opinion; such protests could be and
were repressed as not only wrong but dangerously wrong. The structural injustice of
homophobia imposes, however, a regime of unspeakability, that is, the denial of any
acceptable terms of identity at all. The contemporary reactionary response to rights-
based protest of such structural injustice is an attack on the very claim itself precisely
because and in virtue of its ethical basis as a rights-based protest of the dehumanizing
injustice of cultural unspeakability, invisibility, and marginalization.

---

[335] For further development and defence of this position, see, in general, Richards, *Women, Gays, and the Constitution*, n. 1 above.

[336] See, on this point, Richards, *Conscience and the Constitution*, n. 1 above, at 59.

A politics actuated by such injustice is suspect not only on the same structural grounds as race and gender, but on grounds of the first suspect classification under American public law, religion.[337] The essential terms of this argument have already been presented: claims of gay and lesbian identity are a form of ethically based conscientious conviction entitled to equal respect with other forms of such conviction under the religion clauses of the First Amendment, and there is no compelling secular basis in contemporary circumstances which could justify burdening or abridging this conviction as opposed to others. Elsewhere, I have argued that many constitutional controversies currently in play correspond to the terms of the analysis proposed. In particular, many of these disputes are best understood as unconstitutionally sectarian attacks on gay and lesbian identity as a conscientious conviction entitled to equal respect. Three cases correspond closely to the terms of this analysis: anti-lesbian/gay initiatives, the exclusion of homosexuals from the military, and the exclusion of gays and lesbians from the right to marriage.[338] In all these cases, the constitutionally crucial point is that assertions of gay and lesbian identity, including making claims to justice as a gay or lesbian person entitled to the basic human rights accorded all other persons, are specifically targeted for disadvantage without any adequate secular basis.

THE RATIONALIZATION OF STRUCTURAL INJUSTICE

These interpretive proposals for understanding the right against unjust discrimination define a normative scope and associated limits.[339] Not all basic constitutional values and rights can be understood in terms of these proposals, but some can be. In particular, my account focuses attention on unjust burdens on identity imposed by a background structural injustice of history and culture with two features. First, a class of persons has been denied basic human rights of conscience, speech, intimate life, and work; secondly, such denial is rationalized in terms of dehumanizing stereotypes that, in a vicious circle of self-entrenching injustice, limit both discussion and speakers to the presumptively settled terms of the denial of basic rights. The model for both the understanding of basic rights and the burden of justification required for their just abridgement arises, I suggested, from the argument from toleration (so clearly central to our understanding of both religious liberty and free speech); but the understanding of the structural injustice I describe, while dependent on the argument for toleration, elaborates that argument to condemn an independent constitutional evil, one not limited to unjust abridgement of one right but abridgement of all rights on grounds that remove a class of persons from the category of bearers of human rights. Some cases of religious intolerance are rooted in this structural injustice as well (in my

---

[337] See, on this point, Richards, n. 272 above, at 260, 280.
[338] See, on this point, Richards, *Women, Gays, and the Constitution*, n. 1 above, chs. 7–8.
[339] For further discussion of the limits of these proposals, see Richards, *ibid.*, n. 1 above, 371–3.

view, anti-Semitism and homophobia), but that fact requires special explanation in terms of a background history and culture of particularly focused and aggressively dehumanizing intolerance.

Both the burdens on identity and the background structural injustice inform a principled understanding of the constitutional condemnation of racism, sexism, extreme religious intolerance, and homophobia. In all these cases, the background structural injustice imposes unjust terms of identity on a subjugated group. Though the structural injustice may radiate out to encompass as well material and related disadvantages, merely remedying the latter disadvantages, without more, does not address the roots of the problem, which is a distinctive injury to moral personality.

The idea of identity, in the sense relevant to our concerns here, is not the philosophical problem of identity (in terms of the criteria of mind and/or body for identifying a person as the same over time and space) nor the broadly sociological question of our multiple roles, many of which are uncontroversially socially ascribed. It would, thus, trivialize the evil of burdens on identity to condemn any and all social ascriptions of identity. Rights-based struggle against structural injustice does not renegotiate all the terms of one's personal identity; one's identity as a person is never either infinitely malleable or even desirably regarded as entirely open to choice. Cultural assumptions must always be taken as given if any reasonable criticisms and reforms, including those based on rights-based protest of structural injustice, are to go forward sensibly.

But structural injustice, marked by the two features earlier described, inflicts an injury on aspects of our identity and identifications that are organizing features of our self-understanding of ourselves as persons and moral agents; this is the narrower sense of contestable and contested identity that is our concern here. The pivotally important feature that structures the character of the injustice is its abridgment of basic human rights in general and inalienable rights to conscience and intimate life in particular, that is, denying the very moral powers in terms of which we come to understand and protest basic injustice. Abridgement of conscience and intimate life play the role they do in inflicting this evil because they are so intimately tied up with the sense of ourselves as persons embedded in and shaped by networks of relationships to other persons with the moral powers of rational choice and reasonable deliberation over the convictions and attachments that give shape and meaning to our personal and ethical lives, as lives lived responsibly from conviction. The dehumanization of people, on grounds of race or gender or religion or sexual orientation, imposes objectifying stereotypes of identity (as black or a woman or Jewish or homosexual) that deny these moral powers, indeed, that are rationalized in terms of this denial. In consequence, these stereotypes take on significance in our lives in terms dictated by the underlying injustice, reducing not only life chances but self-conceptions to their terms.

The depth of this genre of injustice is seen in the double consciousness that its most probing critics (like Du Bois, and Friedan, anticipated by Sarah Grimke[340]) identi-

---

[340] On this point, see Richards, *Women, Gays, and the Constitution*, n. 1 above, 100.

fied as among its worst consequences. The imposition of unjust stereotypes of race or gender thus rationalized the abridgement of conscience, imposing on the very terms of one's sense of oneself as an African-American or a woman a devalued self-image of subhumanity. Such lack of free conscience rendered protesting thoughts unthinkable, which entrenched such stereotypes in the consciousness of oppressed and oppressor alike. The awakening sense of injustice was thus understandably articulated in the terms of double consciousness, the inward sense of oneself both in terms of the dominant stereotype and in yet undefined terms of oneself made possible by challenge to the uncritical force the stereotype had enjoyed. This new sense of identity, forged by rights-based protest to the terms of one's dehumanization, must in its nature affirm a basis for self-respect in exactly the moral complexity, experimental openness, and sense of variety and multiple options that dominant stereotypes deaden and stultify.

No small part of the political power of the enforcement of such stereotypes had been twofold: first, their denial of perspectives and voices that might challenge them; and secondly, their lack of reasonable standards in terms of which such injustice might even be understood, let alone protested by thought and action. A vicious circle thus locked human consciousness into a self-perpetuating repetition of unjust stereotypes as the measure of rights and responsibilities. A life lived to the measure of such stereotypes must be as vacant of the consciousness of moral agency and responsibility as maintenance of the rigidity of the stereotypes required (which is not to say entirely vacant of consciousness, even critical consciousness (including irony), in anyone who is human).

Lack of such protesting thoughts and the reasonable critical standards they make possible correspondingly unjustly distort emotional life in creatures, like ourselves, for whom the emotions have important connections to thoughts and beliefs.[341] The unjust force of this indignity is particularly stark in the case of homophobia. Under the structural injustice I call homophobia, the very experience of one's sexuality, as erotically drawn to those of the same sex, must often be experienced in terms of the dominant stereotypes which traditionally enforce homophobia, namely, as an unspeakable threat to one's gender identity let alone one's humanity, thus often as an object of panic and dread. The depth and importance of the human sexuality of sexual orientation may be analogized to that of the natural language we first acquire,[342] as fundamental to our sense of ourselves as a person formed by and living in affective social relationships to other persons. Under the structural injustice of homophobia, our sense of ourselves as homosexual can barely connect to our wider beliefs and convictions, but must live in a psychic ghetto of the mind that corresponds to the cultural space of homophobically mandated unspeakability. One's homosexuality, an effectively forbidden language of sexual experience and sensual bonding, can hardly in such circumstances play the kind of role heterosexuality plays as a language that models and expresses love and friendship in ways that engage our central convictions

---

[341] On the relation of beliefs and feelings, see David A. J. Richards, *A Theory of Reasons for Action* (Clarendon Press, Oxford, 1971), 70–1, 246–7, 252–5, 264–7, 308.

[342] On this point, see Money, n. 13 above, at 11–12, 54, 71, 74, 76, 80, 129–30.

about personal and ethical meaning in living. The enormously popular political reaction to claims of gay rights may be regarded as an attempt to maintain this culturally entrenched difference in the treatment of homosexuality and heterosexuality, a fact conspicuously shown by the focus, as we have seen, of many legal expressions of this attitude in the condemnation of assertions of gay and lesbian identity that protest this difference.

The depth of the problem is, if anything, compounded by the associated abridgement of the basic human right of intimate life, an abridgement also importantly constitutive of all the manifestations of structural injustice we have been concerned with. The right of intimate life plays so fundamental a role as a basic human right, on a par with the right to conscience, because such intimate relations and identifications structure one's sense of self as a person with creative moral powers formed, sustained, and transformed in relations to other persons dealing with many of the same issues of living (the meaning of birth, love, and death) addressed by the right of conscience. As I observed earlier in the discussion of the proper way of understanding the constitutional evil of racism, the nature of the evil of racism was importantly shown by the African-American leaders who protested the evil as still very much active even though they could have passed as white. For them, as for others afflicted by populist prejudices rooted in structural injustice, their protest was against unjust burdens on identifications with persons whom they love and respect; they refused to accept that it could ever be an acceptable condition of equal respect supinely to acquiesce in an unjust stigma placed upon distortions of one's history and heritage. Their protest both broke the silence of such acquiescence and forged reasonable standards of critical assessment in terms of which such historical injustice might be understood, assessed, and protested. It is precisely because American racism was so structured by abridgements of the right to intimate life both during and after slavery that it fundamentally illuminates the role of the abridgement of intimate life in the structural injustice that has been our concern here. Not to be deemed capable of choice of intimate relations (as in the denial of marriage and control of children under slavery) or such choice on equal terms (as under anti-miscegenation laws) was to be deemed sexually subhuman or animalistic. As we earlier saw, similar such abridgements supported the structural injustice of sexism and anti-Semitism, rationalized in terms of objectifying stereotypes of sexuality and gender.

In contemporary circumstances, the most conspicuous example of a still largely intact structural injustice, arising from such abridgement of both the right to conscience and intimate life, is homophobia. The right to sexual intimacy between parties of the same gender is not yet constitutionally recognized, and the right to marriage is disdained by large populist majorities and the demagogic politicians who pander to them. As I earlier observed, the abridgement of the right to conscience to gays and lesbians casts the pall of unspeakability over their intellectual and emotional life, and the further abridgement of the right to intimate life extends this pall beyond thought and emotion to ways of life. A group that, in just protest of the longstanding cultural tradition of their moral subjugation, most needs experimental space to exercise and test their creative moral powers of thought and action meets a reactionary attack on their very claims of justice and even their right to an intimate life. The extent of the injustice may be seen in two of its aspects that, in contrast to some other forms of structural injustice we have studied, remain largely intact.

First, the cultural pall of unspeakability falls not only on the intimate relations of gays and lesbians, but on their intimate relations to others, in particular, their families of origin. Gays and lesbians have as profound identifications with their families of origin as heterosexuals, and as much right to develop, reinterpret, and even deepen those identifications as a reasonable basis for sustaining enduring personal and ethical values in living. However, the terms of their cultural unspeakability often compel disruption of these bonds as the unjust price to be paid for gay and lesbian identity, inflicting a desolating homelessness as the price to be paid for integrity. No culture that claims (as ours proudly does) to respect the right to intimate life should put persons (either parents or children) to such an unjust, morally impoverishing choice. In fact, the kinds of unjust disruptions of family life (both in marriage and in relations of parents to children), that so repel us in the African-American experience of slavery, are today quite self-righteously inflicted on gays and lesbians by Americans who popularly rationalize such flagrant abridgements of the right to intimate life, in a forceful contemporary example of the irrationalist inversions and obfuscations wrought by the paradox of intolerance, by appeals to the very values (family values) they so aggressively attack.

Secondly, the discourse of African-American, Jewish, and feminist protests of the terms of their moral slavery has now given rise to familiar and widely accepted traditions of dissent, many of whose claims now enjoy the status of established constitutional principles.[343] The claims of gay and lesbian identity, because so many of the terms of their moral slavery remain intact, are much more fragile, certainly lacking anything like the strength and durability of the now flourishing traditions of dissent that protest the vestiges of the other forms of moral slavery. In such a situation, gay and lesbian identity enjoys much less cultural support than the merits of its claims of justice would require, remaining exposed, as we have seen, to attacks triggered by its very making protests of the injustice of its terms of moral slavery. It remains largely marginal to the American sense of justice in matters of religion, race, and gender.[344]

In consequence, gay and lesbian identity remains conspicuously vulnerable in yet another way. Its culture of dissent is still so undeveloped and its moral slavery still so largely intact that the very terms of gay and lesbian identity are vulnerable to the stereotypes that have traditionally rationalized their subjugation. Their situation today is perhaps closer to the experience of double consciousness that Du Bois and Friedan discussed than any other group currently is that has historically suffered moral slavery. This may explain the temptation of some gay scientists and activists, earlier noted, to defend the case for gay rights in genetic or biological terms as if such

---

[343] For fuller discussion of these developments, see Richards, *Women, Gays, and the Constitution*, n. 1 above.

[344] See, in general, Alan Wolfe, *One Nation, After All* (Viking, New York, 1998), at 72–81.

explanations of sexual orientation, if true, would or should make any difference to the case for gay rights. But they are not true, and, if true, might, if anything, be used to reimpose the objectifying stereotypes of sexuality and gender identity that the case for gay rights must and does protest. As I earlier observed, biological reductionism was used to rationalize the cultural degradation of African-Americans and women as a separate species and will wreak comparable havoc on lesbians and gays today, as it did to earlier advocates of gay rights in the past, by confirming, rather than challenging, the unjust cultural stereotypes of the inferiority rooted in nature (in this case, biology). Lesbians and gays need responsibly to insist on and to demand our personal and moral identity as lesbian and gay persons, and to resist those unjust and objectifying stereotypes that have stripped us of our powers of free moral personality. Whatever the ætiology of sexual orientation, the normative question remains of what personal and ethical sense a person can reasonably make of such erotic thoughts and feelings, a quest that requires one to question a still largely intact cultural tradition of unspeak-ability that rules such a quest intrinsically unworthy of thought or discussion. The closest analogy to that quest is the religious analogy of the personal quest for reason-able conviction about ultimate values in living. This makes the case for gay rights not less based on established constitutional principles, but more so. The underlying struc-tural injustice is of the same sort as that underlying racism and sexism (indeed, over-laps with aspects of the latter), and its quest for justice, as we have seen, appeals as well to the oldest tradition of constitutional suspectness, namely, suspicion of sectar-ian religious attempts politically to demean such a form of conscientious life without support in acceptably compelling secular state purposes.

Understood in this way, the case for gay rights advances understanding of the com-mon constitutional principles that condemn racism, sexism, anti-Semitism, and homophobia. The evil in each case is directed at identity, and the ground for the evil is a structural injustice rooted in culture and history. The study of the case for gay rights, interpreted in this way, enables us to see clearly not only that immutability and salience are improper bases for constitutional suspectness, but illuminates as well the problematic motivations of this mistaken understanding. It is thus a common feature of all the constitutional evils, rooted in the structural injustice studied here, that the structural injustice, which is rooted in a history and tradition of subjugation (an essentially cultural wrong), is rationalized by alleged facts of nature (whether of race or gender or racialized religion or gendered sexual orientation). This is the origin of the intuition that these wrongs are importantly to be ascribed to an improper weight being placed on facts, more precisely, on immutable and salient facts. It is quite true that the resulting political prejudices self-rationalize themselves in terms of facts. But, as we have seen, there is nothing factual in the traditions of moral subjugation we have examined, each of which inflicts a cultural constructed and maintained wrong. An adequate diagnosis of the problem must thus attend to the cultural conditions that construct and maintain the wrong, not, as it were, to preserve the wrong by main-taining the fiction that it is based on facts. The thesis of immutability and salience is thus in thrall to the view it claims to criticize, supposing that the wrong attaches to facts. The wrong, however, is marked not by its factual basis, but by its unjust construction of what counts as a factual basis, which may be quite remote from anything we would fairly want to describe as rational basis rooted in a fact of nature. The motivation to such an account is thus itself tainted by attempting to preserve a factual basis for such wrongs, when the wrong is, as we have seen, cultural all the way down.

It is precisely a virtue of the case for gay rights, from this perspective, that it does not easily or naturally fit the terms of the conventional understanding of suspect classification analysis in terms of immutability and salience. Of course, as I argued, race and gender, on examination, do not fit the analysis either, but the case for gay rights more obviously fails to do so. It is, indeed, sometimes popularly condemned in these terms as involving choice in a way that, for example, race and gender do not.[345] The challenge for gay rights is not to fit itself to an analysis which is, in any event, inadequate, but to assist in forging a defensible understanding both of its own claims and the related claims of the other manifestations of structural injustice. It is not a disadvantage for such an account, like the one offered and defended here, to put the case for gay rights in terms of the choice of a gay and lesbian conscientious identity. The same Americans who popularly condemn gays reject any such condemnation of people of other faiths or even atheists,[346] a striking sociological fact which suggests a failure precisely to understand that gay and lesbian identity operates at exactly the same level. My account thus has the virtue of pressing critical argument exactly where it should be pressed, on the crucial point that is popularly erased (the ethical convictions at the core of the case for gay rights) and on the structural injustice (the force of the tradition of unspeakability) that supports such erasure. Gay identity is, from this perspective, as much or as little chosen as any conventional religion; religion, the oldest suspect classification, involves the same kinds of choice and is nonetheless fully protected from sectarian burdens; and, on proper analysis, the suspectness of race and gender turn, like religion and sexual orientation, on unjust burdens placed on identity against a certain cultural background. It is a virtue of making the case for gay rights in the terms offered here that it compels us to identify these important common features, thus focusing analysis both on injuries to moral personality and on the cultural construction that motivates such injuries (including unjust popular failures to understand and give weight to these injuries).

There is a depth to such injustice that the theory of double consciousness attempts to articulate. The injustice imposes identifications that degrade essential impulses of moral freedom. The burdens of race, gender, religion, and sexual orientation all fall in this area, abridging, as we have seen, basic human rights. Burdens thus unjustly placed on our very consciousness of ourselves dehumanize because they attack our core humanity, living a life from rational and reasonable conviction. Life lived under the weight of such stereotypes must stultify and degrade moral personality. Accordingly, the protest of such structural injustice is in terms of the self-originating claims of human rights through which we realize and indeed express our humanity,

---

[345] See Alan Wolfe, *One Nation, After All* (Viking, New York, 1998), 73–4, 77–8.
[346] See *ibid.*, 77.

challenging in such empowering reasonable terms the stereotypical identifications that were unjustly imposed.

We need deeper critical understanding of the common grounds used to rationalize such dehumanization if we are to confront the force that it has enjoyed and continues to enjoy over public and private life. Two such important grounds are patterns of dehumanizing sexual stereotyping and the distortion of the public/private distinction. It is a virtue of the study of gay rights that it advances understanding of the role played by both grounds in the support of the structural injustice that is our concern here. Making the case for gay rights confronts and criticizes the role that stereotypical images of sexuality and gender play not only in the dehumanization of homosexuals but in the rationalization as well of the structural injustice underlying racism, sexism, and anti-Semitism. The issue pervades all the forms of structural injustice examined in often interlinking ways.

American racism was importantly constructed, as we have seen, in terms of dehumanized images of black sexuality expressed, under slavery, by laws abridging rights of marriage and custody of children, reducing black slaves to the terms of marketable cattle (reproduction being understood and defined in terms that advanced their market utility for the slave-owner). After slavery, laws against miscegenation were enforced to police the colour line between black men and white women, but not between white men and black women, thus imposing, often through lynchings, a racialized conception of gender (the white woman on her idealized pedestal, black women as sexually available prostitutes) that rationalized the dehumanization of African-American men (as sexual predators) and women (as prostitutes).[347]

The same racialized conception of gender supported American sexism as well, a point cogently noted by Sojourner Truth in her famous speech pointing out that the alleged gender differences that supported unjust treatment of (white) women rested on an idealizing pedestal of delicacy that was belied by the experience of black women.[348] American feminism would only address this problem when, in the spirit of the abolitionist feminism of Sojourner Truth and others, it critically examined the unjust role uncritical conceptions of gender roles (including their racialized character) had been permitted to enjoy in determining the terms of public and private life. Importantly, this realization was crystallized for many American feminists by their own roles in forging stronger anti-racist principles as participants in the civil rights movement.[349] Importantly, such interracial co-operation was, as we saw, interpreted by the parents of these white women as a degradation of their identities as white women (one such father angrily accused his daughter 'of being a whore and chased her out of the house in a drunken rage, shouting that she was disowned'[350]).

Questioning images of gender and sexuality in this way naturally led as well to a comparable critical understanding of the unjust enforcement through law of

---

[347] See, for full discussion of these points, Richards, *Women, Gays, and the Constitution*, n. 1 above, in particular, at 183, 224, 229, 244, 293, 423, 447.

[348] For excerpts, see *ibid.*, n. 1 above, 116–17.

[349] See, on this point, *ibid.*, 228.   [350] See Evans, n. 162 above, at 44.

gendered conceptions of sexuality that had abridged basic human rights of thought, speech, intimate life, and work. Such abridgements had been traditionally defended in terms of the idealizing pedestal of women's superior character and roles. But, in the wake of serious criticism of the racist character of the pedestal, criticism of its sexist character shortly followed. The pedestal was, from this perspective, a cage,[351] dehumanizing women in terms of stereotypical conceptions of their roles solely in terms of the sexual and reproductive interests of men. Second-wave American feminism importantly stated and elaborated the consequences of this criticism in terms of demands for equal respect for the basic human rights of women to conscience, speech, intimate life, and work, whose abridgement was not supported by compelling secular purposes.[352]

Extreme forms of religious intolerance like anti-Semitism were rationalized in terms of images of sexuality and gender drawn from the roles of such stereotypes in both racist and sexist discourse. Religious intolerance was thus rationalized in racist terms of propensities to being a sexual predator or prostitute, and in sexist terms that feminized Jews in the same terms as homosexuals (as women, and fallen women at that).[353]

Introduction of the case for gay rights into serious study of the forms of such structural injustice compels attention to the pervasive force of such dehumanizing images of gender and sexuality in the rationalization of such injustice. The powerful populist resistance to this relatively new human rights struggle crucially rests on the dehumanizing obsession with homosexuality solely in terms of a rather bleakly impersonal interpretation of same-gender sex acts in general, or, as Leo Barsani has observed, some such same-gender sex acts in particular (in particular, sexual penetration of a man), an interpretation that deracinates such sex acts from the life of a person that is recognizably human or humane. The background of such unjust sexualization was, as we saw earlier, the dominant stereotype of the homosexual as a fallen woman, as a prostitute; the terms of such stereotyping are, of course, unjust to sex workers,[354] but they are unjust to homosexuals as well. In the case of homosexuals, such objectification of sex acts crucially isolates them from any of the familiar narratives through which we normally frame our understanding of the role and place of sex acts in a human life; I mean, of course, the narratives of romantic sexual attraction, quest, passion, and love as well as the narratives of connubial tender transparency and mutual support and nurture and those as well of patience in travail and care and solace in illness and before death. It is a mark of the astonishing injustice to homosexual life and experience that these and other humanizing narratives are, as if by fiat, not extended to homosexual eros. Rather, the culture limits the discussion of homosexuality, in

---

[351] See, on this point, Richards, *Women, Gays, and the Constitution*, n. 1 above, 257, 462.

[352] For full discussion of these developments, see *ibid.*

[353] See *ibid.*, n. 1 above, 293, 333–4, 461.

[354] See David A. J. Richards, 'Commercial Sex and the Rights of the Person: A Moral Argument for the Decriminalization of Prostitution', 127 *U Penn. L Rev.* 1195 (1979); on the scapegoating of prostitutes, see Richards, *Women, Gays, and the Constitution*, n. 1 above, 164, 166–7, 169–71, 178, 296, 310, 321–2; on gender stereotyping of prostitutes, *ibid.*, 175–6, 185, 295–6.

contrast to heterosexuality, to one and only one genre, a clinical focus on sex acts historically associated with the trade of sex workers, namely, pornography.[355] What can explain such injustice? As I suggested earlier, it cannot be the non-procreative character of the sex acts that raises public concern, because non-procreative sex for heterosexuals is now conventional and the right to it constitutionalized. The issue, rather, is its challenge to a highly gendered conception of sexuality as if, contrary to fact, sexual love between men or between women could not be or express passionate love and companionship, at the heart of reasonable conviction of what gives personal and ethical meaning to living, in the way it does for heterosexuals. Making the case for gay rights thus compels us to attend to a particularly entrenched form of gender stereotypy and to confront uncritical limits in our conventional understanding that gender stereotypy, whether of men or women, is now constitutionally suspect. If it is suspect, why is this entrenched form of it not suspect as well? The force of an uncritical stereotype is shown by the ease with which it is indulged, a fact shown, as I earlier argued, not only by the wilful nescience of the majority opinion in *Bowers* v. *Hardwick* but by the populist support for the many reactionary responses to the case for gay rights earlier discussed.

The case for gay rights thus compels us critically to attend to the continuing force of the enforcement of a kind of stereotype we now reject, as a matter of constitutional principle, in related areas of constitutional discourse. Indeed, if my earlier analysis of the case for gay rights is correct, we are compelled to attend to what, on analysis, are unprincipled limits in our understanding of now conventional constitutional principles that condemn the expression through public law of religious intolerance and of gender stereotypy, for the case for gay rights appeals justly to these and other such principles. But the case for gay rights invites us, as well, to reflect on why stereotypical images of sexuality and gender so pervade support for the structural injustice that is our concern here.

The answer lies in important facts about human as opposed to animal sexuality, namely, the role of human sexuality in the plastic and symbolic imaginative life of persons not tied to the periodicities of the reproductive cycle.[356] Because of the imaginative depth of sexuality in the life of persons and in their intimate identifications

---

[355] On these historical and related issues, see David A. J. Richards, 'Free Speech and Obscenity Law: Toward a Moral Theory of the First Amendment', 123 *U Penn. L Rev.* 45 (1974).

[356] For important studies of the differences between human and animal sexuality, see Clellan S. Ford and Frank A. Beach, *Patterns of Sexual Behaviour* (Harper & Row, New York, 1951); Irenaus Eibl-Eibesfeldt, *Love and Hate: The Natural History of Behaviour Patterns* (trans. Geoffrey Strachan, Holt, Rinehart, and Winston, New York, 1971). The insight is also central to Freud's exploration of the imaginative role of sexuality in human personality; see Sigmund Freud, '"Civilized" Sexual Morality and Modern Nervous Illness' in James Strachey (ed.), *Standard Edition of the Complete Psychological Works of Sigmund Freud* (Hogarth Press, London, 1959) ix, at 181, 187: 'The sexual instinct . . . is probably more strongly developed in man than in most of the higher animals; it is certainly more constant, since it has almost entirely overcome the periodicity to which it is tied in animals. It places extraordinarily large amounts of force at the disposal of civilized activity, and it does this in virtue of its especially marked characteristic of being able to displace its aim without materially diminishing its intensity. This capacity to exchange its originally sexual aim for another one, which is no longer sexual but which is physically related to the first aim, is called the capacity for sublimation.'

with other persons, we understand our sexuality as a humane resource of transformative moral passion; as Ficino put the point,

But when the loved one loves in return, the lover leads his life in him. Here, surely, is a remarkable circumstance that whenever two people are brought together in mutual affection, one lives in the other and the other in him. In this way they mutually exchange identities; each gives himself to the other in such a way that each receives the other in return . . .

The truth must rather be that each has himself and has the other, too. A has himself, but in B; and B also has himself, but in A. When you love me, you contemplate me, and as I love you, I find myself in your contemplation of me; I recover myself, lost in the first place by own [*sic*] neglect of myself, in you, who preserve me. You do exactly the same in me. And then this, too, is remarkable: that after I have lost myself, as I recover myself through you, I have myself through you, and if I have myself through you, I have you sooner and to a greater degree than I have myself. I am therefore closer to you than I am to myself, since I keep a grasp on myself only through you as a mediary.[357]

Our erotic interests in love, as persons (whatever our sexual orientation), have this kind of imaginative depth whether or not they lead, in any particular case, to reproduction; indeed, the distinctive feature of our (as opposed to animal) sexuality is that we pursue such interests, when they are heterosexual, even in periods of the reproductive cycle when reproduction is not possible. The consequence of this important distinction between human and animal sexuality is that a class of persons may be significantly dehumanized by characterizing their sexuality as, in its nature, more animal than human. The role of images of gender and sexuality in the rationalization of structural injustice may be understood as examples of this phenomenon. In each case, a group was dehumanized by means of stereotypical images (whether of blacks or of women or of Jews) that rendered their sexuality more animal than human; in effect, groups were stripped of their humanity by imposing on them mandatory stereotypes of sexuality and gender whose force turned on denial to them of respect for their moral powers (including the exercise of those powers in sexual love), on this ground rationalizing abridgement of their basic human rights. The means of such dehumanization is a kind of stereotypical sexualization: ascribing to a class of persons exclusively and obsessively sexual or reproductive interests incapable of self-direction in terms of our wider moral powers.

Making the case for gay rights brings this general issue into sharp analytical focus because the longstanding cultural tradition it addresses so dramatically exemplifies the irrationalist enforcement of such sexualization. On the one hand, the tradition includes a doctrine of personal love, like Ficino's (interpreting a similar doctrine in

---

[357] Marsilio Ficino, *Commentary on Plato's Symposium* (trans. and introduction, Sears Reynolds Jayne, University of Missouri, Columbia, Miss., 1944), 144–45. This aspect of Ficino's account should be distinguished from other elements of it which are less defensible, including his sharp distinction of love from physical union (*ibid.*, 130) and his condemnation of the immoderate desire for copulation and unnatural sex (*ibid.*, 143). On Ficino's as well as Pico della Mirandola's possible motives in legitimating forms of homosexual love, see Giovanni Dall'Orto, '"Socratic Love" as a Disguise for Same-Sex Love in the Italian Renaissance', in Kent Gerard and Gert Hekma, *The Pursuit of Sodomy: Male Homosexuality in Renaissance and Enlightenment Europe* (Harrington Park Press, New York, 1989), at 33–65, especially 37–8, 41–4.

Plato[358]), that suggests, if anything, that loving bonds between men realize the full moral meaning of reciprocal human love between equals, as, in Ficino's words, 'they mutually exchange identities'. On the other, the same tradition (Ficino, again following Plato) condemns as unnatural, indeed unspeakable, same-sex relations as such. For Ficino (like Plato), the issue was resolved apparently by the acceptability, indeed idealization of homoerotic love, as the model for love, but not of sex.[359] In our own much more homophobic age, the issue is not even addressed because the dominant stereotype of homosexuality (as a fallen woman, a prostitute) denies even the thinkability of love, let alone sexual love, between men and between women.

The case for gay rights demands that the issue be addressed particularly since the two traditional grounds for the condemnation of same-sex relations (derived from Plato) are no longer constitutionally acceptable, in principle, at least when enforced against heterosexual men and women. If they cannot be legitimately enforced against heterosexuals, they cannot be legitimately enforced, in principle, against homosexuals either. If same-sex relations cannot, for this reason, be legitimately criminalized, then the Plato–Ficino tradition (endorsing homosexual love but not sex) has lost one of its crucial supports; we would have to endorse both homosexual love and sex. But we are living, as I observed, in a much more homophobically irrationalist period, which avoids even thinking about such issues by accepting and enforcing the stereotype of homosexuality as, in its nature, animalistic, focussing obsessionally on a bleakly impersonal interpretation of gay sex acts as if they were not, indeed could not be, expressions of human personality.

The images of gender and sexuality, once so aggressively enforced against African-Americans, women, and Jews, today retain much of their traditional force when popularly enforced against homosexuals. If we want to understand, in stark contemporary terms, the historical power of racism, sexism, and anti-Semitism, we have at hand a useful example for study and comparison, namely, the response of modernist homophobia to claims for gay rights. Such claims include both demands for basic human rights of conscience, speech, intimate life, and work and sceptical scrutiny of laws and policies expressing homophobia rooted in structural injustice. From this perspective, homosexuality is no more exclusively about sex than heterosexuality, as deeply rooted in our humanity and as expressive, on just terms, of our moral powers. The homophobic response to such claims is to distort them in ways that illustrate the force of the paradox of intolerance in contemporary terms, for example, the defence of the

---

[358] See Plato, *Phaedrus*, in *Collected Dialogues of Plato* (ed. Edith Hamilton and Huntington Cairns; trans. by R. Hackworth, Pantheon, New York, 1961), at 476; Plato, *Symposium* (trans. by Michael Joyce), in *ibid.*, 527. Plato appears to have had a highly developed, idealized concept of romantic homosexual love which required that it rarely, if ever, be consummated. Plato, himself homosexual and a celebrant of aim-inhibited romantic homosexual love, appears to have condemned actual homosexual relations, introducing, for the first time anywhere, philosophical arguments for its unnaturalness. Plato, *Laws* (Book VIII) (trans. by A. E. Taylor), 835d–42a, in *ibid.*, 1226, 1401–6. For illuminating discussion of Plato's insistence that romantic love be aim-inhibited and of the question whether Plato believed consummated homosexual acts themselves to be unnatural, see Gregory Vlastos, 'The Individual as an Object of Love in Plato', in *Platonic Studies* (Princeton University Press, Princeton, NJ, 1973), 3, 22–8.

[359] See previous nn. for fuller discussion of and references to Ficino's and Plato's views on this issue.

human rights of gay and lesbian persons is called faction; arguments for such rights, unjust aggression (inverting, like Hitler's anti-Semitism, victims into aggressors); claims for equality, claims of inequality (special rights); sectarian convictions, the measure of human liberty; laws against discrimination, subsidizing any ideology; factual falsities (sexual abuse of the young), truths.[360] The underlying rationale of such injustice is the sexualization of gay and lesbian identity in a dehumanizing way in terms of objectified sex acts with no ostensible connection to human life and personality. The ideological force of this stereotypical objectification is the erasure of what was so clear to Ficino and Plato, namely, that homoeroticism could and did express our imaginative moral powers of mutual love and friendship in ways that engaged and elevated our creative intelligence and sense of enduring personal and ethical value in living. The modernist scapegoating of the homosexual can only self-rationalize such appalling injustice by suppressing the very views and speakers that contest its crassly stereotypical sexualization of homosexuals, thus attacking, as we have seen, the very making of rights-based claims by gays and lesbians. Gays and lesbians must not, from this perspective, speak from and to conscience and a sense of justice. They must be what homophobic ideology requires them to be, not persons but sex acts and only sex acts. The homophobic degradation that James Baldwin experienced as a black gay man at the hands of a white Southerner was of a piece with the degradation of Southern white women participating in the civil rights movement, as prostitutes. Such ideological sexualization of protests of structural injustice remains powerfully operative against claims of gay and lesbian identity today. Many of the arguments against claims of gay and lesbian rights thus turn on an uncritical public common sense shaped by structural homophobia (uncloseted gays and lesbians in the military thus are sexual pedators, and gays and lesbians can no more have the right to marry than animals).[361] What Baldwin learned about the role of homophobia in fulfilling men's 'enormous need to debase other men'[362] remains, perhaps because of the progress we have made against the evil of such sexualization in so many other areas of structural injustice, *painfully* evident today in the popular discourse dismissing gay rights as a heresy to true American values.

There is another feature of the various forms of structural injustice usefully clarified by the case for gay rights. A structural injustice, like racism and sexism, is an affront to human rights both in the public and private spheres that is often rationalized in terms of protecting the values of intimate personal life (one's slave or one's wife as intimately oneself).[363] The sphere of women was thus defined as fixed and limited to private life, and the sphere of African-Americans segregated to an appropriately servile sphere, not extending to public rights and responsibilities. There is an

---

[360] For fuller defence of this position, in terms of a critical assessment of the reasons urged in support of anti-gay/lesbian initiatives, see Richards, *Women, Gays, and the Constitution*, n. 1 above, ch. 7.

[361] See, for elaboration of this argument, *ibid.*, ch. 8.

[362] Baldwin, n. 105 above, 63.

[363] For fuller discussion, see Richards, *Women, Gays, and the Constitution*, n. 1 above, 253, 273–4, 347–8, 367–8.

intimacy to the kinds of despotic control thus rationalized, for the control was often over intimate services in the home, including sexual availability. Such structural injustice was constructed in terms of a distorted interpretation of the public/private distinction; and its remedy required a recasting of the public/private distinction. For example, issues previously regarded as private (like spouse and child abuse) importantly became matters of legitimate public concern.[364]

The structural injustice of homophobia raises the same general issue, but at another, perhaps deeper level that advances understanding of the political dynamics that support structural injustice in general. Homophobia does not limit homosexuality to a private sphere (as with gender) or to a servile sphere (race), but to no legitimate sphere of activity at all, a sphere defined by its unspeakability. Such structural injustice inflicts a deeper injury to moral personality even than race and gender in the sense that no legitimate cultural space at all is allowed to the thoughts, feelings, and actions that express spontaneous erotic feelings and attachments deeply rooted in one's sense of self as a person, let alone to integration of that sense of self into the fabric of convictions about enduring personal and ethical value in living.

Homosexuals, acculturated to the mandate of such unspeakability, live in intimate relation to heterosexuals, both in and outside their families of origin, but under a ban of thoughts, feeling, and action in public and private life that would rightly be regarded as intolerable by contemporary heterosexuals. Under this regime, homosexuals and homosexual activity exist, but as a culturally mandated family secret at the intimate heart of a persisting pattern of gender hierarchy in marriage. As I earlier observed, modernist homophobia (based on scapegoating the homosexual as a fallen woman) arose as an aspect of the cultural construction of gender differences in ostensibly companionate marriage in reactionary reponse to emerging claims of gender equality. Culturally constructed gender differences were thus rationalized as natural to women and men, including the complementarity of such differences that would mandate gender hierarchy in and outside marriage. In particular, the legitimate terms of intimate life (both love and sex) were defined in terms of the opposite gender of the parties, terms of inequality construed as just in virtue of the gender differences natural to intimate life. Men or women, who violated this orthodoxy of love and sex, were necessarily regarded as, respectively, not true men (but women) or not true women (but men). Not only must sex between parties of the same gender be rendered unspeakable, but, more remarkably (in view of the distinguished philosophical tradition on the nature of love between men tracing to Plato and Ficino), love between persons of the same gender. Such love must be excluded from any cultural legitimacy because the parties to it (men, or women, as the case may be) were, within the terms

---

[364] See, e.g., *People* v. *Liberta*, 64 NY 2d 152, 474 NE 2d 567 (NY Ct. App. 1984) (rape in marriage no longer exempt from criminal liability). See, for an important exploration of the normative considerations that motivate growing legal concern with violence in private life, Jane Maslow Cohen, 'Regimes of Private Tyranny: What Do They Mean to Morality and for the Criminal Law?', 57 *U Pitt. L Rev.* 757 (1996).

of the gender orthodoxy), equals (an idea repugnant to the orthodoxy of legitimate love and sex as exclusively between unequals).

The consequence of such unspeakability was the enforcement through law of a conception of family life built upon structural injustice; importantly, the very legitimacy of the unequal terms of companionate marriage, in avowedly egalitarian America, required the total erasure of those forms of intimate relations (between men or between women) that would challenge the terms of inequality in marriage as not mandated by the nature of things. To achieve this ideological end, the privatization of homosexuality was more radically total than that endured by women or African-Americans, inflicting on homosexuality not limitation to a devalued private sphere, but erasure as the unspeakable secret on which the legitimacy of private life, as conventionally understood, depended. The sense of intimacy of homophobia thus arises, as does sexism and racism, from an embattled sense of protecting the legitimate terms of intimate life, here, however, requiring a more extreme privatization of the aggrieved group (homosexuals) in order ideologically to enforce the terms of the devalued private sphere of women. The issue of homosexuality is thus intimately constitutive of the sense of conventional gender identity, of the sense, for example, of protection of one's wife as self-defence of one's self. The force of such structural injustice is shown by the only way it can permit itself to construe the unspeakable challenge to the conventional terms of gender identity, namely, as a degradation of gender identity to what is supposed to be the impersonal sex acts of a prostitute that are chosen for perverse and ostensibly superficial reasons (thus, the emphasis in contemporary homophobia on a consumerist model of the choice of sex acts as having the superficiality of a choice of soap).[365] In particular, homophobia requires that such sex acts cannot, in their nature, have the kinds of deep personal roots of fantasy and longing and moral competence for loving and being loved that dignify the intimate lives among heterosexuals in all their variegated moral complexity. In consequence, homosexuality is equated with the conventional stereotype of prostitution, namely, as objectified consumerist sex acts. It is striking that early modern advocates of gay rights insisted on understanding gay sexuality in terms of some humanizing understanding of the role of homoeroticism in the lives and histories of persons.[366] We may and should critically recognize the degree to which their interpretation of personality was much too much in thrall to the gender stereotypes they should have contested,[367] but their argument surely compels respect when properly understood, as it should be,[368] as a way of challenging the dehumanizing objectification of gay and lesbian sexuality.

[365] See Alan Wolfe, *One Nation, After All* (Viking, New York, 1998), 73–4, 77–8.

[366] See, for further development of this theme, Richards, *Women, Gays, and the Constitution*, n. 1 above, ch. 6.

[367] On male homosexuality as a congenitally abnormal male who is a female 'third sex', see Richards, *Women, Gays, and the Constitution*, n. 1 above, at 305–6, 313, 314, 316, 317, 322, 332, 369.

[368] Michel Foucault's critical account of the resulting pathologization of homosexuality, while certainly true, lacks, in my judgement, interpretive charity of the humanizing impulses behind many of the early gay rights advocates. Foucault thus observed: 'The sodomite had been a temporary aberration; the homosexual now was a species.' See Michel Foucault, *The History of Sexuality* (trans. Robert Hurley, Pantheon, New York, 1978), i, 43.

The contemporary case for gay rights challenges both the terms and consequences of the traditional unspeakability of homosexuality, thus reframing yet again our understanding of the public/private distinction. It challenges its terms by rights-based demands for voice and the reasonable discourse that voice makes possible; it challenges its consequences by insisting on a new conversation in which the choice of homosexuality is no longer homophobically a gratuitous choice of animalistic debasement, but a moral choice of a legitimate form of private and public life on terms of gender equality.

The contemporary case for gay rights thus has available to it a normative resource only incompletely available, at best, to the first generation of advocates of gay rights, namely, rights-based feminism. A case for gay rights, drawing on rights-based feminism, had certainly been made notably by Walt Whitman,[369] and developed by Emma Goldman[370] and Edward Carpenter;[371] all these advocates sought common grounds between arguments for rights-based feminism and gay rights. But the case for rights-based feminism had been morally compromised by strategic alliances (with the temperance and purity movements) based on re-enforcing gender stereotypy as part of the development of suffrage feminism,[372] and figures like Goldman, for example, were notably marginalized by most American feminists of her day.[373] Even Carpenter's remarkably prophetic attempt to unite rights-based feminism with arguments for gay rights was profoundly flawed by the ways in which his arguments indulged and sometimes re-enforced the unjust gender stereotypy of both woman and homosexuals;[374] and other advocates of gay rights were aggressively misogynist.[375] Contemporary rights-based feminism has, however, carried its analysis of the role of gender stereotypy in rationalizing injustice to women far enough reasonably to acknowledge lesbianism as a legitimate feminist alternative;[376] and the case for gay rights may, in ways I earlier suggested, deepen this analysis to criticize, on feminist grounds of principle, the role that gender stereotypy uncritically continues to play in the oppression of both gay men and lesbians.[377]

Indeed, from this perspective, the struggle for gay rights may reasonably be regarded as at the cutting edge of an important criticism of the sexist terms in which family life continues largely to be understood. The dehumanization of homosexuals retains popular appeal when brought into relation to claims for same-sex marriage because, consistently with Freud's observation of the narcissism of small differences,[378] it enables a culture, with a long history of uncritical moral slavery of women

---

[369] See, for development and support of this claim, Richards, *Women, Gays, and the Constitution*, n. 1 above, 297–310.

[370] See, for development and support of this claim, *ibid.*, 173–8, 321, 329–30

[371] See, for development and support of this claim, *ibid.*, 317–27.

[372] For fuller discussion of this point, see *ibid.*, ch. 4.   [373] See, on this point, *ibid.*, 329–30.

[374] See, on these points, *ibid.*, 322–3, 326, 331, 358.

[375] On Otto Weininger, see *ibid.*, 332–6.   [376] See, on this point, *ibid.*, 342–6, 352.

[377] See, for further development of this argument, *ibid.*, ch. 6.

[378] On 'the narcissism of small differences', see Sigmund Freud, *Civilization and its Discontents* in James Strachey (ed. and trans.), *Standard Edition of the Complete Psychological Works of Sigmund Freud* (Hogarth Press, London, 1961), xxi, ch. 5, at 114; see also *Moses and Monotheism*, in *ibid.* (1964), xxiii, at 91.

and homosexuals, not to take seriously, let alone think reasonably about, the growing convergences of heterosexual and homosexual human love in the modern world. These include not only shared economic contributions to the household and convergent styles of non-procreational sex and elaboration of erotic play as an end in itself, but the interest in sex as an expressive bond of companionate relationships of friendship and love as ends in themselves; several partners over a lifetime; when there is interest in children, only in few of the them; and the romantic love of tender and equal companions as the democratized centre of sharing intimate daily life.[379] Indeed, some studies suggest that, if anything, homosexual relationships more fully develop features of egalitarian sharing that are more often the theory than the practice of heterosexual relations.[380] The uncritical ferocity of contemporary political homophobia draws its populist power from the compulsive need to construct Manichean differences where none reasonably exist, thus re-enforcing institutions of gender hierarchy perceived now to be at threat. In particular, as Whitman argued,[381] democratic equality in homosexual intimate life threatens the core of traditional gender roles and the hierarchy central to such roles. Consistent with the paradox of intolerance, the embattled sectarian orthodoxy does not explore such reasonable doubts, but polemically represses them by remaking reality in its own sectarian image of marriage, powerfully deploying the uncritical traditional stereotype of the homosexual as the scapegoat of one's suppressed doubts (excluding the homosexual from the moral community of human rights, including the basic human right to intimate life). Homosexuals are the natural scapegoat for this uncritical feminist backlash,[382] because they, unlike heterosexual women, remain a largely marginalized and despised minority. Traditional sectarian orthodoxy objects as strongly to many of the achievements of the feminist movement (some to the decriminalization of contraception, others to that of abortion, still others to now mainstream feminist issues like ERA[383]),

[379] See, on the continuities among heterosexual and homosexual forms of intimacy in the modern world, in general, Giddens, n. 308 above; D'Emilio and Freedman, n. 308 above, 239–360; Philip Blumstein and Pepper Schwartz, *American Couples* (William Morrow, New York, 1983), 332–545. On declining fertility rates, see Claudia Goldin, *Understanding the Gender Gap: An Economic History of American Women* (Oxford University Press, New York, 1990), at 139–42; on childlessness, see, in general, Tyler May, n. 268 above; on rising divorce rates, see Degler, n. 126 above, 165–8, 175–6. See also Barbara Ehrenreich, Elizabeth Hess, and Gloria Jacobs, *Remaking Love: The Feminization of Sex* (Anchor, New York, 1986); Ann Anitow, Christine Stansell, and Sharon Thompson (eds.), *Powers of Desire* (Monthly Review Press, New York, 1983); Carol S. Vance (ed.), *Pleasure and Danger: Exploring Female Sexuality* (Routledge & Kegan Paul, Boston, Mass., 1984).

[380] On this point, see Susan Moller Okin, 'Sexual Orientation and Gender: Dichotomizing Differences', in David M. Estlund and Martha C. Nussbaum (eds.), *Sex, Preference, and Family: Essays on Law and Nature* (Oxford University Press, New York, 1997), 44–59.

[381] See, for development of this point, Richards, *Women, Gays, and the Constitution*, n. 1 above, 297–310.

[382] See, in general, Susan Faludi, *Backlash: The Undeclared War Against American Women* (Doubleday, New York, 1991); Marilyn French, *The War Against Women* (Penguin, London, 1992).

[383] For some sense of the range of such views and their supporting reasons, see Sherrye Henry, *The Deep Divide: Why American Women Resist Equality* (Macmillan, New York, 1994); Elizabeth Fox-Genovese, *'Feminism Is Not the Story of My Life': How Today's Feminist Elite Has Lost Touch with the Real Concerns of Women* (Doubleday, New York, 1996); *Feminism Without Illusions: A Critique of Individualism* (University of North Carolina Press, Chapel Hill, NC, 1991).

but they have lost many of these battles and the sectarian hard core of the orthodoxy, in fact hostile to feminism and civil rights measures in general,[384] takes its stand strategically where it still can against members of a traditionally stigmatized and silenced minority who are, like the Jews in Europe, easily demonized.[385]

From this perspective, the choice of gay and lesbian identity elaborates the terms of gender equality on deeper grounds of principle. Their experiments in living are of interest not only to them but to the larger culture increasingly concerned, as it is and should be, to forge a conception of both public and private life more consistent with principles of gender equality. Such choice of gay and lesbian identity is, in its nature, an empowering ethical protest of conventional gender stereotypy that enables homosexuals, like heterosexuals, to live as individuals with hearts and minds authentically open to the grace of love. The most illuminating understanding of the distinctive character of this choice is to be drawn from the religious analogy, the right to choose gay and lesbian identity as a matter of conscience.

We understand such issues of conscience in terms of an inalienable right of liberty and the argument for toleration not because we choose our convictions any more than our beliefs in general, but because responsibility for our deepest convictions about value in living expresses the appropriate attitude of respect for the free moral powers of persons. Such responsibility empowers persons to live a life from reasonable conviction, exploring as much as organizing their experience of what gives enduring value to personal and ethical life. The right to liberty of conscience, in the terms protected by the argument for toleration, ensures the requisite moral independence rationally and reasonably to undertake and meet this responsibility free from the unjust imposition of sectarian views. The right to choose gay and lesbian identity is grounded on the right to conscience, thus understood, because only respect for this right ensures the required moral independence in taking responsibility, free of unjust sectarian views unsupported by compelling secular reasons, for convictions about homosexual love as deeply rooted in life experience and personality and the sense of enduring values in living as those about heterosexual love. It is in the nature of this kind of right that respect is accorded for our moral responsibility, as persons, for our reasonable convictions, whatever they are. That persons are thus acknowledged as morally responsible in this arena allows persons to understand, discover, explore, express, develop, revise, and sometimes change their convictions on whatever reasonable terms move them as a matter of conscience; persons are to this extent respected as free to address these issues independent of unjust sectarian impositions that compel or burden such exercise of our moral powers. It does not follow, of course, that the exercise of such freedom of conscience is itself experienced as a gratuitous matter of consumerist whim. More often, our convictions speak with authority, tell us what

[384] For its anti-feminism, see Herman, n. 327 above, 103–10; for its opposition to the civil rights agenda in general, see *ibid.*, at 111–36, 140.

[385] On the analogy of such contemporary homophobia to anti-Semitism, see Herman, n. 327 above, 82–91, 125–8; cf. Pagels, n. 326 above, 102–5. See also, for a useful study of the reactionary populist politics of this group, Chris Bull and John Gallagher, *Perfect Enemies: The Religious Right, the Gay Movement, and the Politics of the 1990's* (Crown Publishers, New York, 1996).

must be done, sometimes even erupt with the force of a power greater than ourselves. Importantly, the very point of guaranteeing such freedom is that conscience is often experienced as the source of reasonable demands or even imperatives of moral personality with an ultimate claim on our convictions. The case for gay rights calls for such responsible freedom for gays and lesbians to confront and meet such demands on terms of justice.

The case for gay rights thus appeals to the moral idea of responsibility for self central to the theory and practice of rights-based constitutional law and government. Both the substantive and procedural guarantees of American constitutional law may reasonably be understood as in service of this moral idea.[386] The moral sense and role of this idea may be sharply drawn and appreciated by contrasting the idea to the picture of human life, as dictated by natural hierarchy, that it criticizes. Such natural hierarchy embeds human life in forms of prescribed status whose force depends on the denial of the moral idea of responsibility for self. The connection between respect for human rights and the idea of responsibility for self may be clarified in terms of two ways that values of human rights protest natural hierarchy. First, human rights ground self-originating claims that challenge the very terms of such hierarchy, in which one's role is externally dictated as exhaustive of meaning in living. Secondly, such claims of human rights also make possible reasonable criticism of the unjust political construction that has rendered such hierarchy ostensibly natural and uncontroversial. I have already discussed the force of such criticism both in terms of the argument for toleration and the theory of structural injustice. The theory of structural injustice thus is a criticism of certain ways in which unjust claims of natural hierarchy have been rationalized, for example, in terms of race or gender. The criticism of such hierarchy, as a naturalization of injustice, affirms the moral idea and value of responsibility for self, claiming one's reasonable moral powers against the stereotypical impositions of natural hierarchy that have blighted critical moral freedom. The case for gay rights, which draws both upon the argument for toleration and the theory of structural injustice, affirms such responsibility for self of gays and lesbians. In particular, such claims protest the traditional naturalization of injustice to homosexuals in terms of dehumanizing stereotypes of the depraved nature of homosexuality. In this way, gays and lesbians take responsibility for defining their personal and ethical lives on terms of justice.

Finally, the case for gay rights invites closer attention to yet another pervasive feature of all the forms of structural injustice studied here, namely, the injuries inflicted on identity are very much supported, on the other side, by the sense of identity (for example, in racism, of whites as superior; or, in sexism, of conventional heterosexual men, as superior). The political power of structural injustice importantly depends on its constitutive power in the formation of such identity in intimate life. Identity, thus formed in intimate relations (as sexism clearly is), has a personal intimacy that, when under attack, construes the attack as a direct threat to self, in particular, invoking the

---

[386] For extended defence of this view, see Richards, n. 272 above.

protection of family values. Study of the case for gay rights, from this perspective, confirms the political power of this dynamic. As I have suggested, gender identity has been formed in intimate relations on terms that enforce gender hierarchy as the measure of intimate life in ostensibly egalitarian America (thus, ideologically compelling the unspeakability of homosexual love); in consequence, the populist reactionary response to the case for gay rights takes the form of resisting alleged unjust aggression against a threatened sense of self, appealing, paradoxically, to family values. As an argument, there is no factual basis for it, and indeed decisive objections to its irrationalism (ideologically transforming, consistent with the paradox of intolerance, victims into aggressors). But the populist appeal of the claim requires explanation. The explanation is the continuing political power of homophobia, as a structural injustice, resting on the tangled sexist ideology that rationalizes this injustice as an ideological support for gender hierarchy in contemporary circumstances.

The absorbing interest of the case for gay rights, in contemporary circumstances, is that it confronts a form of structural injustice that, unlike the other forms we have studied, remains very largely intact. The constitutional principles that now liberally condemn conspicuous forms of racism, sexism, and anti-Semitism have enjoyed only limited, quite recent, application to condemn homophobia.[387] What makes this so striking is that, as we have seen, basic constitutional principles both of conscience and of intimate life and of anti-discrimination fully apply to the laws that continue to disadvantage gay and lesbian people. In particular, the constitutional principles, that now condemn unjust gender stereotypy disadvantageous to both men and women, condemn, as a matter of principle, the important role of gender stereotypy in modernist homophobia. That these issues are barely seen, let alone acted on, suggests the continuing power of the structural injustice of homophobia, which, as it were, exempts—without explanation or any sense of a need for an explanation—gays and lesbians from the principles now aggressively extended to protect the basic rights of all other Americans.

This gap in principles raises larger questions about the integrity of a cluster of constitutional principles, preoccupied with the role of structural injustice in American history and tradition, that are among the principles most central to our sense of ourselves as a people capable of transformative moral growth under the rule of law—a people that struggled constitutionally with itself to understand and remedy the evils of slavery, racism, sexism, and anti-Semitism. The struggle for the rights of gay and lesbians is the retelling in contemporary circumstances of perhaps our most valuable narrative of the struggle to come to know, understand, and act on one's human rights in protest against dehumanizing traditions that have denied one's status as even a bearer of human rights. Such rights-based protest against the terms of one's dehumanization makes the case for gay rights, in its contemporary nature, a struggle to forge a self-respecting identity on terms of justice in the best American tradition of morally transformative constitutional discourse aimed at our most entrenched and popular structural injustices.

---

[387] See *Romer* v. *Evans*, 116 S Ct. 1620 (1996).

The case for gay rights, thus understood, must engage any one seriously interested in the continuing power and authority of American constitutionalism to address fundamental injustices in American public and private life inflicted by the complacent populist tyrannies of democratic majorities that so darkly worried James Madison, our constitutional founder most profoundly engaged by the normative demand to structure legitimate political power to respect the inalienable human right of conscience.[388] Like the related anti-racist and anti-sexist struggles, the struggle for gay and lesbian identity will, as it proceeds, transform American identity as well, deepening and widening the advances we have made on the rights-based grounds of principle that are the birthright of all Americans. For example, corresponding to related advances in our understanding of the scope of anti-racist and anti-sexist principles, admitting gays to the military, on the same fair terms as we have admitted African-Americans and are admitting women, will forge a conception of American citizenship that is more just because it is less complicitous with the construction of injustice (whether racism, sexism, or homophobia). At the end, respect for rights-based protest of the terms of an identity constructed on injustice best defines the American people, as Lincoln believed,[389] as a moral people because capable of moral growth on terms of constitutional principle.

[388] See, for exploration of this issue, Richards, n. 272 above, at 107–30, 147–8, 175–82.
[389] For Lincoln's appeal to 'the light of reason and the love of liberty in this American people', see Robert W. Johannsen (ed.), *The Lincoln–Douglas Debates* (Oxford University Press, New York, 1965), 67.

4

Free Speech as a Remedy for Structural Injustice: Racism

We have now developed the argument for toleration to offer a theory of free speech (Chapter 2) and further elaborated that argument to explicate the structural injustice underlying such constitutional evils as racism, sexism, and homophobia (Chapter 3). Our task now is to integrate these two arguments in service of a deeper understanding of the role free speech plays, as a matter of principle, among the responsible remedies for such structural injustice. The immediate occasion of my analysis is the earlier mentioned scholarly challenge to current American judicial scepticism about the legitimacy of group libel laws as a remedy for such injustice.[1] I have already suggested reasons for believing that such laws violate a proper understanding of free speech principles (Chapter 2), but want now to further deepen this analysis by addressing the assumption, central to the recent scholarly challenge, that such laws responsibly address the underlying evil of structural injustice. I address in this chapter largely the illegitimacy of group libel laws directed against racism in contrast to other remedies that are, in my judgement, legitimate (including affirmative action); in the next chapter, I focus on the related scholarly and judicial defence of anti-obscenity laws (allegedly directed against sexism and homophobia) as well as blasphemy laws, and argue that these are illegitimate for similar reasons. Subsequently, I use the theory of free speech here proposed to criticize current judicial scepticism about laws regulating campaign expenditures and related issues.

An integrated theory of free speech and structural injustice enables us to question the usual premise of discussion of these matters, namely, that they are separable questions. For example, the recent American scholarly challenge crucially assumes that structural injustice can be understood, let alone remedied, independently of the requirements of free speech. It is this largely unexamined assumption that frames the view that the constitutional evil of racism is so great, on the scale of ultimate constitutional values, that its remedy reasonably calls for whatever sacrifices in values of free speech are required. If this assumption were not true, the terms of the scholarly challenge would be radically misconceived. Its programme, ostensibly motivated by remedies for racism, might be self-defeating, precisely because it requires sacrifices of principles of free speech. I propose to argue both that the assumption is false and that remedies for racism, based on its ostensible truth, are self-defeating in a way that should worry anyone seriously committed to advancing reasonable remedies for

---

[1] See, for a recent statement of such a position, Richard Delgado and Jean Stefancic, *Must We Defend the Nazis: Hate Speech, Pornography, and the New First Amendment* (New York University Press, New York, 1997).

structural injustice. Later, I shall generalize this point to include sexism and homophobia as well.

My discussion examines this question from two different, though related, historical perspectives of constitutional theory and practice about this issue: first, the American tradition of interpretive reflection on the longest-lasting written constitution in the world; and secondly, the tradition elsewhere (including under national and regional law as well as public international law) importantly framed by the now universal reasonable sense of normative tragedy in the political success and implementation of the evil of fascist political anti-Semitism under Weimar constitutionalism, its decisive defeat in the Second World War, and the need to reconstruct constitutionalism (both in Germany and elsewhere) accordingly. If we are reasonably to advance both the interpretive understanding and critical evaluation of these two different traditions, we must take seriously both the basic political theory they share (one that now respects both the rights of free speech and the right against unjust discrimination) and the contextual differences, whatever they are, that may illuminate the rather different ways they constitutionally weight these rights in the area of hate speech and related laws. My account begins with a normative defence, on the basis of political theory, of current American interpretive practices, appealing to the interpretive history which, I believe, explains how and why Americans have come reasonably to regard group libel and related laws as striking an unsound balance between basic constitutional rights of free speech and anti-discrimination. On this basis, I then turn to the interpretation and critical evaluation of the other constitutional tradition I have mentioned. My account begins with the reconstruction of German constitutionalism in the wake of the Second World War, focusing, in particular, on the interpretation crucially ascribed to the failure of Weimar constitutionalism in the support of group libel and related laws. Since the alternative understanding within this tradition (about group libel and related laws) importantly draws on the interpretation of these events, presumably its normative evaluation requires an investigation of the cogency of the interpretation. If the interpretation is less reasonably cogent than it is widely supposed to be, that may suggest grounds for critical normative evaluation of various ways in which the interpretation has been used to rationalize the alleged reasonable grounds for trading off the right of free speech against the right of anti-discrimination in support of such laws. My account critically focuses on two such approaches: the appeal to such balancing within national and regional legal systems, and the appeal to it under public international law.

THE AMERICAN PERSPECTIVE

Structural injustice, as earlier analysed (Chapter 3), is entrenched by its two, mutually re-enforcing features: first, the abridgment of basic human rights to a class of persons; and secondly, the dehumanizing stereotypes that unjustly rationalize such abridgment. The abridgment of the basic human rights of conscience and speech crucially shaped and entrenched the terms of such moral slavery in two ways. First, the persons afflicted by such structural injustice were denied the basic human rights of conscience and speech in terms of which they come to know, understand, and act on a sense of conviction that might protest such injustice. Secondly, such abridgement forbade the voices and views that might most reasonably challenge the dehumanizing stereotypes in terms of which such injustice was imposed. The cultural entrenchment of moral slavery in all its forms thus crucially turned on the abridgement of basic human rights of conscience and speech, and cannot reasonably be understood independently of such abridgement.

We can see this structural connection and its consequences quite clearly in the antebellum experience of Jacksonian America that increasingly gave play to an anticonstitutional majoritarianism (protested by Lincoln) that had, both at the state and national levels (with the complicity of Jackson himself), abridged basic human rights of free speech on slavery (its evils and abolition) and racism.[2] The great importance of the abolitionists in American moral, political, and constitutional thought was not only the substantive moral issue on which they aimed to fasten the public mind of the nation, but the mode of argument they demanded as the measure of the integrity of American revolutionary constitutionalism, namely, argument based on the right of free conscience and speech. The abolitionists opposed not only the tyranny of unreflective majoritarian opinion of the age of Jackson, but their voice was its public enemy, the object of the anti-abolitionist mobs. These mobs, often led by Jacksonian community leaders, subjected courageous early abolitionist leaders like Weld and Garrison—who asked only to be heard—to unremitting violence, threats of death, ridicule, and, in the case of Elijah Lovejoy, murder. It was their appeal to conscience that was met by the age of Jackson's repression of free speech at both the state and national levels; such repression deprived the South and, for a long period, the nation of reasonable public discussion of the moral evils of slavery and of the merits and strategies of abolition, thus further entrenching American populist racism. It was the abolitionist attack on the political and constitutional pathology behind the deprivation of these constitutional liberties that eventually was to awaken the public mind of the nation to the underlying constitutional principles of human rights that condemned equally the repression of conscience and the institution of slavery.[3]

The entrenchment of moral slavery in all its forms is crucially linked to such unjustifiable abridgement of the basic human rights of conscience and speech inconsistent with the terms of the argument for toleration. As we have seen (Chapters 2–3), the argument calls for respect for basic human rights (like the inalienable right to conscience), in particular, forbidding the abridgement of such rights on sectarian grounds not reasonably justifiable to all persons in terms of general goods that all persons want irrespective of particular philosophical or religious disagreements about how such goods should be interpreted and weighed. The structural injustice of moral

[2] See David A. J. Richards, *Conscience and the Constitution: History, Theory, and Law of the Reconstruction Amendments* (Princeton University Press, Princeton, NJ, 1993), 51–2.
[3] See *ibid.*, 58–9.

slavery represents a particularly aggravated violation of the terms of the argument for toleration, resting, as it does, on the systematic abridgement of all human rights of a class of persons (thus, denying their status as bearers of such rights) on inadequate grounds. Such inadequate grounds are sectarian in the sense that they unjustly enforce the terms of a political epistemology that rationalizes the abridgement of basic rights. The epistemology is thus enforced by limiting both the terms of argument and the participation of speakers to those supportive of the dominant orthodoxy. Such grounds are inadequate because they not only fail the test of reasonable justification in terms of general goods required for the abridgement of basic human rights, but unjustly rationalize such inadequate grounds by rendering impossible such testing by self-entrenching an insular political epistemology (based on sectarian grounds) as the measure of views and speakers worthy of a hearing. The requirement of compelling secular justification in terms of general goods refuses, as a matter of basic political and constitutional legitimacy, to allow such self-entrenchment of sectarian views as the measure of basic human rights and responsibilities.

Often, as we have seen, the rationalization of such structural injustice involves the paradox of intolerance, thus demonizing as scapegoats the persons who most reasonably challenge the terms of the structural injustice. Such groups of persons, subordinated as moral slaves, exist, in the terms of the dominant political epistemology, not as persons, but as dehumanized stereotypes drained of moral personality—defined in terms of ideological tropes as black or the Jew or woman or the homosexual.[4] I earlier characterized such stereotypical dehumanization, drawing on the theory of double consciousness of Sarah Grimke, Du Bois, and Friedan, as an indignity inflicted on our powers of free moral personality, imposing the unjust terms of moral slavery on identifications constitutive of one's personal and ethical sense of self; the self-entrenching consequence of such injustice is to blight our very moral powers to protest its terms. That is why, in my judgement, abridgement of the basic human rights of conscience and speech so pivotally model the reasonable analysis of structural injustice in all its forms. Such injustice has the cultural depth and intractability which it has because its cultural entrenchment so crucially rests on a long, largely unquestioned history of abridgement of basic human rights of conscience and speech, blighting the free exercise of the moral powers that might protest the terms of such moral slavery (in particular, the dehumanizing stereotypes in terms of which it has been and is rationalized).

It is for these reasons that the analysis of the structural injustice of moral slavery requires intrinsically an analysis of the abridgement of free speech as well (I shall call this the dependence thesis). Such structural injustice in all its forms cannot be reasonably understood independently of the unjust abridgement of principles of freedom of speech. The independence thesis, on which much recent American scholarship rests, is wrong and indefensible. The popularity of this thesis reflects a failure of responsible

---

[4] See, for an important recent study of literary representations in terms of such tropes, Bryan Cheyette (ed.), *Between 'Race' and Culture: Representations of 'the Jew' in English and American Literature* (Stanford University Press, Stanford, Cal., 1996).

scholarship to bring to bear on our understanding of these issues a reasonable use and interpretation of the historical literature on the cultural roots of moral slavery now available.

It should not surprise us, in light of the truth of the dependence thesis, that the demand for free speech has played so powerful a role in the critical attack on structural injustice in all its forms (see Chapter 3). This was not a historical accident, from which we have nothing to learn in our contemporary struggles against the continuing ravages of moral slavery, but an invaluable interpretive legacy about the continuing indispensable role of demands for free speech in any reasonable understanding of the remedies for structural injustice. The reasonable contemporary interpretation of that legacy needs to take seriously the role that the development of a more muscular interpretive understanding of principles of free speech played in the great struggle for human rights, in the areas of both race and gender, in whose achievements (however controversially imperfect) Americans now take such understandable pride. The only political theory of free speech which reasonably can explain and justify this achievement is that based on the argument for toleration (Chapter 2) and the related theory of structural injustice (Chapter 3).

The demand for an expansive understanding of free speech was an important claim of the abolitionist movement because that movement made such fundamental criticisms of the depth and extent of the role structural injustice played in distorting and delegitimating American political and constitutional institutions. An expansive understanding of free speech was thus required along its two dimensions. First, the scope of the protection of free speech could not be limited to the dominant understanding of legitimate politics, precisely because such dominant understanding was so flawed by structural injustice. Rather, the scope of protection of the principle of free speech must extend as broadly as the underlying inalienable right of conscience as required by the argument for toleration and the theory of structural injustice. Since some abolitionists believed such criticism extended not to just conventional slavery but to the moral slavery they associated with both racism and sexism,[5] the scope of protection of the principle of free speech must include all such conscientious criticism. Secondly, the grounds for abridgement of the scope of the principle of free speech could not, either directly or indirectly, legitimate conventional populist distaste for hearing such fundamental criticism of American institutions and practices. Such criticism was, of course, subversive of dominant cultural, political, and constitutional understandings; indeed, such subversive critical advocacy was its normative point, calling the conscience of the nation to account for its failure to respect, on terms of principle, more fundamental constitutionally guaranteed protections of the inalienable human rights of all persons. The abolitionist challenge was so incendiary because it appealed to the fundamental principles of American revolutionary constitutionalism that, following Locke, demanded political and constitutional respect for

---

[5] See, for further development of this argument, David A. J. Richards, *Women, Gays, and the Constitution: The Grounds for Feminism and Gay Rights in Culture and Law* (University of Chicago Press, Chicago, Ill., 1998).

universal human rights as the condition for legitimate government; violation of such fundamental human rights, if egregious and otherwise without remedy, would justify the right to revolution (as it did for the American revolutionaries of 1776 and would again in the ultimate Union justification for the Civil War[6]). The criticism of American slavery (let alone of moral slavery) aroused such repressive populist hostility because it exposed to public thought and debate serious issues that questioned the very legitimacy of popular understandings of American constitutionalism, including the Lockean moral rights of enslaved African-Americans to revolt against the terms of their slavery.

The antebellum populist appeal of such repression of public discussion of issues of slavery and its rightness was anatomized in such terms by Abraham Lincoln as what made Stephen Douglas's politics of popular sovereignty so unacceptable:

> But where is the philosophy or statesmanship which assumes that you can quiet the disturbing element in our society which has disturbed us for more than half a century, which has been the only serious danger that has threatened our institutions—I say, where is the philosophy or statesmanship based on the assumption that we are to quit talking about it, and that the public mind is all at once to cease being agitated by it . . . I ask you if it is not a false philosophy? Is it not a false statesmanship that undertakes to build up a system or policy upon the basis of caring nothing about *the very thing that every body does care the most about?*—a thing which all experience has shown we care a very great deal about?[7]

A public consensus, based on repression of discussion of the issues of constitutional justice (the protection of basic human rights) most worth discussing, was not, Lincoln argued, a 'philosophy or statesmanship' worthy of American revolutionary constitutionalism. As Lincoln elsewhere elaborated his point of rights-based constitutional morality against Douglas:

> Judge Douglas is going back to the era of our Revolution, and to the extent of his ability, muzzling the cannon which thunders its annual joyous return. When he invites any people, willing to have slavery, to establish it, he is blowing out the moral lights around us. When he says he 'cares not whether slavery is voted down or voted up'—that it is a sacred right of self-government—he is, in my judgment, penetrating the human soul and eradicating the light of reason and the love of liberty in this American people.[8]

Many antebellum abolitionists (especially the most radical such advocates like Garrison) were, of course, anxious to deny that their advocacy supported violent exercise of the right to revolt. But, the combination of Garrisonian radical moral criticism (including both anti-racism and anti-sexism) with pacifism[9] was hardly convincing to all abolitionists, let alone to their critics. But even against such worries about legitimating slave revolts and the like, abolitionist demands for an expansive protection of

---

[6] See, on this point, Richards, *Conscience and the Constitution*, n. 2 above.

[7] Abraham Lincoln, in Robert W. Johannsen (ed.), *The Lincoln–Douglas Debates* (Oxford University Press, New York, 1965), at 315.

[8] See *ibid.*, 67.

[9] See, on this point, Richards, *Conscience and the Constitution*, n. 2 above, 91–2.

speech refused to accept the legitimacy of abridging free speech on grounds of public distaste for their fundamentally subversive, even revolutionary, character. Rather, from the perspective of the argument for toleration (fundamental to abolitionist theory and practice[10]), such grounds were illegitimately sectarian attempts to truncate human rights to the measure of the dominant political orthodoxy, not exposing the orthodoxy to reasonable assessment in terms of the values of basic human rights fundamental to the demands of political legitimacy of American revolutionary constitutionalism.

Such abolitionist understanding of the principle of free speech, once so politically marginal, even eccentric, is today the measure of judicially enforceable constitutional principles of free speech in part because its terms of principle (in both its dimensions) have played an indispensable role in the progressive remedy of forms of structural injustice now condemned by constitutional principles.[11] African-American criticism of the depth and extent of American racism, for example, was thus energized by an aggressive and expansive use of free speech, increasingly protected by the American judiciary, in the criticism of the cultural entrenchment of this form of structural injustice, including criticism of interpretively mistaken opinions of the Supreme Court of the United States (Chapter 3). Current judicial protection both of subversive advocacy and group libel, as protected speech, are important and defensible features of this development (Chapter 2). The grounds for protection of subversive advocacy should now be obvious: conscientious criticism of basic American institutions (including its constitutionalism), as fundamentally wrong (indeed worthy of revolt), is exactly the criticism most needed to expose the otherwise unspoken rights-based issues of conscience that most require discussion under a constitutionalism committed to the protection of universal human rights as a requirement of politically legitimate government. The point is not that such claims are always right, but that they expose to public discussion and debate conscientious convictions about those issues (for example, about structural injustice) which raise that most fundamental question of constitutionally legitimate government. It is exactly because majoritarian conventional democratic politics does not adequately raise such fundamental issues of conscience that the argument from democracy so poorly captures the grounds for the American principle of free speech as we understand and honour it today.

The right of free speech plays the role it did and continues to do in the struggles against structural injustice earlier discussed (Chapter 3) because the right was understood and claimed often in rights-based criticism of what counted as legitimate majoritarian politics. In particular, for groups on whom structural injustice has been inflicted, claims based on the right of free speech in both its dimensions empowered protest of the terms of their moral slavery. In the terms of the analysis of such protests earlier developed (Chapter 3), such protests to the unjust terms imposed on personal

---

[10] See Richards, *Conscience and the Constitution*, n. 2 above, 91–2, ch.3.
[11] See, in general, Richards, *Women, Gays, and the Constitution*, n. 5 above.

and ethical identity transformed identity, both demanding self-respecting recognition of one's status as bearers of human rights and debunking the dehumanizing stereotypes unjustly imposed on identity. The criticism of such stereotypes, as we have seen, questions the deep cultural assumptions in terms of which such stereotypes have been uncritically framed. Such assumptions importantly include both the ways in which groups are sexualized and the ways in which issues of structural injustice are rendered invisible by their privatization into the very terms of private (as opposed to public) life. The ethical protest of such assumptions must, in its nature, be addressed to culture broadly understood, much of which traditionally remains outside the conventional understanding of politics. Indeed, the identity-transforming character of such protest often self-consciously rejects ordinary politics, as Garrisonian abolitionists did in the antebellum period,[12] because its aims are personal and ethical in a way in which politics often is not. Both the argument for toleration and the theory of structural injustice,[13] in terms of which such abolitionists understood and advanced their purposes, thus addressed the ways in which entrenched injustice corrupted conscience itself, disabling otherwise good people from recognizing, let alone addressing, the rights-denying evils of structural injustice. Such protest addresses, in its nature, the public mind of its culture, as reflected in all its dimensions—the arts and literature (high and low), science (hard and soft), religion (mainstream and marginal), love and family life (conventional and unconventional), work (public and private), and the like. It questions the ways in which all these dimensions have been unjustly complicitous with the construction of structural injustice, and often innovates new cultural forms that recognize and address such injustice. In particular, the identity-transforming protest of the terms of one's moral slavery thus often takes the form of the construction of new imaginative spaces (as in the Harlem renaissance[14]) through which the ravages of such injustice may be made visible and challenged. I call the manifold forms of such ethical protest the politics of identity because such rights-based protest of the terms of one's moral slavery precisely makes a public and highly controversial issue of what had previously been invisible, unspoken, and, sometimes, unspeakable. Such politics of identity must, in the nature of its claims, address and often eventually impact on politics as conventionally understood, but both its claims and its criticisms are altogether more culturally profound and pervasive, altering the very terms of private as well as public life.

The muscular contemporary American judicial understanding of the right of free speech in both its dimensions crucially arises from its protection of such politics of identity. This understanding properly includes not only the inclusion of subversive advocacy in the scope of protected speech (for reasons already examined), but group

---

[12] See Richards, *Conscience and the Constitution*, n. 2 above, 91–5.
[13] See, for fuller exploration of these points, *ibid.*, ch. 3; Richards, *Women, Gays, and the Constitution*, n. 5 above, chs. 2–3.
[14] See, for an important recent study, George Hutchinson, *The Harlem Renaissance in Black and White* (Belknap Press of Harvard University Press, Cambridge, Mass., 1995).

libel as well.[15] Such laws make it a criminal and/or civil wrong to engage in defamation of racial, ethnic, or religious groups. Such laws require a demonstration that claims made about certain groups subject its members to a false disparagement of social esteem like the harm inflicted on a person by a libel of him as an individual. Persons do, of course, often associate their self-esteem with groups with which they identify, and thus experience injury to such esteem when the group is denigrated.[16] But, the legal protection of this interest by group libel laws, on the analogy with individual libel, is defective in ways of the gravest constitutional concern. Individual libel actions have two distinctive features: they require the publication of false facts, often known to be false, and thus not expressive of conviction; and belief in such false facts by the audience disparages the reputation of the individual expressly written or spoken about. But the communications, restricted by group libel, express general conscientious views of speakers and audiences, whose nature and effect both depend on evaluative conceptions. Group libel actions, in contrast to individual libel actions, require the state to make abstract evaluative judgements about the value of what is said and about the legitimacy of the objection taken to the assertions. These state judgements about the nature and effect of communicative utterances place group libel laws at the heart of the values of free speech. In effect, a broad range of personal grievances at hearing conscientious views opposed to one's own (and rebuttable as such) triggers state prohibitions. Inevitably, such laws impose state restrictions in the core area of evaluative conceptions appealing to the moral powers of speakers and audiences on the basis of state judgements of the worth of such conceptions, thus usurping the sovereign moral judgement of the people.[17]

Such state usurpation of moral judgement is not of less but of more concern from the perspective of the legitimate role of free speech in the ethical empowerment of the politics of identity. Group libel laws thus rest on enforceable state judgements of group harm in the domain of conviction, judgements that interpret what can and should count as the stereotypical harms inflicted by structural injustice. Persons are,

---

[15] Despite earlier views to the contrary (*Beauharnais* v. *Illinois*, 343 US 250 [1952]), cases such as *Brandenburg* v. *Ohio*, 395 US 444 (1969), which strike down subversive advocacy statutes applied to speech fomenting racial and religious hatred and bigotry, suggest that group libel statutes directed against the expression of false racial or religious stereotypes, as such, would be similarly unconstitutional. See also *Collin* v. *Smith*, 578 F 2d 1197 (1978), cert.den., 439 US 916 (1978), holding unconstitutional the attempts of Skokie, Illinois, a heavily Jewish community, to stop a pending march of the Nazi party at Skokie; *R.A.V.* v. *City of St. Paul*, 505 US 377 (1992), holding unconstitutional a city ordinance condemning placing on public or private property a symbol that arouses anger on the basis of race, colour, creed, religion, or gender, here applied to a cross-burning on a black family's lawn.

[16] For a classic statement and defence of this interest as worthy of legal protection, see David Riesman, 'Democracy and Defamation: Control of Group Libel', 42 *Colum. L Rev.* 727 (1942); 'Democracy and Defamation: Fair Game and Fair Comment I', 42 *Colum. L Rev.* 1085 (1942); 'Democracy and Defamation: Fair Game and Fair Comment II', 42 *Colum. L Rev.* 1282 (1942). For a more recent defence, urging largely informal dispute remedies as the best solution, see Richard L. Abel, *Speaking Respect Respecting Speech* (University of Chicago Press, Chicago, Ill., 1998).

[17] For my earlier criticism of these laws, see David A. J. Richards, *Toleration and the Constitution* (Oxford University Press, New York, 1986), 190–3; for a similar criticism, see Henry Kalven, Jr., *The Negro and the First Amendment* (University of Chicago Press, Chicago, Ill., 1965), 7–64.

on grounds of moral paternalism, protected from such alleged harms, but the alleged protection does not reasonably address or contest the role unjust stereotypes in fact play in the support of structural injustice. Rather, such majoritarian judgements of group harm, enforced through law in the domain of speech, mandate a kind of ortho-doxy of appropriate tribalization in the terms of public discourse. Public claims allegedly disrespectful of groups are subject to state prohibition. But this empowers the state to determine not only what discourse is properly respectful and what not, but what groups are entitled to such protection and what are not. But such state-enforced judgements introduce stereotypical political orthodoxies as the measure of human identity, thus removing from public discourse precisely the contest of such stereotypical boundaries that a free people often most reasonably requires, in partic-ular, the persons afflicted by a pervasive culture of structural injustice. The identity of no moral person (including the persons afflicted by this injustice) can be exhaus-tively defined by their ethnicity or race or gender or sexual preference or any of the other terms of common group identification familiar today, some of which we con-demn as grounded in injustice. Such protest of injustice targets the social force such group identifications often have today because they unreasonably diminish both the range of diversity and individuality that exist within such groups and the similarities between members of such groups and the groups with which they are contrasted. To enforce such identifications through law in the domain of conscience, on the osten-sible ground of protecting groups from unjust insult, defeats its aim: in attempting to protect groups from unjust insult, it enforces and does not deconstruct the under-lying injustice; for, it disempowers the voices and claims of those subject to unjust subordination in the exercise of reasonable discourse that best challenges the dehu-manizing stereotypes that support structural injustice. Such state censorship of a range of discourse (alleged to inflict group harms) stifles the empowering protests of individuals to that discourse through which they express, demand, and define their individuality as persons against such stereotypical classifications.[18]

Such protest in one's own voice of the terms of one's dehumanized moral slavery is as epistemologically important for members of the subordinated group as it is for the larger society, for it is hearing one's own voice in such protest, on the basis of the principle of free speech, that enables one to hear one's self as a moral person, not as a stereotype. From this perspective, it is precisely the groups that the state may regard itself as most reasonably protecting from group libel (the most historically stigmatized groups, like people of colour in the United States, or Jews in Europe, or women and gays and lesbians everywhere) that should, as a matter of free speech principle, most reasonably be constitutionally immunized from such allegedly protective state power.

---

[18] On the important strand of American free speech thought emphasizing expressive authenticity, see Steven H. Shiffrin, *The First Amendment, Democracy, and Romance* (Harvard University Press, Cambridge, Mass., 1990). Unfortunately, Shiffrin wrongly isolates this romantic Emersonian strand of thought from the neo-Kantian theorists, like myself, who find in American neo-abolitionist transcendentalism a clear and enduring strand of Kantian thought, argument, and practice. See Richards, *Conscience and the Constitution*, n. 2 above.

Ralph Ellison's *Invisible Man* pleaded for racial justice in America in these eloquent terms: '[o]ur task is that of making ourselves individuals. The conscience of a race is the gift of its individuals.'[19] If the struggle against the stereotypical indignities of racism (or anti-Semitism or sexism or homophobia) is essentially a struggle for individuality, free speech rightly requires that the terms of emancipation must be the empowering responsibility of individuals, including the voluntary organizations through which they define themselves and their struggle. Otherwise, ethical protest degenerates into a tribalism that may uncritically, in the name of rectifying one prejudice (racism), inflict another (anti-Semitism).[20] What groups ostensibly gain by such laws in esteem, they lose in further entrenching the terms of the structural injustice that afflicts them.

The politics of identity arises from ethically transformative protest of the terms of one's moral slavery. It is the very making of such rights-based claims, in one's own voice, that challenges one's dehumanization as not a bearer of human rights, making space for the free exercise of one's moral powers in the reasonable criticism of such structural injustice. Only a principle of free speech, which insists on equal treatment of all conscientious convictions, ensures both the legitimacy and the integrity of such politics of identity in the understanding and remedy of structural injustice.

On the one hand, in terms of legitimacy, it alone assures all contestants to these debates the normatively required respect for each and every person's right to conscience, which is inalienable in the sense that it is each person's responsibility (not to be surrendered to any other person, let alone to the state); such equality in the domain of conscience, particularly in areas of ongoing controversy and debate over basic questions of justice, expresses the standpoint of public reason that aspires, to the extent feasible, to legitimate political power (including criticisms and reforms thereof) in terms that can be reasonably justified to all, as free and equal persons and citizens.[21] A history and culture of structural injustice, of the sort that I earlier called moral slavery (Chapter 3), depends for its power on an often deeply popular consensus (rooted in longstanding traditions) that has unreasonably rendered certain persons and claims invisible and unspeakable (abridging their right to conscience). Reasonably to subject such pervasive cultural patterns to criticism, as structural unjust, requires, as an internal condition of the democratic legitimacy of its claims (based on the inalienable right to conscience), that all persons be addressed in the terms of equal respect in the domain of conviction, namely, as persons to be persuaded. Otherwise, the politics of identity abandons the standpoint which not only gives legitimacy to its claims, but addresses those who fundamentally disagree on the terms of equal respect that they

[19] Ralph Ellison, *Invisible Man* (Vintage, New York, 1989), at 354.
[20] For a recent claim along these lines, see Daniel A. Farber and Suzanna Sherry, *Beyond All Reason: The Radical Assault on Truth in American Law* (Oxford University Press, New York, 1997), at 57–9, 80–4, 103–5.
[21] See, for development of this contractualist theme, Richards, *Toleration and the Constitution*, n. 17 above.

can accept or come to accept as treating them reasonably and thus inviting reasonable reconsideration of their views on such grounds.

On the other hand, from the perspective of integrity, such egalitarian responsibility empowers the reasonable demands and criticisms of the politics of identity from a more demanding critical standpoint morally independent of the state; such moral independence affords a public standpoint of impartiality that promotes more reasonable public discussion and debate, on terms of principle, of the dehumanizing stereotypes that unjustly rationalize the cultural entrenchment of structural injustice; it better ensures, even (as I have argued) from the standpoint of those subjected to such stereotypes, that those stereotypes are more reasonably contested as the insult to individuality that they are. Such stereotypes of race or gender or gendered sexuality naturalize injustice in complex cultural constructions that often mask the fact of their unjust cultural construction. We need more, not less, open and robust discussion and debate about such cultural constructions. The kind of state power invoked by group libel laws, precisely because it claims a transparent understanding of what counts as a group harm in the domain of conscience, unreasonably censors such debate when it is most needed. The state (so complicitous with the construction of structural injustice) has no such transparent understanding in this domain that it can legitimately claim. Only the most robust and free discussion of these issues can reasonably confront us with the cultural depth and complexity of structural injustice, implicating, as we have seen (Chapter 3), not only abridgements of the right to conscience and speech but the rights to intimate life and work as well through the enforcement of dehumanizing stereotypes of unjust sexualization that often privatize such injustice. It is, as earlier noted, an important cultural fact about the entrenchment of such structural injustice that its political force has been traditionally unspoken and even unspeakable. The American principle of free speech has played the role it has in the understanding and remedy of such entrenchment by insisting on both the right and responsibility of protesting voice as alone adequate reasonably to break the silence that entrenches structural injustice.

I earlier argued for the truth of the dependence thesis in the sense that structural injustice depends on abridgement of the right to free speech; we may now extend the thesis to include as well both the understanding and remedy of structural injustice. The observance of the principle of free speech, in the terms I have defended it, does not retard the remedy of structural injustice; it is, rather, the term of principle that guarantees both the legitimacy and integrity of the politics of identity so important to advancing the understanding and remedy of structural injustice.

These concerns for the legitimacy and integrity of the politics of identity may be most vivid for a pluralistic, largely immigrant culture like that of the United States in which the structural injustice of American cultural racism has played so prominent a role. Generations of Americans have recurrently had to endure the ordeal of Americanization, encountering nativist prejudice against their ethnic group and determining how, if at all, their identity as Americans would interact with their identity as African-Americans or as immigrants from Italy or Eastern Europe, and the like.

In particular, the terms of Americanization often included requirements of complicity by new immigrants with the terms of American racism. As Rogers M. Smith has recently made clear in his magisterial study of this question,[22] American constitutional culture has throughout its history had two conflicting strands: first, principles of liberal nationalism that, in principle, extend basic human rights to all persons consistent with the argument for toleration, and secondly, patterns of structural injustice (racism, sexism, and homophobia) that structure national identity in terms of such injustice. As Smith painfully shows, liberal principles have not progressively been in the ascendant, but liberal progress (the Civil War and Reconstruction Amendments) followed by perhaps the most reactionary period of political racism in our history, including during the so-called Progressive Era.[23] Americans concealed these ugly facts from ourselves by the naturalization of structural injustice, the claim that such injustice is not something for which they have any moral responsibility but rather is differential treatment rooted in nature. To challenge such naturalization of injustice was to question nothing less than national honour. For this reason, the terms of Americanization of new immigrants patriotically precluded any such challenge.[24]

If I am right about this, any form of structural injustice will be most threatening when its terms are most conspicuously likely to challenge such naturalization of injustice. The victims of racism that I call (in the terms introduced in Chapter 2) nonvisibly black (for example, Italian immigrants from Southern and Jewish immigrants from Eastern Europe during the period 1880–1920) raised this issue acutely, particularly when they came from European cultures that were, in the way of thinking typical of late nineteenth-century Americans, at least not obviously inferior to American culture. Their subordination did not rest on the usual obvious natural fact (skin colour) taken to be an apodictic marker of subordination, but rather on cultural differences (including more tolerant religious and racial attitudes) that conflicted with dominant American views. The very existence of such groups in America, at least if conceived as equals of other groups, thus reasonably raised the question which the naturalization of injustice requires not to be raised, namely, the cultural entrenchment of structural injustice. What was thus obvious to Henry James about the cultural processes that had transformed Southern Italians into Italian-Americans threatened the whole structure of American racism:[25] if this were true about Italian-Americans (or Jews), it might be true of 'the Negro and the Chinaman'[26] as well; and Americans would have to face moral responsibilities that their uncritical racism, as the

---

[22] See, in general, Rogers M. Smith, *Civic Ideals: Conflicting Visions of Citizenship in US History* (Yale University Press, New Haven, Conn., 1997).

[23] See *ibid.*, 347–469.

[24] For fuller discussion of this and related points, see David A. J. Richards, *Italian American: The Racializing of an Ethnic Identity* (New York University Press, New York, 1999).

[25] For James's comments on this point, see Henry James, *Collected Travel Writings: Great Britain and America* (Library of America, New York, 1993), 'The American Scene', 353–736, especially at 432–63; for commentary, see David A. J. Richards, *Italian American: The Racializing of an Ethnic Identity* (New York University Press, New York, 1999), at 181–3.

[26] See Henry James, n. 25 above, at 462.

Southern Italian philosopher Benedetto Croce had acutely observed about Italian racism,[27] enabled them to avoid (supposing that what was, in fact, complicity with cultural injustice was required by nature). Such groups, whose very existence as equals challenged the legitimacy of American racism, *must* thus be degraded as racist inferiors unworthy of attention, and their Americanization required that they be '100 per cent Americanized',[28] in effect, suppressing any suggestion of the equal dignity, let alone political value of their cultural traditions.

Structural injustice arises, as we have seen, pivotally from the abridgment of basic human rights of conscience and speech, which limit speakers and speech to the terms compatible with the underlying injustice. The non-visibly black class of victims of racism might, by protest of the structural injustice, conspicuously make clear its cultural character, reasonably debunking in their own voice the unjust cultural stereotypes that had naturalized injustice. To avoid such a devastating ideological threat to the sense of American nationalism, racist pressure was unjustly imposed on them uncritically to accept the flawed terms of American nationalism, and certainly not to protest it; both the political repression of any suggestion of dissent (drawing on alternative cultural traditions) and the crusade of Americanization made this quite repressively clear to the new immigrants. Such a Faustian bargain was perhaps particularly easy to accept in a historical period when the unjust construction of American racism was so little publicly understood, let alone discussed. Dominant American views might thus easily be accepted particularly when such attitudes allowed a non-visibly black group at least to experience uncritically some sense of racial privilege over the visibly black,[29] a form of what Du Bois called a 'public and psychological wage'.[30] This sense of privilege was even supported by ostensible legal doctrines about who could count as 'white' for purposes of naturalization (Italians were white for this purpose although not, after 1924, for purposes of immigration).[31] The price, however, for such privilege over blacks was often accepting a range of opportunities on discriminatory terms, including, as we have seen, forgoing exercise of basic rights of conscience and speech. As Frederick Douglass had earlier put the same point about the Irish:

Every hour sees us elbowed out of some employment to make room for some newly-arrived emigrant from the Emerald Isle, whose hunger and color entitle him to special favour. These white men are becoming houseservants, cooks, stewards, waiters, and flunkies. For aught I see

[27] See for citations and discussion, Richards, n. 25 above, 107–9.

[28] See John Higham, *Strangers in the Land: Patterns of American Nativism 1860–1925* (Rutgers University Press, New Brunswick, NJ, 1988), at 242.

[29] See, on this point, Ann Douglas, *Terrible Honesty: Mongrel Manhattan in the 1920s* (Farrar, Straus and Giroux, New York, 1995), 303–9; see, on the importance of racial privilege in the construction of American racism, Barbara J. Flagg, *Was Blind But Now I See: White Race Consciousness and the Law* (New York University Press, New York, 1998).

[30] See W. E. B. Du Bois, *Black Reconstruction in America 1860–1880* (Atheneum, New York, 1962) (originally published, 1934), at 700. For illuminating development of this analysis, see David R. Roediger, *The Wages of Whiteness: Race and the Making of the American Working Class* (Verso, New York, 1991).

[31] See, for illuminating discussion of this body of law, Ian F. Haney Lopez, *White By Law: The Legal Construction of Race* (New York University Press, New York, 1996), especially 104–6.

they adjust themselves to their stations with all proper humility. If they cannot rise to the dignity of white men, they show that they can fall to the degradation of black men . . . In assuming our avocation, [the Irishman] has also assumed our degradation.[32]

Sometimes, such complicity even took the form, as in the performance of Irish immigrants as blackface minstrel entertainers, of affirming a common whiteness, even during periods of anti-immigrant hysteria, on the basis of indulging racist stereotypes of African-Americans.[33] In general, we may understand the unjust terms of the Americanization of immigrants to include such patterns of complicity with and accommodation to American racism. The minstrel phenomenon (white skins wearing black masks) exemplifies a more general dynamic of such acculturation: white skins wearing masks (concealing and suppressing multicultural identity) to affirm, rather than challenge, the unjust privilege of whiteness under American cultural racism.

Americans, whatever their ethnicity or race or gender or sexual preference, reasonably strive to be individuals, but individuals enriched by the cultural depth of their diverse heritages or the struggle reasonably to reinterpret constructively their heritages against the background of growing understanding of the impact of American structural injustice on their sense of identity (as reflected, for example, not only in ethnic studies but the development of women's and gay studies[34]). The American principle of free speech, as I have defended it here, affords the reasonable terms in which many Americans, including those who are not people of colour, increasingly break the traditional silence imposed on their Americanized sense of ethnic identity to give voice to reasonable discourse on the importance of retaining and rediscovering a sense of multicultural identity on terms of justice as a way of subjecting American nationality to more fundamental criticism for its entrenched patterns of structural injustice.[35] It is precisely because the American principle of free speech debars a state role in the domain of conviction about these issues that such voices and claims responsibly engage in such fundamental criticism of the traditional understanding of American identity. This development further supports the reasons of con-

[32] Quoted in Noel Ignatiev, *How the Irish Became White* (Routledge, New York, 1995), at 111.

[33] See, for probing commentary on this phenomenon of white skins and black masks, David R. Roediger, *The Wages of Whiteness: Race and the Making of the American Working Class* (Verso, London, 1991), 116–27. On the comparable phenomenon of black skins and white masks, see Frantz Fanon, *Black Skin, White Masks* (trans. Charles Lam Markmann, Grove Weidenfeld, New York, 1967).

[34] See, in general, Richards, n. 5 above. For an important development in the genre of gay studies, see Jonathan Dollimore, *Sexual Dissidence: Augustine to Wilde, Freud to Foucault* (Clarendon Press, Oxford, 1991).

[35] See, for recent studies along these lines, Karen Brodkin, *How Jews Became White Folks and What That Says about Race in America* (Rutgers University Press, New Brunswick, NJ, 1998); Matthew Frye Jacobson, *Whiteness of a Different Color: European Immigrants and the Alchemy of Race* (Harvard University Press, Cambridge, Mass., 1998); Maurice Berger, *White Lies: Race and the Myths of Whiteness* (Farrar, Straus, Giroux, New York, 1999); Marianna de Marco Torgovnick, *Crossing Ocean Parkway* (University of Chicago Press, Chicago, Ill., 1996); Richards, n. 25 above. For important related studies, see Richard Dyer, *White* (Routledge, London, 1997); Toni Morrison, *Playing in the Dark: Whiteness and the Literary Imagination* (Vintage Books New York, 1993); Richard Delgado and Jean Stefancic, *Critical White Studies: Looking Behind the Mirror* (Temple University Press, Philadelphia, Penn., 1997).

stitutional principle that require both subversive advocacy and group libel laws to be alike condemned as violations of the principle of free speech: such laws stifle precisely the politics of identity that reasonably raises the most fundamental questions of the degree to which American institutions entrench structural injustice. American experience shows how the principle of free speech, thus understood, supports a diverse and robust public culture, affording Americans the freedom and rationality critically to reflect on the values and disvalues of their American and their ethnic and other identities and to weave together a sufficiently complex tapestry adequate to express the authentic moral identity of a free person. This is not the American bleached WASP, but the critically self-conscious multicultural American who weds convictions of universal human rights to the cultural and human depth such rights, properly understood, make possible.

The principle of free speech plays the role it has and does in a reasonable politics of identity because of the normative links of its principle to the underlying inalienable right to conscience as articulated by the argument for toleration and the theory of structural injustice. The cultural entrenchment of structural injustice crucially turns on both the abridgement of the basic human right of conscience of a class of persons and the irrationalist stereotypes that rationalize such abridgement. The politics of identity, grounded in the right to free speech commensurate with the underlying right to conscience, addresses both wrongs: it demands the right and responsibility of protest, and it thus reasonably criticizes the uncritical force dehumanizing stereotypes have been unjustly allowed to enjoy. On the grounds of such protest, further remedies for structural injustice are, of course, reasonable. Nothing in the argument proposed here debars such remedies in any way; indeed, the role for free speech in the politics of identity, here defended, clarifies both how and why such remedies should be pursued.

It is an important feature of the way in which my account links together the theories of toleration and of structural injustice that it takes seriously the ways in which pervasive patterns of structural injustice have been entrenched by abridgement of basic human rights that were and are ostensibly constitutionally guaranteed to all persons. Such entrenchment thus required, for its rationalization, the massive suppression of the voices and claims that most reasonably would challenge its injustice, in particular, the voices and claims of those subordinated by dehumanizing stereotypes of race or gender or sexualized gender. Constitutional protection of the basic rights of voice of such groups, on terms of the principle of free speech here defended, has brought into reasonable public discourse and subjected to criticism institutional patterns (for example, segregation and anti-miscegenation laws) that unjustly enforced such stereotypes. Importantly, such voices and claims (for example, Harriet Jacobs on the dehumanization of women of colour under slavery[36] or Richard Wright on the Southern racist culture of terror and humiliation after slavery[37]) humanized the

---

[36] See Harriet A. Jacobs, *Incidents in the Life of a Slave Girl Written by Herself* (ed. Jean Fagan Yellin, Harvard University Press, Cambridge, Mass., 1987).
[37] See Richard Wright, *Black Boy* (Perennial Classics, New York, 1998).

experience of subordination under structural injustice, both by breaking the silence imposed by crude racist stereotypes and suggesting the extent and depth of the cultural and political problem of structural injustice that confronted Americans. Such discourse is the discovery procedure for the understanding and remedy of structural injustice, a discovery, as I have insisted, as epistemologically important and ethically empowering for members of subordinated groups as it is for the larger society; and it is part of the discovery that one take seriously the reactionary forces that seek to limit or cabin both understanding and remedy of the underlying problem (including strategies of using one subjugated group to scapegoat another). If the roots of structural injustice are as interconnected and mutually supporting as they appear to be (see Chapter 3), one cannot do justice to one manifestation of structural injustice without attempting to do justice to all. If, for example, unjust gender stereotypes play a crucial role in enforcing both unjust stereotypes both of race and of sexual orientation (see Chapter 3), we need more, not fewer, dissenting voices and claims to enlarge our responsible sense of both the understanding and remedy of structural injustice. We need not the enforcement in the domain of conviction of slogans condemning group libel, which claim a transparent and secure understanding that the state usually conspicuously lacks, but the conditions of free speech, as I have defended them, that responsibly confront us with the voices and claims that make clearer to us how far we have yet to go in both the understanding and remedy of structural injustice.

Such points may seem obvious, but they have not been to the recent American scholars who have urged rethinking the unconstitutionality of group libel laws in order better to combat structural injustice. Such scholars believe that such laws not only better combat racism and related evils, but suggest that defence of such laws must itself exemplify a refusal to take seriously reasonable remedies for structural injustice;[38] one formulation of this objection even claims that, if group libel laws are constitutionally suspect, so too must be judicial decisions and laws that strike down racial segregation and anti-miscegenation laws and other forms of racial discrimination.[39] Each claim requires careful examination.

The first claim is asserted axiomatically: group libel laws *must* remedy structural injustice in virtue of the content of group libels expressing, for example, racial or religious hatred. The axiomatic force of the claim dissolves, however, on analysis. First, the claim assumes a competence in the state to identify transparently what counts as such a libel in the domain of conscience, which is, as I have argued, undefended and quite indefensible. Secondly, it assumes, from an already controversial claim about what counts as group libel, that such claims, as claims, inflict harm. But this assumption conflates two questions that the principle of free speech, rooted in the inalienable right to conscience, correctly separates, namely, the content of conscientious conviction and inflicting secular harms on persons. Jefferson, in his defence of

---

[38] See, for a compendium of such views, Mari J. Matsuda *et al.*, *Words That Wound: Critical Race Theory, Assaultive Speech, and the First Amendment* (Westview Press, Boulder, Colo., 1993).

[39] See Charles R. Lawrence III, 'If He Hollers Let Him Go: Regulating Racist Speech on Campus', *ibid.*, at 53–88.

religious liberty of conscience, marked the same distinction, observing, as we earlier
saw (Chapter 2), 'it is time enough for the rightful purposes of civil government for
its officers to interfere when principles break out into overt acts against peace and
good order'; the normal means for rebuttal of noxious belief, consistent with respect
for the right of conscience, is 'free argument and debate'.[40] As he wrote elsewhere: 'it
does me no injury for my neighbor to say there are twenty gods, or no god. It neither
picks my pocket nor breaks my leg.'[41] The contemporary American law of free speech
(rooted in liberty of conscience and the argument for toleration, see Chapter 2)
defensibly uses the same distinction (conviction versus action) to mark the scope and
limits of protection of free speech.

The distinction does not rest on the false supposition, sometimes ascribed to
defenders of the American principle of free speech by its critics,[42] that speech in the
domain of action never harms whereas action may and does harm. But, it does defensibly rest on the kinds of harms, or frustration of interests, that speech in the domain
of conviction as opposed to actions inflicts. Speech in the domain of conviction, as I
have defined it (Chapter 2), expresses and communicates general evaluative views to
which, in some cases, members of the audience take offence, rooted in frustration of
(and thus harm to) interests we have in groups or ideas being treated with respect.
The kinds of harms to which such expressions sometimes give rise are, however, in
two respects normatively different from the harms inflicted by action (for example,
Jefferson's examples of harms to property (pickpocketing) and personal injury (breaking one's leg)). First, such harms (their disrespectful character) inhere in the exercise
of the inalienable right to conscience itself, and cannot, consistent with respect for its
exercise (including the moral powers exercised in the politics of identity), be a ground
for its abridgement; rather, to the extent that we regard conscience as properly a basic
human right that is constitutionally protected, we reasonably want its exercise to be
not subject to intimidation or otherwise chilled but freely expressive of one's convictions, whatever they are. In contrast, state action, in protection of general goods like
life and property, abridges neither conscience nor any other basic right, but reasonably protects a basic right on terms of justice. Secondly, the harms in hearing speech
in the domain of conviction inhere in the audience's evaluative responses to the
speech, and, for this reason, responsive arguments of conviction by the audience can,
in principle, meet and defeat its claims, and thus expunge its harm in terms that are
consistent with equal respect for the right of conscience of all persons. In contrast, the
harms from unjust theft or injury are harms to interests (in property and bodily security), on which the state may reasonably act without implicating any such normative
concerns.

---

[40] Julian P. Boyd (ed.), *The Papers of Thomas Jefferson, 1777–1779* (Princeton University Press,
Princeton, NJ, 1950), ii, 546.
[41] Thomas Jefferson, *Notes on the State of Virginia* (ed. William Peden, University of North Carolina
Press, Chapel Hill, NC, 1955).
[42] For a form of this criticism, see Stanley Fish, *There's No Such Thing as Free Speech and It's a Good
Thing, Too* (Oxford University Press, New York, 1994), 102–33.

The state may and should, on this view, act to prevent the infliction of secular harms from action, but the principle of free speech demands scepticism about state judgements about harms inhering in convictions and speech expressing such convictions unless and until there is a clear and present danger of such secular harms. As I have elsewhere observed,[43] persons are not propositions or the propositions they believe; and it is a vicious political fallacy to assume that our contempt for false evaluative convictions may justly be applied to contempt for the persons who conscientiously hold and express such views. Such persons are not, as if by definition, outside the civilizing community of humane discourse. There is legitimate political power to deal with those who move beyond conviction to overt acts which threaten the rights of others. Not all those who entertain such convictions do so, and many lacking such convictions will threaten such acts. The principle of free speech insists that the mere offence taken at convictions cannot be the measure of a clear and present danger sufficient to justify the abridgement of speech.

The highly demanding American requirements for satisfaction of the 'clear and present danger' test, namely, the danger of some imminent, non-rebuttable, and very grave secular harm,[44] make sense, as a matter of basic constitutional principle, as a way of ensuring that mere offence, without more, cannot be an acceptable ground for state abridgement of advocacy of conscientious claims in public contexts clearly consistent with the purposes of free speech. The hostility of an audience to conscientious claims made in such contexts cannot, consistently with this principle, justify abridgement of the right of the speaker; rather, the constitutional burden should be placed on the state to protect speakers from hostile audiences, rather than to protect audiences from offensive speech.[45] Not all contexts are, of course, consistent with the purposes of free speech; for example, some forms of *ad hominem* harassment fall outside the principle of free speech, involving, as they do, coercively assaultive personal threats that are addressed in a face-to-face manner and addressed to an individual unable to avoid the assaultive message; such verbal assaults of violence are, in their nature, imminent, non-rebuttable, and intrinsically harmful to rights of personal security. Such coercive threats are not within the scope of the principle of free speech concerned to protect the free exercise of disagreement in convictions, not assaultive targeted threats to personal security and tranquillity.[46] Consistently with this principle, it does not follow from the fact that a person is offended by a general remark made by another in a public forum that such offence can, in itself, suffice for the abridgement of speech in the domain of conviction.

Nothing in this argument supports the view that persons thus offended are, as it were, constitutionally compelled to take these views as true or valid or defensible. On

---

[43] See Richards, n. 17 above, 192.   [44] See, on this point, *ibid.*, 178–87.

[45] For a striking example of the contrasting treatment of otherwise similar factual contexts, with *Edwards* v. *South Carolina*, 372 US 229 (1963), cf. *Feiner* v. *New York*, 340 US 315 (1951).

[46] See, for illuminating studies of these issues, Wojciech Sadurski, 'Racial Vilification, Psychic Harm, and Affirmative Action', in Tom Campbell and Wojciech Sadurski, *Freedom of Communication* (Dartmouth, Aldershot, 1994), at 77–93; Kent Greenawalt, *Fighting Words: Individuals, Communities, and Liberties of Speech* (Princeton University Press, Princeton, NJ, 1995).

the contrary, the argument is that only attempts by such persons, including forms of group organization, reasonably to respond to and rebut such insults in their own voice address and remedy the underlying stereotypical attitudes that such unjust insults often reflect. The interposition of the state into the domain of conviction (as opposed to action) disempowers the indispensable role of the politics of identity in protesting the terms of one's moral slavery, thus dignifying one's claims to respect as a person. It is such politics, not the state censorship that impedes it, that accords equal respect as a person and citizen (for further development of this point, see Chapter 6).

It is revealing that sometimes the axiomatic claim (that group libel laws must remedy structural injustice) is interpreted as a way of squaring the principle of free speech of the First Amendment with the guarantee of equal protection of the Fourteenth Amendment.[47] The idea appears to be that group libels instantiate the prejudices condemned by equal protection, and are thus overall (interpreting free speech in light of equal protection) less worthy of constitutional protection. The argument, of course, proves too much, encompassing surely much conventional religious conviction that is at least sometimes racist and quite often sexist and homophobic, let alone anti-Semitic. The argument is no more plausible if further elaborated, as it sometimes is,[48] in terms of the role such libels allegedly play in silencing dissent. Allegation here masks not merely lack of evidence, but our cumulative historical experience to the contrary (the American principle of free speech has advanced both the legitimacy and integrity of the politics of identity; the experience of other nations with group libel laws, applied in Britain, for example, to advocacy by black power leaders, suggests such laws, if anything, delegitimate the politics of identity[49]). Nothing in the Fourteenth Amendment, properly understood, repeals the principle of free speech based on the argument for toleration. Indeed, as many scholars have made clear,[50] the central principle of free speech requires, consistently with the argument for toleration, an equal respect for all forms of conscience, an equal protection in the domain of conscience further elaborated and certainly not repealed by the equal protection clause of the Fourteenth Amendment. The theory of structural injustice, which elaborates the argument for toleration, best explains how they are related.

Equal protection crucially requires equal respect for basic human rights, including rights of conscience and speech, and the theory of structural injustice explains the inadequate grounds, constitutionally condemned as suspect, in terms of which groups of persons have been unjustly denied such rights. The guarantee of free speech

[47] See, e.g., Owen M. Fiss, *The Irony of Free Speech* (Harvard University Press, Cambridge, Mass., 1996), 25–6.

[48] See *ibid.*

[49] See, on this point, Nadine Strossen, 'Regulating Racist Speech on Campus', in Gates *et al.*, *Speaking of Race, Speaking of Sex: Hate Speech, Civil Rights and Civil Liberties* (New York University Press, New York, 1994), at 225–6; Kent Greenawalt, *Fighting Words: Individuals, Communities, and Liberties of Speech* (Princeton University Press, Princeton, NJ, 1995), at 145; on the Canadian judicial treatment of such laws, see Greenawalt, *ibid.*, 64–70.

[50] See Kenneth I. Karst, 'Equality as a Central Principle of the First Amendment', 43 *U Chi. L Rev.* 20 (1975).

to such groups, on terms of principle, is one of the requirements of equal protection, and so too is equal protection of other basic human rights. Free speech, thus guaranteed, plays the role of decision procedure for both the understanding and remedy of structural injustice, that is, for the guarantee of other basic human rights.

Nothing in the argument for toleration or the theory of structural injustice supports the claim that the unconstitutionality of group libel laws also casts into doubt the judicial decisions and laws opposing American apartheid. The theory of structural injustice brings the argument for toleration to bear on the criticism of an unjust pattern of cultural entrenchment, which, of course, includes abridgement of the principle of free speech, but of much else besides. The proper understanding of the remedy for such structural injustice includes, as I have argued, a principle of free speech that extends to group libel laws, but also the deconstruction of the practices (including racial segregation and anti-miscegenation laws) that both abridged basic human rights and rationalized such structural injustice. It was, as we have seen (Chapter 3), an important feature of the arguments of the politics of identity, on the basis of the American principle of free speech, that such rationalization importantly turned on cultural practices (like apartheid) that masked structural injustice as facts of nature. Such practices were certainly not understood as convictions or speech expressing such convictions, though, like all practices, they were based on, indeed gave expression to, convictions. To say that these practices are, on critical examination, importantly cultural and are unjust (imposing harms on a class of persons for inadequate reasons) is not to say that they are, as group libel laws are, understood by both speakers and audiences to be communicatively addressed to the domain of conscientious conviction. Otherwise, the guarantees of free speech (extending to all convictions, whether true or false) would protect as well all policies based on such convictions (whether just or unjust), which is absurd (eliding the basic distinction between conviction and action fundamental to the theory of toleration); in effect, everything cultural becomes speech; a principle of free speech that thus condemns everything is as vacuous as one that condemns nothing. The principle of free speech addresses communications understood by speakers and audiences to be addressed to the domain of conviction, imposing a high burden of constitutional scepticism on state judgements of the worth of convictions in this domain unless there is a clear and present danger of secular harms. Nothing in the reasonable understanding of the basis or scope of this scepticism extends to the judicial decisions and policies attacking American apartheid, which impose secular harms (depriving persons of basic human rights) within the domain of action. Rather, the principle of free speech, as I have defended its scope and limits, has advanced understanding of the cultural entrenchment of such structural injustice (what I earlier called the naturalization of injustice) and the appropriateness of remedies therefore including the decisions and laws invalidating the cultural practices of American apartheid.

The principle of free speech is consistent with a robust state power to prevent secular harms, including the harms inflicted by violation of basic human rights. One such basic human right is the right against unjust discrimination, and structural injustice defines the corresponding harm. Its harms include both the systematic abridgement of basic human rights to a class of persons and the inadequate grounds of stereotypical dehumanization that rationalize such abridgement. The state, itself complicitous with such structural injustice, has both the legitimate power and responsibility to take measures to remedy such harms. As I have argued, such measures certainly include the constitutional invalidation of both race-based segregation and anti-miscegenation laws, both of which importantly constructed the stereotypical dehumanization in terms of which abridgement of basic rights was rationalized. Such laws importantly abridged basic human rights like the right to education and to intimate life, depriving the subordinated group of fair access to such rights. Such deprivations fall in the domain of action, and are thus well within the legitimate power of the liberal state. The same theory of equal protection, that requires equal respect for speech, requires as well equal respect for other basic rights, and appropriate remedies for these rights.

Such remedies importantly included a public responsibility, consistent with the equal protection clause of the Fourteenth Amendment, to advance basic education in democratic values like toleration of minorities and anti-discrimination, including the forms of desegregation mandates required by *Brown* v. *Board of Education*.[51] Such mandates remedy the long American history of apartheid by insisting that basic education no longer reflect and reinforce such racial barriers but affirm a common education in values of mutual respect; in this way, these mandates remedy one of the important ways in which dehumanizing stereotypes of race were enforced as the unjust basis for structural injustice. Other reasonable remedies include a curriculum which educates in the values of equal respect, including some historical sense of the American construction of structural injustice and the struggles to overcome and correct it. Education of this sort must include, to do justice to such struggles, a sense of the importance and responsibilities of free speech, including, especially when students are more mature, the values of academic freedom. A reasonable balance must be struck between insisting on civility in discourse in academic environments without compromising the important free speech values of academic freedom, which are also part of the mission of liberal education in a free society.[52]

Appropriate remedies, based on secular harms, also include the passage and enforcement of anti-discrimination laws applicable in both the public and private spheres. Discriminatory actions inflict the harm of depriving people of their equal rights and opportunities on inadequate grounds. The structural injustice which underlies such harms, is enforced in part by the ways in which it privatizes injustice (Chapter 3). Accordingly, the laws forbidding the infliction of such harms must apply

[51] 347 US 483 (1954).
[52] For criticism of some recent university speech codes for not striking a balance properly sensitive to values of free speech, see Ronald Dworkin, *Freedom's Law: The Moral Reading of the American Constitution* (Harvard University Press, Cambridge, Mass., 1996), 244–60. See also Nadine Strossen, 'Regulating Racist Speech on Campus: A Modest Proposal?', in Gates, Jr. *et al.*, n. 49 above, 181–256.

both in the public and private sphere because this scope is alone adequate to remedy the nature of the harm inflicted.

There is, further, no sound reason of moral or constitutional principle why, where appropriate, affirmative action should not be an appropriate remedy for the cultural entrenchment of structural injustice. As I earlier argued (Chapter 3), the principle underlying suspect classification analysis under the equal protection clause of the Fourteenth Amendment cannot reasonably be interpreted in terms of an immutable and salient characteristic, an interpretation that would render constitutionally suspect any use of such a characteristic (including in ameliorative affirmative action plans). Rather, the principle of suspect classification analysis condemns the expression through law of the dehumanizing prejudices that rationalize structural injustice. Affirmative action programmes do not violate this principle but better effectuate it when they give appropriate weight to, for example, racial classifications as a remedy for the force such prejudices have uncritically been permitted to enjoy in limiting access to basic rights, opportunities, and resources. In particular, such programmes reasonably remedy the harms of such injustice when they give appropriate weight to the unjust cultural force race has been permitted to enjoy in framing remedies for structural injustice, for example, race-sensitive opening of opportunities appropriately to rectify a culture of racist exclusion and marginalization.

There is, finally, a compelling secular basis for the exercise of state power aggressively to protect citizens from actions threatening the rights of others (including inchoate crimes like conspiracy) motivated by irrational hatred and prejudice. While groups that advocate racist dehumanization cannot, consistently with free speech principles, be subjected to penalty for such advocacy, there are often other acceptable grounds on which they may be subject to law, including taking steps in concert, subject to the law of conspiracy, to inflict harms on racial minorities. Thus, while all justices of the Supreme Court agreed on diverse grounds that a form of group libel law could not constitutionally be enforced against a cross burned on the lawn of a black family, they also conceded that such acts could have constitutionally been prosecuted on other grounds, including terroristic threats, arson, and criminal damage to property.[53] Criminal conspiracy laws are another such legitimate remedy for actions taken in concert that purpose harm to racial and other minorities.

The American constitutional objection to group libel laws is based on their failure reasonably to meet the standards set by the argument of principle that we call free speech. The unconstitutionality of group libel and similar laws leaves open, indeed stimulates and encourages both the legitimacy and integrity of the politics of identity, for example, the kind of rebuttal of racist and anti-Semitic speech so prominently part of the American political landscape through the activities of such organizations as the NAACP, the Anti-Defamation League, and many others.

---

[53] See *R.A.V.* v. *City of St. Paul*, 505 US 377 (1992).

I recognize that there is venerable authority for not extending the principle of toleration to the intolerant[54] and that the modernist European nightmare of anti-Semitism[55] might be supposed to offer continuing contemporary support for such a view at least in circumstances comparable to those of Weimar Germany (in fact, as we shall see, the Weimar democracy did not even-handedly protect the free speech of the right and the left, and certainly did not use the legitimate powers it had to protect rights at threat from racist injustices[56]). Most contemporary constitutional democracies, including, as we have seen (Chapter 2), Germany itself, understandably take the view that the institutions of constitutionalism must self-defensively protect themselves against the modernist demons of populist racism by refusing such groups certain constitutional liberties. On this view, limitations in free speech protection foster, against the historical background of the powerful role of populist racist fascism in European politics leading to the Second World War, a much needed public education in constitutional values, making precisely the kind of statement that must be made about the ultimate ethical values of respect for the human dignity of all persons.

American free speech law undoubtedly has its grave critical defects;[57] but its view of group libel offers a plausible alternative interpretation of the principle of free speech to the common view elsewhere about group libel. American interpretive experience suggests that a sound argument of principle not only protects such anti-constitutional speech (for the reasons already examined at length), but, properly understood, renders such protection a more effective instrument of ultimate public education in enduring constitutional values, in particular, the place of the basic human rights of conscience and speech in a free and democratic society of equal citizens. In American circumstances, the principle of free speech—extended to blatantly racist and anti-Semitic advocates like the KKK[58]—has remarkably energized and empowered the battle for racial justice and religious toleration under the rule of law, a story ably told by Harry Kalven in *The Negro and the First Amendment*.[59] An American constitutionalist, like Kalven, would defend our position as a matter of

---

[54] For useful discussion, see John Rawls, *A Theory of Justice* (Harvard University Press, Cambridge, Mass., 1971), 216–21.

[55] See Raul Hilberg, *The Destruction of the European Jews*, 3 vols. (Holmes and Meier, New York, 1985).

[56] For useful discussion of those circumstances and their background, see Peter Pulzer, *The Rise of Political Anti-Semitism in Germany and Austria* (Cambridge, Mass.: Harvard University Press, 1988); Jacob Katz, *From Destruction to Destruction: Anti-Semitism, 1700–1933* (Harvard University Press, Cambridge, Mass., 1980).

[57] The treatment by the US Supreme Court of the relationship between free speech and economic power is one of the areas of the gravest doubt both as a matter of sound interpretation of American history and as an argument of democratic political theory. For elaboration of this view, see Richards, n. 17 above, 215–19. In this domain, the German constitutional theory of the duty to protect rights, including economic rights, may be a much better interpretation of the theory of constitutional legitimacy that both Germany and the United States share. For a recent, often compelling, critique of the Supreme Court's treatment of campaign financing and related matters along these lines, see Mark A. Graber, *Transforming Free Speech: The Ambiguous Legacy of Civil Libertarianism* (University of California Press, Berkeley, Calif., 1991).

[58] See *Brandenburg* v. *Ohio*, 395 US 444 (1969); cf. *Collin* v. *Smith*, 578 F 2d. 1197 (1978), cert. denied 439 US 916 (1978) (American Nazi Party).

[59] See Kalven, n. 17 above.

principle.[60] An argument of principle based on respect for conscience must understand the moral ground on which it stands, one which includes in its conception of what a community of principle is all persons who conscientiously exercise their moral powers and who recognize their ultimate responsibility to depend on themselves (not the state) to exercise their moral powers in defence of rights. The principle of free speech rests on the basic human right of each citizen, consistent with the like equal right of all, to be the ultimate critic of the legitimacy of state power. The principles of our tolerance are most in need when the dissent is most radical, not when it is most conventional. Our commitment to this kind of free testing of the legitimacy of our institutions will be measured by the degree to which we extend our right of free thought even to the radical dissent of moral barbarians who would provoke us to their immorally exclusive measure of insularity, parochialism, and faction. Our principles are, I believe, best and most reasonably affirmed when we resist the temptation to respond to bigots in kind and insist on embracing them in an inclusive moral community that recognizes in all persons what some of them might wilfully deny to others, the equality of all persons as free and reasonable members of a political community of principle. Protecting the rights of the speakers and speech we hate affirms the deeper fraternal bonds of a political community based on universal human rights. In the case of the right of free speech, the response, as a matter of principle, to hate should be, if not the inhuman demands of universal love, at least the humane demands of tolerance and mutual respect.

PERSPECTIVES UNDER NATIONAL AND REGIONAL LAW IN THE SHADOW OF WEIMAR

The constitutional legitimacy of group libel and related laws under the national law of other peoples has been crucially framed by the European project of constitutional reconstruction, both national and regional, in the wake of the Second World War. The project of reconstruction was conceived as a normative response to the defective European political and constitutional institutions that Hitler manipulated in service of his populist aims of political racism self-consciously at war with respect for human rights, culminating in the Holocaust; Europe's most brutal and brutalizing century required a constitutional diagnosis of what had gone so wrong and what responsibly must be done in response to such wrong.[61] Any reasonable such diagnosis must consider the background and sources of the political power of anti-Semitism that Hitler used to unify the German people in service of his imperialistic and ultimately genocidal aims.[62]

[60] See also, in general, Harry Kalven, Jr., *A Worthy Tradition: Freedom of Speech in America* (Harper & Row, New York, 1988).
[61] For an illuminating general study of Europe's most brutal century from this perspective, see Mark Mazower, *Dark Continent: Europe's Twentieth Century* (Alfred A. Knopf, New York, 1999).
[62] For an illuminating and balanced recent review of the literature on the degree of support for and understanding by the German people of Hitler's aims (including the Holocaust, surrounded, as it

I earlier discussed the background of modern anti-Semitism in the religious intolerance of Christian anti-Semitism and argued that its structural injustice explains, as the American abolitionists clearly saw, the injustice of American slavery and racism (both Jews and people of colour as scapegoats of forms of religious or political self-doubt, Chapter 3). Hitler's anti-Semitism assumes and elaborates this background in the context of German culture and history, in particular, a romantic conception of authentic ethnic-cultural nationality that negatively defined itself by its cultural resistance to the French doctrine of universal human rights and its most profound German exponent, Immanuel Kant[63] (in Italy, Mussolini was correspondingly to defend fascism as the antithesis of the principles of the French revolution of 1789, principles of free speech, liberty of conscience, and equality before the law[64]). The analogy to American pro-slavery constitutionalism is striking: Calhoun defined Southern constitutional identity in terms of cultural resistance to Jefferson's rights-based Declaration of Independence.[65] In nineteenth-century Europe, culture was the rallying call of national identity—culture often understood in terms of linguistic unity as the basis of a larger cultural and ultimate national unity (thus, Pan-Germanism). German national unity was increasingly identified with the forging of a cultural orthodoxy centring on the purity of the German language, its ancient 'Aryan' myths,[66] its high culture. This search for cultural unity arose in part in reaction to the French imperialistic and assimilationist interpretation of universal human rights. That history invited the search for an alternative, linguistically and culturally centred concept of national unity.

But, cultural unity—when hostile to universal human rights—is, as under southern slavery in the United States, an unstable, highly unprincipled, and sometimes ethically regressive basis for national unity. It may unreasonably enforce highly sectarian values by deadly polemical reaction to its imagined spiritual enemies; and it is all too comfortable to identify those enemies with a group already historically degraded as culturally inferior. Blacks were this group in America, culminating in Justice Taney's definition of American national identity in *Dred Scott* in terms of white supremacy;[67] in Europe, this role was performed by Jews, a highly vulnerable, historically stigmatized cultural minority—the paradigm case of cultural heresy. In the German case,

ostensibly was, by official secrecy), see Inga Clendinnen, *Reading the Holocaust* (Cambridge University Press, Cambridge, 1999).

[63] See, for a persuasive interpretation of German nationalism along these lines, Liah Greenfeld, *Nationalism: Five Roads to Modernity* (Harvard University Press, Cambridge, Mass., 1992), at 277–395. For a specific focus on the contrasting definitions of citizenship in Germany and France, see Rogers Brubaker, *Citizenship and Nationhood in France and Germany* (Harvard University Press, Cambridge, Mass., 1992). On Kant's rights-based political philosophy, see Patrick Riley, *Kant's Political Philosophy* (Rowman & Littlefield, Totowa, NJ, 1983); on Rousseau's influence on Kant, see Ernst Cassirer, *The Question of Jean-Jacques Rousseau* (trans. Peter Gay, Yale University Press, New Haven, Conn., 1989).

[64] See Denis Mack Smith, *Mussolini* (Vintage, New York, 1983), 140

[65] See Richards, n. 2 above, 32.

[66] For a superb treatment, see Leon Poliakov, *The Aryan Myth: A History of Racist and Nationalist Ideas in Europe* (trans. Edmund Howard, Sussex University Press, London, 1971).

[67] Taney thus wrote: 'They [African-Americans] had . . . no right which the white man was bound to respect': *Dred Scott v. Sanford*, 19 How. 393 (1857), at 407.

where there was little solid, humane historical background of moral pluralism on which to build, romantic æsthetic values increasingly dominated over ethical ones. Italy's Mussolini, in contrast, had the history of Roman pluralistic tolerance of Jews to appeal to in rebuking Hitler's very German anti-Semitism, and only acquiesced in complicity with such anti-Semitism under pressure from Hitler, by then his indispensable ally (leading to notable resistance by the people of Italy).[68] Richard Wagner, a major influence on the development of German anti-Semitism, thus preposterously regarded his artistic genius as sufficient to entitle him to articulate, as a prophetic moral leader such as Lincoln, an ethical vision for the German people in the Aryan myth embodied in _Parsifal._ Such a confusion of the categories of æsthetic and ethical leadership reflects the underlying crisis in ethical and political culture.[69]

The force of this crisis in German constitutional culture was prominently exemplified in the period of Weimar constitutionalism by the constitutional theory of Carl Schmitt. Schmitt's complicity with the Nazis[70] places him, with Heidegger,[71] among the leading intellectuals of their period exemplifying the culture that made Hitler both thinkable and acceptable; the interest of Schmitt in particular is his pivotal role as a leading constitutional theorist highly critical of Weimar constitutionalism.

Schmitt's critique was based on a rights-sceptical theory of the ineliminable nature of political power as based on polarities of friends and enemies[72] in which political sovereignty was ultimately defined by 'the orientation toward the possible extreme case of an actual battle against a real enemy'.[73] For Schmitt, consistent with the German nationalistic tradition he reflects, these polarities were founded on retaining the purity of the nation's already constitutive ethnic homogeneity, requiring, as the condition of national integrity, 'first homogeneity and second—if the need arises— elimination or eradication of heterogeneity'.[74] His criticism of Weimar constitutionalism was not its political democracy, but its liberalism, its demand for a kind of rights-based equal treatment that was inconsistent with the friend–enemy polarities of politics as such.[75] From this perspective, the rights-based demand for liberal dialogue and mutual respect (centring on respect for rights of conscience, free speech,

[68] On Mussolini's rejection of anti-Semitism, see Poliakov, n. 66 above, 70. On the striking history of the Italians, in not persecuting and sometimes protecting Jews both in Italy and in the territories they occupied, see Susan Zuccotti, _The Italians and the Holocaust: Persecution, Rescue, Survival_ (Basic Books, New York, 1987); Meir Michaelis, _Mussolini and the Jews: German–Italian relations and the Jewish Question in Italy, 1922–1945_ (Clarendon Press, Oxford, 1978); and Jonathan Steinberg, _All or Nothing The Axis and the Holocaust, 1941–1943_ (Routledge, London, 1990).

[69] See _ibid._ See also Leon Poliakov, _The History of Anti-Semitism_ (trans. Miriam Kochan, Vanguard Press, New York, 1975), iii, ch. 11.

[70] See Joseph W. Bendersky, _Carl Schmitt: Theorist for the Reich_ (Princeton University Press, Princeton, NJ, 1983).

[71] See Victor Farias, _Heideigger and Nazism_ (Temple University Press, Philadelphia, Penn., 1989).

[72] See Carl Schmitt, _The Concept of the Political_ (trans. George Schwab, Rutgers University Press, New Brunswick, NJ, 1976), at 26.

[73] See _ibid._, at 39.

[74] See Carl Schmitt, _The Crisis of Parliamentary Democracy_ (trans. Ellen Kennedy, The MIT Press, Cambridge, Mass., 1985), at 9.

[75] See Schmitt, n. 74 above, at 8–13.

and association) were a kind of anti-politics, fundamentally inconsistent with the exigencies of political action as such.[76] Liberalism was, for Schmitt, thus unacceptable as a political theory for the same reason that he had earlier argued German political romanticism was unacceptable: its passivism when political action was required.[77]

Schmitt could characterize his views as democratic, albeit illiberal, on the basis of a positivistic interpretation of the ultimate basis for political legitimacy, namely, the will of a people to act politically. The interpretation is positivistic because, in contrast to both the American and French rights-based conceptions of popular sovereignty,[78] the will of the people was amorally defined, for Schmitt, by however a people bonded themselves as a homogeneous unit against an enemy in possible war irrespective of 'ideals or norms of justice'.[79] The view was supposedly democratic because it defined legitimate politics as whatever was the authentic expression of the people's will so understood.

Of course, thus mystically understood, democracy would not necessarily be defined even by respect for minimal conditions of majority rule expressed through regular and fair elections.[80] Schmitt thus famously argued for the broadest possible construction of executive powers under Article 48 of the Weimar constitution not as an expression of majority rule or democratic processes (which it would often frustrate), but in order to allow expression of politically decisive action that would preserve national integrity against what Schmitt took to be the anti-German forces of disorder (including the democratic expression of such forces through electoral politics).[81] The crucial point about healthy politics, for Schmitt, was not its reasonableness, but its wilful decisiveness: '[l]ooked at normatively, the decision emanates from nothingness.'[82] Such nothingness could, in principle, validate anything.[83]

Schmitt's theory of politics, understood as a descriptive theory of political psychology, is not, as such, inconsistent with liberal constitutionalism. Indeed, a form of such a theory (Madison's theory of faction) plays a prominent role among the ingredients of American revolutionary constitutionalism.[84] For Madison, however, the fact of factionalized group psychology in politics is just that: an ineliminable fact of political psychology as such. The task of liberal constitutionalism is not to deny facts (in the way French constitutionalism apparently did), but to take them seriously in

---

[76] See Schmitt, n. 72 above, at 69–93.

[77] See Carl Schmitt, *Political Romanticism* (trans. Guy Oakes, The MIT Press, Cambridge, Mass., 1986).

[78] See, on this point, Richards, n. 25 above, 39–44.   [79] See Schmitt, n. 72 above, 49.

[80] For fuller exploration of the nature of democratic processes, see Robert A. Dahl, *Democracy and Its Critics* (Yale University Press, New Haven, Conn., 1989).

[81] See Carl Schmitt, *Political Theology* (trans. George Schwab, Harvard University Press, Cambridge, Mass., 1985), at 11–12; for background, see George Schwab's introduction at pp. xix–xxiii.

[82] See Schmitt, n. 81 above, 31–2.

[83] Consistent with this view, after Hitler's accession to power, Schmitt would publicly defend the legality of Hitler's purges as appropriately decisive action to preserve national integrity. See Joseph Bendersky, *Carl Schmitt: Theorist for the Reich* (Princeton University Press, Princeton, NJ, 1983), at 212–18.

[84] For fuller discussion, see David A. J. Richards, *Foundations of American Constitutionalism* (Oxford University Press, New York, 1989), 32–9.

the construction of constitutional institutions that would use facts in the design of institutions that would better achieve the normative ends of liberal constitutionalism, respect for human rights and the public interest.

But Schmitt interprets such facts not descriptively, but normatively. He gives these facts a normative interpretation that rests not on the facts, but on normative assumptions of what appears superficially to be a radical, indeed avowedly nihilistic rights scepticism: 'an absolute decision created out of nothingness.'[85] On the basis of this scepticism, the recommended course is to resist any appeal to such universalistic constraints on national aspirations and to follow the leader who best expresses national authenticity. The underlying normative assumptions, while certainly nihilistic about rights, are not, however, ultimately normatively nihilistic. If they were ultimately nihilistic, any choice might be as good as any other. But Schmitt offers us one choice as clearly the one demanded, namely, respect for the person who is most politically decisive in uniting a people against its putative enemies. That is a normative choice that has had its self-conscious defenders in political philosophy since Callicles defended the view in Plato's *Gorgias*:[86] namely, the worship of power. Schmitt, however, offers no normative argument, indeed wilfully denies the need for one, because he fails to understand that he has taken and indeed defended a normative choice.

Schmitt's incoherence was during this period publicly echoed to similar effect by the philosopher, Martin Heidegger: the self-conscious appeal to moral nihilism is offered as a ground for following the mandates of the most politically powerful and nationally unifying man of the hour, to wit, Adolf Hitler.[87] The argument made in both cases cannot be defended, because it is fundamentally incoherent and therefore indefensible. But both the argument and its appeal can be understood against the historical background of German nationalism to which I earlier made reference. German national cultural identity was forged, as we have seen, in negative opposition to ideas of universal equal human rights, an opposition that had been philosophically deepened for Heidegger in particular by what he took to be Nietzsche's nihilistic attack on these ideas.[88] Both Schmitt and Heidegger profoundly identify with this negatively defined German cultural tradition as the communitarian source of all affirmative value in living. Their appeal to moral nihilism was thus self-understood as the therapeutic rejection of discredited ideas of universal human rights; in contrast,

---

[85] See Schmitt, n. 81 above, 66.

[86] See Plato, *Gorgias* (trans. Walter Hamilton, Penguin, Harmondsworth, 1973).

[87] For a persuasive argument that Schmitt and Heidegger share a common position on these normative issues, see Richard Wolin, *The Politics of Being: The Political Thought of Martin Heidegger* (Columbia University Press, New York, 1990), at 29–30, 31–2, 38, 39–40, 106; see also Pierre Bourdieu, *The Political Ontology of Martin Heidegger* (trans. Peter Collier, Polity Press, Cambridge, 1991). On Heidegger's complicity with Nazism, see, in general, Victor Farias, *Heidegger and Nazism* (Temple University Press, Philadelphia, Penn., 1989); cf. Jean-Francois Lyotard, *Heidegger and 'the Jews'* (trans. Andreas Michel and Mark Roberts, University of Minnesota Press, Minneapolis, Minn., 1990). For a sympathetic and probing account of Heidegger's contributions to other areas of philosophy, see Hubert L. Dreyfus, *Being-in-the-World: A Commentary on Heidegger's Being and Time, Division I* (The MIT Press, Cambridge, Mass., 1991).

[88] On Neitzsche's profound influence on Heidegger, see Wolin, n. 87 above, 98, 141–2.

obedience to the mandates of the nationally unifying man of the hour was interpreted as the way of preserving what they took to be the only ultimate value in living, the cultural tradition of the German people. Heidegger thus quite clearly weds a person's solitary pursuit of personal authenticity with a passivist subordination to the communitarian demands of the hour, an interpretation of the essential historical-cultural values of German culture as expressed by the supposedly great political interpretive artist of the hour, Adolf Hitler.[89]

As I earlier remarked, cultural unity—when hostile to universal human rights—can be an ethically regressive basis for national unity, founding national unity on forms of religious, ethnic, or racial subjugation. The European form of this, anti-Semitism, arose in the context of the tense relationship between emerging European principles of universal human rights, sponsored by the French Revolution, and nineteenth-century struggles for a sense of national identity and self-determination. When the French Revolution took the form of Napoleonic world revolution, these forces became fatally contradictory. The emancipation of the Jews occurred in this tense environment and became over time its most terrible victim. The Jews, whose emancipation was sponsored by an appeal to universal human rights,[90] were identified with a culture hostile to the emergence of national self-determination.[91] Their very attempts at assimilation into that culture were, according to this view, marks of the degraded inability for true national culture.

In Germany, political anti-Semitism became, under Hitler's leadership, the very core of the success of Nazi politics in a nation humiliated by the triumphant democracies in the First World War.[92] Nazism was self-consciously at war with the idea and practice of human rights, including the institutions of constitutional government motivated by the construction of a politics of public reason that respects human rights.[93] Schmitt's constitutional theory was congenial to these aims because his normative theory of politics, based both on rights scepticism and the polarity of friends and enemies, would amorally permit war against any enemy, no matter how unjust, to be the basis of authentic national identity. Hitler's irrationalist and immoral war against the Jews would thus be legitimate precisely because it attacked human rights (identified, as we have seen, with the Jews) and afforded the kind of enemy that unified the German people as a people.

The exigent question for European constitutional reconstruction, in the wake of the Second World War and public recognition of the role political racism played in both Hitler's means and ends, was a diagnosis of the political and constitutional

---

[89] See *ibid.*, 60–1.

[90] See Arthur Hertzberg, *The French Enlightenment and the Jews* (Columbia University Press, New York, 1990).

[91] See Uriel Tal, *Christians and Jews in Germany* (trans. Noah Jonathan Jacobs, Cornell University Press, Ithaca, NY, 1975).

[92] See Peter Pulzer, *The Rise of Political Anti-Semitism in Germany and Austria* (rev. edn., Harvard University Press, Cambridge, Mass., 1988); Jacob Katz, *From Prejudice to Destruction* (Harvard University Press, Cambridge, Mass., 1980).

[93] See Hannah Arendt, *The Origins of Totalitarianism* (Harcourt Brace Jovanovich, New York, 1973).

structures that facilitated his grisly successes and the proposal of constitutional rules of transition that would, in light of that diagnosis, forge national and regional structures that would, in contrast, render politics in Europe respectful of basic human rights. Of course, historical memory was itself in this period already controversial, corresponding to the terms of the Cold War that saw East Germany turn to the remedy of Communist dictatorship and West Germany to the rights-based democratic constitutionalism of the Basic Law[94] (with the end of the Cold War, Germany has been unified on terms of the Basic Law[95]). For the framers of the Basic Law, historical memory focused on an interpretation of the flaws in Weimar constitutionalism (including the executive powers under Article 48), Germany's first experiment in ostensibly rights-based democratic constitutionalism (lasting for fourteen years, from 1918 to 1932, when Hitler comes to power, appointed as Chancellor in 1933 by President Hindenburg).[96] While building on Weimar constitutionalism, the Basic Law has, in contrast, entrenched a stable and working democratic system of political parties and institutionalized powers of judicial supremacy in the Constitutional Court that have both protected basic human rights and monitored Germany's federal system.[97] I focus here on its provisions regarding basic rights relevant to my argument, namely, those legitimating group libel laws and defending militant democracy by forbidding anti-democratic parties (Chapter 2).

Such a project of constitutional reconstruction must be reasonably interpreted contextually as rules of transition. The argument of political theory that I have offered regarding the relationship of the right of free speech and the right against unjust discrimination makes interpretive and normative sense in the American context, but may apply differently in other contexts, in particular, those of constitutional transition now under consideration. Within the terms of my argument, the constitutional reconstruction of Germany in 1949 may be interpreted as part of the larger process (beginning with the Nuremberg trials and allied deNazification policies[98]) of understanding and remedy of the degree to which German culture, politics, and constitutionalism had politically unleashed the worst monsters of entrenched patterns of structural injustice on Europe and the world. The constitutional provisions, allowing the Constitutional Court to bar anti-democratic parties, may be contextually under-

[94] See, in general, Jeffrey Herf, *Divided Memory: The Nazi Past in the Two Germanys* (Harvard University Press, Cambridge, Mass., 1997).
[95] See, on this point, Peter E. Quint, *The Imperfect Union: Constitutional Structures of German Unification* (Princeton University Press, Princeton, NJ, 1997).
[96] See, in general, Detlev J. Peukert, *The Weimar Republic: The Crisis of Classical Modernity* (trans. Richard Deveson, Hill and Wang, New York, 1987).
[97] See, for an illuminating overview, David P. Currie, *The Constitutional of the Federal Republic of Germany* (University of Chicago Press, Chicago, Ill., 1994).
[98] See, on these points, Detlef Junker, Manfred F. Boemeke, and Janine Micunek (eds.), *Cornerstone of Democracy: The West German Grundgesetz, 1949–1989* (German Historical Institute, Washington, DC, 1995); Constantine FitzGibbon, *Denazification* (W. W. Norton, New York, 1969); Tom Bower, *The Pledge Betrayed: American and Britain and the Denazification of Postwar Germany* (Doubleday, Garden City, NY, 1982); Carl-Christoph Schwietzer, Detlev Karsten, Robert Spencer, R. Taylor Cole, Donald Kommers, and Anthony Nicholls, *Politics and Government in Germany, 1944–1994* (Berghahn Books, Providence, RI, 1995).

stood as short-term rules of transition from the power of such parties under Weimar, whose methods of brutal terror, violence, and political murder must have been all too palpably alive in the memory of Germans in 1949; importantly, the Constitutional Court barred such parties only twice and fairly close to the Nazi period, in 1952 (a neo-Nazi party) and 1956 (Communist Party);[99] with a more stable experience of democratic politics, these provisions have, quite reasonably, fallen into desuetude.

The legitimacy and continuing use of group libel laws in Germany are, however, a quite different matter. Such laws have a long history in Germany, including under Weimar, and play an important continuing role in contemporary German legal culture. The only difference is that, whereas under previous law such actions had been disallowed against anti-Semitic insults,[100] such insults are now prominently actionable (as, for example, the criminal law against the 'lie of Auschwitz' of 1985).[101] A more radical rethinking of German law on this question had been proposed. The American military leader in post-war Germany, General Lucius D. Clay, had responded in 1947 to the draft proposal of Jewish groups for a 'Bill to Combat Incitement Against Jews' by deploring anti-Semitism but not supporting the draft legislation, since 'such legislation, in seeking to suppress oral and written statements, would undoubtedly be considered unconstitutional in the United States; and it is wholly at variance with the American belief that the public good is best advanced in the long run by the free expression of ideas, however misguided or odious the particular opinions might be'.[102]

American constitutional law on this issue has, as we have seen, much more appeal than many of its critics suppose; but it is surely not at all surprising, in the wake of the Second World War, that German public law chose the road, retaining group libel, more continuous with its traditions. What is not at all historically clear is that its decision reflected any deep analysis of the history and culture that had made political anti-Semitism so powerful a means and end for German nationalism under Hitler. Germans, notoriously in the wake of the Second World War, refused to accept responsibility for the ravages of National Socialism,[103] and the abandonment of denazification left a civil service highly compromised by complicity with Nazism;[104]

---

[99] See, for discussion, Currie, n. 97 above, 215–21.

[100] On the limits on such group libel actions for libels of Jews as a group, see Cyril Levitt, 'Under the Shadow of Weimar: What Are the Lessons for the Modern Democracies?', in Louis Greenspan and Cyril Levitt (eds.), *Under the Shadow of Weimar: Democracy, Law and Racial Incitement in Six Countries* (Praeger, Westport, Conn., 1993), 15–37, at 27–31.

[101] See, for pertinent discussion, Juliane Wetzel, 'The Judicial Treatment of Incitement against Ethnic Groups and the Denial of National Socialist Mass Murder in the Federal Republic of Germany', in Greenspan and Levitt (eds.), n. 100 above, 83–106, at 95–103.

[102] Cited at 225, Frank Stern, 'The Historic Triangle: Occupiers, Germans and Jews in Postwar Germany', in Robert G. Moeller (ed.), *West Germany under Reconstruction: Politics, Society, and Culture in the Adenauer Era* (The University of Michigan Press, Ann Arbor, Mich., 1997), at 199–229.

[103] See Josef Foschepoth, 'German Reaction to Defeat and Occupation', in Moeller (ed.), n. 102 above, 73–89.

[104] See Curt Garner, 'Public Service Personnel in West Germany in the 1950's: Controversial Policy Decisions and their Effects on Social Composition, Gender Structure, and the Role of Former Nazis', in Moeller (ed.), n. 102 above, 135–95.

anti-Semitic attitudes even without Jews retained a powerful populist hold on Germans.[105] Correspondingly, Konrad Adenauer, Germany's post-war leader from the occupation until he left the chancellor's office in 1963:

considered the West and Christianity unambiguously positive traditions. Yet just as he had ignored the issue of anti-Semitism in his otherwise highly critical view of modern German history, he also had nothing to say about centuries-old tradition of Christian anti-Semitism and the contribution it had made to German and National Socialist anti-Semitism . . . His reluctance to examine critically the anti-Semitic components of the Christian tradition or the role of the Catholic Church during the Third Reich remained significant blind spots of postwar West German conservatism.[106]

From this perspective, the retention of group libel laws (even as extended to Jews as a group) suggests much more a conservative impulse of continuity with longstanding German legal and cultural traditions than it does a critical understanding and remedy of anti-Semitism as a political and constitutional evil entrenched in German culture and history.

Nothing perhaps makes this clearer than the way in which, as if self-evidently, Germany's current group libel laws were assumed to be dictated by the lessons of Weimar's defective constitutionalism. The case is simply not that reasonably clear. Weimar's laws against incitement to class hatred and religious hatred were successfully used to defend Jews against anti-Semitism; but the pervasive bias (including anti-Semitism) of officials during this period led to many injustices,[107] and the lack of availability of group libel laws on fair terms to Jews as a group expressed and enforced cultural anti-Semitism. The history does not suggest, however, that even the availability of group libel laws to Jews would, in light of the problem of official bias, have made a significant difference. If anything, the very expansive character of Germany's individual and group libel laws may have been an important legal incentive to the development of political anti-Semitism, aggressively used, as they were, by Hitler's supporters, among others, to advance their cause in highly publicized trials.[108] Hitler himself famously used his own Munich trial for treason in 1924[109] and the Leipzig trial of army officers for treason in 1930[110] as stages for highly successful propaganda, sometimes deferentially encouraged and even stage managed by presiding officials.[111] Such deference by authoritarian elites (including, as we have seen, the support of leading intellectuals like Schmitt and Heideigger) included a

---

[105] See Frank Stern, 'The Historic Triangle: Occupiers, Germans and Jews in Postwar Germany', in Moeller (ed.), n. 102 above, 199–229; Constantin Goschler, 'The Attitude towards Jews in Bavaria after the Second World War', *ibid.*, 231–49.

[106] Jeffrey Herf, *Divided Memory: The Nazi Past in the Two Germanys* (Harvard University Press, Cambridge, Mass., 1997), 216–17, 272–80.

[107] See, on this point, Peukert, n. 96 above, 222–3.

[108] See, on all the above points, Cyril Levitt. 'Under the Shadow of Weimar', in Greenspan and Levitt (eds.), n. 100 above, 15–37.

[109] See, for illuminating discussion, Ian Kershaw, *Hitler 1889–1936: Hubris* (W. W. Norton, New York, 1998), at 216–17, 235–9, 262.   [110] See *ibid.*, 337–8.

[111] See, for further discussion of this point, Alan Bullock, *Hitler; A Study in Tyranny* (rev. edn., Harper & Row, New York, 1962), at 113–20.

remarkable degree of practical immunity from prosecution for an immorally ruthless and dynamic minority engaged in both conspiracies to act and acts of political violence, terror, and murder,[112] all well within the legitimate power and responsibility of the state to condemn and punish. The political legitimation of such a politics of terror and violence laid the groundwork, when Hitler took power, for the extinction of civil liberties and the state terror and mass murder that was to follow.[113] The unholy alliance between a ruthless minority of terror (the Nazis) and authoritarian elites, all hostile to democratic rights-based constitutionalism, warred on and finally destroyed the republican constitutionalism of Weimar that they had always despised.[114]

The Weimar Republic was 'a democracy without democrats',[115] a fact shown by its failure to respect the principle of free speech both in its scope and in its limits. Authorities, as we have seen, blatantly favoured the speech of right-wing politicians like Hitler over others, violating the principle of equal respect for speakers and speech. Much more importantly, such authorities grotesquely legitimated both criminal conspiracies to act and actions of terror, violence, and political murder, failing to protect the basic rights of citizens to life, personal security, and the like. Carl Schmitt's theory of politics, earlier discussed, both reflected and defended the increasingly dominant anti-democratic ideology of contempt for the very idea of reasonable democratic dialogue between equals at the core of rights-based constitutional government. That ideology warred on the basic right of free speech as I have defended it in this work, regarding the very idea of deliberative dialogue between equals as inconsistent with the essence of politics, as Schmitt understood it, namely, the coercive struggle of friends against enemies (Hitler's political anti-Semitism, as both means and end, fits Schmitt's prescription for legitimate political power exactly). It is hardly surprising that Schmitt was not only, as we have seen, the leading constitutional defender of expansive executive powers under Article 48 of the Weimar constitution but would publicly *defend* Hitler's use of state-sponsored murders in the Night of the Long Knives in 1934; the title of his speech was, 'The Führer Protects the Law'.[116] Legitimacy in politics, on this view, is ruthless violence against putative enemies.

Such a ruthlessly amoral conception of legitimate politics is, of course, fundamentally at war with the conception of liberal political theory, in which the legitimacy of political power turns on respect for basic human rights. Free speech plays the defensible role it does in liberal constitutionalism because it exposes to reasonable public discussion and debate precisely the issues of respect for basic human rights on which the legitimacy of liberal government turns (including, as we have seen, the understanding and remedy of structural injustice). In contrast, Hitler, who confessed an

[112] See, e.g., Kershaw, n. 109 above, 120, 170–80, 287, 368, 381–3, 409.
[113] See *ibid.*, 435, 454–64, 459, 471–5, 500, 559–73.
[114] On the importance of the complicity of authoritarian elites in the rise of Hitler, see Peukert, n. 96 above, 261.
[115] Cited in Levitt, n. 108 above, 32.   [116] See Kershaw, n. 109 above, 521.

attraction early in his life to parliamentary democracy,[117] learned his contempt for democratic dialogue from watching the Reichsrat (the Austro-Hungarian parliament) in which representatives, speaking in mutually unintelligible languages, never sought consensus, but minorities used insults and violence to bully and intimidate; the use of terror and violence by ruthless ideological minorities was the model for Hitler's politics.[118] It was a politics, like that of Schmitt, very much at war with the principle of free speech and its associated conception of democratic dialogue among equals. The amoral conception of a constitutional scholar, like Schmitt, could only have succeeded to the degree it did under Weimar by wholesale mockery and contempt, not only by mass politicians like Hitler but by complicitous authoritarian elites, of the right of free speech and the issues of rights-based legitimacy that it places at stage centre of political discussion and debate. Constitutional institutions (including officials and elites) like those of Weimar, so little concerned with defending the right of free speech, cast a legitimating shadow on a bullying mass politics of terror and violence constructed on structural injustice (political anti-Semitism).

There is thus little in the political history of Weimar that reasonably compels the current interpretation of free speech, favoured in Germany and elsewhere, that renders group libel laws outside the protection of free speech; indeed, if anything, as I earlier suggested, a reasonable case could be made to exactly the opposite effect. Germany's contemporary use of these laws is, in fact, continuous with its legal traditions, and their constitutional legitimacy in Germany was not framed during a period when German leaders and people were yet ready critically to address their responsibility for the role anti-Semitism played in Hitler's grisly populist politics. With the passage of time, however, events suggest greater German openness to such discourse.[119]

It is thus an opportune time to raise and investigate the questions of political theory that I have posed in this book. If nothing in the history of Weimar reasonably compels the view of group libel now taken in Germany and elsewhere, does political theory? The interpretation of American experience, in light of such political theory, supports a reading of the right of free speech (hostile to both subversive advocacy and group libel laws) that appeals to the legitimacy and integrity of the politics of identity in the understanding and remedy of structural injustice. Political theory, applied in one way in American circumstances, may apply in a different way in other circumstances. We can best assess these matters by focusing on the three kinds of arguments used in the defence of group libel laws: first, the weight German law accords group interests in reputation as rights to be weighted against the right of free speech; second, the weight, in Canada and elsewhere, accorded the right of equal protection as a right to be balanced against the right to free speech; and third, the justification of such laws, as in Britain, to control public order.

---

[117] See, on this point, Brigitte Hamann, *Hitler's Vienna: a Dictatorship's Apprenticeship* (trans. Thomas Thornton, Oxford University Press, New York, 1999), at 120.

[118] See, on this point, *ibid.*, at 116–32.

[119] On relevant developments, see Herf, n. 106 above, 334–72.

Current German law, as we have seen (Chapter 2), regards group libel laws as striking an appropriate balance between the right of free speech and the right of persons to respect for their group identities; and the European Commission has upheld such laws on similar grounds under the European Convention on Human Rights.[120] The constitutional balance struck, in the assessment of such laws by the German Constitutional Court, is well illustrated by the *Holocaust Denial Case* (1994)[121] and the *Historical Fabrication Case* (1994).[122] The former case involved a meeting at which a revisionist historian denied that the mass extermination of the Jews during the Third Reich ever happened; the latter involved a book that did not deny the occurrence of the Holocaust, but argued that Germany was not to blame for the outbreak of the Second World War. The Constitutional Court found the former Holocaust denial to be a false fact not protected by the right of free speech and justified by protecting Jews from unjust insult; on the other hand, the Court deemed the latter a false interpretation, within the constitutional protected sphere of opinion, and thus not subject to abridgement. These cases can surely not be squared on the ground that one involved a fact and the other an opinion (as the Constitutional Court supposes). In both cases, unreasonably false interpretive claims about the historical record are proposed, and in both cases such claims express conviction and thus should be entitled to constitutional protection. Further, in both cases, Jews as a group might reasonably regard both claims as unjustly disrespectful of their identity and historical experience of profound injustice. Why, if there is no difference of principle in the protection of speech, should their claims, as claims of group libel, be weighed differently as constitutional interests?

The German law against the 'lie of Auschwitz' of 1985,[123] like the comparable French law of 1990 making it a crime to contest 'the existence of one or several crimes against humanity as defined in Article 6 of the Statute of the International Military

[120] See, for pertinent discussion, Stephen J. Roth, 'The Law of Six Countries: An Analytical Comparison', in Greenspan and Levitt (eds.), n. 100 above, 177–211, at 189–90.

[121] *Holocaust Denial Case* (1994) 90 BVerfGE 241, translated at 382–7, Donald K. Kommers, *The Constitutional Jurisprudence of the Federal Republic of Germany* (2nd edn., Duke University Press, Durham, NC, 1997).

[122] *Historical Fabrication Case* (1994) 90 BVerfGE 1, noted at *ibid.*, 387.

[123] In Germany the case law relating to the implementation of Arts. 130 and 185 of the Criminal Code has led to the conviction of authors who deny the Holocaust; the new wording of Art. 194(1) of the Criminal Code allows a prosecution for insult to be instituted without a petition 'if the insulted person was persecuted as a member of a group under the National-Socialist regime or another violent and arbitrary dominance, if the group is part of the population and if the insult is connected with such a persecution'. See Roger Errera, 'Group Libel, Hate Speech, and other Fighting Words: Civility and the Uses of Law', in Basil S. Markesinis (ed.), *Law Making, Law Finding and Law Shaping: The Diverse Influences* (The Clifford Chance Lectures Vol. 2, Oxford University Press, Oxford, 1997), 43–51, at 47–8. See, for pertinent discussion, Juliane Wetzel, 'The Judicial Treatment of Incitement against Ethnic Groups and the Denial of National Socialist Mass Murder in the Federal Republic of Germany', in Greenspan and Levitt (eds.), n. 100 above, 83–106, at 95–103; Eric Stein, 'History Against Free Speech: The New German Law Against the "Auschwitz"—and Other—"Lies"', 85 *Mich. L Rev.* 277 (1986).

Tribunal',[124] reflect growing readiness in both Germany and France critically to assess the role political anti-Semitism played in both nations before, during, and after the Second World War;[125] comparable laws exist in Switzerland, Austria, and Israel.[126] From the perspective of political theory, the question with respect to these and other such laws must be whether, in contemporary circumstances, they justifiably interpret the relationship between the right to free speech and the right against unjust discrimination as basic rights of constitutional law. There are two reasons of principle for having doubts on this score. First, as I earlier suggested (Chapter 2), by effectively exiling certain convictions from the community of legitimate discourse, such laws reinforce rather than contest the ideology of friends and enemies that has, in the history of both nations, been so inimical to respect for human rights as the test for the legitimacy of laws under constitutional government. If political education in liberal values is the ostensible point of these laws, their means subverts their ends. Secondly, such laws in contemporary circumstances, alleged to rest on combating the evil of unjust discrimination, in fact undermine the legitimacy and integrity of the politics of identity in the understanding and remedy of structural injustice.

Consider, for example, the German Constitutional Court's defence of such laws when they are directed against false facts. As I earlier noted, these false facts here are, in contrast to lies or fraud, believed to be true and so believed as part of general interpretive convictions. This brings abridgement of such speech into the core, not the periphery, of the right to conscience as a human and constitutional right. If it would not be acceptable on such grounds to criminalize religious conviction because based on false facts, why should convictions of Holocaust denial be, as a matter of constitutional principle, treated differently? Presumably, what is, intuitively, thought to be different is that such convictions are not only deeply unreasonable and even immoral, but conspicuously, even defiantly display the workings of structural injustice, to wit, European anti-Semitism. But is this a difference worthy of constitutional respect? Religious convictions have historically been attacked and abridged on precisely such grounds, a tradition which we should reasonably reject today as failing to accord equal respect in the domain of conviction. Perhaps, Holocaust denial may be thought properly isolated for special treatment because it so displays an evil that nations with a now acknowledged history and culture of anti-Semitism want now to condemn,

---

[124] France, Art. 24 of the French Law on the Press (since 1990), cited by Lawrence Douglas, 'Policing the Past: Holocaust Denial and the Law', in Robert C. Post (ed.), *Censorship and Silencing: Practices of Cultural Regulation* (The Getty Research Institute, Los Angeles, Cal., 1998), at 67–87, 74. For further commentary on this and related French laws, see Roger Errera, 'French Law and Racial Incitement: On the Necessity and Limits of the Legal Responses', in Greenspan and Levitt (eds.), n. 100 above, 39–62.

[125] On the French experience under Vichy, see Richard Weisberg, *Vichy Law and the Holocaust in France* (New York University Press, New York, 1996).

[126] See Swiss Penal Code, Art. 261; Austrian Law no. 148, 1992; Israel, Denial of Holocaust (Prohibition Law) 5746–1986. See Errera, n. 123 above, at 47. On related developments in Italian law, see Giorgio Sacerdoti, 'Italian Legislation and Case Law on Racial and Religious Hatred and Group Libel: International Aspects' (1992) 22 *Israel Yearbook on Human Rights*, 229–42.

and condemn unequivocally.[127] But, if the point is that the right of free speech may for this contextual reason yield to the right against unjust discrimination, the point, from the perspective of political theory, subverts itself.

We need to remind ourselves what structural injustice is and why political anti-Semitism has long been taken by its critics (including the American abolitionists) as a kind of model for the ways in which such injustice has been constructed and sustained (Chapter 3). Such structural injustice reflects a long history and culture that abridges the basic human rights of a class of persons, and unjustly rationalizes such treatment on terms of a normatively circular abridgement of basic rights (for example, forbidding voices and views that might reasonably contest the dehumanizing stereotypes in terms of which such treatment is rationalized). Such injustice often arises within a tradition (like Christianity) now subject to reasonable doubts about some of its doctrines; rather than entertaining and reasonably discussing such doubts in order better to arrive at the truth, it paradoxically frustrates such inquiry by engaging in the irrationalist scapegoating of groups subject to a history of structural injustice (for example, African-Americans in the United States as slaves, Jews in Europe as the slaves of Christians'). Political anti-Semitism in twentieth-century Europe reflects and elaborates a long history of such Christian anti-Semitism, developed, as by Hitler in terms of racist pseudo-science, to construct an internal enemy in terms of which any reasonable doubts about the terms of German nationalism might be suppressed, rationalizing both his totalitarianism and imperialism as necessary steps against the enemy. Consistent with the paradox of intolerance, unjust victims were thus ideologically transformed into aggressive enemies, and, on this irrationalist ground, genocide rationalized as self-defence. It is, from this perspective on the history and culture of structural injustice, fundamental that such injustice feeds on the irrationalist distortion of facts.

If we are reasonably to understand and remedy such structural injustice, we need more, not less, reasonable exposure and discussion of the degree to which Holocaust denial is *believed*; and the kind of censorship—endorsed by Holocaust denial and related laws—impedes both the legitimacy and integrity of such reasonable discourse. It impedes its legitimacy because, by failing to guarantee equal respect to all in the domain of conviction, it abandons the standpoint of equal respect that the liberal state must extend to all persons, as persons, whatever their convictions. It frustrates the integrity of such reasonable discourse because it introduces modes of state inquiry into facts that have the unintended consequence, which Hitler so brilliantly manipulated, of lending reasonable credibility to views that have none;[128] the prosecution in France of Le Pen for violation of such laws, including an acquittal and conviction, suggests the continuing contemporary vitality of this strategy under such

---

[127] See, for defence of this position, David Kretzmer, 'Free Speech and Racism', 8 *Cardozo L Rev.* 445 (1987); Thomas David Jones, *Human Rights: Group Defamation, Freedom of Expression and the Law of Nations* (Martinus Nijhoff Publishers, The Hague, 1998).

[128] See, for an illuminating development of this position, Lawrence Douglas, 'Policing the Past: Holocaust Denial and the Law', in Post (ed.), n. 124 above, 67–87.

ill-considered laws, in effect, legitimating the imitation by a modern political racist of Hitler's grisly example.[129] Contemporary advocates of Holocaust denial crave such fora because such fora accord their views a polemical impression of legitimacy and integrity which, in fact, they wholly lack.[130] Nothing in a principled understanding of either the right of free speech or the right against unjust discrimination requires that their polemical irrationalism be thus assisted. Holocaust denial and related laws, ostensibly directed at structural injustice, only further entrench it, not least by a shallow political symbolism that, in apparently condemning such evils, distracts from the deeper reasonable inquiry into the history and culture of European structural injustice.

We need more, not less, free speech in this domain, both in America and in Europe, because only such speech empowers the understanding and remedy of structural injustice at the deep levels at which it continues politically to operate. I have already observed the many significant structural analogies between American racism and European anti-Semitism, which suggests the urgency of a comparative study of political evils like racism as a pervasive problem of legitimate government in the modern world. European racism and related evils may urgently require a comparable analysis. Hitler's political anti-Semitism thus self-consciously built on long-familiar European practices of imperialism rationalized by a racism that sometimes took genocidal forms.[131] Germany came relatively late to European colonialism;[132] and Hitler, invoking British imperialism in India as model,[133] rationalized his imperialism in terms of extending this colonial project to Europe and eastward.[134] Hitler's political anti-Semitism was, from this larger European perspective, a grotesque elaboration of the European imperialism motored by racism directed at people of colour in Africa and Asia (in contrast, Mussolini's fascist racist imperialism in Africa, albeit motivated by his racialization of the Italian people of the South whom he proposed to colonize in Africa, was, by European standards, much more conventional[135]). Hitler's political anti-Semitism, on the basis of pseudo-science, racialized the Jews (Europeans and not people of colour) as yet another subhuman people, but since living in Europe, requiring expulsion, subjugation, and extermination as required by Germany's colonial imperium (including comparable treatment of inferior Slavic peoples) over Eastern Europe.[136] Hitler's political anti-Semitism starkly illustrates the irrationalism of racism, its gargantuan appetite for whatever false fantasies serve its ends (including racializing, if necessary, people not of colour). Americans have considerable experi-

[129] See Errera, n. 124 above, at 50, 54. Even Errera, who in general defends such laws in a French context, believes that the 1990 Holocaust denial law was 'unnecessary and unwise': *ibid.*, at 56.

[130] See, in general, Deborah Lipstadt, *Denying the Holocaust: The Growing Assault on Truth and Memory* (Plume, New York, 1994).

[131] See, in general, Sven Lindqvist, *Exterminate All the Brutes* (trans. Joan Tate, The New York Press, New York, 1996); Mazower, n. 61 above, 71–5, 100.

[132] See Lindqvist, n. 131 above, 154.		[133] See Mazower, n. 61 above, 146–7.

[134] See Kershaw, n. 109 above, 275, 288.

[135] See Mazower, n. 61 above, 71–5; on Mussolini's racist contempt for the Italian people of the Mezzogiorno and its role in his imperialist ambitions in Africa, see Richards, n. 25 above, 105–15.

[136] See Mazower, n. 61 above, 71–5.

ence with a similar pattern of injustice, reflected both in the racialization of immigrants (earlier discussed) and in racist proposals to colonize African-Americans abroad or segregate them at home.[137] We need more, not less, reasonable discourse about these pervasive and mutually influential structural injustices in European and American culture, including their structural linkages to issues of gender and sexuality (Chapter 3). There is every reason to believe that such discourse would be enhanced by respect for a principle of free speech which empowered a politics of identity that would advance the legitimacy and integrity of the understanding and remedy of structural injustices in Europe, including still entrenched patterns of racism, recently targeting immigrant people of colour.[138] If Europeans are now reasonably interested in the understanding and remedy of the entrenchment of such racism in their culture (reflected in nativist violence against immigrants),[139] they will need not the shallow and self-defeating symbolism of group libel laws, but a regime of free speech which confronts them with the depth of the still largely undiscussed cultural problem. Such discourse may make possible sometimes painful but much needed reasonable rethinking of and remedies for largely unquestioned conceptions of ethnic nationalism (as, for example, in Germany[140]).

EUROPEAN COURT OF HUMAN RIGHTS

Laws, like those of Germany and elsewhere that constitutionally protect interests in group identity at the expense of free speech, may enhance the respect of existing groups, but they do not, as they claim, advance either the understanding or remedy of structural injustice. Such laws necessarily implicate the state in endorsing what counts as a group and what respect is owed to such groups. Such judgements will, of course, track conventional understanding of these matters in the culture, and thus enlist the state in the support of the dominant group pluralism. Consider, for example, the protection of interests in religious group identity (as by traditional blasphemy laws) appealed to by Austria in justifying suppression of a film that would offend Roman Catholics; the European Court of Human Rights, in upholding the constitutionality of the law under the European Convention, appealed to the weight reasonably accorded to such group interests in the pertinent clause allowing reasonable limits on the constitutionally protected right of free speech under Article 10(2) (Chapter 2).[141] Protection of such conventional group interests not only enlists the

---

[137] For the abolitionist attack on such proposals, see Richards, n. 2 above, 82 ff., 99, 152, 173; for Lincoln's support of such proposals, see *ibid.*, 81, 152.

[138] See Mazower, n. 61 above, 321–3, 345–50.

[139] See, on this point, *Legal Instruments to Combat Racism and Xenophobia* (Commission of the European Communities, Brussels, 1992).

[140] See Michael J. Baun, 'The Federal Republic of Germany', in Daniel P. Franklin and Michael J. Baun (eds.), *Political Culture and Constitutionalism: A Comparative Approach* (M. E. Sharpe, Armonk, NY, 1995), 79–97, at 92–4. For a recent political development in line with this recommendation, see Roger Cohen, 'Germany Makes Citizenship Easier for Foreigners to Get', *New York Times*, 22 May 1999, A–3.

[141] See *Otto-Preminger-Institut* v. *Austria* (1995) 19 EHRR 34 (Ct.).

state in the political support of such dominant groups, but it endorses such views as the ground for state censorship in the domain of conviction. But it is precisely such dominant views that may be implicated in the history and culture of structural injustice. In effect, such protection privileges conventional groups over the unconventional dissenting voices that often engage in the politics of identity, protesting patterns of structural injustice that often rested on the stereotypical dehumanization and repression of such voices. If such dominant views are the measure of the right of free speech, we undercut the empowering role of such speech precisely when it is most legitimately needed, namely, promoting the understanding and remedy of structural injustice. Whatever may be the justification of laws protecting group identity, it cannot reasonably be that they advance the understanding and remedy of structural injustice; if such laws claim reasonably to require sacrifices of the right of free speech better to combat evils like anti-Semitism, they are incoherent and self-defeating. Such laws enforce conventional understandings in the domain of conviction, repressing the protesting voices that reasonably confront the public mind of the community with the entrenchment of structural injustice. The point is perhaps obvious when we consider the role of religious or conventional views of gender and sexuality, more generally, in the structural injustices of sexism and homophobia, a matter to be discussed in the next chapter;[142] but, the point applies equally to the diagnosis and remedy of anti-Semitism.

Hitler's version of political anti-Semitism was importantly influenced by his early admiration for the political successes in Austria of Dr Karl Lueger's version of Christian anti-Semitism, rooted in Catholic ideology;[143] Hitler never officially left the Catholic Church of his youth, but he despised its universalistic institutions as inconsistent with German ethnic nationalism.[144] But both the roots and appeal of his political anti-Semitism importantly drew upon strands of Christian anti-Semitism, including Lueger's version that used political anti-Semitism to forge an Austrian political nationalism identified with a hegemonic Catholicism. Hitler carried Lueger's means and ends one step further by forging a political anti-Semitism that established ethnic, allegedly race-based nationalism as an ultimate value. No critical understanding of the political power of Hitler's means and ends can be achieved without taking seriously the traditional role Christian anti-Semitism played in legitimating such a politics of scapegoating. It is for this reason, as we earlier saw, that Konrad Adenauer's indictment of fascism as fundamentally anti-Christian failed reasonably to come to terms with the diagnosis and remedy of anti-Semitism in German culture. Correspondingly, allowing such group interests to be the measure of free speech does not, for this reason, advance either the understanding or remedy of structural injustice.

---

[142] See, for an exploration of this point in the German context, Robert G. Moeller, 'The Homosexual Man Is a "Man", the Homosexual Woman Is a "Woman": Sex, Society, and the Law in Postwar Germany', in Moeller (ed.), n. 102 above, 251–84.

[143] See Hamann, n. 117 above, 280–91, 302.

[144] See *ibid.*, at 249–50.

CANADIAN LAW

There is yet another way in which group libel laws have been justified as consistent with free speech, namely, that such laws strike an appropriate or reasonable balance between the constitutional right of free speech and that of equal protection. We earlier examined and criticized a form of this argument in American thought, and now must consider whether the argument, as developed under the national and regional law of other peoples, is any more defensible.

The leading Canadian case, *R.* v. *Keegstra*,[145] illustrates this form of argument. Keegstra, an Alberta high school teacher, was charged under section 319(2) of the Criminal Code with wilfully promoting hatred against a group (Jews) by communicating anti-Semitic statements to his students. The Supreme Court of Canada held, by four to three, that the statute, while abridging constitutionally protected speech under section 2(b) of the Canadian Charter of Rights and Freedoms, was justified under the limitation clause of section 1 ('reasonable limits prescribed by law as can be demonstrably justified in a free and democratic society').[146] Chief Justice Dickson, writing for the Court, distinguished the Canadian from the American approach by appeal to section 1 interpreted in light of 'the international commitment to eradicate hate propaganda and, most importantly, the special role given equality and multiculturalism in the Canadian Constitution'.[147] This special role is, for the majority,[148] specified by section 15 (guaranteeing 'equal protection and equal benefit of the law without discrimination . . . based on race, national and ethnic origin, colour, religion, sex, age or mental or physical disability'[149]) and section 27 (requiring interpretation of the Charter 'consistent with the preservation and enhancement of the multicultural heritage of Canadians'[150]). The argument of the Court thus interprets the weight to be accorded the right of free speech in terms of weight to be given, *inter alia*, the right against unjust discrimination. Chief Justice Dickson construes the weight to be accorded the latter right in terms of harms as follows: '[t]he threat to the self-dignity of target group members is thus matched by the possibility that prejudiced messages will gain some credence, with the attendant result of discrimination, and perhaps even violence, against minority groups in Canadian society'.[151] That such harms are credible is shown by 'the triumphs of impudent propaganda such as Hitler's'.[152] In later assessing the balance to be struck between the right of free speech and the right against unjust discrimination, the Court denies that the expression condemned by the criminal statutes is 'closely linked to the rationale' underlying the free speech guarantee.[153] In particular, the statute does not, in the view of Dickson, implicate or seriously compromise any of the three rationales for free expression: its instrumental uses in advancing truth and the common good,[154] autonomous

---

[145] *R.* v. *Keegstra*, 3 Can. SCR 697 (1990).
[147] *Ibid.*, at 743.
[150] *Ibid.*
[153] Cited in *ibid.*, at 762.

[148] See *ibid.*, at 755.
[151] Cited in *ibid.*, at 748.
[154] *Ibid.*, 762.

[146] Cited in *ibid.*, 716.
[149] Cited in *ibid.*, at 717.
[152] Cited in *ibid.*, at 747.

self-expression,[155] or political speech essential to democracy.[156] The Court concedes '[t]he suppression of hate propaganda undeniably muzzles the participation of a few individuals in the democratic process, and hence detracts somewhat from free expression values, but the degree of limitation is not substantial'.[157] Such muzzling condemns speakers and speech 'wholly inimical to the democratic aspirations of the free expression guarantee'[158] and advances the speakers and speech that 'best encourage the protection of values central to freedom of expression, while simultaneously demonstrating dislike for the vision forwarded by hate-mongers'.[159]

The Canadian Supreme Court offers an argument in *R.* v. *Keegstra* no different in substance from that earlier examined in German constitutional jurisprudence. Its interpretation of both the right of free speech and the right against unjust discrimination uncritically endorses the weight to be accorded to group identities. This becomes painfully clear in the way the Court defends its inadequate understanding of free speech in terms of both a question-begging conception of democracy (and thus of the democratic argument) and the autonomy rationale. Its appeal to democratic values, as the measure of free speech, illustrates the inadequacy of the argument from democracy as a theory of free speech, because it fails to take seriously the roots of free speech in the equal respect for the inalienable right to conscience. Its discussion of the autonomy rationale, which calls for respect for this basic human right of morally independent conscience, is even worse. For example, the Court raises only to dismiss the relevance of the autonomy rationale for free speech in the following terms: 'such self-autonomy stems in large part from one's ability to articulate and nurture an identity derived from membership in a cultural or religious group. The message put forth by individuals who fall within the ambit of s. 319(2) represents a most extreme opposition to the idea that members of identifiable groups should enjoy this aspect of the s. 2(b) benefit.'[160] This claim would be sociologically silly if it were meant to deny that anti-Semitic groups are not groups, but it makes sense if it means to endorse conventional groups in which Canadian cultural pluralism takes national pride. However, understood in these terms, its very orientation to conventional groups, as the measure of free speech, shows no normative understanding of the role the inalienable right to conscience plays both in the theory of toleration and the theory of structural injustice. In the long history of the struggle both for free speech and against structural injustice, it has been small and unconventional individuals and minorities (like the American radical abolitionists) who both demanded their right to speak and be heard and, in that voice, subjected to fundamental criticism the ways in which conventional groups (including dominant churches) had formed themselves on the basic of structural injustice (the subjugation of African-Americans or of Jews) (Chapter 3). On the view taken of free speech by the Canadian Supreme Court, the normative weight to be accorded the right to conscience simply disappears in its unfounded absorption in the endorsement of the dominant Canadian identities in

---

155 *R.* v. *Keegstra*, 3 Can. SCR 697, 762 (1990).   156 *Ibid.*, 762–3.   157 *Ibid.*, 763.
158 *Ibid.*, 764.   159 *Ibid.*   160 *Ibid.*, 763.

which the Chief Justice, as a Canadian, takes an understandable pride. Such considerations of national pride should not, however, be the measure of the judicial enter-
prise under a constitution ostensibly committed to the protection of universal human
rights.

Similar critical difficulties attach to the way in which the Court weights the harms
it associates with the constitutionally guaranteed right against unjust discrimination.
The Court construes these harms in terms of unjust insults to one's sense of group
identity, and crucially conceives these harms in terms of the possibility that they will
be believed or even acted on. But the Court thus legitimates the wholly improper role
of the state in the domain of conviction of determining what counts as a group worthy of respect, disempowering the politics of identity that, by reasonably contesting
unjust stereotypes, advances both the understanding and remedy of structural injustice. This does not advance, but frustrates, protection of the right against unjust discrimination. Its framing of its argument about harm in this way betrays, at the same
time, the right of free speech. As we saw earlier, the normative ground for the protection of speech (in contrast to action) rests on the distinctive character of the harms
in speech (as opposed to action). First, such harms (their disrespectful character)
inhere in the exercise of the inalienable right to conscience itself, and cannot, consistent with respect for its exercise (including the moral powers exercised in the politics
of identity), be a ground for its abridgement; secondly, the harms in hearing speech
in the domain of conviction inhere in the audience's evaluative responses to the
speech, and, for this reason, responsive arguments of conviction by the audience can,
in principle, meet and defeat its claims, and thus expunge its harm in terms that are
consistent with equal respect for the right of conscience of all persons. But the
Canadian Supreme Court endorses as harms entitled to decisive constitutional weight
what, consistently with respect for this distinction, cannot reasonably count as such.

The harms, as the Court construes them, inhere in the speech and in its persuasive
appeal to audiences, which not only fails to respect the convictions of the speakers but
shows contempt for the judgement of audiences, both in blatant violation of the operative principle of equal respect in the domain of conviction; the persuasiveness of
speech cannot, in principle, be an acceptable ground for the abridgement of speech,
as the Canadian Supreme Court apparently supposes.[161] The success of Hitler's propaganda is not to the point in light of Weimar's blatant failure to respect the principle of free speech in either its scope or its limits. If the appeal to Weimar is bad
enough as interpretive authority for Germany, it has no purchase whatsoever on the
long experience of Canadian democratic constitutionalism. There can be no reasonable claim that, in the Canadian context, protests of anti-Semitism cannot and will
not be vigilantly made, nor that such protests cannot and will not be heard and given
reasonable weight. And there is quite good reason to believe that state censorship in
this domain will, if anything, disempower both the legitimacy and integrity of such

---

[161] See, on this point, David A. Strauss, 'Persuasion, Autonomy, and Freedom of Expression', 91
Colum. L Rev. 334 (1991).

politics of identity in the understanding and remedy of structural injustice.[162] The right of free speech and the right against unjust discrimination are not, as the Canadian Supreme Court supposes, normatively separable; they are structurally linked so that the abridgement of one impairs the other as well. In effect, the Court spuriously supposes that securing less public discussion of issues of racial conflict is an acceptable measure of a decrease in racial discrimination itself.[163] On the contrary, the principle of free speech, properly understood, indispensably advances both the understanding and remedy of structural injustice. Such remedies include ample constitutional grounds for the state responsibly to intervene in protecting the right from unjust discrimination in the domain of action.

Of course, it complicates one's judgement about *R. v. Keegstra* that its facts involve a forum (namely, teaching in high school) in which the state has a legitimate interest in imparting constitutional values, including both the right of free speech and the right against unjust discrimination. Education under liberal constitutionalism must impart its basic values of tolerance and mutual respect; it is a fundamental misunderstanding of both the role of both free speech and liberal education to suppose that such education should or must be open to all views, including views (like Holocaust denial) for which nothing can be reasonably said.[164] Teaching anti-Semitism, in the way Keegstra evidently did, is an abuse of his educational responsibilities as a teacher, and he could and should, on that ground, have reasonably been dismissed. The application of a criminal statute to his teaching may be regarded as a closer case,[165] certainly not as constitutionally objectionable as the application of such a statute to a more conventional public forum of discourse and discussion; the Canadian Supreme Court, however, expressly declined the invitation to draw any such distinctions.[166]

Judicial views on these constitutional issues are not, of course, monolithic either in Canada or elsewhere. *Keegstra*, for example, is a closely divided case (four to three), which itself indicates a substantial body of contrary judicial opinion in Canada about the underlying issues of free speech; in another case, *R. v. Zundel*,[167] a similarly closely divided Canadian Supreme Court held (four to three) unconstitutional, on vagueness grounds, Criminal Code, section 181, prohibiting wilful publication of false news, applied to Zundel's pamphlet advocating Holocaust denial. In contrast to

---

[162] See, for complementary views, Terry Heinrichs, 'Censorship as free speech! Free Expression Values and the Logic of Silencing in R. v. Keegstra', 36 *Alberta L Rev.* 835 (1998); Calvin R. Massey, 'Hate Speech, Cultural Diversity, and the Foundational Paradigms of Free Expression', 40 *UCLA L Rev.* 103 (1992); Robert C. Post, 'Free Speech and Religious, Racial, and Sexual Harassment: Racist Speech, Democracy, and the First Amendment', 32 *Wm. And Mary L Rev.* 267 (1991).

[163] See, for evidence on this point, Jeffrey G. Reitz, 'Less Racial Discrimination in Canada, or Simply Less Racial Conflict?: Implications of Comparisons with Britain', 14 *Canadian Public Policy* 424 (1988).

[164] See, on this point, Lipstadt, n. 130 above, 183–208.

[165] On balance, my own considered judgement would regard such a criminal statute as constitutionally improper, in light of the reasonable and less restrictive alternative of firing.

[166] See *R. v. Keegstra*, 3 Can. SCR 697, 773 (1990). But see *Attis* v. *Board of School Trustees*, 1 Can. SCR 825 (1996) (school board transfer of public school teacher to non-teaching role, for having made anti-Semitic statements in off-duty hours, held constitutional; but school board prohibition on making such statements held unconstitutrional).

[167] See *R. v. Zundel*, 2 Can. SCR 731 (1992).

the German Constitutional Court, Justice McLachlin, writing for the Canadian Supreme Court, quite properly analysed such conscientious statements of false facts as protected speech[168] and then found the statute unreasonably overbroad because not narrowly tailored to a legitimate state purpose[169] (the Court, however, reserved the possible constitutionality of a more narrowly drawn Holocaust denial statute, like that of Germany[170]). Similarly, although group libel laws have been regarded as constitutionally acceptable in other jurisdictions, there is a developing body of distinguished judicial practice that has questioned at least some applications of these laws; the European Court of Human Rights has thus struck down Denmark's attempt to apply its hate speech law to a journalist who interviewed on television a group that made derogatory remarks about immigrants and ethnic groups[171] and the Israeli Supreme Court struck down the limitations imposed by the Israeli Broadcasting Authority on broadcasting the racist opinions of Rabbi Meir Kahane, an elected member of the Knesset.[172] My argument offers reasons of political theory both in support of such growing internal constitutional doubts and in support of extending such criticism further.

BRITISH AND ISRAELI LAW

There is one final form of group libel law that we should examine, namely, a law, like that in Britain, more narrowly directed at threats to public order in the following general terms:

A person who uses threatening, abusive or insulting words or behaviour, or displays any written material which is threatening, abusive or insulting, is guilty of an offence if—
(a) he intends thereby to stir up racial hatred, or
(b) having regard to all the circumstances racial hatred is likely to be stirred up thereby.[173]

The statute, as specifically directed at racial incitement, dates from 1965,[174] and has gone through a number of revisions before reaching its current form in 1986;[175] but, in all its forms, the statute has required the procedural requirement that a prosecution could only be brought by the Attorney General, or with his consent, which has effectively limited the number of prosecutions brought. The design of this requirement was to enable the government to avoid petty prosecutions and focus on only

---

[168] See *ibid.*, 751–60.   [169] See *ibid.*, 760–78.   [170] See *ibid.*, at 767.
[171] See *Jersild* v. *Denmark* (1995) 19 EHRR 1 (Ct.); see also *Castells* v. *Spain* (1992) 14 EHRR 445 (Ct.) (striking down criminal prosecution, for insulting the government, of Basque national senator for newspaper article about murders in the Basque country that he argued were not adequately prosecuted by the government, claiming 'behind these acts can only be the Government').
[172] See *Meir Kahane* v. *The Broadcasting Authority* 41(3) PD 225 (1987) reprinted in English translation in Itzhak Zamir and Allen Zysblat, *Public Law in Israel* (Clarendon Press, Oxford, 1996), 74–107.
[173] Public Order Act 1986, s. 18.
[174] See, on the 1965 statute and its background, Anthony Lester and Geoffrey Bindman, *Race and Law in Great Britain* (Harvard University Press, Cambridge, Mass., 1972), at 343–74.
[175] See, for illuminating history of its background and various revisions, Kenneth Lasson, 'Racism in Great Britain: Drawing the Line on Free Speech', 7 *Boston College Third World LJ* 161 (1987); see also W. J. Wolffe, 'Values in Conflict: Incitement to Racial Hatred and the Public Order Act 1986' [1987] *Public Law* 85.

what it perceived as the most serious forms of racist propaganda, as well as to institutionalize a safeguard (consent of the Attorney General) against proceedings that would penalize legitimate controversy.[176]

The British statute, both in its substance and procedure, more narrowly confines group libel actions than the previous statutes we have now examined, focusing on abusive or threatening words that give offence to minorities. It is not, however, a fighting words or breach of the peace statute of the sort that, appropriately limited, would satisfy the American clear and present danger test.[177] It was, rather, expressly passed by Parliament to prohibit anti-Semitic and other insults that would not be actionable under Britain's statutes condemning incitement to violence.[178] While the requirement of the Attorney General's consent has appreciably limited the prosecutions that have been brought, those that have been brought do not, to say the least, inspire confidence that a proper balance has been struck between the right of free speech and the right against unjust discrimination. The Court of Appeal quashed one such prosecution of a 17-year-old labourer for attaching a racialist tract to the front door of an MP's home; the Court found that the youth's actions did not constitute distribution to the public within the then terms of the statute.[179] A successful prosecution was brought against the leader of the National Socialist Movement and an associate for distribution of a pamphlet 'The Coloured Invasion', but other successful prosecutions were brought against black leaders for anti-white insults at small meetings in Reading and Hyde Park; as a result of the latter prosecutions, the racialist utterances were widely reported in the British press (whereas the prosecution of the National Socialist leader had received little attention).[180] Yet another prosecution was brought against four members of the Racial Preservation Society for distributing the newsletter of the Society that spoke about the dangers of race mixing and the threat to white Britain from the increasing coloured population; the court became a forum for the discussion of the effects of miscegenation, and the defendants were acquitted.[181] More recently, a prosecution was successfully brought against the Dowager Lady Birdwood, an elderly woman who publishes a periodical called *Choice* that argues for sending blacks and Jews back where they came from.[182] The Court of Appeal, in rejecting her appeal against conviction, reviewed Lady Birdwood's testimony and questioning at trial in ways that suggest (to a foreign observer) the pathos

[176] See Lasson, n. 175 above, 167.

[177] On fighting words, with *Chaplinsky* v. *New Hampshire*, 315 US 568 (1942) (breach of the peace statute may be constitutionally applied to fighting words like 'damned fascist'), cf. *Gooding* v. *Wilson*, 405 US 518 (1972) (statute, condemning opprobrious words tending to breach of peace, struck down as overbroad). On breach of the peace, with *Feiner* v. *New York*, 340 US 315 (1961) (disorderly conduct conviction upheld against speaker who refused to obey police orders), cf. *Edwards* v. *South Carolina*, 372 US 229 (1963) (breach of peace convictions of civil rights demonstrators on state grounds held unconstitutional).

[178] See, on this point, Lester and Bindman, n. 174 above, 344–67. For how demanding requirements for incitement should be, consistently with respect for civil liberties, see Ruth Gavison, 'Incitement and the Limits of Law', in Post (ed.), n. 124 above, at 43–65.

[179] *R.* v. *Britton* [1967] 2 QB 51.   [180] See Lester and Bindman, n. 174 above, 368–9.
[181] See *ibid.*, 369–71.   [182] On Lady Birdwood, see Lasson, n. 175 above, 178.

and absurdity of trials of this sort. For example, when Lady Birdwood questioned whether the Holocaust occurred, this led the judge to say:

Even the Germans admit that the Holocaust took place now, do they not?

   The appellant answered:

Yes, of course they pay reparations but I still feel there is something wrong and in any case, as I said—
Q. What you just said was that in your view it never took place?
A. Yes.
Q. I am just wondering why the Germans admit it if it did not happen?
A. Well, I wonder too. I do.

Or, when the judge queried Birdwood about her motives as follows:

Have I got this right, Lady Birdwood; one of the objects of this booklet, you say, is to encourage, in order to get some sort of dialogue going and dialogue principally between Christians and Jews?
A. Yes your Honour. This is the way I started out doing this job was to try and get a dialogue.
Q. What about this chapter, because this chapter is asking for the expulsion of both Blacks and Jews, is it not?
A. Yes, it sounds like a contradiction.
Q. If that came to pass there would not be anybody to have a dialogue with?
A. That is quite true, your Honour.

Or, when questioned about her use of the word 'satanic':

Q. Did you consider the word satanic to be an emotive word?
A. Not particularly because it's used so often now. I think it's quite a usual word.
Q. It means of the devil, does it not?
A. Yes, devilish.
Q. Did you consider that to be insulting or abusive?
A. No. Well, I don't when it's implied [*sic*] to me.

   Then Judge Pownall said:

If somebody told you that you were a satanic old thing, would you not think that insulting?
A. I've lived too long, your Honour, you know.
Q. You mean you are past insult?
A. I think I am almost, and there are so many insults now these days taken under this cover word racism, racist, people are getting perhaps used to it now. I mean, if you're looking perhaps for an insult, you know, your mind's dwelling on insults and perhaps you might think it was, I don't know, but it doesn't strike me that way at all.[183]

---

[183] *R.* v. *Birdwood*, Court of Appeal (Criminal Division), 11 Apr. 1995, available on LEXIS, UK Library, ENGCAS file, transcript: John Larking, at 7–8. The charges against Lady Birdwood were eventually dropped on 19 Jan. 1998, after the Attorney General signed an order to halt the proceedings against her, since Lady Birdwood was found not to have the mental capacity to stand trial. See Stuart Miller, 'Lady Birdwood's Failing Memory Brings Early End to Racism Trial', *Guardian*, 20 Jan. 1998, 6.

If this is the best one can do with a narrowly confined group libel statute, it supports my case that such laws are not worth the price they exact in compromising protection of both the right of free speech and the right against unjust discrimination. The compromise in the principle of free speech should be obvious: all these prosecutions are brought against speech expressive of conscientious conviction, and on grounds of what counts as the respect properly owed to a group that, as Lady Birdwood cogently observes, can mean anything and nothing. But these cases show how such laws compromise the right against unjust discrimination as well. They were brought, for example, against wholly conscientious attempts of ethnic minorities to speak in their own voice about structural injustice, and thus disempower the discourse that best contests pervasive patterns of structural injustice that remain otherwise invisible; the application of such laws in Israel to Palestinian advocacy[184] or in South Africa to anti-apartheid advocacy[185] or in Sri Lanka to the Tamil minority[186] or India to the Muslim minority[187] or in New South Wales to Aborigines[188] suggests how structurally pervasive this problem is. Such laws also have unacceptable consequences in legitimating and even encouraging racist speech. For one thing, the terms of such laws, targeting blatantly insulting forms of speech, have the perverse consequence of legitimating speech that is more sanitized and thus, though equally or more racist, more broadly attractive and appealing.[189] For another, each such prosecution (whether successful or not), by virtue of the very nature of due process of law, gives a fair hearing to views that do not deserve such a hearing, and thus improperly legitimates them, sometimes (as in the case of the indomitable Lady Birdwood) renders them perversely sympathetic; indeed, acquittals put the state's mark of approval on views it claims to condemn. In some cases, as we have seen, racist views meant for a small audience are thus given, by the perverse gift of an allegedly anti-racist law, a national audience; in others, the very illegitimacy of such laws, on the ground of com-

---

[184] See, on this point, Joshua Schoffman, 'Legislation Against Racist Incitement in Israel: A 1992 Appraisal', in Sandra Colliver (ed.), *Striking a Balance: Hate Speech, Freedom of Expression and Non-discrimination* (Article 19, International Centre against Censorship, London, and Human Rights Centre, University of Essex, 1992), 192–6, at 194–5.

[185] See Gilbert J. Marcus, 'Racial Hostility: The South African Experience', in Coliver (ed.), n. 184 above, 208–22. On the situation in the new South Africa, see Lene Johannessen, 'Should Censorship of Racist Publications have a Place in the New South Africa?', in *ibid.*, 223–37.

[186] See Sunila Abeyesekera and Kenneth L. Cain, 'Incitement to Inter-Ethnic Hatred in Sri Lanka', in *ibid.*, 238–44.

[187] See, in general, Venkat Eswaran, 'Advocacy of National, Racial, and Religious Hatred: The Indian Experience', in *ibid.*, 171–81; see also Anthony Chase, '"Pakistan or the Cemetery": Muslim Minority Rights in Contemporary India', 16 *BC Third World LJ* 35 (1966); see also Anthony Chase, 'Legal Guardians: Islamic Law, International Law, Human Rights Law, and the Salman Rushdie Affair', 11 *Am. UJ Int'l L & Pol'y* 375, 423–4 (1996).

[188] See, on this point, Wojciech Sadurski, 'Racial Vilification, Psychic Harm, and Affirmative Action', n. 46 above, pp. 90–1; for relevant background, see Kate Eastman, 'Racial Vilification: The Australian Experience,' in Coliver, (ed.), n. 184 above, 75–81; Kitty Eggerking, 'Australia: The Role of the Media in Perpetuating Racism', in *ibid.*, 82–6; Sharyn Ch'ang, 'Legislating Against Racism: Racial Vilification Laws in New South Wales', *ibid.*, 87–105.

[189] See, for evidence of this consequence in the case of Britain, Lester and Bindman, n. 174 above, 371–3.

promising the right of free speech, affords an incentive to the very practices it means to discourage. One British commentator concluded that the statute 'has probably been adverse to race relations in Britain'.[190] Another commentator astutely observes:

the comparison can be taken further if we look at the events of the 'Skokie-Nazi' cases in the United States in 1977 and compare them with similar happenings regarding the English National Front and the Irish Republican Army in the United Kingdom. The Skokie cases were well litigated and found many freedoms of protest, but it is interesting to note that the Nazis never marched in Skokie. Although English law prohibits a large number of the behaviours that the courts finally allowed in the Skokie cases, many of those behaviours were occurring on marches in England at the time—marches that *did* take place.[191]

This observation suggests an important consequence of the principle of free speech as I have defended it in this book. The consequence of its prohibition of state censorship in the domain of conviction is to render the conscientious judgements of people generally in civil society all the more powerful because now responsible for exercising their reasonable moral powers, for example, in condemning and contesting conscientious views with which they disagree. American experience, under the principle of free speech I have defended here, illustrates this consequence in ways that further clarify its structural connections to vindicating the right against unjust discrimination. In effect, this principle of free speech disempowers the state in the domain of conviction, but much empowers public opinion in this domain in ways that subject racist advocates to ongoing criticism and debate that may more effectively control their behaviour than group libel laws. In light of the argument I have made, comparative experience in Britain and elsewhere appears reasonably to support the same conclusion.

The experience of Israel, a British-style parliamentary democracy who adopted laws in this area very much on the British model, also supports this conclusion. Israel strengthened its existing sedition and group defamation laws to include a law against racial incitement in 1986 very much in response to the growing importance in Israel of the racist politics of Rabbi Meir Kahane, who had been elected to the Knesset; the new law required, like Britain's, the consent of the attorney general for prosecution and had a similar focus on racial incitement;[192] correlative legislation banned racist parties from the Knesset.[193] As if to create balance between these laws (directed

[190] See *ibid.*, 374.

[191] See Avrom Sherr, 'Incitement to Racial Hatred in England', in Greenspan and Levitt (eds.), n. 100 above, 63–82, at 80.

[192] See Israel, Penal Code Amendment Law (No. 2), 1986.

[193] See Israel, Basic Law: The Knesset sec. 7(a), amended in Basic Law: The Knesset Amend. No. 9, 1155 Sefer Hahukim (SH) 196 (1985); Israel, Knesset Elections Law, 1969 sec. 63, 23 L.S.I.110 (consolidated version), amended in 1155 SH 196 (1985). For good studies of both the racial incitement law and the laws banning racist parties, see Eliezer Lederman and Mala Tabory, 'Criminalization of Racial Incitement in Israel', 24 *Stan. J of International Law* 55 (1988); Mala Tabory, 'Legislation Against Incitement to Racism in Israel' (1987) 17 *Israel Yearbook on Human Rights* 270–99; David Kretzmer, 'Racial Hatred in Israel' (1992) 22 *Israel Yearbook on Human Rights* 243–59; Gerald Cromer, 'The Prevention of Racial Incitement in Israel', in Greenspan and Levitt (eds.), n. 100 above, 131–481; Raphael Cohen-Almagor, *The Boundaries of Liberty and Tolerance: The Struggle Against Kahanism in Israel* (University Press of Florida, Gainesville, Flo., 1994).

against the racism of Jews), Israel's 'Denial of Holocaust (Prohibition) Law' outlaws the 'denying or diminishing the proportion' of 'crimes against the Jewish people or crimes against humanity', if done 'with intent to defend the perpetrators of those acts or to express sympathy or identification with them'; also outlawed are statements that are positive toward such acts ('expressing praise or sympathy for or identification with . . . ').[194] The ostensible purpose of legislation of this sort was to make a statement of political education, one that 'reinforced anti-racist ideology and influenced modes of behaviour through its normative proscription against racism'.[195] But legislation, thus designed to rule out equally both advocacy of racism against the Palestinians and comparable anti-Semitic advocacy (Holocaust denial) against the Jews, has, strikingly, led to only one conviction under the racial incitement law, that of an Arab for distributing anti-government propaganda.[196] What may most charitably be said about such legislation is that its end (encompassing both Jews and Arabs in a common discourse of anti-racism) was estimable; but its means, censorship in the domain of conviction, subverted its ends. Kahane's disqualification from the Knesset and assassination in November 1990 had a very detrimental effect on the fortunes of his Kach Party, but the lack of prosecution of either Kahane or any other Jewish leader for racial incitement put the stamp of legitimacy on such views, some of which were adopted by other political parties.[197] More importantly, the attempt of dominant Israeli political elites to demonize both Kahane and Holocaust advocates, as similarly outside the scope of Israeli toleration, subverts the legitimacy and integrity of the politics of identity of the ordinary people of Israel (Jewish and Palestinian) to engage in a reasonable dialogue, as democratic equals, about the political power structural injustice invisibly enjoys as an unjust force in their politics, Jewish and Palestinian, as it does in the politics of all peoples.[198] A measure of free speech, thus based on a political ideology of friends and enemies (like that of Schmitt), enforces, as in Germany, the divisions in national identity that it claims to transcend.

THE PERSPECTIVE OF PUBLIC INTERNATIONAL LAW

The Canadian Supreme Court in *R.* v. *Keegstra* also supported its interpretive and normative argument by appealing to developments in public international law since the Second World War, most notably, the requirement of Article 4(a) of the International Convention on the Elimination of All Forms of Racial Discrimination that states 'declare an offence punishable by law all dissemination of ideas based on

---

[194] See Israel, Denial of Holocaust (Prohibition Law) 5746–1986, cited at 200, in Stephen J. Roth, 'The Laws of Six Countries: An Analytical Comparison', in Greenspan and Levitt (eds.), n. 100 above, 177–211.

[195] See Lederman and Tabory, n. 193 above, at 83.

[196] See Joshua Schoffman, 'Legislation Against Racist Incitement in Israel: A 1992 Appraisal', in Coliver (ed.), n. 184 above, 192–6, at 194–5.

[197] See, on this point, Cromer, n. 193 above, at 145–6.

[198] See, on this point, Schoffman, n. 196 above, 192–6.

racial superiority or hatred, incitement to racial discrimination';[199] similar developments in Italian law (as elsewhere) have been prodded by such doctrines of public international law.[200] These developments, initiated by the Charter of the United Nations in 1945[201] and the Universal Declaration of Human Rights in 1948,[202] represent a constitutional reconstruction of public international law analogous to those at the national and regional levels as a response to the institutional defects that led to the atrocities of the Second World War. Associated developments include the Convention on the Prevention and Punishment of Genocide (1948),[203] the International Covenant on Civil and Political Rights (1966),[204] the International Covenant on Economic, Social and Cultural Rights (1966),[205] and others.[206] The development within public international law of a normative and legal discourse about the role respect for basic human rights does and should play in the legitimacy of government complements, of course, the constitutional discourse to this effect at the national and regional levels. The normative political theory of democratic constitutionalism, previously operative in only a few nations before the Second World War, is now much more strongly entrenched legally both nationally and regionally, and public international law itself now appeals to and develops the implications of this theory.

My topic is a narrow one within this complementary national, regional, and international discourse. Section 4(a) of the Convention on the Elimination of all Forms of Racial Discrimination appears to require group libel laws that, on the argument I have made, arguably does not draw the correct implications from the background political theory of human rights that it takes itself to be implementing (in the next chapter, I will develop a similar criticism about the role the International Covenant on Political and Civil Rights has played in legitimation of the law of blasphemy). How, interpretively and normatively, are we to understand this discrepancy, and what implications should this understanding have for the way we assess the approach to this question at the national and regional levels (for example, the approach taken by the Canadian Supreme Court in *Keegstra*).

One natural way to address this issue is to appeal to contextual differences along the lines suggested by my colleague, Theodore Meron:

> The different approach in the United States [from that required by the Convention] should not be explained on constitutional grounds alone. It also reflects, at least in recent history, the feeling of confidence and security in a developed and relatively stable society that, while failing

[199] Cited in *R.* v. *Keegstra*, n. 145 above, at 751.

[200] See, on this point, Giorgio Sacerdoti, 'Italian Legislation and Case Law on Racial and Religious Hatred and Group Libel: International Aspects' (1992) 22 *Israel Yearbook on Human Rights* 229–42.

[201] See Bahiyyih G. Tahzib, *Freedom of Religion or Belief: Ensuring Effective International Legal Protection* (Martinus Nijhoff Publishers, The Hague, 1996), at 66–70.

[202] See *ibid.*, 70–81.

[203] See Natan Lerner, *Group Rights and Discrimination in International Law* (Martinus Nijhoff Publishers, Dordrecht, 1991), at 141–6.

[204] See Tahzib, n. 201 above, 81–92.   [205] See *ibid.*, 92–3.

[206] See, e.g., *ibid.*, at 99–121.

to eradicate racism, has found orderly means of dealing with its racial problems, as well as the traditional preference for individual freedoms over the regulatory power of the state. In some other countries, however, activities and organizations that in the United States would often be regarded as creating only a marginal possibility of violence and threat to public order might be regarded as a clear and present danger. If certain provisions of the Convention are overbroad when viewed against the U.S. social and legal systems, it does not necessarily follow that they are overbroad for some of the other countries.[207]

The normative political theory of human rights has an abstract character that may reasonably be contextualized differently, and there is thus certainly theoretical space for the kind of reconciliation that Meron proposes. But such reconciliation can only be plausible if we are reasonably satisfied, to start with, that the Convention embodies a normatively coherently conception of the political theory that it claims to implement. There are two reasons for doubt on this score, both of which relate to questions about the internal coherence of the Convention.

First, the sense of the need for the Convention arose from the adoption by the General Assembly of the United Nations in 1960 of Resolution 1510 (XV), condemning all manifestations and practices of racial, religious, and ethnic hatred in all spheres of the life of society, as violations of the United Nations Charter and the Universal Declaration of Human Rights; the resolution 'was adopted after the attention of the United Nations had been drawn to an outburst of anti-Semitic incidents in several parts of the world, in 1959 and 1960'.[208] The Convention, adopted by the General Assembly in 1965,[209] limits, however, its condemnation to racial or ethnic discrimination, not addressing, except incidentally,[210] the issues of religious discrimination and intolerance which importantly gave rise to the expressions of political anti-Semitism that were the occasion for conceiving the need for the Convention; moreover, the expansive obligations of Article 4(a) were proposed and importantly supported by the representatives of the Soviet Union and Poland over the narrower proposals of the United States[211] and were a rallying point for nations in the then Communist bloc for the allegiance of the large bloc of African and Asian nations.[212] The processes giving rise to Article 4(a) of the Convention are thus very much normatively distorted by the issues of the Cold War. On the one hand, the Soviet bloc thus marginalized what, in light of the Second World War, should have been the normatively central issues of anti-Semitism (not only because of its hostility to Israel but

---

[207] See Theodore Meron, 'The Meaning and Reach of the International Convention on the Elimination of All Forms of Racial Discrimination', 79 *American J Int'l Law* 283 (1985), at 298–9.

[208] See Natan Lerner, *The U.N. Convention on the Elimination of all Forms of Racial Discrimination* (Sijthoff & Noordhoff, Alphen aan den Rijn, 1980), at 1.

[209] See *ibid.*, 6.

[210] The Israeli representative to the Third Committee, drafting the Convention, noted, in this connection, 'that it should be borne in mind that the religious and ethnic aspects of discrimination were often closely interrelated', *ibid.*, 10.

[211] See, on this point, *ibid.*, at p. 44.

[212] See, on the background of the drafting and adoption of Art. 4, *ibid.*, 43–53.

because of its own entrenched traditions of cultural anti-Semitism[213]); on the other hand, the nations in Africa and Asia, with a history of enduring racist colonialism at the hands of the nations of Europe, could have such structural injustice condemned without confronting the degree to which their own cultures, by not according respect for the basic human rights of conscience and speech, may entrench such structural injustice.[214] It is hard to believe, in the wake of our current understanding of Soviet Communism,[215] that one today can regard Article 4(a), rooted in such myopia, as entitled to reasonable weight in contemporary circumstances.

Secondly, such normative myopia is only made possible if, in the discussion of issues of structural injustice, one effectively abridges the basic human rights of conscience and speech that, appropriately guaranteed, make such reasonable discourse possible (the politics of identity). The failure of the Convention appropriately to weight the right of free speech in relation to the right against unjust discrimination is thus at one with its failure to take seriously the right against religious intolerance.[216] The abridgement of the right to toleration was, as we have seen (Chapter 3), culturally constitutive of racism; and appropriate guarantees of such toleration (including free speech) have been crucial both to the understanding and remedy of racism. Against this background, the claim of public international law to condemn racism but not to condemn religious intolerance reflects an incoherent and self-defeating conception of what the evil of racism is. It is surely a compelling point, about the inadequate current state of the consensus of public international law on these issues, that the international public law guarantees of religious liberty are still comparatively undeveloped; the United Nations 1960 resolution, earlier mentioned, called for such guarantees against both racial and religious hatred; the Convention on the Elimination of all Forms of Racial Discrimination followed quickly in 1965, but the promised guarantee of religious liberty was the much later (1981) and much weaker Declaration on the Elimination of all Forms of Intolerance and of Discrimination Based on Religion or Belief.[217] For example, at the insistence of

---

[213] See, for background on this point, Mala Tabory and M. Zvi, 'Racial Prejudice and Incitement to Hatred Against Jews in the USSR: Legal and Political Aspects' (1992) 22 *Israel Yearbook on Human Rights* 169–91; for post-Soviet developments, see Yuri Luryi and Alexander Lyubechansky, 'Soviet/Russian Legislation Against National or Racial Hatred and Discrimination', *Review of Central and East European Law*, vol. 20, no. 2, 217–31 (1994); Yuri Rechetov, 'Incitement of National Enmity in the Context of International Law, Foreign and Soviet Practice' (1992) 22 *Israel Yearbook on Human Rights* 155–68.

[214] See, on this point in African cultures, Kwame Anthony Appiah, *In My Father's House: Africa in the Philosophy of Culture* (Oxford University Press, New York, 1992); on Asian cultures, see Amy L. Chua, 'Markets, Democracy, and Ethnicity: Towards a New Paradigm for Law and Development', 108 *Yale LJ* 1 (1998).

[215] See, on this point, Francois Furet, *The Passing of an Illusion: The Idea of Communism in the Twentieth Century* (trans. Deborah Furet, University of Chicago Press, Chicago, Ill., 1999).

[216] On the generality of this failure to take seriously the right against religious intolerance (including under national laws), see Kevin Boyle, 'Religious Intolerance and the Incitement of Hatred', in Coliver (ed.), n. 184 above, 61–71.

[217] See, for pertinent discussion, Tahzib, n. 201 above, 165–89.

Islamic states, the Preamble omits express guarantee of the right to change one's religion or belief.[218]

Article 4(a) of the Convention thus rests on a normative incoherence in its understanding of the nature and weight of the basic human right of free speech and the right against unjust discrimination. As we have seen (Chapter 3), the understanding and remedy of structural injustice (required by the right against unjust discrimination) turns on the theory of toleration, which requires the full protection of both the right of conscience and of speech on the terms earlier defended. To suggest that the right of conscience and of speech can and should be compromised in the interest of advancing the right against unjust discrimination is, incoherently, to frustrate both basic human rights. Public international law is trapped in this dilemma because the conditions of reasonable consensus on sound principles of public international law in this area apparently do not at this time obtain. We should not, however, claim that the consensus that exists (at least on Article 4(a)) is defensible. It is not. For this reason of compelling political theory, national and regional law improperly gives interpretive and normative weight to public international law when it dilutes its conception of free speech and anti-discrimination to the measure of Article 4(a).

---

[218] See Tahzib, n. 201 above, 167. On the inadequate state of the protection of religious liberty under national laws, see Elizabeth Odio Benito, *Elimination of all Forms of Intolerance and Discrimination Based on Religion or Belief* (United Nations, New York, 1989).

5

Free Speech as a Remedy for Structural Injustice:
Sexism and Homophobia

I have now developed both the argument for toleration and the theory of structural injustice to both explain and justify the role of a certain interpretation of the principle of free speech as a remedy for the structural injustice of racism. The argument included the development of the argument for toleration both to explain the principle of free speech and a further elaboration to explicate the nature of structural injustice and the role free speech played among its reasonable remedies. On this basis, I contested two views of the relationship of this interpretation of free speech and structural injustice: first, that they are normatively independent; and secondly, that the principle of free speech, modified to validate group libel laws, reasonably would remedy a structural injustice like racism. Thus, I both defended the dependence thesis (structural injustice depends on the abridgment of free speech) and argued that the proposed modification would, if anything, be self-defeating as a reasonable remedy for racism. The thesis was illustrated with reference to American constitutional jurisprudence and then brought critically to bear on the rather different views under other systems of national and regional law and under public international law.

I want now to generalize the scope of this structure of argument to justify an interpretation of free speech as a remedy for the structural injustice of sexism and homophobia in the following stages. I defend the dependence thesis by showing the pivotal role the abridgment of free speech played in the cultural entrenchment of sexism and homophobia. In particular, I focus in this chapter on two issues: first, the role anti-obscenity laws crucially played in the repression of the reasonable politics of identity of feminism and gay rights; and secondly, the role blasphemy laws currently play. With respect to the former, I examine critically the inspiration of the scholarly revival of interest in the constitutionality of group libel laws, namely, a related development arising within feminism that sought to ascribe such a group libel to women in pornography and, on this ground, to repress it.[1] My critical examination of this latter argument generalizes the argument of the previous chapter to make a similar case about the role of free speech as a remedy for the structural injustice of sexism and homophobia. Such anti-pornography arguments not only fail to remedy the structural injustice of sexism and homophobia; they worsen it in ways that should be of concern to anyone absorbed in constructing reasonable remedies for such structural injustice; these problems are, I argue, illustrated in the recent adoption by the Canadian Supreme Court of the view here criticized. I then turn to the related issue

[1] See, on the importance of this inspiration, Mari J. Matsuda *et al.*, *Words that Wound: Critical Race Theory, Assaultive Speech, and the First Amendment* (Westview Press, Boulder, Colo., 1993), at 22–3, 62, 64, 74, 79, 108–9.

of the blasphemy laws, which are, I argue, forms of group libel laws that are questionable on the same grounds; my focus will be on the role these laws have played in the Salman Rushdie case and in the repression of advocacy of gay rights in Britain, comparing the quite different approaches taken in Britain and the United States with respect to rather similar, allegedly blasphemous advocacy by gay artists. The normative force of my criticism is directed at the continuing acceptability of such blasphemy laws under both national and regional systems of law and under public international law.

OBSCENITY LAWS

As earlier suggested (Chapter 3), the theory of structural injustice, as applied to sexism and homophobia, was developed in the United States as part of second-wave feminism as an interpretation of the arguments of antebellum abolitionist feminists who argued that slavery, racism, and sexism rested on a common structural injustice.[2] The argument of toleration, elaborated by abolitionist feminists to include slavery, racism, and sexism, suggested dimensions of argument that focused on both the basic human rights that had been unjustly denied to a class of persons (as non-bearers of human rights) and on the inadequate sectarian grounds that rationalized such abridgments of basic rights. These two dimensions defined the structural injustice I earlier called moral slavery.

It is fundamental to the kind of criticism that the argument for toleration has brought to American racism and sexism that the political power of these ideologies rested on dehumanizing cultural stereotypes that abridged basic human rights of moral personality, including, prominently, the right to conscience and free speech. Such basic human rights are culture-creating rights, affording appropriate space for the free exercise of our powers of moral personality in responsibly creating, forging, sustaining the cultural and institutional forms through which we reasonably find and sustain permanent humane value in living both for ourselves and, if the values are reasonable and enduring, for later generations. Systematic abridgment of these rights is the fundamental insult and indignity that it is because of the role the free exercise of such rights plays in self-respect for our creative moral freedom to originate claims and reasonably to forge and sustain the cultural forms of life that give enduring personal sense and moral meaning to living a life as a responsible moral agent. Persons systematically deprived of such rights, in a constitutional community like the United States that otherwise respects such rights, are denationalized as both persons and citizens: useful as tools are useful, lovable and amusing as pets are, but not equal subjects of rights and responsibility and thus members of the constitutional community. Accordingly, any serious attention to such structural injustice requires correlative

---

[2] For elaboration of this argument, see David A. J. Richards, *Women, Gays, and the Constitution: The Grounds for Feminism and Gay Rights in Culture and Law* (University of Chicago Press, Chicago, Ill., 1998), chs. 3, 5.

attention to the role abridgment of such basic rights played in the cultural entrenchment of such injustice.

The tradition of rights-based feminism, from Wollstonecraft[3] to Sarah Grimke[4] to Lucretia Mott to Elizabeth Stanton,[5] has given central weight, consistent with the centrality of the inalienable right to conscience in the argument for toleration, to claims for equal rights to conscience and correlative rights to equal educational opportunity (including, as Wollstonecraft argued, integrated public education[6]). For Grimke[7] and Mott,[8] the argument focused on the equal right of women to be scholars, theologians, and ministers and thus to bring their moral independence to bear on the criticism of misogynist Bible interpretation and the political power it had unjustly been allowed to enjoy; Stanton published *The Woman's Bible* very much in this spirit.[9] Women had in nineteenth-century American culture used constitutional guarantees of religious liberty not only in forging, as Grimke and Mott did, abolitionist feminist dissent within a religion like Quakerism that traditionally accorded a more central role to women in the works of conscience,[10] but in generating and fostering either highly personal forms of spirituality like that of Sojourner Truth[11] or religious organizations founded by women like Shakerism, Christian Science, and spiritualism.[12] But the censure of Stanton by the suffrage movement she had founded[13] suggests the degree to which suffrage feminism had compromised the argument for toleration that had made it normatively possible, cramping

---

[3] See, on this point, *ibid.*, 63–71.   [4] See *ibid.*, 81–102.

[5] See *ibid.*, 102–15.

[6] See Mary Wollstonecraft, 'A Vindication of the Rights of Woman', in *The Works of Mary Wollstonecraft* (ed. Janet Todd and Marilyn Butler, 1790, New York University Press, New York, 1989), v, 65–266.

[7] See Richards, n. 2 above, 96–8, 104.   [8] See *ibid.*, 103–4.

[9] See Mary D. Pellauer, *Toward a Tradition of Feminist Theology: The Religious Social Thought of Elizabeth Cady Stanton, Susan B. Anthony, and Anna Howard Shaw* (Carlson Publishing Inc., Brooklyn, NY, 1991).

[10] See, in general, Margaret Hope Bacon, *Mothers of Feminism: The Story of Quaker Women in America* (Harper & Row, San Francisco, Cal., 1989).

[11] See Jacquelyn Grant, *White Women's Christ and Black Women's Jesus: Feminist Christology and Womanist Response* (Scholars Press, Atlanta, Ga., 1989), at 214, 219–20, 222.

[12] See, in general, Susan Starr Sered, *Priestess, Mother, Sacred Sister: Religions Dominated by Women* (Oxford University Press, New York, 1994). On spiritualism in particular, see Ann Braude, *Radical Spirits: Spiritualism and Women's Rights in Nineteenth-Century America* (Beacon Press, Boston, Mass., 1995); on Shakerism, see Nardi Reeder Campion, *Ann the Word: The Life of Mother Ann Lee, Founder of the Shakers* (Little, Brown, Boston, Mass., 1976); Lawrence Foster, *Women, Family, and Utopia: Communal Experiments of the Shakers, the Oneida Community, and the Mormons* (Syracuse University Press, Syracuse, NY, 1991), at 17–71; Henri Desroche, *The American Shakers: From Neo-Christianity to Presocialism* (trans. John K. Savacool, University of Massachusetts Press, Amherst, Mass., 1971); Marjorie Procter-Smith, *Women in Shaker Community and Worship: A Feminist Analysis of the Uses of Religious Symbolism* (Edwin Mellen Press, Lewiston, NY, 1985); Stephen J. Stein, *The Shaker Experience in America* (Yale University Press, New Haven, Conn., 1992); Jean M. Humez, *Mother's First-Born Daughters: Early Shaker Writings on Women and Religion* (Indiana University Press, Bloomington, Ind., 1993); Louis J. Kern, *An Ordered Love: Sex Roles and Sexuality in Victorian Utopias—the Shakers, the Mormons, and the Oneida Community* (University of North Carolina Press, Chapel Hill, NC, 1981), at 71–136.

[13] For discussion of this point, see Richards, n. 2 above, 154–5.

the scope of acceptable feminist conscience to the sectarian measure of a Frances Willard.[14]

An important background condition for the emergence of second-wave feminism after the Second World War was thus not only the increasing numbers of American women who worked,[15] but the formative cultural importance of the increasingly powerful insistence of the Supreme Court during this period that, consistent with the guarantees of both religious free exercise and anti-establishment in the First Amendment, the state not engage in or support what in contemporary circumstances was sectarian religious teaching, but extend respect to all forms of conscience, secular and religious.[16] While these doctrinal developments did not deal specifically with issues of gender or gender roles, they affirmed principles that affirmed limits on legitimate state power in the enforcement of sectarian purposes that were of generative importance in the constitutional legitimation of new forms of conscientious dissent, both anti-racist and anti-sexist, that rested on such grounds. In the areas of free speech and privacy, interpretations of such principles were reasonably extended specifically to protect the rights of women.

Equal respect for rights of conscience also required that constitutional attention be paid, as it had in the area of race, to forms of state-imposed segregation that were inconsistent with equal educational opportunity. It was no accident that the NAACP had focused its anti-racist litigation strategy on first attacking such segregation in basic public education.[17] Consistent with the Boasian theory of the cultural construction of racism, no set of institutions could be more fundamental in framing such racism than the basic public school education which artificially divided and stigmatized minority students on grounds of race. Accordingly, the needed remedial statement of inclusion into the common culture on equal terms was eloquently made by integration of the basic institutions of universal public education. The Supreme Court has decided two cases that, consistent with Betty Friedan's early application of

---

[14] For fuller discussion, see Richards, n. 2 above, 149–55. See also, in general, Betty A. DeBerg, *Ungodly Women: Gender and the First Wave of American Fundamentalism* (Fortress Press, Minneapolis, Min., 1990).

[15] See William H. Chafe, *The Paradox of Change: American Women in the 20th Century* (Oxford University Press, New York, 1991), 166–72, 188–92.

[16] Important anti-establishment cases include *McCollum* v. *Board of Education*, 333 US 203 (1948) (release time for religious education unconstitutional) (cf. *Zorach* v. *Clauson*, 343 US 306 (1952) (not unconstitutional if release time is for religious teaching off site)); *Engel* v. *Vitale*, 370 US 421 (1962); *Abington School Dist.* v. *Schempp*, 374 US 203 (1963) (requirements of sectarian prayers unconstitutional); *Epperson* v. *Arkansas*, 393 US 97 (1968) (banning teaching Darwin unconstitutional). Important free exercise cases include *United States* v. *Ballard*, 322 US 78 (1944) (truth or falsity of religious belief not subject to state inquiry); *Torcaso* v. *Watkins*, 367 US 488 (1960) (requirement that officials must swear belief in God held unconstitutional); *United States* v. *Seeger*, 380 US 163 (1965) (conscientious exemption for those who object to all wars must extend to all beliefs, religious and non-religious); *Welsh* v. *United States*, 398 US 333 (1970) (similar finding); but cf. *Gillette* v. *United States*, 401 US 437 (1970) (failure to exempt selective conscientious objectors supported by adequate secular purpose). For commentary on these developments, see, in general, David A. J. Richards, *Toleration and the Constitution* (Oxford University Press, New York, 1986), at 67–162.

[17] See, in general, Mark Tushnet, *The NAACP's Legal Strategy against Segregated Education, 1925–1950* (University of North Carolina Press, Chapel Hill, NC, 1967).

our growing anti-racist worries about separate-but-equal to anti-sexism as well,[18] suggest common concerns in the area of gender.

In 1982 in *Mississippi University for Women* v. *Hogan,*[19] the Court in a five to four decision sustained a male's constitutional challenge to the State's policy of excluding men from the Mississippi University for Women (MUW) School of Nursing. Justice Powell in his dissent emphasized not only that co-educational public nursing schools were open to Hogan, but that the American practice of single-sex schools was supported by a long history that has only recently been largely abandoned[20] and that served today legitimate values of educational diversity.[21] Justice O'Connor, writing for the Court, found that the State's primary justification for the single-sex admissions policy of MUW, namely, compensation for discrimination against women, was disingenuous. There was no showing that women lacked opportunities to obtain training in nursing that would call for such a policy. Instead, 'MUW's policy of excluding males from admission to the School of Nursing tends to perpetuate the stereotyped view of nursing as an exclusively woman's job'.[22] That was objectionable because it 'lends credibility to the old view that women, not men, should become nurses, and makes the assumption that nursing is a field for women a self-fulfilling prophecy'.[23] In effect, a traditional conception of gender roles, itself based on denying equal educational opportunities to women, could not, *pace* Justice Powell, be a constitutionally reasonable measure of equal opportunity today. Justice O'Connor's scepticism about the enforcement 'of fixed notions concerning the roles and abilities of males and females'[24] in the educational context suggests the same Boasian themes we have already identified in the area of racial segregation, only now transposed into the key of gender. Inclusion of women into the common culture, on terms of equal respect for conscience, suggests at least a strong presumption of integrated educational opportunities.

The recent decision of the Supreme Court, by a seven to one majority, in *United States* v. *Virginia*[25] has, if anything, strengthened this presumption. The Virginia Military Institute (VMI) was the sole single-sex institution among Virginia's current institutions of higher learning; its exclusion of women was based on its purposes (the production of citizen-soldiers for leadership in civilian and military life) and its highly demanding, adversarial mode of education based on English public schools. Invoking the tests of Justice O'Connor's opinion in *Hogan,* Justice Ginsberg, writing for the Court, examined VMI's justifications for single-sex admissions and found them not to rest on compensatory purposes but on once traditional 'views about women's proper place'[26] that, themselves reflecting historical patterns of discrimination, may not be a reasonable measure of opportunity today.[27] In reaching this assessment, Justice Ginsberg noted the parallel historical uses of arguments, like those of VMI, to

---

[18] See Betty Friedan, *The Feminine Mystique* (Penguin, London, 1982), at 157–9.
[19] *Mississippi University for Women* v. *Hogan,* 458 US 718 (1982).   [20] See *ibid.,* 736–39.
[21] See *ibid.,* at 745.   [22] *Ibid.,* 729.   [23] *Ibid.,* 730.
[24] *Ibid.,* 725.   [25] See *United States* v. *Virginia,* 116 S Ct. 2264 (1996).
[26] See *ibid.,* 2277.   [27] See *ibid.,* 2280.

rationalize the exclusion of women from higher education[28] as well as from the practice of law, from law and medical schools, and from policing.[29] In all these cases,
'women's categorical exclusion, in total disregard of their individual merit'[30] failed to
do justice to women 'as citizens in our American democracy equal in stature to
men'.[31] The inclusion of women into VMI was called for on the same ground that,
in *Sweatt* v. *Painter*,[32] blacks were admitted to the University of Texas Law School:
only integration into common public educational institutions can do justice to the
equal rights of women as persons.[33]

If both the construction and remedy of the structural injustice of sexism thus clus-
tered around the right to conscience, both the abridgment and remedy of the right to
free speech play a comparably important role. The use of anti-obscenity laws exemplifies these points clearly in both the areas of sexism and homophobia.

Obscenity laws played a powerful censorious role against a wide range of dissenting late nineteenth- and early twentieth-century views on matters of sexuality and
gender, including against the poems of Whitman,[34] the advocacy of free love by
Victoria Woodhull,[35] Ezra Heywood,[36] and Lois Weisbrooker,[37] the advocacy of
contraception and abortion by Margaret Sanger,[38] and similar such advocacy, including of consensual homosexuality, by Emma Goldman.[39] Assessed from this historical
perspective, obscenity law (applied, as it was, to conscientious rights-based protest
against the dominant orthodoxy of sexuality and gender) was the main weapon to
abridge the fundamental rights of free speech of dissenters to the gender orthodoxy
of the gilded age, including rights-based feminists like Woodhull, Sanger, and
Goldman and their allies.[40] Such abridgements of rights of free speech compromised,
in turn, the more basic right to conscience, on which the right to free speech is often
grounded.[41] A number of highly conscientious dissenting speakers and the dissenting
convictions they held were subject to repression on the ground that they contested
the dominant majoritarian orthodoxy of gender and sexuality. The consequences
were devastating to them and to American public discourse and debate; no one could
reasonably be expected to even undertake such debate when they saw the consequences to a Woodhull or a Goldman. Rather, the message was either to go silent or
to self-censor and accommodate one's views and public image to the mainstream in
order to make progress on one issue (Sanger's strategy on contraception).[42] The

---

[28] See *United States* v. *Virginia*, 116 S Ct. 2277–8.   [29] See *ibid.*, 2280–2.

[30] See *ibid.*, 2282.   [31] See *ibid.*, 2282.

[32] See *Sweatt* v. *Painter*, 339 US 629 (1950).

[33] See *United States* v. *Virginia*, 116 S Ct. at 2285–6.

[34] See, on this point, Richards, n. 2 above, 14, 238, 298.

[35] See, on this point, *ibid.*, 161, 238, 239.   [36] See, on this point, *ibid.*, 163.

[37] See, on this point, *ibid.*, 163.

[38] See, on this point, *ibid.*, 156, 178, 179, 181, 238, 334.

[39] See, on this point, *ibid.*, 156, 181, 238, 239, 329.

[40] See, on the nature of their rights-based claims and the reactionary repressive response thereto, *ibid.*,
155–81.

[41] For elaboration on this point, see Richards, n. 16 above, 166–74.

[42] See, on this point, Richards, n. 2 above, 178–81.

growing marginalization of rights-based feminism in favour of suffrage feminism (in alliance with the temperance movement and purity leagues[43]) was thus by no means the consequence of fair discourse and debate, but rather of a highly cynical, blatantly unconstitutional political manipulation of the agenda of public debate and discussion. Such manipulation politically privileged the normative theory of gender roles of Catharine Beecher[44] and Frances Willard[45] and actively repressed dissenting views with the full force of criminal law and (in the case of Emma Goldman) also exiled her abroad.[46] The rights-based vision of abolitionist feminism was thus compromised in ways that advanced not only racism[47] but sexism as well.[48] A nation, which in the antebellum period sustained a public stage, at least outside the South, for the radical moral criticism of a Garrison or the Grimke sisters[49] could not in the twentieth century extend similar constitutional civility to the comparably rights-based moral protests of an Emma Goldman against the shallow conventionalities of the gilded age.

The consequences of such censorship were, if anything, more devastating for any serious American discussion of the case for gay rights, a case that had been classically made in the nineteenth century by an American, widely admired abroad as a prophet of the case for gay rights, namely, Walt Whitman.[50] The role that the interpretation of Whitman played in the development of European thought self-consciously about homosexuality as such had no correlative development in Whitman's own country. A homosexual subculture flourished in cities like New York in the period 1890–1940,[51] but one American commentator noted with dismay in 1913: '[i]t is rather odd that homosexuals, at least in America, do not regard Whitman as one of themselves or brag about him.'[52] Europeans (the British Edward Carpenter prominent among them[53]), not Americans, in the early twentieth century publicly connected Whitman with homosexuality.[54] Whitman played a role within the thriving New York City gay subculture in arguments for a more masculine interpretation of homosexual love[55] or as evidence of a larger gay culture;[56] the Spanish gay poet, Federico Garcia Lorca, made this latter point ('the faggots, Walt Whitman, point you out') in his harrowing 'Ode to Whitman' written on the basis of the Spanish gay poet's visit to New York City during this period.[57] But Lorca's dark picture of gay life in early twentieth-century New York City drew a devastating comparison about the

[43] See, on this point, *ibid.*, 153–5. [44] On Beecher's views, see *ibid.*, 72–8.
[45] On Willard's views, see *ibid.*, 149–52. [46] See, on this point, *ibid.*, 181.
[47] See, on this point, *ibid.*, 182–90. [48] See, on this point, *ibid.*, 141–81, 190–8.
[49] See, on this point, *ibid.*, chs. 2–3.
[50] See, on Whitman and his impact abroad, *ibid.*, 297–327.
[51] See, in general, George Chauncey, *Gay New York: Gender, Urban Culture, and the Making of the Gay Male World 1890–1940* (BasicBooks, New York, 1994).
[52] Quoted in David Reynolds, *Walt Whitman's America* (Knopf, New York, 1995), 579.
[53] See, on this point, Richards, n. 2 above, 317–27.
[54] See Reynolds, n. 52 above, 579. [55] See 104–5, George Chauncey, n. 51 above.
[56] See *ibid.*, 284–5.
[57] See Federico Garcia Lorca, *Poet in New York* (trans. Greg Simon and Steven White, Noonday Press, New York, 1998), 155–63, at 157; I am grateful to Prof. Jose Luis Colomer, who brought this poem and its significance to my attention during a recent visit to New York City from Madrid.

Free Speech and the Politics of Identity

repressive state of American culture in this period by its ironic counterpoint to Whitman's generously optimistic antebellum vision of the promise that gay life in his beloved New York City held for democratic life in America, concluding:

> And you, lovely Walt Whitman, stay asleep on the Hudson's banks
> with your beard toward the pole, openhanded.
> Soft clay or snow, your tongue calls for
> comrades to keep watch over your unbodied gazelle.
> Sleep on, nothing remains.
> Dancing walls stir the prairies
> and America drowns itself in machinery and lament.[58]

The published texts using Whitman to address the larger culture in explicitly gay affirmative terms were mainly European, in particular, those of Carpenter.[59] Ironically, whatever self-conscious political organization there was around the issues of gay rights during this period in the United States (for example, the short-lived homosexual-rights group, the Society for Human Rights, organized by the writer Henry Gerber in Chicago in 1924) was inspired by travels in Europe, in particular, Carpenter's books and the work of the German homosexual emancipationist Magnus Hirschfeld; Gerber's group was promptly suppressed by the Chicago police.[60] In 1932 Gerber denounced American repression in contrast to European (in particular, French and German) toleration. He noted that many 'homosexuals live in happy, blissful unions, especially in Europe, where homosexuals are unmolested as long as they mind their own business, and are not, as in England and in the United States, driven to the underworld of perversions and crime for satisfaction of their very real craving for love'.[61]

If Whitman was not during this period self-consciously invoked in America (as he was in Europe) as the democratic prophet of homosexual love, he was notably invoked as a source of inspiration for the development of more inclusively democratic American culture by leading figures in the Harlem renaissance and associated movements of black and socialist emancipation.[62] Both the black gay critic, Alain Locke, and the poet, Langston Hughes, interpreted Whitman as making possible a distinctive form of black protest and art, one that, in Locke's case, self-consciously included a revolt against American puritanism.[63] Even if covertly, Whitman thus was interpreted by leading gay figures in the ongoing American anti-racist struggle as making possible a distinctive procedure and substance of critical voice and protest.

---

[58] See Federico Garcia Lorca, *Poet in New York*, 163.
[59] See Chauncey, n. 51 above, 107, 144, 231, 284, 285.   [60] See *ibid.*, 144–5.
[61] Quoted in *ibid.*, 144–5.
[62] For an informative treatment of this influence, see George Hutchinson, *The Harlem Renaissance in Black and White* (Harvard University Press, Cambridge, Mass., 1995), at 40–1, 107–10, 138–9, 141, 150, 251–6, 282–5, 319, 410, 414–16.
[63] On the appeal of Whitman for Locke along these lines, see *ibid.*, 40–1, 109–10, 282–3; on the appeal of Whitman for Hughes, see *ibid.*, 414–16.

The repressiveness of American political culture during this period was very much framed by a development we have already explored and criticized at some length, the compromises of rights-based principle wrought by the alliance of suffrage feminism with the temperance and the purity movements. We have already discussed the obscenity prosecutions of advocates of free love and contraception, and should observe as well the correlative striking success of the purity movement in the repression of prostitution.[64] In the gender symbolism current in the period, advocacy of homosexuality was certainly regarded as obscene, and homosexual activity construed as prostitution[65] ('gay', for example, etymologically derived from the self-referring slang of female prostitutes[66]). After their success in repressing prostitution proper,[67] the purity leagues turned their repressive focus on gay activity, and were as generally uncontradicted in their sectarian political moralism there as they had been earlier.[68]

The exception that proves the rule was, of course, Emma Goldman. Goldman was a publicly articulate advocate not only of the right to contraception but of homosexuality,[69] and acknowledged the influence on her thought of the poetry of Whitman.[70] The authorities would not 'tolerate her speaking publicly on homosexuality and on how to practice birth control',[71] using obscenity prosecutions to silence her; she was eventually deported. Her advocacy of these positions was very much of a piece with her opposition to both suffrage feminism and the purity movement. The obsessional focus of suffrage feminism on voting rights, including its alliance with the temperance and purity movements, had led to its outright hostility to the deeper issues of women's human rights, including the rights to economic independence and to love.[72] The purity leagues had unjustly demonized prostitution, enforcing on society at large a sectarian conception of gender and sexuality that rationalized, rather than contested, the abridgment of basic human rights of women.[73] If any person were capable of forging in America the kind of 'comrade-alliances'[74] between homosexuals and women that Carpenter had earlier urged in Britain, it was and would have been Goldman. But, in America, Goldman's views were interpreted as those of an anti-feminist (meaning an anti-suffrage feminist) and an anti-American to boot. There was no public space in America, whose once searing abolitionist feminist vision of the

---

[64] On this latter development, see, in general, Timothy J. Gilfoyle, *City of Eros: New York City, Prostitution, and the Commercialization of Sex, 1790–1920* (W. W. Norton, New York, 1992).

[65] See Chauncey, n. 51 above, 61, 67, 69–70, 81–5, 97, 185–6, 286.

[66] See Chauncey, n. 51 above, 286.   [67] See, on this point, Richards, n. 2 above, 165–7.

[68] See Chauncey, n. 51 above, 138–41, 143, 146–9.   [69] See *ibid.*, 231–2.

[70] See Richard Drinnon, *Rebel in Paradise: A Biography of Emma Goldman* (University of Chicago Press, Chicago, Ill., 1961), at 160–2; see also Richard and Anna Maria Drinnon, *Nowhere at Home: Letters from Exile of Emma Goldman and Alexander Berkman* (Schocken, New York, 1975), at 140–1.

[71] See Alix Shulman, 'The Most Dangerous Woman in the World', in Emma Goldman, *The Traffic in Women and Other Essays on Feminism* (Times Change Press, New York, 1970), 5–15, at 13.

[72] For important statements of this position, see Emma Goldman, 'Woman Suffrage', at 195–211, and 'The Tragedy of Woman's Emancipation', at 213–25 of *Anarchism and Other Essays* (ed. Richard Drinnon, Dover, New York, 1969).

[73] For important statements of this position, see Emma Goldman, 'The Hypocrisy of Puritanism', at 167–76, and 'The Traffic in Women', at 177–94 of *ibid.*

[74] See, on this point, Richards, n. 2 above, 324.

human rights of women had been trivialized to the measure of suffrage feminism, for Emma Goldman and the alternative rights-based feminist tradition that she might, interpreting Whitman (as Carpenter had), have eloquently embodied for Americans. Carpenter's proposed rights-based alliances between women and homosexuals could hardly be even plausible in America in light of the trajectory of suffrage feminism into increasing hostility to rights-based feminism as such. A culture of American censorship had rendered Goldman's inspiration, Whitman, as Edith Wharton sadly noted, an obscenity to be 'kept under lock and key, and brought out, like tobacco, only in the absence of the ladies', to whom the name of Walt Whitman was unmentionable, if not utterly unknown.[75] While Whitman was an influence on women artists like Wharton and Kate Chopin,[76] this was very much against the grain of America's repressive conception of women's proper roles.

This repressive culture of censorship effectively cut off any possibility of exploring links between arguments for feminism and gay rights (Radclyffe Hall's explicitly lesbian novel, for example, had been declared obscene[77]) until the revival of second-wave feminism. Undoubtedly, there were strong, sometimes implicitly or explicitly lesbian connections among various women involved in the struggles of abolitionist and suffrage feminism and their aftermath, but their practice could not, in this repressive cultural environment, be theorized and publicly defended, as it would later be, as a lesbian alternative central to rights-based feminism.[78] Gertrude Stein could in France develop a hermetic style that we now understand to encode lesbian material,[79] as could Virginia Woolf in Britain.[80] And Woolf would implicitly draw upon her lesbian experience[81] to write her important feminist statement, *A Room of One's Own*.[82] The later development of lesbian feminism, as an interpretation of second-wave feminism, thus importantly had its roots in the lesbian practice, if not the explicit theory, of these earlier feminists.[83]

Reasonable exploration of the common links between feminism and gay rights was not helped by the fact that leading European advocates of more humane treatment of homosexuals (Ulrichs, Symonds, Ellis, and even Carpenter himself[84]), let alone

---

[75] See Edith Wharton, *The Uncollected Critical Writings* (ed. Frederick Wegener, Princeton University Press, Princeton, NJ, 1996), at 282.

[76] See Kenneth M. Price, *Whitman and Tradition: The Poet in His Century* (Yale University Press, New Haven, Conn., 1990), at 114–21.

[77] See Una, Lady Troubridge, *The Life and Death of Radclyffe Hall* (Hammond, London, 1961), at 93–4.

[78] For an important general treatment see Lillian Faderman, *Surpassing the Love of Men: Romantic Friendship and Love Between Women from the Renaissance to the Present* (William Morrow, New York, 1981), at 145–415. See also Lillian Faderman, *Odd Girls and Twilight Lovers: A History of Lesbian Life in Twentieth-Century America* (Columbia University Press, New York, 1991).

[79] On Stein, see Lillian Faderman (ed.), *Chloe Plus Olivia: An Anthology of Lesbian Literature from the Seventeenth Century to the Present* (Viking, New York, 1994), at 452–9.

[80] On Woolf, see *ibid.*, 489–97. See, in general, for many other examples, Faderman (ed.), n. 79 above, 17–544.

[81] See *ibid.*, at 491–2.

[82] See Virginia Woolf, *A Room of One's Own* (Harcourt, Brace, New York, 1929).

[83] On the development of lesbian feminism, see Richards, n. 2 above, 342–6.

[84] See, on this point, *ibid.*, 305–6, 313, 314, 316, 317, 322–3, 332, 369.

respected European psychiatrists like Richard von Krafft-Ebing, had advocated a model of homosexuality as a congenital abnormality, in Krafft-Ebing's case, linked to a Lamarckian history of past ancestors' hypersexualized degeneracy.[85] While Krafft-Ebing, like the pro-gay advocates, called for decriminalization of homosexuality on the ground of a psychiatric abnormality for which the agent bore no responsibility,[86] the model itself often re-enforced, rather than contested the stereotypes on which the traditional moral reprobation of homosexuality uncritically rested. Krafft-Ebing had thus idealized monogamous, heterosexual marriage in terms worthy of the American anti-polygamy movement;[87] and, Ulrichs's model of gay men (as women) and lesbians (as men)[88] replicated the traditionally stereotypical grounds for moral reprobation (a degradation of men to women, or women to men).

Gender-stereotypical interpretations of homosexuality were thus, if anything, hardened into medical granite, and could themselves easily be uncritically used by some pro-gay advocates as the basis for rationalizing disdain for the opposite gender: the man who identified with other men was more valuable as a man or manly, the woman with other women more valuable as a woman or womanly.[89] Such misogyny, on the part of gay affirmative advocates, further widened the yawning chasm between them and feminists of the period, who could hardly find any reasonable common ground in what amounted to unjust mutual contempt between the two groups.

The most extraordinary development of such an interpretation into a radical metaphysical misogyny was Otto Weininger's *Sex and Character*[90] (compared to Weininger, Schopenhauer's notorious misogyny was moderate[91]). Interpreting his own homosexuality in Ulrichs's terms,[92] Weininger not only advocated decriminalization of homosexuality[93] and its health as a human adaptation,[94] but morally idealized the contributions of gays and lesbians to human culture. His argument postulated that all people have differing components of the mutually exclusive properties, male and female, and that maximum sexual attraction was determined by a

---

[85] See Richard von Krafft-Ebing, *Psychopathia Sexualis* (first published in German, 1886, trans. Franklin S. Klaf, Bell Publishing Co., New York, 1965), 186–307. Krafft-Ebing revised his views in 1901 to the effect that homosexuality was not a manifestation of degeneracy or pathology, but could occur in otherwise normal subjects. But the retraction written shortly before his death did little to alter the impression on the public of the twelve editions of his book that was translated into many languages. See Wayne R. Dynes (ed.), *Encyclopedia of Homosexuality* (Garland Publishing, Inc., New York, 1990), i, 668–9.

[86] See von Krafft-Ebing, n. 85 above, 334–5, 381–8.

[87] See, for illuminating discussion, Sander L. Gilman, *Difference and Pathology: Stereotypes of Sexuality, Race, and Madness* (Cornell University Press, Ithaca, NY, 1985), at 197–8; on the anti-polygamy movement, see Richards, n. 2 above, 171–2.

[88] On Ulrichs, see *ibid.*, 305.

[89] See Elaine Showalter, *Sexual Anarchy: Gender and Culture in the Fin De Siecle* (St. Martin's Press, New York, 1993), at 172–4; Bram Dijkstra, *Idols of Perversity: Fantasies of Feminine Evil in Fine-de-Siecle Culture* (Oxford University Press, New York, 1986), at 200–9.

[90] See Otto Weininger, *Sex and Character* (William Heinemann, London, 1907).

[91] See Arthur Schopenhauer, 'On Women', *Essays and Aphorisms* (trans. R. J. Hollindale, Penguin, Harmondsworth, 1970), 80–8.

[92] See *ibid.*, 45–52. On Weininger's life and early suicide, see David Abrahamsen, *The Mind and Death of a Genius* (Columbia University Press, New York, 1946).

[93] See *ibid.*, 51.   [94] See *ibid.*, 46–7 (citing Krafft-Ebing's change of view on this issue).

person seeking in the other what he or she lacks in these properties[95] (a homosexual man, predominantly feminine, thus sought men because they best complemented his needs for masculinity). Gay men, having less need for women, were more ethically impartial about issues of gender[96] (lesbians were morally superior because they were masculine[97]), and on this basis Weininger rationalized as metaphysical truths highly personal misogynist fantasies of women as sexually rapacious,[98] lacking a soul[99] or any of the properties of the soul (including memory, identity, and logic[100]), and therefore lacking the Kantian capacity for ethics.[101] Ostensible moral reasoning in women was duplicitous,[102] parroting,[103] a hysterical parody.[104] The 'nullity and inanity of women'[105] explained, in turn, the feminized inferiority of non-Aryan races[106] and of the Jews (Weininger was also Jewish).[107] The only hope for humankind (both men and women), preserving the uniquely masculine competence for high culture and Kantian ethics untainted by feminine hypersexualized degradation of our higher powers, would be to give up coitus.[108]

This farrago would be more amusing and less disturbing had it not been taken so seriously in general (reading Weininger, for example, pivotally influenced Ludwig Wittgenstein[109] and shaped the thought of Sigmund Freud[110]) and in particular used as a way of discrediting the emancipation of women, properly understood, in Weininger's terms, as 'a prostitute emancipation'.[111] The American feminist, Charlotte Perkins Gilman, was baffled at the book's paradoxical marriage of elevated metaphysical ideality with the crudest sexist stereotyping of women: 'a mystical exaltation of the ideal, with an unspeakable grossness in apprehension of the real'.[112] A feminist like Gilman could barely understand, let alone find common ground with, a gay affirmative advocate like Weininger, whose affirmation of homosexuality required the radical dehumanization of women, blacks, and Jews. That even Carpenter could endorse Weininger's model, as serving the goals of the homosexual rights movement, indicates the extent of the problem.[113]

---

[95] See Weininger, n. 90 above, 29–31.   [96] See *ibid.*, 57.
[97] See *ibid.*, 66.   [98] See *ibid.*, 88–9, 92, 102.
[99] See *ibid.*, 186–213.   [100] See *ibid.*, 145–22.
[101] Weininger uses Kantian ethics as his model; see *ibid.*, 153–62, 177, 210, 331.
[102] See *ibid.*, 260.   [103] See *ibid.*, 262–3.
[104] See *ibid.*, 278.   [105] See *ibid.*, 294.   [106] See *ibid.*, 302.
[107] See *ibid.*, 306. For Weininger on Chamberlain, see *ibid.*, 303, 312, 314, 325, 328; on Richard Wagner and German anti-Semitism, see *ibid.*, 304–6, 319, 344; on Jewish anti-Semitism, see *ibid.*, 304.
[108] See *ibid.*, 336–7, 343, 345–7.
[109] See, e.g., Ray Monk, *Ludwig Wittgenstein: The Duty of Genius* (Free Press, New York, 1990), at 19–25.
[110] See Sander L. Gilman, *Freud, Race, and Gender* (Princeton University Press, Princeton, NJ, 1993), 77–92, 154; *Jewish Self-Hatred: Anti-Semitism and the Hidden Language of the Jews* (Johns Hopkins University Press, Baltimore, Md., 1986), at 250–1, 267–9, 293–4.
[111] See Weininger, n. 90 above, 332; on not giving women suffrage, see *ibid.*, 339. See, in general, on homosexual anti-feminism during this period, Dijkstra, n. 89 above, 200–9.
[112] See Charlotte Perkins Gilman, 'Dr. Weininger's "Sex and Character"', in *The Critic*, vol. XLVIII, no. 5 (May, 1906), 387–417, at 416.
[113] See Edward Carpenter, *The Intermediate Sex: A Study of Human Evolution and Transfiguration* (Mitchell Kennerley, New York, 1912), at 5, 155–6. For Carpenter on women's primitiveness, see Dijkstra, n. 89 above, 242–3.

The case of Weininger brings out in more dramatic form a problematic feature of all the gay affirmative views we have so far examined, their uncritical dependence on a model of homosexuality that reflects, rather than contests, the unjust gender stereotyping to which homosexuals have been subjected in particular and women subjected in general. Such attempts to characterize the difference between homosexuals and heterosexuals in gender stereotypical terms end up enforcing, not contesting the unjust sexist stereotypes to which gays and lesbians have been subjected, and thus subvert the rights-based case for gay and lesbian identity while, for this very reason, they advance the rights-denying evils of sexism, racism, and anti-Semitism.

In effect, Weininger's argument starkly illustrates in a different context the general rights-denying normative dynamic of abandoning a principled normative perspective on the platform of human rights. The failure of political abolitionists to condemn sexism on the same basis as racism rendered their anti-racism shallow and culturally reinforced the degradation of women;[114] the compromise by suffrage feminists of anti-racist principles worsened American racism and rendered their anti-sexism increasingly vapid; their abandonment of rights-based feminism in general led not only to their uncritical idealization of unjust gender roles, but to their aggressive war on basic claims to human rights of women, including various aspects of the right to love, as Sanger bitterly complained.[115] Similarly, Weininger's idealization of a gender-stereotypical interpretation of homosexuality not only failed to address the central issues in the abridgement of the human rights of gays and lesbians, but enforced uncritical gender stereotypes of women as morally depraved as the basis for the dehumanization of women, racial minorities, and Jews. The study of Weininger, a classic figure in the history of European anti-Semitism (including Jewish anti-Semitism),[116] thus offers generative insights as well into the intersectionality of the unjust cultural and political construction of irrationalist prejudices based, as they often are, on rights-denying culturally and politically enforced stereotypes of difference.

Anti-Semitism, as we earlier saw (Chapter 3), was regarded as a paradigm exemplar of such irrationalist prejudice by the American radical abolitionists because its history so clearly exemplified the intolerance condemned by a principled understanding of the argument for toleration: first, the abridgement of the basic rights of a group; and secondly, the rationalization of such abridgment on grounds that were themselves the viciously circular consequences of the history of such abridgment. The radical abolitionists generalized this analysis to condemn racism as well, and the abolitionist feminists among them extended the theory, as we have seen, to sexism as well. In all these cases, the viciously circular history in question had dehumanized an entire class of persons from their status as bearers of basic human rights in terms of unjust cultural

---

[114]   See, on this point, Richards, n. 2 above, 126–41.
[115]   See Margaret Sanger, *Woman and the New Race* (first published, 1920) (Maxwell Reprint Company, Elmsford, NY, 1969), at 2, 94–5, 186–97, 210–11.
[116]   For useful general studies, see Gilman, n. 87 above; Gilman, *Jewish Self-Hatred: Anti-Semitism*, n. 110 above; Sander L. Gilman, *Disease and Representation: Images of Illness from Madness to AIDS* (Cornell University Press, Ithaca, NY, 1988); Gilman, *Freud, Race, and Gender*, n. 110 above.

stereotypes enforced through law and public opinion. The irrationalist political force of such prejudices was shown by the ways in which any doubts that might now be raised about the political order resting on such unjust stereotypes (in light of movements self-consciously opposing anti-Semitism, racism, and sexism) were not reasonably allowed debate and discussion, consistent with respect for human rights and the role of public reason in constitutionally legitimate politics. Rather, the paradox of intolerance aggressively repressed any such doubts through the illegitimate enforcement at large of now embattled sectarian readings of facts and values that remade reality in their own irrationalist image. Victims were thus imaginatively transformed into aggressors, slavery into freedom, terror and even genocide into self-defence.

Weininger's pivotal use of gender stereotypy dehumanized not only women, non-Aryans, and Jews, but, as I earlier suggested, homosexuals as well. His argument thus illustrates the rights-denying intersectionality of such prejudices, the common ways in which they are enforced, and the ease with which, once the platform of human rights is abandoned, such prejudices are uncritically re-enforced and allowed much more aggressive scope in their war against the theory and practice of human rights well beyond any dream of their original proponent. In periods when roles are under debate in light of reasonable rights-based pressure for change, the very foundations of personal as well as political identity are put at risk, one's sense of oneself, for example, as a man and American (or British, or whatever).[117] In the absence of any strong institutions or consensus protective of human rights (including a robust principle of free speech), identity—personal and national—knows no limits in hardening itself against change by constructing an often highly gendered national identity, rooted in unjust gender stereotypes, that constructs its personal and national identity, as fascist Germany certainly did, in stereotypical hatred of traditionally dehumanized groups, in particular, Jews and homosexuals.[118] The Nazi campaign against homosexuality included, for example, the criminalization of 'a kiss, an embrace, even homosexual fantasies'.[119] Weininger, a Jew and an advocate of homosexuality, had culturally legitimated precisely the rights-denying stereotypes on the basis of which this sav-

---

[117] For the important recent literature on this topic, see, in general, Mark C. Carnes and Clyde Griffen (eds.), *Meanings for Manhood: Constructions of Masculinity in Victorian America* (University of Chicago Press, Chicago, Ill., 1990); David D. Gilmore, *Manhood in the Making: Cultural Concepts of Masculinity* (Yale University Press, New Haven, Conn., 1990); Harry Brod (ed.), *The Making of Masculinities: The New Men's Studies* (Routledge, New York, 1987); R. W. Connell, *Masculinities* (University of California Press, Berkeley, Cal., 1995); Michael Kimmel, *Manhood in America: A Cultural History* (Free Press, New York, 1996).

[118] For important recent treatments, see, in general, George L. Mosse, *Nationalism and Sexuality: Middle-Class Morality and Sexual Norms in Modern Europe* (University of Wisconsin Press, Madison, Wisc., 1985); *The Image of Man: The Creation of Modern Masculinity* (Oxford University Press, New York, 1996); Andrew Parker, Mary Russo, Doris Sommer, and Patricia Yaeger (eds.), *Nationalisms and Sexualities* (Routledge, New York, 1992).

[119] See James D. Steakley, *The Homosexual Emancipation Movement in Germany* (Arno Press, New York, 1975) at 110.

agery against Jews and homosexuals, knowing no constraints of human rights, worked its tyrannical will.[120]

A central feature of such dehumanization in the modern era was, as we earlier saw in the development of both racism and sexism and see again in Weininger, its reinterpretation in terms of an abusive science of race or gender or sexuality.[121] As one astute historian of this period observed: '[t]o combat the already diminishing influence of the orthodox religious conceptions which had formed a solid basis for antidiscriminatory activity in the fields of sex and race at mid-century, evolutionary theory had arrived in the nick of time, a resplendent white knight in the service of discrimination.'[122] No argument was more abusive in this way than the translation of what had traditionally been a sectarian argument of moral condemnation (for example, of Jews as heretics) into the pseudo-scientific discourse of degeneration or madness.[123] The blatantly rights-denying character of such claims is transparent when Jewish madness was adduced as the discrediting explanation for their claims of basic rights[124] or medical claims of disease or insanity used in response to claims of women's rights.[125] The effect was, of course, exactly the same as the traditional sectarian ideological views: reducing the scope of legitimate public discussion to its own sectarian measure, excluding, in principle, any claim of Jews or women to originate claims of basic human rights in their own voice.

The same indignity was inflicted on homosexuals in the United States during much of the twentieth century. Advocacy on behalf of the rights of gays and lesbians was, as we have seen, quashed by obscenity and related police prosecutions. No fair discussion by homosexuals in their own voice was tolerable during a period when such arguments by African-Americans and women were increasingly allowed fuller critical scope. The deepest damage to the normative possibility of such gay and lesbian conscientious voice was inflicted, however, by establishment American psychiatry. Freud and his early followers had offered a surprisingly subtle and compassionate view of homosexuality as one of a wide variety of healthy outcomes of psychosexual development; but, in America, psychoanalysis changed from an open-minded and humane study to an increasingly insular and sectarian orthodoxy whose view of sexual preference as a mental disease reflected more American moral orthodoxy than it did careful empirical study. After some internal struggle, only in 1973 did the Board of Trustees of the American Psychiatric Association decide to remove

---

[120] See Mosse, *Nationalism and Sexuality*, n. 118 above, at 17, 145–6. For Himmler on the need for rigid gender roles, see *ibid.*, 162–70. See, in general, for Weininger's influence on Nazi anti-Semitism, Nancy A. Harrowitz and Barbara Hyams (eds.), *Jews and Gender: Responses to Otto Weininger* (Temple University Press, Philadelphia, Pa., 1996).

[121] See, in general, Stephen Jay Gould, *The Mismeasure of Man* (W. W. Norton, New York, 1981).

[122] See Dijkstra, n. 89 above, 164.

[123] See Gilman, *Jewish Self-Hatred*, n. 110 above, at 211–12.

[124] See Gilman, n. 87 above, 152–3, 162; *Freud, Race, and Gender*, n. 110 above, at 113.

[125] See G. J. Barker-Benfield, *The Horrors of the Half-Known Life: Male Attitudes Toward Women and Sexuality in Nineteenth-Century America* (Harper & Row, New York, 1976), at 84–90, 122–6, 189–93, 206–14.

homosexuality from the *Diagnostic and Statistical Manual of Psychiatric Disorders.*[126] This development was very much an outgrowth of a new American struggle to understand and elaborate the human and civil rights of African-Americans and women and the impact of that struggle on forging claims of human and constitutional rights by gay and lesbian persons.

A prominent feature of that development in all these domains was a more robust protection of free speech, which made possible a politics of identity of African-Americans, women, and, more recently, gays and lesbians that could challenge the terms of their moral slavery, including what had previously been ignored, the common and often interlinked grounds of structural injustice.

The suggestion of stronger judicial protections for freedom of speech began in the United States in 1918 in the dissent of Justices Holmes (joined by Justice Brandeis) to a federal Espionage Age criminal prosecution for protests of American participation in the First World War in *Abrams* v. *United States*[127] (Emma Goldman was also successfully prosecuted for her anti-war and anti-draft advocacy under one of these statutes[128]). Holmes and Brandeis persisted in their pathbreaking dissents in several important later cases,[129] but the view began to command majorities on clear First Amendment grounds[130] only in 1937 in cases protecting the rights of dissent of American Communists, one of which crucially involved anti-racist dissent in Georgia that was subject to the death penalty.[131] With some backtracking,[132] the federal judiciary later elaborated even stronger protections of free speech (including the protection of group libel) often in the context of protecting the legitimacy and integrity of the rights of conscience and dissent of the anti-racist civil rights movement.[133] On

[126] See, for an excellent study of this development, its criticism, and its change, Kenneth Lewes, *The Psychoanalytic Theory of Male Homosexuality* (Simon and Schuster, New York, 1988). See also Ronald Bayer, *Homosexuality and American Psychiatry: The Politics of Diagnosis* (Basic Books, New York, 1981).

[127] See *Abrams* v. *United States*, 250 US 616 (1919).

[128] See Drinnon, n. 70 above, at 184–99.

[129] See, in particular, *Gitlow* v. *New York*, 268 US 652 (1925) (Holmes J, dissenting, joined by Brandeis J); *Whitney* v. *California*, 274 US 357 (1927) (Brandeis J, concurring, joined by Holmes, J).

[130] See the earlier case of *Fiske* v. *Kansas*, 274 US 380 (1927) (application of state criminal syndicalism statute to the terms of the preamble to the IWW constitution found to lack any due process factual support).

[131] See *Herndon* v. *Lowry*, 301 US 242 (1937) (5–4 decision holding unconstitutional on free speech and vagueness grounds conviction for anti-racist civil rights advocacy of black member of American Communist Party under state anti-incitment-to-insurrection statute). See also *De Jonge* v. *Oregon*, 299 US 353 (1937) (criminal prosecution under state criminal syndicalism statute of member of Communist Party for assisting in public meeting held unconstitutional under First Amendment).

[132] See, most notably, *Dennis* v. *United States*, 341 US 494 (1951) (federal Smith Act, making criminal organization and teaching of Communist Party for advocacy of overthrow of government, held facially constitutional). But see *Yates* v. *United States*, 354 US 298 (1957) (Smith Act unconstitutional as applied); *Noto* v. *United States*, 367 US 290 (1961) (similar finding); cf. *Scales* v. *United States*, 367 US 203 (1961) (Smith Act constitutional as applied). But see also *Brandenburg* v. *Ohio*, 395 US 444 (1969) (state criminal syndicalism statute, making criminal advocacy of overthrow of government, held unconstitutional).

[133] Notable examples include *Edwards* v. *California*, 372 US 229 (1963) (breach of peace prosecution of civil rights demonstrators on grounds of South Carolina State House held unconstitutional); *New York Times* v. *Sullivan*, 376 US 254 (1964) (libel action for false reporting of *New York Times* of Martin Luther King's protests in Alabama held unconstitutional); *Cox* v. *Louisiana*, 379 US 536 (1965) (criminal

this clearly correct view, the measure of constitutional protection for conscientiously dissenting speech could not be the dominant orthodoxy that it challenged, for that would trivialize the protection of free speech to whatever massaged the prejudices of dominant majorities. Rather, as the judicial protection of the increasingly successful anti-racist advocacy of the civil rights movement showed, it was the speech most critical of and offensive to the dominant orthodoxy in the United States that most needed to be publicly questioned and challenged if the unjust, indeed unconstitutional, basis for such racism was to be publicly understood as the rights-denying evil it was and remedially addressed with an appropriate sense of communal ethical responsibility.

No laws had been more aggressively used against the claims of rights-based feminism and of gay rights than anti-obscenity laws. As David Rabban has recently made clear in his important study of this period,[134] advocates had largely unsuccessfully questioned the constitutionality of such laws during the late nineteenth and early twentieth century, constituting what Rabban calls a lost libertarian tradition of free speech well worth recovering as a way of understanding the grounds for our contemporary worries about theories of free speech (including the argument for democracy) that have traditionally marginalized such dissent. My analysis here is convergent with and supplementary to Rabban's historical recovery of a tradition of free speech, largely disfavoured during the progressive era that saw important judicial arguments (often in dissent, but eventually commanding majorities), as we have seen, increasingly hospitable to anti-war and eventually anti-racist dissent (the protection of both subversive advocacy and group libel are important landmarks in this development for reasons discussed in Chapter 4). While this more liberal theory of free speech is implicit in both the protection of subversive advocacy and group libel, it moves forthrightly into much greater judicial favour roughly congruent with the growing judicial protection of the dissenting claims of rights-based feminism and eventually advocates of gay rights.

We can observe this development quite clearly in the growing judicial scepticism of the obscenity laws that had previously been used, as we have seen, to silence such conscientious rights-based dissent from the dominant orthodoxy of gender and sexuality. In 1957 in *Roth* v. *United States*,[135] the Supreme Court, addressing the abstract question of whether obscene material was constitutionally protected, attempted to preserve the traditional immunity of obscene materials from free speech scrutiny. However, subsequent cases required it to address the more concrete

---

prosecution of civil rights demonstration for breach of peace and obstructing public passages held unconstitutional); *Brown* v. *Louisiana*, 383 US 131 (1966) (breach of peace conviction for black sit-in of segregated public library held unconstitutional); *Shuttlesworth* v. *Birmingham*, 394 US 147 (1969) (state ordinance, requiring permit before civil rights demonstration could take place, held unconstitutional); *Street* v. *New York*, 394 US 576 (1969) (state prosecution for use of burning flag to protest murder of civil rights leader in Mississippi held unconstitutional).

[134] See, in general, David M. Rabban, *Free Speech in Its Forgotten Years* (Cambridge University Press, Cambridge, 1997).

[135] See *Roth* v. *United States, Alberts* v. *California*, 354 US 476 (1957).

question whether certain materials were or were not obscene, and thus, within *Roth*, did not or did raise free speech questions. During this period, as issues of gender and sexuality became more publicly contested and contestable, the Supreme Court began constitutionally to reverse obscenity prosecutions on diverse constitutional theories none of which commanded a majority of the Court.[136] The view that commanded most support focused on whether the material had exclusively prurient appeal, was offensive to national community standards of sexual representation, and utterly lacked redeeming social value (excluding prurience from counting as such social value).[137] Increasingly, under this standard, only hard-core pornography could be constitutionally repressed. In 1973 in *Miller* v. *California*[138] and *Paris Adult Theatre I* v. *Slaton*,[139] the Court, by a five to four majority, narrowly retained the structure of *Roth* but limited the scope of the constitutionally obscene effectively to hard-core pornographic depictions of sexual organs (coming to climax) that appealed exclusively to prurient interest, violated local community standards, and lacked serious value (excluding its prurient value); Justice Brennan, the original author of *Roth*, admitted his earlier abstract view that obscene versus non-obscene material could be distinguished without compromising free speech interests had proven untenable, and dissented. American public law has thus increasingly acknowledged the collision of traditional obscenity law with the values of free speech, and consequently constitutionally narrowed the scope of what could legitimately be prosecuted under these obscenity laws.

The American constitutional debate over obscenity law has been, first, a struggle over how appropriately to narrow the scope of what could constitutionally count as obscene and thus be immune from free speech analysis, and, secondly, whether, as a category immune from free speech analysis, it should be narrowed to the vanishing point. The development of Justice Brennan's thought, for example, reflects this chronology exactly. Both these interpretive developments aim to protect the basic conscientiously dissenting rights of free speech on matters of gender and sexuality that have historically been abridged by the abusively repressive use of obscenity laws. Proponents of these two interpretive perspectives disagree about precisely how those rights should be understood; both largely agree, however, that all the historical prosecutions for obscenity so far discussed could not be reached under an appropriately narrowed conception of obscenity. That clearly reflects the important emphasis now accorded, against the background of historical repression, to one of the basic rights claimed by rights-based feminism.

It remains to discuss which view is most consistent with the concerns of rights-based feminism as we can now understand them in the historical perspective of the repressive uses of obscenity law against serious discussion of matters of gender and sexuality largely raised by rights-based feminists or their allies. Catharine MacKinnon

---

[136] See *Redrup* v. *New York*, 386 US 767 (1967).
[137] See *Memoirs* v. *Massachusetts*, 383 US 413 (1966).
[138] See *Miller* v. *California*, 413 US 15 (1973).
[139] See *Paris Adult Theatre I* v. *Slaton*, 413 US 49 (1973).

has been a notable critic of traditional obscenity law (because it targets eroticism as such), and would certainly repudiate many laws which could constitutionally be used in the way traditional obscenity law was against rights-based feminists. But, she has urged, on self-consciously feminist grounds, that obscenity law be functionally reconstructed in terms of sexual representations whose availability harms the civil rights of women, portraying them in degraded, sexually objectified ways that disable men from regarding women as persons and claimants to equal civil rights; such representations may be repressed on the ground that no basic right is thus infringed and the unjust subordination of women is combated.[140] MacKinnon was thus the architect, with Andrea Dworkin, of an Indianapolis civil rights ordinance that used her revised definition of pornography, an ordinance that was later struck down as unconstitutional (on the ground that its definition did not satisfy the *Miller* guidelines, and thus unconstitutionally abridged protected speech).[141] American public law has thus expressly refused to accept MacKinnon's interpretation of group-based harms to women as a constitutional ground for the abridgment of speech in this domain; and I shall hereinafter take this rejection as a distinctive feature of the American public law of obscenity analogous to its refusal to accept the legitimacy of such group-based harms as an adequate constitutional basis for group libel and blasphemy laws.

The Canadian Supreme Court has, however, unanimously accepted MacKinnon's approach not in the form of a civil rights ordinance, but as the constitutional measure of criminalization of obscene materials. In *R. v. Butler*,[142] the Court reviewed the constitutionality of obscenity provisions of the Criminal Code[143] in light of the Charter's guarantees of free speech. Justice Sopinka, writing for the Court, began by construing the statutory prohibition of dissemination of obscene materials to apply to explicit sexual depictions that harmed people exposed to them, that is, predisposed 'persons to act in an anti-social manner as, for example, the physical or mental mistreatment of women by men, or, what is perhaps debatable, the reverse'.[144] Depictions of sex with violence 'almost always'[145] inflict such harms and are therefore obscene; depictions of sex without violence are obscene if they are degrading or dehumanizing and the risk of such harms is substantial; depictions of sex without violence and that are not degrading are not obscene.[146] Citing *Keegstra* on the expansive scope of protected speech, the Court found that the obscenity law, thus construed, abridged the protected sphere of free speech under section 2(b) of the Charter,[147] and then turned to the assessment of whether the statute was justified under the

[140] See, in general, Catharine A. MacKinnon, *Only Words* (Harvard University Press, Cambridge, Mass., 1993). See also Catharine A. MacKinnon, *Feminism Unmodified: Discourses on Life and Law* (Harvard University Press, Cambridge, Mass., 1987), at 127–213; *Toward a Feminist Theory of the State* (Harvard University Press, Cambridge, Mass., 1989), at 195–214.
[141] See *American Booksellers Ass'n v. Hudnut*, 771 F 2d 323 (7th Cir. 1985), aff'd, 475 US 1001 (1986).
[142] See *R. v. Butler*, 1 Can. SCR 452 (1992). See also *R. v. Mara*, 148 DLR 4th 75 (1997) (criminal statute, condemning indecent performances in public places, may constitutionally be manager of establishment who knows lap dancing will be conducted there).
[143] See Canada, Criminal Code, s. 163, cited in *R. v. Butler*, n. 142 above, at 469–71.
[144] *R. v. Butler*, n. 142 above, at 485. [145] *Ibid.*, 485.
[146] See *ibid.*, 483–5. [147] See *ibid.*, 488.

limitation clause of section 1. The Court took the view, in line with MacKinnon's argument in this area, that the traditional rationale for these laws (namely, upholding conventional moral standards) did not reasonably justify them in contemporary circumstances.[148] However, such laws were reasonably justified on the ground that they prevented harms, namely, the depiction of sexuality in ways that reinforced 'male–female stereotypes to the detriment of both sexes'.[149] Justice Sopinka explicitly analogized the constitutional weight of these harms to those from hate speech previously acknowledged in *Keegstra*,[150] '[t]he threat to the self-dignity of target group members . . . matched by the possibility that prejudiced messages will gain credence'.[151] Obscene pornography like hate speech, on this view, is group libel, 'a significant portion of the population is humiliated by its gross misrepresentations';[152] while the Court acknowledged that 'a direct link between obscenity and harm to society may be difficult', it concluded that 'it is reasonable to presume that exposure to images bears a causal relationship to changes in attitudes and beliefs'.[153] The Court notes however, in passing, that this argument does not apply to 'good pornography'[154] whose objective is 'the celebration of sexuality'.[155]

The Canadian Supreme Court's claim to be able to distinguish constitutionally bad from good pornography raises an issue of principle that concerns many feminists. Nan Hunter, Sylvia Law, and Nadine Strossen have, on self-consciously feminist grounds, urged that the position more consistent with the rights of women would be neither to use nor to revise the current constitutional conception of obscenity, but to get rid of it altogether (all restrictions on sexually explicit material should be subjected to free speech analysis). They object to MacKinnon's conception, in particular, because it reintroduces the power of state censorship allegedly to protect women from moral harms that reinforces, rather than rebuts, sexist stereotypes of women in the long and now largely constitutionally repudiated tradition of protective legislation for women.[156] It would be one thing for women themselves to organize to combat any sexist material (whether sexually explicit or not), but quite a different matter to empower the state to make inherently controversial interpretive judgements about the degradation of women. The record in Canada, for example, has been that the state power of censorhip has been used largely against gay and lesbian materials, not the mainstream heterosexually oriented hard-core pornographic materials that are MacKinnon's real concern.[157]

---

[148] See *R.* v. *Butler*, n. 142 above, at 491–3.
[149] See *ibid.*, 493, citing with approval the Report on Pornography by the House of Commons Standing Committee on Justice and Legal Affairs (MacGuigan Report) (Queen's Printer, Ottawa, 22 Mar. 1978, at 18: 4).
[150] See *R.* v. *Butler*, n. 142 above at 496, 501–3.   [151] See *ibid.*, 496 (citing *Keegstra*).
[152] See *ibid.*, 501.   [153] See *ibid.*, 502.
[154] See *ibid.*, 500 (citing West).   [155] See *ibid.*, 500.
[156] See Nan D. Hunter and Sylvia Law, 'The FACT Brief', reprinted in Lisa Duggan and Nan D. Hunter, *Sex, Sexual Dissent, and Political Culture* (Routledge, New York, 1995); Nadine Strossen, *Defending Pornography: Free Speech, Sex, and the Fight for Women's Rights* (Scribner, New York, 1995).
[157] See *ibid.*, 229–46.

This result is, in light of the argument adopted by the Canadian Supreme Court, not surprising. Obscenity law, whatever its more circumscribed or revised form, requires interpretive judgements to be made by the state about the worth or value of sexually explicit materials on the ground that they embody or elicit erotic fantasies that are inconsistent with proper sexuality or appropriate gender roles. A theory of the obscene is a theory of the unnatural in matters of sex or gender.[158] It should not be at all surprising that Canada's revised obscenity laws have given expression to a traditional conception of the unnatural that regards homosexuality as intrinsically degrading, not at all the more enlightened conception of MacKinnon or Dworkin.

The Canadian test for the constitutionally obscene is whether explicit sexual depictions include violence or are otherwise humiliating or degrading. But what counts as humiliating or degrading must depend precisely on the conventional moral standards that MacKinnon and the Canadian Supreme Court both deny can be a constitutionally adequate basis for law. Obscenity proscecutions raise basic issues of constitutional principle if these prosecutions are based, as they appear to be in Canada, on judgements about the disrespectful character of the putatively obscene materials and of the thoughts and experiences to which use of such materials leads. It does not dispel, but only aggravates, the issue of free speech principle to redescribe the putative evils in terms of the degradation of women as such. That argument clearly places obscenity prosecutions, as the Canadian Supreme Court acknowledges, in the framework of group libel[159] and, for that reason, renders them altogether more constitutionally problematic.[160]

Group libel laws are so constitutionally problematic because the character of the harms, appealed to as a basis for law, are precisely the alleged harms that cannot, in principle, be an adequate basis for the abridgement of speech absent a clear and present danger (Chapter 4). Such harms are not an adequate basis for abridgement of speech for two reasons. First, such harms (their disrespectful character) inhere in the exercise of the inalienable right to conscience itself, and cannot, consistently with respect for its exercise (including the moral powers exercised in the politics of identity), be a ground for its abridgement; secondly, the harms in hearing speech in the domain of conviction inhere in the audience's evaluative responses to the speech (not to independent evidence of clear and present dangers), and, for this reason, responsive arguments of conviction by the audience can, in principle, meet and defeat its claims, and thus expunge its harm in terms that are consistent with equal respect for the right of conscience of all persons. The politics of identity on this view alone both

---

[158] See, on this and related points, David A. J. Richards, 'Free Speech and Obscenity Law: Toward a Moral Theory of the First Amendment', 123 *U Pa. L Rev.* 45 (1974).

[159] MacKinnon quite clearly sees and espouses this analogy; see *Feminism Unmodified*, n. 140 above, at 156–7.

[160] This argument assumes that group libel laws are or should be constitutionally problematic for the reasons already discussed in Ch. 4. The constitutionalism of nations like Canada, which accept the legitimacy of group libel laws, has at least been consistent in extending the analogy to obscene materials. The same cannot be said of the United States, whose constitutionalism rejects group libel laws but accepts anti-obscenity laws.

adequately contests and rebuts such stereotypical harms consistent with both respect for the right of conscience and speech and the right against unjust discrimination.

Obscenity laws are, on the Canadian Supreme Court's view of them, group libel laws, directed at protecting women as a class from insults inhering in the character of the sexual depictions; it views such insults as the reasonable ground for state abridgment though it concedes there is no compelling evidence of a clear and present danger of harms. But, such state-endorsed judgements of group harms are themselves stereotypical in precisely the way that entrenches and does not contest the underlying structural injustice of sexism and homophobia.

Why are certain pornographic images of women (as opposed to others, the Court's 'good pornography') taken to express disrespect for women? Why pornographic images as opposed to depictions of women in religion or advertising? The idea must be that certain pornographic images (as opposed to others) morally degrade women intrinsically from their status as full persons and as bearers of equal rights. But even to state the claim is reasonably to contest it. Pornographic images (in contrast to conventional group libel claims) make no such express claims as such. The claim that they do is a controversial interpretive claim, ascribing to producers and users of these materials (whether men or women) condemned moral attitudes (a kind of corrupt conscience), quite like the motivation for group libel laws. Sexism, like other forms of structural injustice, rests, as we have seen (Chapter 3), on unjust stereotypical sexualization, but, as the feminists critical of MacKinnon and Dworkin have argued, such stereotyping may be reasonably understood in terms of the cultural entrenchment of narrowly mandatory sexual and gender roles for women (exclusively as wives and mothers) that abridge, among other rights, their right to control their intimate lives as sexual beings. Such feminists correctly point out the role that the conventional sexist ideology of the good as opposed to the bad woman has played in the unjust repression of pioneering feminist claims to respect for basic rights, including, within feminism, the use of this ideology unjustly to scapegoat and marginalize such dissent, for example, what I have elsewhere called the Wollstonecraft repudiation (dismissing Wollstonecraft's brilliant arguments of liberal political theory because of her unconventional sexual life[161]). Such abridgment of women's sexual voice has devastating consequences for their creative and intellectual lives, as Freud, who was certainly no feminist, saw with such remarkable psychological clarity.[162] The attempt within fem-

---

[161] See, on this point, Richards, n. 2 above 63–73, 176, 197, 235.

[162] Freud observed: 'The relationship between the amount of sublimation possible and the amount of sexual activity necessary naturally varies from person to person and even from one calling to another. An abstinent artist is hardly conceivable . . . The harmful results which the strict demand for abstinence before marriage produces in women's natures are quite especially apparent . . . Not only does it forbid sexual intercourse and set a high premium on the preservation of female chastity, but it also protects the young woman from temptation as she grows up, by keeping her ignorant of all the facts of the part she is to play and by not tolerating any impulse of love in her which cannot lead to marriage . . . Their upbringing forbids their concerning themselves intellectually with sexual problems though they nevertheless feel extremely curious about them, and frightens them by condemning such curiosity as unwomanly and a sign of a sinful disposition . . . I think that the undoubted intellectual inferiority of so many women can rather be traced back to the inhibition of thought necessitated by sexual suppression': Sigmund Freud, ' "Civilized" Sexual

inism to repress such sexual voice has accordingly repressed some of its most morally independent and profound exponents. The anti-pornography movement has a similarly reactionary basis and appeal. It should be resisted because it rests on the unjust gender stereotypes that have so familiarly intimidated and silenced women about the issues of sexuality and gender central to their subordination. The aims of rights-based feminism are frustrated, not advanced, by such censorship. We need not misguided state censorship, but more, not less, reasonable discussion by women and men not only of their attraction to pornographic materials, but of the larger traditions of nudity in art and their role in shaping erotic experience in very different ways. A frank conversation about such experience could open the minds and hearts of men and women, heterosexual and homosexual, to how and why erotic experience sometimes objectifies its object, sometimes acknowledges the will and intentions of the beloved, sometimes even dignifies her or his sexual agency.[163] From the perspective of such frank conversation about erotic life, pornographic materials may come to be regarded in quite different ways, sometimes, indeed, emancipatory of the unjustly stunted and starved sexual interests of women as well as men (heterosexual as well as homosexual), an emancipation of interests that many persons of conscience (profoundly concerned with traditional injustices in the areas of gender and sexuality) increasingly take now to be central to a life well and humanely lived.[164]

A constitutional test, that turns on conventional understanding of what is degrading or dehumanizing to women, uses precisely the unjust gender stereotypes that have culturally entrenched the structural injustice of sexism as the measure of legitimate censorship; this is Orwellian Newspeak, unjustly entrenching sexism in the name of fighting sexism. The patronizing and rather sexist appeal to stereotypical anxieties about sexual fantasy, as the root of all evil, marginalizes reasonable discourse among free women and men about the injuries inflicted on both by the profound cultural entrenchment of sexism and homophobia, including, of course, what should be unacceptable and legally prohibited and prosecuted forms of sexual violence and exploitation.[165] The crucial appeal to such stereotypes, in the very structure of the approach urged on and adopted by the Canadian Supreme Court, was, of course, designed to appeal to the judgment on such matters of the conventional, largely male and heterosexual judges who would decide the case. It bespeaks the *depth* of the problem, on feminist grounds, with the Canadian approach that one of the lawyers responsible

Morality and Modern Nervous Illness', in James Strachey (ed.), *Standard Edition of the Complete Psychological Works of Sigmund Freud* (Hogarth Press, London, 1959), 197–9. I am indebted for this point to conversations with Carol Gilligan.

[163] See, for illuminating discussion along these lines of the different roles of the nude in Western high art, John Berger, *Ways of Seeing* (Penguin, London, 1972), at 45–64; Rona Goffen, *Titian's Women* (Yale University Press, New Haven, Conn., 1997).

[164] See, in general, Varda Burstyn (ed.), *Women Against Censorship* (Douglas & McIntrye, Vancouver, 1985).

[165] See, for an excellent recent discussion which shows that such discourse is feasible, Stephen J. Schulhofer, *Unwanted Sex: The Culture of Intimidation and the Failure of Law* (Harvard University Press, Cambridge, Mass., 1998).

for the successful litigation strategy, Kathleen E. Mahoney, later explained how they persuaded the Court in the following terms:

How did we do it? We showed them the porn—and among the seized videos were some horrifically violent and degrading gay movies. We made the point that the abused men in these films were being treated like women—and the judges got it. Otherwise, men can't put themselves in our shoes.[166]

This strategy essentially used the judges' homophobic prejudices to elicit from them the desired repugnance for heterosexual pornography, taking their prejudices against what they saw depicted in gay male pornography as the interpretive measure of how they should construe what was mainly of concern to Mahoney (as it was to MacKinnon), namely, reading heterosexual pornography as degrading. In effect, the judges were asked to consult their own feelings about pornography meant for homosexuals as the appropriate standard for judging pornography for heterosexuals. But this grotesque strategy expressly underwrote and indeed legitimated the judge's homophobia by self-consciously making the point that 'the abused men in these films were being treated like women'. As Jeffrey Sherman cogently observes, '[t]he men in the gay pornographic film were not being treated like women; they were being treated like gay men'.[167] The judgement (being treated like a woman) is an interpretive judgement, plausible to the judges because it validated a stereotypical prejudice at the heart of homophobia (that gay sex treats a man as a woman, see Chapter 3); and this judgement (prejudiced as it is) is offered as the measure of allegedly *good* judgement about explicit depictions of heterosexual sexuality. It is nothing of the sort. This argument scandalously uses, indeed enforces, the still largely culturally invisible but nonetheless unjust role of gender stereotypes in homophobia as the model for justice, or the reasons of justice for the censorship of depictions of heterosexual sexuality. This does justice neither to heterosexual nor homosexual sexuality, underwriting, as it does, one irrationalism (the traditional stereotype of homosexuality) in service of another (the stereotype of sexually active women as degraded). More importantly, from the perspective of its ostensible aims of justice to women, it uncritically enforces unjust gender stereotypes against heterosexual men and women, but it crucially does so by enforcing injustice against homosexuals. It is no accident that this vaunted victory for feminism led to the repression not of heterosexual pornography (the rather obsessional purpose of its advocates), but to that of gays and lesbians. In short, such censorship, held legitimate by the Canadian Supreme Court, did nothing to stem the tide of heterosexual pornography, but was used aggressively to attack the basic rights of the homosexual minority. If this is a victory for feminism, then, to paraphrase an observation made by Justice Black in a related context, another such victory and feminism is undone.[168]

---

[166] Cited in Jeffrey G. Sherman, 'Love Speech: The Social Utility of Pornography', 47 *Stan. L Rev.* 661, at 690 (1995).

[167] See *ibid.*, 691.

[168] See *Beauharnais* v. *Illinois*, 343 US 250, 275 (1952) (Black J, dissenting) ('Another such victory and I am undone') (criticizing majority's holding of constitutionality of group libel law).

We need to ask seriously: how could such a bad argument be plausible to a unanimous Canadian Supreme Court when the comparable group libel case, *Keegstra*, at least reflected a closely divided (four to three) Court? The most reasonable explanatory hypothesis is that the structural injustice of sexism and homophobia, in contrast to that of anti-Semitism and racism, is still so largely culturally entrenched that its unjust force remains largely invisible. It is for this reason that the appeal to unjust gender stereotypes had such plausibility, particularly when the appeal was used in ways that were alleged to protect heterosexual women but in a mode that crucially depended, for its imaginative plausibility, on the marginalization of the sexual experience of the most despised sexual minorities, lesbians and gay men.[169] The Canadian experience illustrates quite clearly the perils of censorship grounded on group-based harms to any reasonable understanding and remedy of structural injustice; such censorship, particularly in the areas where rights-based discourse about the terms of structural injustice is not yet well understood or discussed, entrenches, rather than subverts, the terms of such injustice. Its appeal manipulatively draws upon and reinforces the still largely unchallenged populist political force of gender stereotypes, including a paternalism in the domain of conviction that, in the name of combating sexism, illustrates its patronizing contempt for the empowered sexual voice of free women and men. Heterosexual male judges, asked to consult their feelings about homosexual sexual depictions, are asked to make those feelings the criterion for the group libel to women from heterosexual sexual depictions; a fantasy of a fantasy thus becomes the measure of censorship by law. To rationalize such injustice, facts and values are inverted: censorship, that denies voice, protects voice;[170] injustice becomes the measure of justice; oppression of freedom. Constitutionally fundamental distinctions of principle, between censorship in the domain of conviction and reasonable regulations of actions, are elided and obfuscated, including fallaciously ascribing to pornography a performative power (as a kind of religious or judicial ritual) that it no more possesses than any other depiction or representation (whether in art or religion or advertising), all of which are clearly constitutionally protected from state censorship in the domain of conviction. In effect, anxieties about sexual fantasy have been imaginatively transformed into actions in order to rationalize censorship that should, as a matter of basic constitutional principle, be unacceptable in a free and rational society.[171]

[169] See, on this important point, Jeffrey G. Sherman, 'Love Speech: The Social Utility of Pornography', 47 *Stan. L Rev.* 661 (1995); Andrea Loux, 'Idols and Icons: Catharine MacKinnon and Freedom of Expression in North America', 6 *Feminist Legal Studies* 85 (1998). See also Bettina Quistgaard, 'Pornography, Harm, and Censorship: A Feminist (Re)vision of the Right to Freedom of Expression', 52 *U of Toronto Faculty of Law Review* 132 (1993); Annalise Acron, 'Case Comment and Note: Harm, Community Tolerance, and the Indecent: A Discussion of R. v. Mara', 36 *Alberta L Rev.* 258 (1997).
[170] See, e.g., Owen M. Fiss, *The Irony of Free Speech: Liberalism Divided* (Harvard University Press, Cambridge, Mass., 1993), at 16–17, 26; Frank I. Michelman, 'Conceptions of Democracy in American Constitutional Argument: The Case of Pornography Regulation', 56 *Tenn. L Rev.* 291, 295–6 (1989).
[171] See, for powerful criticism of MacKinnon's position along these lines, Wojciech Sadurski, 'On "Seeing Speech Through an Equality Lens": A Critique of Egalitarian Arguments for Suppression of Hate Speech and Pornography' (1996) 16 *Oxford Journal of Legal Studies*, 713–23.

The appeal of such a strategy, including to a unanimous Canadian Supreme Court, suggests how powerfully intact the structural injustice of sexism and homophobia remain, illustrating yet again how the reactionary support of such injustice requires the distortion of facts and values of the paradox of intolerance, repressing, on irrationalist grounds, the discourse of the politics of identity that reasonably advances the understanding and remedy of structural injustice. In fact, as we have seen, the rights of one unjustly treated group are thus bargained away allegedly to advance the rights of another such group (as if the struggle for human rights is or must be a kind of zero sum game); such tactics of advancing one group, by scapegoating another, advance the rights of neither, but only further entrench what both groups most urgently need, a free and reasonable discourse about the unjust role that gender stereotypes have traditionally played in the abridgement of the basic human rights of all persons, including the right to intimate life. What is needed is not misguided state censorship, but a regime of free speech that empowers the politics of identity reasonably to contest the unjust force that such stereotypes continue to enjoy in public and private life.

In the case of gays and lesbians, who are protesting a tradition that rendered their sexuality literally unspeakable and thus sometimes unthinkable, availability of such pornographic materials may play an indispensable and wholly just normative role (which heterosexuals understandably often can barely understand) in imaginative images of the beauty and power of homosexual sexual love, liberating and empowering resources of thought and feeling and of moral voice, rooted in intimate relations of love and friendship, that enable gays and lesbians better to protest the terms of their moral slavery and to live ethically and authentically as free men and women.[172] Such materials express conscientious convictions about the values of sexuality and gender, protesting the dominant political orthodoxy, through images that are powerfully communicative and no less worthy of constitutional protection than other images that appeal to, enliven, and expand our erotic and sensual imaginations, sense of beauty, and cultivated artistic and ethical responsive intelligence.[173] Indeed, nonpornographic material (not only advertising, but traditional religious views of women's nature and role) may be more degrading, more debilitating of the integrity and autonomy of women (as well as gays and lesbians) as creative moral agents. In this maelstrom of increasingly free and reasonable debate about the sources of the unjust subjugation of women and gays, enforceable state judgements of the worthlessness or disvalue of certain thought and speech enforce intrinsically controversial *interpretive* judgements based on the dominant sexually repressive and now highly questionable political orthodoxy about issues of sexuality and gender; they do so precisely in the way (on the putative ground of a corruption of conscience) that, on grounds of free speech, we have good reason to suspect unreasonably to limit discussion and debate on these matters and deprive persons of their inalienable rights of thought, experience, and discussion. To deny that such laws abridge rights of conscience is unrea-

---

[172] See, on this important point, Strossen, n. 156 above, 167–70; Sherman, n. 169 above.
[173] See, on this and related points, Richards, n. 158 above.

sonably to circumscribe the scope of protected conscience to the measure of majoritarian views of the good life. Human rights, trimmed to the measure of such majoritarian judgements, lack their proper force precisely in the area where, as a matter of constitutional principle, they are most exigently required (namely, protection of the human rights of minorities), because they disempower both the legitimacy and integrity of the transgressive voice raised in protest of structural injustice.[174]

No such conception, no matter what its ostensibly appealing form in the abstract, has any place as a ground for censorship in a free society in contemporary circumstances, certainly not in a society with our history that now self-critically claims to respect the rights of women. No group, except perhaps gays and lesbians, has suffered more acutely than heterosexual women from the imposition on them of traditional roles in sexuality and gender, or been more often silenced and intimidated by the invocation of the unnatural in response to any legitimate form of dissent from such roles (including the cultivation of erotic imagination on their own terms). It does not advance rights-based feminism, but compromises it, to ascribe stereotypically to any communicative material in the area of sexuality or gender a depersonalized procrustean meaning or simplistic causal script (life simply imitating pornographic art) in the place of the varied imaginative lives of persons, the different roles sexually explicit materials play in such lives[175] and, in light of such variety, the lack of any reliable evidence of a causal significance of harm to women.[176] If we are interested in the understanding and remedy of the structural injustice of sexism and homophobia, we need not censorship, but the politics of identity which alone offers the empowering voices and reasonable discourse that contest and rebut the political force gender stereotypes have played in the subordination of women as well as gays and lesbians.

MacKinnon's proposal rests on a form of anti-subordination argument, but it is a quite bad anti-subordination argument. First, it assumes that no weighty free speech rights of the person (rights central to rights-based feminism) are at stake, but, as feminists have argued against MacKinnon, such rights are at stake, namely, rights of women autonomously to define and express their own erotic imaginations free of the unjust imposition of illegitimate stereotypes of proper gender roles; the Canadian experience with constitutional acceptance of MacKinnon's approach (on this basis, censoring gay and lesbian materials) confirms this worry, and is highly relevant to understanding the free speech issues reasonably at stake in the modern world. Secondly, her argument demonizes the harms from such materials in ways that impartial evidence does not support and that should raise worries that (like the purity movement) one's polemics, based on the search for a shallow, scapegoating populist consensus as a basis for political solidarity, are perversely enforcing subordination, not advancing anti-subordination. Thirdly, her argument assumes an undefended view of the focal importance of pornographic material in enforcing the subordination of women in contrast to other more reasonable understandings of such sources of

---

[174] See, on this point, Amy Adler, 'What's Left?: Hate Speech, Pornography, and the Problem for Artistic Expression', 84 *Calif. L Rev.* 1499 (1996).

[175] See Strossen, n. 156 above, 142–60.   [176] See *ibid.*, 253–6, 272–3.

subordination (for example, the illegitimate enforcement of sectarian religious or mythological views, or the systemically unjust economic subordination of women in family and job roles). A rights-based feminism needs not to indulge yet another mythological stereotype of gender, but to contest and subvert them precisely because they do not do justice to individualized moral personality and experience. The use of such stereotypes in this discourse uncritically repeats the mistake of a Catharine Beecher or Frances Willard,[177] namely, the appeal to a polemical mythology of gender, to which women have superior access, that has been the traditional rationale of gender inequality, not its clear-eyed and sharp-tongued reasonable moral critic on grounds of human rights and demanding standards of public reason. Our attention, like Willard's, is thus distracted from the intractable sectarian sources of gender inequality (which are left unexamined, and sometimes re-enforced), to an unreal issue whose pursuit, like the temperance or purity movements, retards, rather than advances human rights.[178]

We see in this area a replication of exactly the worries about group libel laws discussed earlier (Chapter 4). All forms of structural injustice (racism, anti-Semitism, sexism, and homophobia) importantly turn on the abridgment of the basic human right of free speech (the dependence thesis). The protection of free speech properly extends to all forms of group libel laws (including anti-pornography laws) because only that scope of protection guarantees both the legitimacy and integrity of the politics of identity as one of the reasonable remedies for structural injustice. These concerns apply, *a fortiori*, to the group libel laws alleged to combat sexism and homophobia because, on examination, such laws, as we have seen, call for, if anything, even more reasonably controversial interpretive judgements about group harms than those ascribed to conscientious expressions of racism or anti-Semitism. We have available a long history of the use of obscenity laws against the claims of both rights-based feminism and gay rights, which is highly relevant to understanding the magnitude of these risks in contemporary circumstances. Redefining obscenity in terms of controversial interpretive judgements of group harms, if anything, exacerbates these risks, precisely because such state-enforced judgements of stereotypical harms retard, as we have seen, serious attention to sexism and demonstrably exacerbate homophobia. Such state censorship of a range of discourse enforces rather than contests stereotypical identifications, stifling the empowering protests of individuals through which they express, demand, and define their individuality as persons against such stereotypical classifications.

This argument, of course, applies only within its properly understood domain of reasonable application. It does not apply, for example, to the domain of action in which the state has the right and responsibility to protect heterosexual women as well as gays and lesbians from unjust discrimination and from forms of unjust coercion to

---

[177] On the analogy of MacKinnon's arguments to those of the temperance movement, see Strossen, n. 156 above, at 269.

[178] Cf. Strossen, n. 156 above, 261–2, 266.

sex that should be both socially and legally sanctioned.[179] Even within the domain of speech, the argument does not apply to appropriate limits on speech in workplace contexts which are not properly analysed as public fora for reasonable public discussion and debate. Indeed, for this reason, remedies for structural injustice may include appropriate protections applicable to the workplace and, within reasonable limits, to education.[180] Such remedies, in my judgement, reasonably include, as Catharine MacKinnon was (to her distinguished credit) among the first to argue, appropriate legal actions for sexual harassment of both men and women, heterosexual and homosexual, in these and other similar contexts that are wholly inconsistent with the legitimate purposes of the workplace or of education.[181]

BLASPHEMY LAWS

These constitutional worries about group libel and obscenity laws apply, for the same reason, to the still widespread constitutional acceptability of blasphemy laws. Such laws protect, in their nature, group religious identity from insult, and thus raise the same sorts of issues of constitutional principle that we have now discussed at some length; current American constitutional scepticism about these laws, like its comparable views on group libel law, rests on sound grounds of political theory (under American law based constitutionally on the anti-establishment clause of the First Amendment, forbidding the state in this way from lending its support to sectarian religious conviction).[182] My concern in this book has been to offer and defend a

[179] See, for an able and illuminating discussion of the inadequacies of current law in this area, with which I substantially agree, Stephan J. Schulhofer, *Unwanted Sex: The Culture of Intimidation and the Failure of Law* (Harvard University Press, Cambridge, Mass., 1998).

[180] For criticism of some recent university speech codes for not striking a reasonable balance properly sensitive to values of free speech, see Ronald Dworkin, *Freedom's Law: The Moral Reading of the American Constitution* (Harvard University Press, Cambridge, Mass., 1996), 244–60. See also Nadine Strossen, 'Regulating Racist Speech on Campus: A Modest Proposal?', in Henry Louis Gates, Jr. *et al.*, *Speaking of Race, Speaking of Sex: Hate Speech, Civil Rights, and Civil Liberties* (New York University Press, New York, 1994), 181–256.

[181] This would and should include, in my judgement, prohibitions and regulations directed against the *ad hominem* use of pornographic material in a work environment to intimidate women or men, heterosexually or homosexually. Such a work environment is not in this case properly understood as a public forum for free speech purposes, and may therefore reasonably be subjected to forms of prohibition and regulation of speech that would raise constitutional issues of free speech in a public forum. On public forums, see Richards, n. 16 above, at 219–26. See, for illuminating treatment of free speech issues arising in workplace harassment contexts, Kent Greenawalt, *Fighting Words: Individuals, Communities, and Liberties of Speech* (Princeton University Press, Princeton, NJ, 1995), 77–96. On the wrong of sexual harassment, see Katherine M. Franke, 'What's Wrong With Sexual Harassment?', 49 *Stan. L Rev.* 691 (1997). For Catharine MacKinnon's important seminal contribution to understanding this problem, see Catharine A. MacKinnon, *Sexual Harassment of Working Women* (Yale University Press, New Haven, Conn., 1979).

[182] See, for full discussion of the background and character of the American constitutional view, resting on the anti-establishment clause of the First Amendment, Leonard W. Levy, *Blasphemy: Verbal Offense Against the Sacred, From Moses to Salman Rushdie* (Alfred A. Knopf, New York, 1993), 522–33, commenting, *inter alia*, on *Burstyn v. Wilson*, 343 US 495 (1952) (censorship of film as sacrilege, held unconstitutional); Robert C. Post, 'Cultural Heterogeneity and Law: Pornography, Blasphemy, and the First Amendment,'

political theory that structurally integrates interpretive and normative understanding of the right to free speech and the right against unjust discrimination. As we saw earlier (Chapter 4), the criminal prosecution of blasphemy, held by the European Court of Human Rights to be constitutionally acceptable,[183] may be regarded as objectionable not only on the ground of free speech but on the ground of impeding the role of the politics of identity in the reasonable understanding and remedy of structural injustice. My focus there was on the role such unjust censorship plays in impeding the politics of identity in combating anti-Semitism. The failure in post-war Germany of Konrad Adenauer to address the role Christian anti-Semitism played in Hitler's anti-Semitism is symptomatic of the failure of Germany, notwithstanding its group libel laws, responsibly to address the structural injustice of anti-Semitism in German culture and politics. For the same reason, the use of blasphemy laws, which enlist the state's power in the repression of speech offensive to dominant religious identities, privileges group identity at the constitutionally unacceptable price of abridging the exercise of the inalienable right of conscience in reasonable discourse about the political evil of Christian anti-Semitism and the role it played in the construction of the structural injustice of anti-Semitism as the ghastly force in European politics that it became in the twentieth century.

The point is not limited to the role of the politics of identity in the understanding and remedy of anti-Semitism, but applies to racism in general and, importantly, to sexism and homophobia. Reasonable discourse about the degree to which religion in Europe was implicated in its racism and imperialism cannot, if European nations are responsibly concerned to protect the right against unjust discrimination, be subject to censorship by blasphemy laws, which limit reasonable debate exactly where it may be most painfully and reasonably required. The forms of structural injustice are, moreover, mutually supporting (Chapter 3), and the same argument constitutionally condemns such laws for the role they play in the censorship of the politics of identity about sexism and homophobia as well. It was no accident, for this reason, that Germany's quite narrow post-war understanding of the scope of reasonable discourse about anti-Semitism would manifest itself in the uncritical continuity of its treatment of gay men, reflecting and enforcing Nazi views of male homosexuality; the murder of homosexuals in the Holocaust was not acknowledged, and the stronger criminal prohibitions of the Nazi era were not repealed, indeed were validated, by the German Constitutional Court; criminal sanctions for consensual sex between men over the age of 21 were only lifted by the Bundestag in 1969.[184]

---

76 *Calif. L Rev.* 297 (1988). See, for further historical background, Leonard W. Levy, *Treason Against God: A History of the Offense of Blasphemy* (Schocken Books, New York, 1981).

[183] See *Otto-Preminger-Institut* v. *Austria* (1995) 19 EHRR 34 (Ct.) (1994) (repression of film at request of Roman Catholic diocese, under Austrian blasphemy law, held constitutional).

[184] See, for an illuminating treatment of this matter, Robert G. Moeller, 'The Homosexual Man Is a "Man", the Homosexual Woman Is a "Woman": Sex, Society, and the Law in Postwar West Germany', in Robert G. Moeller (ed.), *West Germany under Construction: Politics, Society, and Culture in the Adenauer Era* (University of Michigan Press, Ann Arbor, Mich., 1997), at 251–84; on the decriminalization, see *ibid.*, 282.

As a normative argument of political theory, this argument is not limited to the circumstances of the United States or Europe. If the human right of free speech and the right against unjust discrimination are structurally connected (as I have argued), then blasphemy laws are inconsistent with a sound understanding of how these rights are related; their claim to protect religious groups from unjust insult not only abridges the human right of free speech but entrenches patterns of structural injustice condemned by the right against unjust discrimination. Perhaps the most dramatic recent example of the ongoing and aggressive threat of laws of this sort to respect for human rights (at the national, regional, and international levels) is the Salman Rushdie affair.[185]

The repressive sectarian uproar against Salman Rushdie's novel, *The Satanic Verses*,[186] began not in theocratic Iran, but in constitutionally democratic India even before the book's official British publication, on 26 September 1988. Two Indian magazines provided reviews of the book, excerpts, and interviews with the author, who, now a British citizen living in Britain, had been born to a Muslim family in India, which later moved to Pakistan.[187] Two Muslim members of the Indian parliament, not liking what they read about the book (and refusing to read it themselves), began a campaign to have the novel banned in India; the gravamen of the charges of sacrilege against the novel centred on its narration, based on reputable historical sources, of verses of the Qur'an that originally endorsed polytheism and then were retracted when Muhammad saw them as coming from Satan, not God.[188] The repressive efforts of the Indian politicians met with almost instant success; under a ruling of the Indian Customs Act, the Finance Ministry prohibited the book on 5 October 1988. Democratic India was the first country to ban the book,[189] followed shortly by Pakistan. In both cases, subsequent to the banning of the book, Rushdie-related violence led to deaths—in India, the deaths of fourteen people and the injury of scores more; in Pakistan, seven deaths.[190] Virtually every government with a Muslim majority or plurality, except secular Turkey,[191] also banned the book, as did a number of governments with substantial minorities, including Papua New Guinea, Thailand, India, Sri Lanka, Kenya, Tanzania, Liberia, Sierra Leone, and South Africa; two nations with negligible Muslim populations banned the book as well (Japan and Venezuela).[192] Ayatollah Khomeini, the theocratic leader of Iran, interposed himself responsively into an already unfolding scenario of state censorship and violent street riots (in Great Britain, South Africa, Pakistan, and India[193]), including already extant death threats to Rushdie and book burnings by Muslim communities in Britain;[194] in February of 1989, Khomeini issued his *fatwa*, calling 'on all zealous Muslims to execute' Rushdie and his publishers 'so that no one else will dare to insult the Muslim

---

[185] See, for illuminating discussion, Daniel Pipes, *The Rushdie Affair: The Novel, the Ayatollah, and the West* (a Birch Lane Press Book, New York, 1990).
[186] See Salman Rushdie, *Satanic Verses* (Henry Holt and Company, New York, 1988).
[187] See Pipes, n. 185 above, 41–3. [188] See *ibid.*, 56–62.
[189] See *ibid.*, 19–20. [190] See *ibid.*, 209. [191] See *ibid.*, 145–6.
[192] See *ibid.*, 143. [193] See *ibid.*, 98. [194] See *ibid.*, 19–26.

sanctities'.[195] The procedural and substantive legality under Islamic law of the *fatwa* was widely contested within the Islamic scholarly community,[196] and was sufficiently disproportionate that it has been plausibly argued that, as an act of state-endorsed sectarian religious terrorism (incitement to murder), it was in violation of public international law.[197]

Khomeini's *fatwa* certainly illustrates, in the starkest possible terms, the political uses to which blasphemy, as a punishable offence, may aggressively be put in service of forging a sectarian political nationalism, attempting thus to establish Khomeini's credentials as the true ideological leader (against the internal challenge to Islam of the scepticism represented by the bicultural Rushdie) of the Muslims in Great Britain, South Africa, Pakistan, and India who took to the streets before he issued his *fatwa*.[198] My critical normative interest is not, however, in Khomeini's politics, but in the larger constitutional assumptions about the legitimacy of blasphemy and related laws (under national and regional law and public international law), which allowed so many more mainstream political leaders (including the politicians in India and elsewhere who started the pattern of censorship) to believe it was appropriate to engage in such bullying tactics of repression and intimidation.

The constitutional rationale for such tactics is the assumption that blasphemy and related laws, like group libel laws, strike a reasonable balance between the right of free speech and the right against unjust discrimination (in this case, religious discrimination or intolerance). For example, Articles 19 and 20 of the International Covenant on Civil and Political Rights articulate this balance as a matter of public international law. Thus, Article 19 protects the right of free speech but subject to limitations based on respect of rights and reputation of others, and protection of 'national security', 'public order', and 'morals';[199] and Article 20 holds that 'any advocacy of national, racial, or religious hatred that constitutes incitement to discrimination, hostility or violence shall be prohibited by law'.[200] Though the matter is not free from doubt, blasphemy laws may be regarded as consistent with Article 19 and even required by Article 20.[201] But this view—shared in many national and regional legal systems as well as possibly under public international law—disastrously legitimates state censorship on sectarian religious grounds, and thus abridges not only the right to conscience and speech but what respect for these rights makes possible, reasonable discourse about the diagnosis and remedy of structural injustice. To this extent, this inadequacy in the International Covenant on Civil and Political Rights confirms my earlier criticism about a similar inadequacy in the scope of the Convention on the Elimination of All Forms of Racial Discrimination, namely, the failure of international public law

---

[195] Quoted at Pipes, n. 185 above, 27.   [196] See *ibid.*, 87–95.

[197] See, in general, Anthony Chase, 'Legal Guardians: Islamic Law, International Law, Human Rights Law, and the Salman Rushdie Affair', 11 *Am. UJ Int'l L & Pol'y* 375 (1996).

[198] On Khomeini's motives, see Pipes, n. 185 above, 95–104.

[199] See Anthony Chase, 'Legal Guardians: Islamic Law, International Law, Human Rights Law, and the Salman Rushdie Affair', 11 *Am. UJ Int'l L & Pol'y* 375, 414 (1996).

[200] See *ibid.*, 417–24.

[201] For a statement and criticism of this interpretive position, see *ibid.*, 414–22.

adequately to give weight to the normative force of rights to conscience and to speech as basic human rights (Chapter 4). The censorship of blasphemy, underwritten by the International Covenant on Civil and Political Rights, is objectionable for the same reasons as the censorship of group libel, required by the Convention on the Elimination of All Forms of Racial Discrimination.[202]

The consequences of such censorship, as the Rushdie affair surely teaches, are not a reasonable dialogue among equals about justice, respect for human rights and the public good, but the entrenchment and legitimation of the irrationalist politics of sectarian religion that feeds on scapegoating and the violent repression of dissenters (including state-sponsored religious intolerance of Rushdie). It leads, as in India and elsewhere, to the legitimation of a politics of rigid and impermeable group identities, aggressively hostile to any suggestion of questions of reasonable doubt about traditional religious authority. Such a politics of ideological terror, alleged to protect religious identity, in fact reinforces the structural injustice of religious intolerance and often related prejudices (including racism, sexism, and homophobia).[203] The abridgement of the right of free speech thus also abridges the right against unjust discrimination, including the right against religious discrimination.

It surely supports this argument of normative political theory that the censorship, so quickly imposed in constitutionally democratic India, stimulated the worst Rushdie-related violence anywhere, including the deaths of fourteen people and the injury of scores more.[204] Holding such an abridgement of speech in the domain of conviction to a demanding standard of a clear and present danger underwrites a reasonable public consensus on the terms of democratic dialogue among equals in a free and democratic society; in particular, people thus come to understand, as part of their political education in constitutional essentials, that ideological disagreement is never enough either for state censorship or bullying group violence as political tactics. In contrast, the Indian legitimation of such censorship, on grounds *not* held to a demanding standard of a clear and present danger, perversely unleashed such dangers, underwriting an aggressive politics of sectarian religious identity (politically manipulated by the leaders of such groups to their own advantage) that is among the sources of the communal violence that has now reached levels in India not seen since the partition of India and Pakistan.[205] Political identity, whether of majority Hindu or

---

[202] On the generality of the failure to take seriously the right against religious intolerance (under both international public law and national law), see Kevin Boyle, 'Religious Intolerance and the Incitement of Hatred', in Sandra Coliver (ed.), *Striking a Balance: Hate Speech, Freedom of Expression and Non-discrimination* (Article 19, International Centre against Censorship, London, and Human Rights Centre, University of Essex, 1992), at 61–71. On the experience of Northern Ireland in extending hate speech prohibitions to religious intolerance, see Therese Murphy, 'Incitement to Hatred: Lessons from Northern Ireland', in *ibid.*, 263–8.

[203] On the role of Arab countries in supporting the publication of anti-Semitic literature like the Protocols of the Elders of Zion, see Pipes, n. 185 above, 109–10.

[204] See, on this point, Chase, n. 199 above; Pipes, n. 185 above, at 209–11.

[205] See, in general, Venkat Eswaran, 'Advocacy of National, Racial and Religious Hatred: The Indian Experience', in Coliver (ed.), n. 202 above, 171–81; Anthony Chase, '"Pakistan or the Cemetery?": Muslim Minority Rights in Contemporary India', 16 *BC Third World L.* 35 (1996).

minority Muslim, is constitutionally entrenched in terms of sectarian religion, not allegiance to respect for basic human rights of all persons. The consequence is a sense of political community, like that of India today, increasingly rooted in a sectarian Hindi nationalism aggressively hostile to respect for the rights of the Muslim minority.[206]

It is, of course, quite true that some religious traditions, like Islam, have not had the long historical experience of the Christian West in the internal development, within its religious as well as political thought, of traditions of separation of church and state,[207] but it would be a mistake to underestimate the degree to which, even within Islam (or in other non-Western traditions), there is an internal diversity of interpretive sources of authority that may be a reasonable basis for the normative appeal of arguments of political theory grounded on respect for basic human rights like the right of free speech and the right against unjust discrimination.[208] Western countries might, however, in light of their traditions, reasonably be held to a more demanding standard of respect for such basic human rights.

The United States and the nations of Western Europe, including Britain (which protected Rushdie from the threat of assassination), did not, of course, ban Rushdie's novel (though the Canadian government temporarily banned imports as hate literature, until the Prohibited Importations Branch found it did not constitute such literature[209]). But, Britain, in particular, faced a challenge from its Muslim population in light of Britain's own blasphemy law, which raises important issues of constitutional principle that indicate even Western countries fall unreasonably short of the normative standards we should demand of them. Under the British common law of criminal blasphemy, a successful prosecution took place in *Gay News* v. *United Kingdom*.[210] The arguments in this case, virtually the same as those made by British Muslims about *The Satanic Verses*, were applied (three to two) by the United Kingdom's House of Lords, Britain highest appellate court,[211] and accepted by the European Commission on Human Rights.[212] The *Gay News* case was Britain's first prosecution for blasphemy in over fifty years. The case involved a poem published in *Gay News* magazine, which depicted Jesus as homosexual, 'well hung', and engaged in sex with a Roman centurion after his crucifixion.[213] Interestingly, from a comparative perspective on *The Satanic Verses*, the decision held that a publication is blasphe-

[206] See, on this point, Chase, ' "Pakistan or the Cemetery?": Muslim Minority Rights in Contemporary India', 16 *BC Third World L.* 35 (1996).

[207] See Pipes, n. 185 above, 74; on the development of this tradition in the Christian West, see, in general, Richards, n. 16 above.

[208] See, on this point, Chase, n. 199 above, 429–34. For the theological support for a liberal tradition within Islam, see Abdullahi Ahmed An-Na'im, *Toward an Islamic Reformation: Civil Liberties, Human Rights, and International Law* (Syracuse University Press, Syracuse, NY 1990).

[209] Pipes, n. 185 above, 157.

[210] *Gay News* v. *United Kingdom* (1983) 5 EHRR 123 (Comm.).

[211] *Whitehouse* v. *Lemon* [1979] AC 617 (defining a blasphemous libel as 'a matter calculated to outrage the feeling of Christians').

[212] *Gay News* v. *United Kingdom* (1983) 5 EHRR 123 (Comm.).

[213] James Kirkup, 'The Love that Dares to Speak Its Name', *Gay News*, June 1976, at 26.

mous if it 'contains any contemptuous reviling, scurrilous or ludicrous matter relating to God, Jesus Christ, or the Bible or to the formularies of the Church of England. It is not blasphemous if . . . the publication is couched in decent and temperate language. The test is to be applied is as to the manner.'[214]

On appeal to the European Commission on Human Rights as a violation of Article 10 of the European Convention on Human Rights regarding free expression, the application was deemed inadmissible, a view in line with the later decision to similar effect of the European Court of Human Rights.[215] The European Commission 'decided that the restriction imposed upon the applicant's freedom of expression was necessary under Article 10(2) for the protection of the rights of others. People had a right not to be offended in their religious feelings by publications.'[216]

In light of the *Gay News* precedent, British Muslims reasonably thought they had a good case for banning the ostensibly derogatory views in *The Satanic Verses*. In *R. v. Chief Metropolitan Stipendiary Magistrate, ex parte Choudhury*, however, British courts affirmed that British law applied only to blasphemy against Christianity.[217] The allegations of blasphemous libel and seditious libel against Rushdie and his publishers were, for this reason, summarily dismissed. The court held that even if it were free to extend the law to cover other religions, it would not do so as it would be impossible to set clear limits on such an extension.[218] The European Commission on Human Rights also refused the case, saying that the United Kingdom did not violate its obligation to protect the European Convention's rights against discrimination, and there was no positive obligation to protect Muslims from blasphemy.[219]

The *Gay News* and *Rushdie* cases bespeak blatantly unjust treatment. Upholding the protections against blasphemy for individual Christians and denying them to Muslims violates any reasonable interpretation of the basic human right against unjust discrimination. Unfortunately, this hypocrisy was quite apparent to many British Muslims and fed a sense of alienation from British and European institutions. If courts—an impartial forum for the peaceful resolution of conflicts—are only open on an unequal basis, there is a sense of just grievance which leads aggrieved groups to take to the streets and engage in demonstrations designed to be publicly notorious and thus gain attention. This is yet another example of how the protection of one group's sectarian religious values—be they majority or minority—alienates other groups from engaging in civil and political society. Such alienation stimulates polarized reactions and rationalizes the most inflexible forms of communal identity.

One solution to this problem would be that suggested in the opinion of Lord Scarman in the House of Lords' judgment in the *Gay News* case.[220] Lord Scarman

---

[214] *Whitehouse* v. *Lemon* [1979] AC 661–5.

[215] See *Otto-Preminger-Institut* v. *Austria* (1995) 19 EHRR 34 (Ct.) (1994) (repression of film at request of Roman Catholic diocese, under Austrian blasphemy law, held constitutional).

[216] See Kevin Boyle, 'Religious Intolerance and the Incitement of Hatred', in Coliver (ed.), n. 202 above, 61–71, at 67.

[217] *R.* v. *Chief Metropolitan Stipendiary Magistrate, ex parte Choudhury* [1990] 3 WLR 986.   [218] *Ibid.*

[219] *Choudhury* v. *The United Kingdom*, App. No. 17439/1990 (1991) 12 *Hum. Rt. LJ* 172.

[220] *Whitehouse* v. *Lemon* [1979] AC 617.

was willing to assume that Lemon could establish 'that he had no intention to shock Christian believers' and had published 'the poem not to offend Christians but to comfort practising homosexuals by encouraging them to feel that there was room for them in the Christian religion'.[221] But Scarman found Lemon's intent to be irrelevant, because the point of blasphemy law was 'to protect religious feeling from outrage and insult'.[222] He rejected the notion that blasphemy was criminal because of its tendency to cause of breach of the peace. It is 'a jejune exercise', he said, 'to speculate whether an outraged Christian would feel provoked by the words and illustration in this case to commit a breach of peace. I hope, and happen to believe, that most, true to their Christian principles, would not allow themselves to be so provoked.'[223] It is because, for Scarman, blasphemy protects religious sensibility, as an end in itself, that 'the character of the words published matter; but not the motive of the author or publisher'.[224] If in Kirkup's poem 'the argument for acceptance and welcome of homosexuals within the loving fold of the Christian faith had been advanced "in a sober and temperate . . . style," . . . there could have been no criminal offence committed'.[225] But for Scarman 'the jury (with every justification) had rejected this view of the poem and drawing'.[226]

Lord Scarman's rejection of the requirement of intent followed from his view of 'legal policy in the society of today'; in his view, that policy should find a 'way forward for a successful plural society'.[227] Although Scarman, as a judge, could not expand the common law crime of blasphemy to protect the religious feelings of non-Christians, he wanted to use the *Lemon* case as a platform to urge that the common law be changed, consistent with views of Muslims in the wake of the Rushdie case,[228] by legislation to protect the sensibilities of all religious groups. His repudiation of the requirement of intent reflected this ambition. He made this point clearly at the beginning of his judgment:

My Lords, I do not subscribe to the view that the common law offence of blasphemous libel serves no useful purpose in the modern law. On the contrary, I think that there is a case for legislation extending it to protect the religious beliefs and feelings of non-Christians . . . In an increasingly plural society such as that of modern Britain it is necessary not only to respect the differing beliefs, feelings and practices of all but also to protect them from scurrility, vilification, ridicule, and contempt . . . When in the 19th century Lord Macaulay protested in Parliament against the way the blasphemy laws were then administered, he added (Speeches, p. 116): 'If I were a judge in India, I should have no scruple about punishing a Christian who should pollute a mosque.' . . . When Macaulay became a legislator in India, he saw to it that the law protected the religious feelings of all. I have permitted myself these general observations at the outset of my opinion because, my Lords, they determine my approach to this appeal. I will not lend my voice to a view of the law relating to blasphemous libel which would render it a dead letter, or diminish its efficacy to protect religious feeling from outrage and insult. My

---

[221] *Whitehouse* v. *Lemon* [1979] AC 660.   [222] *Ibid.*, 658.   [223] *Ibid.*, 662.

[224] *Ibid.*, 665 (citation omitted).   [225] *Ibid.*, 662 (citation omitted).   [226] *Ibid.*

[227] *Whitehouse* v. *Lemon* [1979] AC 664–5.

[228] See, e.g., Bhikhu Parekh, 'Group Libel and Freedom of Expression: Thoughts on the Rushdie Affair', in Coliver (ed.), n. 202 above, 358–62.

criticism of the common law offence of blasphemy is not that it exists but that it is not sufficiently comprehensive. It is shackled by the chains of history.[229]

Lord Scarman offers a conception of blasphemy law no longer unjustly rationalized as a question-begging sectarian consequence of Britain's establishment of the
Anglican Church as the state church,[230] but enlarged by statute to achieve pluralism.
But, pluralism is importantly thus defined in terms of existing group identities, which
such a statute, like the comparable group libel statutes earlier discussed (Chapter 4),
makes the basis of state censorship in the domain of conviction. In effect, the sensibilities of well-established religions are made the measure of censorship at the expense
of the inalienable right of any dissenter from such religions to speak her or his mind.
For exactly the same reasons we canvassed earlier, this cannot be reasonably justified
on the basis either of the right of free speech or of the right against unjust discrimination. My earlier discussions have focused on the damage such laws do to reasonable
discussion and debate about the structural injustice of religious intolerance (including anti-Semitism) and racism; I now explore the same point in terms of the way such
laws, as in the *Gay News* case itself, self-righteously are invoked (pandering to uncritical majoritarian sensibilities) unjustly to entrench the structural injustice of homophobia.

I begin with Scarman's ostensible rationale of such laws, applied to publication of
Kirkup's poem, in terms of a style/substance distinction. The weakness of the distinction, from the perspective of both the right of free speech and right against unjust
discrimination, is illustrated by a literary work like that prosecuted in the *Gay News*
case. To say that a gay poet, like Kirkup, could without penalty have produced a
scholarly study on Jesus of Nazareth's attitude to homosexuality, making in academic
style substantially the same points Kirkup makes in his robustly earthy and sensual
poem, is to say Kirkup should not have written a poem adequate to his convictions
about the sources of the structural injustice of homophobia. This is to do justice neither to the right of free expression nor to the reasonable role such expression plays in
the struggle for voice and reasonable discourse against the background of a tradition
of repressive structural injustice like homophobia which has depended on the silencing of such conviction and such sexual voice. In particular, it is to enlist the state to
enforce an interpretive view of a dominant religious identity which, though traditional, is now reasonably contestable even among believers of conviction and, moreover, contestable precisely in the area and in the terms (namely, matters of sexuality
and gender) that the state refuses, dogmatically, to acknowledge as subject to reasonable debate. The state may no more interpose in this arena, as the measure of legitimate debate, the interpretive views of dominant Christians than it may, against
Rushdie, the interpretive views of Islamic believers about the inerrancy of their

---

[229] *Whitehouse* v. *Lemon* [1979] AC 658.
[230] See, for British tradition on this point, Peter Cumper, 'Religious Human Rights in the World
Today: A Report on the 1994 Atlanta Conference: Legal perspectives on Religious Human Rights Today:
Religious Human Rights in the United Kingdom', 10 *Emory Int'l L Rev.* 115 (1996).

scriptures. To understand the issues of constitutional principle at stake here, we need to be clear about the role a strand of Christianity played in the construction of the injustice of homophobia (analogous to the role of Christian anti-Semitism in modern anti-Semitism).

Human cultures have dealt very differently with homosexuality as an erotic preference. Ancient Greek culture, as we have seen, not only tolerated, but idealized pederastic male homosexual relations as central elements in Greek pedagogy and artistic and political culture.[231] Christian moral teaching, sharply critical of Greek sexual morality, went well beyond the traditional Pagan distaste for men taking the passive (female) role in being penetrated by another man (the active role was quite a different matter[232]) to a remarkably cruel reprobation of homosexual relations as such:

For the first time in history, in 390 [Common Era], the Roman people witnessed the public burning of male prostitutes, dragged from the homosexual brothels of Rome. The Emperor Theodosius' edict (preserved in full, significantly by a writer anxious to prove the agreement of the Mosaic with the Roman laws) shows clearly, in the very incoherence of its moral indignation, the slow turning of the tide. For a male to play a female role, by allowing himself to become the passive partner in a sexual act, had long been repugnant . . . But it was now assumed to be equally shocking that a soul allotted in perpetuity to the 'sacrosanct dwelling-place' of a recognizably male body should have tried to force that body into female poses.[233]

Christian moral thought on sexuality and gender had implicit within it a valuation of asexuality (or the renunciation of sexuality) which made a moral space possible for a theory and practice treating women as persons and as equals.[234] Such a suspension of gender differences might reasonably have been interpreted to justify gender equality and even more humane treatment of homosexual love as a variation on the theme of gender equality. Certainly, abolitionist feminist women in the antebellum period in America interpreted their Christian convictions as mandating gender equality, and some gay Christians today not unreasonably interpret their tradition as requiring

[231] Important studies include William Armstrong Percy III, *Pederasty and Pedagogy in Archaic Greece* (University of Illinois Press, Urbana, Ill., 1996); K. J. Dover, *Greek Popular Morality in the Time of Plato and Aristotle* (Basil Blackwell, Oxford, 1974); Kenneth J. Dover, *Greek Homosexuality* (Duckworth, London, 1978); Kenneth J. Dover, 'Greek Homosexuality and Initiation', in K. J. Dover, *The Greeks and their Legacy* (Blackwell, Oxford, 1988), at 115–34; Peter Green, 'Sex and Classical Literature', in Peter Green, *Classical Bearings: Interpreting Ancient History and Culture* (Thames and Hudson, New York, 1989), at 130–50; Eva Cantarella, *Bisexuality in the Ancient World* (trans. Cormac O'Cuilleanain, Yale University Press, New Haven, Conn., 1992); David M. Halperin, *One Hundred Years of Homosexuality: And Other Essays on Greek Love* (Routledge, New York, 1990); David M. Halperin, John J. Winkler, and Froma I. Zeitlin (eds.), *Before Sexuality: The Construction of Erotic Experience in the Ancient Greek World* (Princeton University Press, Princeton, NJ, 1990).
[232] See Peter Brown, *The Body and Society: Men, Women and Sexual Renunciation in Early Christianity* (Columbia University Press, New York, 1988), at 30.
[233] See *ibid.*, 383. For the text of Theodosius's edict, see Derrick Sherwin Bailey, *Homosexuality and the Western Christian Tradition* (originally published, 1955) (Archon Books, Hamden, Conn., 1975), at 71–2.
[234] See Brown, n. 232 above, 118–19, 146, 170, 288, 369–71.

recognition of the dignity of homosexual love.[235] But the idea of gender equality in early Christianity was increasingly interpreted in otherworldly terms without relevance to gender roles in this world, indeed hardening the impermeability of gender roles in this world (as the edict of Theodosius clearly does). And while there were periods of relative tolerance of homosexuals,[236] the dominant religious and political culture of Christian Europe was given classic legal expression for Americans at the founding of their republic by William Blackstone's hesitation to even discuss something 'the very mention of which is a disgrace to human nature . . . a crime not fit to be named; *"peccatum illud horrible, inter christianos non nominandum"* '.[237] Citing with approval Constantine's sanguinary edict,[238] Blackstone grounded capital punishment for the offence not only in 'the voice of nature and of reason' but 'the express law of God' in the biblical 'destruction of two cities by fire from heaven', a punishment imitated by 'our antient [*sic*] law . . . by commanding such miscreants to be burnt to death'.[239] By Blackstone's time, however, the standard capital punishment applied to this crime as it did to other capital offences was hanging.[240] Such legal enforcement of Christian reprobation of homosexuality was the basic framework within which the later development of various interpretations of such condemnation in Western thought must be understood, as a fixed point of moral and legal thought not subject to reasonable doubt or discussion.

During this long period of quite punitive reprobation, homosexual activity existed outside the law, as a kind of ultimate heresy in religion[241] or treason in law,[242] and took the form, as it did in renaissance Venice, of sometimes barbarously punished active partners (burned alive or after decapitation) and much less severely punished passive (often younger) partners (sometimes including sodomy with women).[243] Homosexual activity was thus interpreted as an atavistic vestige of animalistic sexual

---

[235] See, for an important such view, mustering historical evidence in its support, John Boswell, *Christianity, Social Tolerance, and Homosexuality* (University of Chicago Press, Chicago, Ill., 1980); for more recent studies, rather more critical of the Christian tradition but also urging rethinking of these issues on grounds internal to the Christian tradition, see Bernadette J. Brooten, *Love Between Women: Early Christian Responses to Female Homoeroticism* (University of Chicago Press, Chicago, Ill., 1996); Mark D. Jordan, *The Invention of Sodomy in Christian Theology* (University of Chicago Press, Chicago, Ill., 1997). For more popular forms of advocacy along these lines, see Andrew Sullivan, *Virtually Normal: An Argument About Homosexuality* (Knopf, New York, 1995); Bruce Bawer, *A Place at the Table: The Gay Individual in American Society* (Poseidon Press, New York, 1993); Bruce Bawer, *Beyond Queer: Challenging Gay Left Orthodoxy* (Free Press, New York, 1996).

[236] For the historical evidence on this point, see Boswell, n. 235 above.

[237] See William Blackstone, *Commentaries on the Laws of England* (facsimile of first edition of 1765–9) (University of Chicago Press, Chicago, Ill., 1979), iv, 215–16.

[238] The edict called for 'exquisite punishment'; see text cited in Bailey, n. 233 above, at 70; Theodosius's later edict explicitly called for 'avenging flames in the sight of the people', text cited in *ibid.*, at 72.

[239] See *ibid.*, 216.   [240] See *ibid.*

[241] See Alan Bray, *Homosexuality in Renaissance England* (Gay Men's Press, London, 1982), at 19, 65.

[242] See *ibid.*, 20.

[243] See Guido Ruggiero, *The Boundaries of Eros: Sex Crime and Sexuality in Renaissance Venice* (Oxford University Press, New York, 1985), at 109–45; for a useful comparison, see Michael Rocke, *Forbidden Friendship: Homosexuality and Male Culture in Renaissance Florence* (Oxford University Press, New York, 1996).

barbarism at war with civilization as such. Its presence, as the tolerated cultural form of the berdache among the Amerindians of the New World,[244] was thus one of the aspects of those cultures that, like the powerful role of women[245] or cannibalism,[246] simply outraged European colonialists; such uncritical outrage led them, sometimes through the prism of their own sectarian convictions, to interpret Amerindian cultures as barbarous and thus rationalized the normative judgement that the Amerindians were, in Aristotle's terms, natural slaves, who might justly be enslaved.[247] From this undiscriminating perspective, Amerindian sodomy was conflated, as a form of diabolic evil in the Amerindians, with cannibalism.[248] This perspective rationalized as well related judgements notably in the minds of the Spanish conquerors in particular (in light of Spain's powerfully irrationalist inquisitorial anti-Semitism and expulsion of the Jews in 1492, the year of Columbus's discovery of America for the Spanish monarchy[249]); these included the judgements of the Amerindians as women,[250] as diabolic heretics like the Jews (thus, also subject to inquisitions),[251] and, prophetically for the later history of American slavery and racism, as the descendants of comparably degraded African cultures.[252] Similarly, in British North America, the Amerindians were analogized to the Jews[253] (as well as to the Irish[254]). Such reinforcing prejudices (homophobia, sexism, anti-Semitism, racism) naturally laid the foundation, in turn, for developing forms of Spanish and British racism and the later enslavement of Africans; their African culture was interpreted also as involving comparably degraded forms of intimate life (for example, allegations of selling children[255] and sexual incontinence[256]) that rationalized their natural slavery. Indeed, the largely successful rebuttal of the argument of natural slavery of the Amerindians by Los Casas was companioned with the quite uncritical

---

[244] The berdache was a man, who cross-dressed and lived as a woman, who was valued for shamanic and other powers in Amerindian cultures, living sometimes as the wife of another man. For important treatments of the violent European reaction to this cultural role in Amerindian cultures, see Walter L. Williams, *The Spirit and the Flesh: Sexual Diversity in American Indian Culture* (Beacon Press, Boston, Mass., 1986); Richard C. Trexler, *Sex and Conquest: Gendered Violence, Political Order, and the European Conquest of the Americas* (Cornell University Press, Ithaca, NY, 1995); Rudi C. Bleys, *The Geography of Perversion: Male-to-Male Sexual Behaviour Outside the West and the Ethnographic Imagination, 1750–1918* (New York University Press, New York, 1995).

[245] See Anthony Pagden, *The Fall of Natural Man: The American Indian and the Origins of Comparative Ethnology* (Cambridge University Press, Cambridge, 1982), at 52–3.

[246] See *ibid.*, 86.

[247] See Pagden, n. 245 above, 86, 174–9. See also Williams, n. 244 above; Trexler, n. 244 above; Bleys, n. 244 above.

[248] See Fernando Cervantes, *The Devil in the New World: The Impact of Diabolism in New Spain* (Yale University Press, New Haven, Conn., 1994), 9, 29–30.

[249] For an important recent study of Spanish anti-Semitism, suggesting a much earlier racialized interpretation of the prejudice than previously supposed, see B. Netanyahu, *The Origins of the Inquisition in Fifteenth Century Spain* (Random House, New York, 1995).

[250] See Pagden, n. 245 above, 43–4, 46, 116.   [251] See Cervantes, n. 248 above, 39.

[252] See Pagden, n. 245 above, 174–9.

[253] See Alden T. Vaughan, *Roots of American Racism: Essays on the Colonial Experience* (Oxford University Press, New York, 1995), at 49–57.

[254] See *ibid.*, 42.   [255] See Pagden, n. 245 above, 161, 174–9.

[256] See Vaughan, n. 253 above, 164–5.

application of such arguments to Africans.[257] Such attitudes of reprobation rested on the European rejection of any cultural legitimation of the homosexual role (largely understood in terms of men having sex with boys) as an animalistic barbarism.

However, the stigmatized cultural role of the homosexual in European cultures in the eighteenth and nineteenth centuries underwent a significant change, associated with the development of urban anonymity and a new ethics of gender relations, from a man who had sex with boys and women to men in subcultures who 'are effeminate members of a third or intermediate gender, who surrender their rights to be treated as dominant males, and are exposed instead to a merited contempt as a species of male whore'.[258] Homosexual activity was, if anything, even more persecuted, as it was in Britain, because it now took more publicly organized subcultural forms.[259] But persecution now had a different focus. The sodomite was labelled a 'he-whore', a transvestite, and was no longer a promiscuous rake 'but a species of outcast woman of the lowest standing'.[260] Randolph Trumbach has eloquently explained this development in terms of rising anxieties about gender associated with 'the rise of the egalitarian family':

The degree of equality between men and women, and parents and children, that resulted from companionate marriage and closer attachment to one's children, raised profound anxiety in both men and women. The anxiety resulted in a compromise with full equality that historians have called domesticity. Men and women were equal, but they were supposed to live in separate spheres, he dominant in the economy, she in the home. Women were no longer supposed to have bodies which were inferior copies of men's; instead, as Thomas Laqueur has shown, their bodies were now seen to be biologically different; and of course, on these differences could be founded supposed inescapable differences in gender role, despite the morality of equality.[261]

The cultural transformation of the homosexual role was very much a form of symbolic scapegoating to rigidify the new pattern of gender roles:

[T]he transvestite was a wall that guaranteed the permanent, lifelong separation of the majority of men and women, in societies where their relative equality must have been a perpetual

[257] See, in general, Pagden, n. 245 above; Vaughan, n. 253 above.
[258] See Randolph Trumbach, 'Gender and the Homosexual Role in Modern Western Culture: The 18th and 19th Centuries Compared', in Dennis Altman *et al.*, *Homosexuality, Which Homosexuality?* (DMP Publishers, London, 1989), 149–69 at 153. See also Randolph Trumbach, 'Sex, Gender, and Sexual Identity in Modern Culture: Male Sodomy and Female Prostitution in Enlightenment London', in John C. Fout (ed.), *Forbidden History: The State, Society, and the Regulation of Sexuality in Modern Europe* (University of Chicago Press, Chicago, Ill., 1992), 89–106; Randolph Trumbach, 'The Birth of the Queen: Sodomy and the Emergence of Gender Equality in Modern Culture, 1660–1750', in Martin Bauml Duberman *et al.* (eds.), *Hidden from History: Reclaiming the Gay and Lesbian Past* (New American Books, New York, 1989), 129–40; Randolph Trumbach, 'The Original and Development of the Modern Lesbian Role in the Western Gender System: Northwestern Europe and the United States, 1750–1990' (1994) 20 *Historical Reflections* 288–320; Randolph Trumbach, *Sex and the Gender Revolution: Volume One Heterosexuality and the Third Gender in Enlightenment London* (University of Chicago Press, Chicago, Ill., 1998); Alan Bray, *Homosexuality in Renaissance England* (GMP Publishers, Ltd., London, 1982).
[259] See Bray, n. 258 above, 81–114.
[260] See Trumbach, 'Gender and the Homosexual Role in Modern Western Culture', n. 258 above, 157.
[261] See *ibid.*, 155. See also Thomas Laqueur, *Making Sex: Body and Gender from the Greeks to Freud* (Harvard University Press, Cambridge, Mass., 1990).

danger to patriarchy. A minority of adult males were allowed to be passive, but the over-whelming majority of males can never have had the experience of being sexually submissive in their boyhood. The transvestite was the dike that held back the flood of true equality between men and women, where both genders would experience power and submission in equal degrees. All women in societies with transvestites experienced sexual domination all their lives, but only the transvestite minority of males ever did so.[262]

This cultural construction of the homosexual role guaranteed that men lived 'in a sphere completely separated by biological nature from women':[263] only women desired men in the appropriately subordinated mode. An ostensible man, who vio-lated this norm, was simply not a man, but a woman. By the late nineteenth century, women too were drawn into this normative world: a woman desiring a woman must be a man.[264]

As George Chauncey had made clear about the later development of this role in the United States, male homosexuals and prostitutes were culturally assimilated: indeed, the word 'gay', applying originally to prostitutes, was transposed to homo-sexuals.[265] The American cultural construction of the male homosexual as a female prostitute powerfully re-enforced the embattled normative theory of radically differ-ent spheres of gender in ways our earlier discussion of the purity movement has already explored (Chapter 5). As we saw there, to immunize women's traditional nor-mative sphere from the rights-based scepticism of abolitionist feminism, a reactionary moral and political epistemology of gender roles was defended and aggressively used against dissenting views, including those of advocates of free love. Women's norma-tive sphere was, from this perspective, religiously idealized as the source of a superior maternal morality, which was to stand as judge over lesser rights-based moralities. Such a sectarian religion of rigid gender orthodoxy made its idealization of intimately domestic maternal purity the measure of what could count as a woman and degraded dissenters to this conception as fallen non-women, thus the scapegoating of the pros-titute as outside the reasonable scope of what a woman, as such, could do or be. The male homosexual, traditionally even more culturally marginalized, was the dissident to male gender that the female prostitute was to her gender: the male homosexual's love for other men not only challenged the male gender norm of aggressive competi-tion with other men but its very object (love between men) unspeakably affirmed what the traditional model of heterosexual love anxiously did not want even to dis-cuss, let alone debate (real equality in love). Such embattled sectarian anxieties fas-tened on the most symbolically marginal form of dissenting gender role (male homosexuality), and mythologically erased homosexual love in light of its sectarian image of gender hierarchy as the essence of anything that could even count as roman-

---

[262] See Trumbach, 'Gender and the Homosexual Role in Modern Western Culture', n. 258 above, 155.
[263] See *ibid.*, 156.   [264] See *ibid.*, 156
[265] See George Chauncey, *Gay New York: Gender, Urban Culture, and the Making of the Gay Male World 1890–1940* (BasicBooks, New York, 1994), at 61, 67, 69–70, 81–5, 97, 185–6, 286. On 'gay' applying to prostitutes, see Timothy J. Gilfoyle, *City of Eros: New York City, Prostitution, and the Commercialization of Sex, 1790–1920* (W. W. Norton, New York, 1992), at 157.

tic love: the very idea of homosexual love was a conceptual absurdity, an unnatural act, which made such a man loving another man doubly disgraced and stigmatized, not a man, and, as a woman, a fallen woman. The measure of the even greater dehumanization of the homosexual over the prostitute was this double disgrace, so disgraceful, indeed, that its disgrace could not even be spoken.

An ideology of gender roles, very much embattled against the rights-based doubts of abolitionist feminism, enforced its sectarian orthodoxy by remaking reality in its own mythological image. The measure of its mythologizing character was its frenzied reinterpretation of the traditional unspeakability of the homosexual role (its role as never to have voice) in terms of the image of the most degraded of women, dehumanized as a sexual animal owed nothing by the community of civil discourse. In a constitutional community otherwise committed to human rights, it was easy enough not to extend such rights to women if an appropriate idealization could ostensibly invest them, in exchange, with a higher moral value. It was quite another matter not to extend such rights to men (and often white men at that). That could be rationalized only by ascribing to such men, already traditionally voiceless as heretics and traitors to moral and religious community, a more radical dehumanization that would, as it were, legitimate their exile from the realm of the publicly speakable and thus of the thinkable or the imaginable. The homosexual thus was the placeholder for the most threatening anxieties and doubts of the embattled hierarchy of gender at the intimate heart of self-consciously egalitarian America and Britain. Such creatures had at all costs to keep their degraded and silenced place in the hierarchical order of things if that order was to remain so unconscious of itself as in normative contradiction to American and British equal liberty.

It is against this repressive background, in which a strand of longstanding Christian moral thought plays a prominent role, that we may reasonably understand why both the right of free speech and the right against unjust discrimination must condemn the use of blasphemy laws as in the *Gay News* case. Such laws use the sensibilities of dominant religious identities as the measure of both the speakers and claims that may be politically tolerated. But strands of dominant religious traditions, like Christianity, have often been implicated in the construction and enforcement of structural injustice. In fact, in light of such massive cultural and legal repression of the very speakability of homosexuality, there is probably no area of contemporary structural injustice more uncritically entrenched than homophobia. It is for this reason that both the legitimacy and integrity of the politics of identity, central to the case for gay rights (Chapter 3), depends on a robust understanding of the scope of protection of free speech (sceptical of all forms of group libel laws, including blasphemy laws) that places on gays and lesbians the responsibility reasonably to protest in their own voice the terms of their moral slavery. Such responsibility includes for gay artists, like Kirkup, often speaking in a frankly sexual voice about the essentially sexual repression one has unjustly experienced at the hands of a dominant and still much loved religious tradition. Not to speak about this injustice in Kirkup's sensual vocabulary of Jesus's message of love, interpreted as love rooted in and expressive of his homoerotic sexual humanity, is not to speak both in the voice and about the issues that reason-ably demand public discussion and debate. Why, exactly, can Jesus's sexual human-ity (as a loving person) not reasonably include homosexuality?[266] This is not, as Lord Scarman mistakenly supposes, a matter of style that can be reasonably removed with-out impairing substance; it goes to the very heart of the matter to truncate dissent about denial of sexual voice and sexual life to the asexual terms of the culturally hege-monic religious tradition whose justice, in this arena, is now in reasonable dispute, among believers and the society at large.

It illuminates the normative issues of comparative public law and culture to con-trast the *Gay News* case in Britain with the similarly motivated attempts to repress in America the production of Terrence McNally's play, *Corpus Christi.*[267] It is surely of interest that almost any attempt by an artiste to deal with the sexuality of Jesus of Nazareth leads to attempts at censorship, including the largely unsuccessful attempts to censor Martin Scorsese's film 'The Last Temptation of Christ', based on the novel by Nikos Kazantzakis.[268] If Scorsese's artistic exploration of Jesus of Nazareth's imag-inative attraction to heterosexual marriage, in fact admired by some orthodox Christians,[269] was the object of sectarian censorship, gay artistes like Kirkup and McNally, who explore Jesus's homosexuality, are the objects of much stronger repres-sive forces. In America (unlike Britain), there was no serious issue, under current con-stitutional law, of political or legal censorship of the production of McNally's play at the Manhattan Theatre Club, but there was, at least initially, its functional equiva-lent; the production was initially cancelled in light of a campaign against the play led by the Catholic League for Religious and Civil Rights and subsequent anonymous threats to bomb the theatre if the production went forward. The ire of the Catholic League, like the Indian politicians in the Rushdie affair, had been aroused (without reading or seeing the condemned work) by an article in the *New York Post* with the headline 'Gay Jesus May Star on B'Way' and containing anonymous accounts of people at a reading of the play saying it featured a Jesus-like character 'who has sex with his apostles'.[270] The Manhattan Theatre Club, after significant public protest against its actions by playwrights (including the withdrawal by Athol Fugard of a new

---

[266] On the importance of Jesus's sexual humanity in the representation of his Christian message, see Leo Steinberg, *The Sexuality of Christ in Renaissance Art and in Modern Oblivion* (University of Chicago Press, Chicago, Ill., 1996).

[267] See Terrence McNally, *Corpus Christi* (Grove Press, New York, 1998).

[268] See Nikos Kazantzakis, *The Last Temptation of Christ* (trans. P. A. Bien, Simon & Schuster, New York, 1988). On censorship of the movie in Chile and Argentina, see Howard LaFranchi, 'In Conservative Chile, What You See Isn't What you Get', *The Christian Science Monitor*, 29 Nov. 1996, International Section, 7; US Department of State, Chile Country Report on Human Rights Practices for 1996, Department of State Human Rights Country Reports (Government Printing Office, Washington, DC, Feb. 1997), at 9–11; on the attempt to censor the movie by a Florida community, see Associated Press, 'Judge Overturns Ban on Film', *New York Times*, 11 Sept. 1988, sec. 1, 34; on related attempts in Oklahoma, see *Committee for the First Amendment* v. *John Campbell*, 962 F 2d 1516 (10th Cir. 1992) and *Cummins* v. *Campbell*, 44 F 3d 847 (10th Cir. 1994); on the banning of advertisements of the movie on the London subway system, see 'London Cool to "Temptation"', *New York Times*, 10 Sept. 1988, sec. 1–16.

[269] See Revd. Andrew Greeley, 'Blasphemy or Artistry?', *New York Times*, 14 Aug. 1988, sec. 2–1.

[270] See Ralph Blumenthal, 'Canceled Play May Be Staged,' *New York Times*, 28 May 1998, E–1.

play scheduled for production[271]) and many other New Yorkers, reversed its cancellation and the production, which sold out, went forward without incident (though with what count in New York as extraordinary security measures and rather decorous protests outside the theatre).[272] New York theatre became, in consequence, altogether more interesting to many New Yorkers, who certainly did not attend the play because it was well reviewed (which it was not[273]).

From the perspective of the *Gay News* case in Britain, what is of interest in these events is the character of the play and of the sectarian religious motives to repress it. *Corpus Christi* is the work of a gay artist who depicts Joshua (Jesus) as a homosexual lover of his disciples and his death as motivated by the priestly caste's homophobic hatred of such love. The interest of the play, from the perspective of the politics of identity, is its interpretation of Christian redemptive love as an expression of homosexual love and its corresponding interpretation of the homicidal hatred directed at Jesus as homophobia (the irrationalist scapegoating of a form of personally redemptive love).[274] The author's protest against the role of Christianity in the unjust construction of homophobia speaks in a sexual voice, a voice which responsibly addresses and indeed analyses the terms of the injustice, namely, as unleashing what is, on McNally's interpretation of Christianity, an unChristian hatred of love. McNally's indictment includes criticism, based on an interpretation of Jesus's defence from stoning of the woman taken in adultery,[275] of the intolerant scapegoating by gays of homosexual prostitutes.[276]

The nature of the repressive ire against the play's production is revealed in the terms that the columnist Patrick J. Buchanan used of the play: 'nothing less than a hate crime of modernity directed against Christians, the moral equivalent of Nazis marching through Skokie.'[277] What offends or shocks in this way is 'that Christ may have been gay and may had sex with some of his disciples'.[278] Buchanan refuses to entertain the interpretive possibility of such a view, indeed regards the very saying of it as group libel. It is surely of interest that Buchanan's ire in the United States, like that of Mrs Whitehouse in Britain, was aroused by an interpretive claim by a gay artist about the role of Jesus's homosexuality in his redemptive mission of love. What makes the interposition of blasphemy laws into such conscientious disagreements so unacceptable, from the perspective of respect for the human rights of both speech and against unjust discrimination, is that such laws inexorably enlist the state in determining which of the views is the group worthy of protection. The claims of Buchanan

---

[271] See *ibid.*

[272] See Peter Applebome, 'Ideas & Trends; Blasphemy? Again? Somebody's Praying for a Hit', *New York Times*, 18 Oct. 1998, sec. 4–4.

[273] See, e.g., Ben Brantley, 'Nice Young Man and Disciples Appeal for Tolerance', *New York Times*, 14 Oct. 1998, E–1; Vincent Canby, 'Battered and Broker, So That She May Rise', *New York Times*, 18 Oct. 1998, sec. 2–9.

[274] On this point, see McNally, n. 267 above, 65.   [275] See John 8: 1–11.

[276] See, on this point, McNally, n. 267 above, 53–6.   [277] See Applebome, n. 272 above.

[278] See Michael Scammell, 'Film; Why Not Let the Show Go On, Then Rebut It?', *New York Times*, 20 Sept. 1998, sec. 2–27.

or Mrs Whitehouse are as much group libellous of Kirkup or McNally as the claims of these gay artistes are to them. The state has no legitimate role to play in the censorship of such reasonable controversies about the scope and content of now reasonably controversial religious traditions.

The American approach quite properly demanded that both the Catholic League and McNally not only reasonably confront their profound disagreements in conviction but do so in a way that ultimately appeals to the reasonable democratic judgement of people in general. It is not always easy to confront such disagreements, to be compelled to take seriously and respond reasonably to people with whom one fundamentally disagrees in the domain of conviction. But disempowering the state in this domain, as American constitutional law requires on grounds of principle, empowers the American people reasonably to confront the questions of justice that most urgently require their understanding and remedy.

The great normative mistake of the state engaging in censorship in this domain is hardening and polarizing the sense of conventional group identity, often in ways that legitimate not the good democratic judgement of the people at large but the manipulative and bullying political power of traditional leaders over their groups, including those within the group who would otherwise reasonably dissent on terms of justice. We need to recall that the historical roots of the normative demands of the post-war national, regional, and international reasonable consensus on respect for basic human rights lay in the argument for toleration, later elaborated into the theory of structural injustice. The constitutional importance of the argument for toleration to politics was its diagnosis of the abuse of political power to entrench sectarian orthodoxies by the unjust limitation of basic human rights to the speakers and views supportive of the dominant orthodoxy. Indeed, such a corrupt politics fed on the unjust abridgment of human rights of the persons and views that would most reasonably contest its injustice often by scapegoating such groups in terms of dehumanizing stereotypes of religion or race or gender or gendered sexuality. The paradox of intolerance supported this pathology: precisely when such a sectarian tradition is most reasonably open to doubt about the basic justice of its terms, it paradoxically repressed the persons and views most likely reasonably to raise and explore the doubts most worthy of full and fair discussion. We have now examined a range of contemporary cases which powerfully illustrate the unjust role that blasphemy laws continue to play in enforcing the paradox of intolerance in the modern world. It is surely important to emphasize that it is the tool invariably resorted to precisely when sectarian religions are open to the most reasonable doubt about their injustice, including their role in enforcing structural injustice (whether anti-Semitism, or religious intolerance, or racism, or sexism, or homophobia).

Once a political culture allows, as a matter of principle, banning material offensive to religious groups, it legitimates the role of political leaders of such groups, whether the Indian Muslim politicians or Khomeini in the Rushdie affair or Mrs Whitehouse in the *Gay News* case or Patrick Buchanan in the matter of *Corpus Christi*, to bully and intimidate those who reasonably disagree. The alleged justification of such abridgment of free speech in terms of protecting the rights of others distorts and subverts the language and thought of human rights in ways inconsistent with normative political theory. The right of free speech is structurally linked to the right against unjust discrimination. The abridgment of human rights by blasphemy laws thus wreaks havoc on any reasonable discourse among democratic equals about the understanding and remedy of structural injustice. To the extent that constitutional law— both under national and regional law and under public international law—protects basic human rights of speech and against unjust discrimination, blasphemy laws must be regarded as self-defeating and incoherent.

Nothing in this argument for a robust principle of free speech in the domain of conscience limits the scope of reasonable remedies for sexism and homophobia analogous to those earlier discussed as remedies for racism (Chapter 4). Indeed, the guarantee of the principle of free speech is, I have suggested, justified by its role in advancing the legitimacy and integrity of the politics of identity in the understanding and remedy of structural injustice. On this basis, we may reasonably come to an understanding that both sexism and homophobia inflict secular harms on persons in the domain of action, and, as such, may reasonably be addressed by analogous remedies for discrimination on the basis of gender and sexual orientation, including, where appropriate, desegregation, educational reforms, anti-discrimination laws and policies, affirmative action, and prohibition of acts (including conspiracies) motivated by irrational prejudices rooted in structural injustice.

If the discourse of comparative public law plays a reasonable role, as I have suggested, in understanding the normative weight to be accorded free speech in constitutional democracies, such discourse will advance as well both the reasonable understanding of and remedies for structural injustice. American constitutional law may have much to learn from such discourse. While the American judiciary now accepts what I have here defended as the most normatively defensible principle of free speech, it came to this understanding only after the Second World War; indeed, in some areas (for example, the discussion of homosexuality), as we have seen, American censorship has been much more oppressive than in Britain or Europe. Against this cultural background, it should not be surprising that, especially in the area of gay rights but others as well, American constitutionalism has much to learn from discussions elsewhere. For example, the European Court of Human Rights has properly extended the human right of intimate life to protect consensual homosexual sexuality from sectarian religious condemnation[279] in a way that the United States Supreme Court has so far declined to do.[280] And the Canadian Supreme Court has recently correctly interpreted the right against unjust discrimination to include sexual orientation and extended such protection into an area (spousal benefits on dissolution of the intimate relationship[281]) not yet approached by the United States Supreme

---

[279] See *Dudgeon* v. *United Kingdom* (1982) 4 EHRR 149 (Ct.).

[280] See *Bowers* v. *Hardwick*, 478 US 186 (1986).

[281] See *M* v. *H.*, 1999 Can. Sup. Ct. Lexis 28 (20 May 1999) (holding unconstitutional Ontario law that allows married and unmarried opposite-sex couples, but not same-sex couples, to receive benefits on

Court.[282] Comparative public law is not and should not be a one-way street. If American constitutionalism has some things to teach, it has yet much to learn (more on this point in the concluding chapter that follows).

To summarize, the principle of free speech, as defended here in terms of the argument for toleration and theory of structural injustice, is not independent of structural injustice (the dependence thesis). Indeed, a demanding interpretation of its principle (sceptical of state enforced judgements of group harms in the domain of conscience) advances the understanding and remedy of such structural injustice by the conditions it imposes on the legitimacy and integrity of the politics of identity. We have now explored the implications of this analysis for the group related harms that are, I have suggested, the basis for both obscenity and blasphemy laws. Both laws (like the group libel laws earlier discussed, Chapter 4) should, on grounds of the relationship between the right of free speech and the right against unjust discrimination, no longer be normatively acceptable.

dissolution of the relationship). See, for an important introduction to the use of comparative public law in the study of these issues, Robert Wintemute, *Sexual Orientation and Human Rights: The United States Constitution, the European Convention, and The Canadian Charter* (Clarendon Press, Oxford, 1995).

[282] See, e.g., *Romer* v. *Evans*, 116 S Ct. 1620 (1996) (amendment to Colorado state constitution, repealing and prohibiting all ordinances that protected on grounds of sexual preference, held unconstitutional).

6

The Scope and Limits of Free Speech and the Promise of Comparative Public Law

I have now offered and elaborated an account of free speech one of whose features has been its defence of the distinctive American principle of free speech that includes laws against group libel, obscenity, and blasphemy within the scope of protection of free speech. My concern has been both to explain and defend an important interpretive development of American public law in terms of its role in a development with which it has recently been supposed to be in conflict, namely, the identification and remedy of structural injustice as a constitutional evil. I have argued that this assumption of conflict is false, that structural injustice depends on abridgment of free speech (the dependence thesis), and that the robust American protection of speech is one among the reasonable remedies for structural injustice for reasons now discussed and illustrated at length. A theory of this sort has a certain scope, but it also has limits. Its scope is, on my view, its protection of the domain of conviction from state censorship not on consequentialist grounds (whether utilitarian or perfectionism) nor to protect democracy, but to protect the exercise of the inalienable right to conscience on terms of the argument for toleration and the theory of structural injustice. Only this scope of protection of speech empowers the legitimacy and integrity of the politics of identity in the understanding and remedy of structural injustice. On this basis, I have argued that any group-based harm (whether group libel or obscenity law or blasphemy law) cannot, in principle, be a ground for the abridgment of speech absent a clear and present danger of harms. But this view of free speech, while normatively demanding within its scope of application, does not apply outside its domain of conviction. It does not, as I have insisted at several points, apply in the domain of action, and thus many laws aimed at the remedy of structural injustice are both necessary and proper within this domain.

I would now like, in this brief concluding chapter, further to develop the normative and interpretive implications of my account for the question of the limits of free speech and the promise of comparative public law. Such an analysis usefully reviews the character of the argument I have made, clarifying not only its terms but its normative and interpretive power. My account was thus developed as a matter of normative political theory (Chapter 2), and its implications for legal doctrine explored as an interpretation of certain striking post-Second World War interpretive developments in American constitutional law, both in the law protecting the right of free speech and the right against unjust discrimination (Chapters 3–5). It was against this normative and interpretive backdrop that I offered a normative criticism of other systems of national and regional law and public international law (in their views of the legitimacy of laws condemning group libel, obscenity, and blasphemy) on the ground that their acceptance of group-based harms, as a reason for abridging free speech, reflected an incoherent view that the abridgment of the right of free speech was necessary to advance the right against unjust discrimination (Chapters 4–5). But if my normative political theory makes possible fruitful investigation of comparative public law as a discourse about the relationship among basic human rights, sometimes its critical normative force may suggest American public law is in some area deeply defective and the views of other legal systems offer a better view of the underlying issues of the constitutional protection of basic human rights.

THE LIMITS OF THE PRINCIPLE OF FREE SPEECH

There are many areas of current free speech law where I believe an argument of this sort could reasonably be made, for example, the dominant weight American law, in contrast to the constitutional law of other nations, currently gives the right of free speech over the right to informational privacy or over the right to a fair trial.[1] But perhaps the most serious such defect is the weight currently accorded the right of free speech in the United States in the area of attempts to regulate campaign contributions and expenditures. I shall argue that the theory of free speech here proposed offers a better critical understanding of why the current judicial view of these matters is interpretively mistaken than competitor views, in particular, the argument from democracy.[2]

In *Buckley* v. *Valeo*,[3] the Supreme Court considered the constitutionality of the Federal Election Campaign Act of 1971 (as amended in 1974), which imposed, *inter alia*, limitations on both the amounts that could be contributed to presidential campaigns, and the amounts that could be spent on such campaigns by candidates and by independent groups on behalf of candidates. The crucial theme in the assessment of these two limitations was the Court's view of legitimate and illegitimate state purposes. Anti-corruption was a quite legitimate such purpose; equalizing political power was a constitutionally illegitimate purpose. The Court thus legitimated the campaign limitations since they did not inhibit central free speech interests but did advance the

---

[1]   e.g., with the controlling normative weight accorded the right of free speech over the right to privacy in *Cox Broadcasting Corp.* v. *Cohn*, 420 US 469 (1975) (name of rape victim in court records may be broadcast) and *Florida Star* v. *B.J.F.*, 491 US 524 (1989) (name of rape victim not in court records but police department press room may be published), cf. *Lebach Case* (1973) 35 BVerfGE 202 (television broadcast of documentary of convicted criminal, including reference to his homosexual tendencies, may be enjoined to protect right to private life), translated in Donald P. Kommers, *The Constitutional Jurisprudence of the Federal Republic of Germany* (2nd edn., Duke University Press, Durham, NC, 1997), at 416–19. On the very different views on the proper balance between the right of free speech and the right to a fair trial in the United States and Britain, see Eric Barendt, *Freedom of Speech* (Clarendon Press, Oxford, 1985), at 223–9.

[2]   Much of my critical argument of *Buckley* here was first stated in David A. J. Richards, *Toleration and the Constitution* (Oxford University Press, New York, 1986), 215–19. I develop here more extensively the implications of the argument for the criticism of the argument from democracy.

[3]   *Buckley* v. *Valeo*, 414 US 1 (1976).

constitutionally legitimate purpose of discouraging corruption. The Court, however, struck down the expenditure limitations because they inhibited free speech interests and they did not reasonably pursue the anti-corruption purpose (expenditure by 'independent' groups, for example, were not co-ordinated with the candidate's campaign in a way that would encourage improper commitments by the candidate to them). The expenditure limits did reasonably pursue an equalizing purpose, but that purpose was constitutionally illegitimate.[4]

The pivotal premise of this case is that the aim of equalizing the power and impact of money on the democratic political process is, in constitutional principle, illegitimate. A restriction on expenditures, translated into a restriction on the communications that those expenditures support, is, on this view, a diminution of speech. This, so the argument goes, violates free speech values, for how can a lowering of speech activity by the state be consistent with the rich and robust communicative activity protected by the First Amendment from state inhibition and restriction? The judicial statement of the view is rhetorically dismissive of equalizing aims for such reasons:

the concept that government may restrict the speech of some elements of our society in order to enhance the relative voice of others is wholly foreign to the First Amendment, which was designed 'to secure "the widest possible dissemination of information from diverse and antagonistic sources" '.[5]

There is a sleight of hand in this inference from expenditure limits to less speech to a violation of free speech, namely, a blankly aggregative conception of free speech no matter what the law and its purposes that has the incidental effect of reducing such aggregates. More is better, no matter what the distributive effects and consequences, and any incidental restraint on speech must therefore be condemned. But the Court's view is subject to three interconnected objections: first, the internal coherence of its own rationale; secondly, its disregard of pertinent authority to the contrary; and thirdly, its questionable political theory.

How, exactly, does a restriction on expenditures diminish diverse sources of speech? The idea perhaps makes some sense as applied to marginal political parties

---

[4] A case to similar effect is *First National Bank of Boston* v. *Bellotti*, 435 US 765 (1978). In this case, the Supreme Court considered and invalidated, by a narrow 5 to 4 majority, a Massachusetts criminal law prohibiting certain expenditures by banks and business corporations for the purpose of influencing the vote on referendum proposals, in this case a proposed state constitutional amendment to authorize a graduated individual income tax. Consistent with *Buckley*, any equalizing purpose of the statute was disallowed by the Court, since it inhibited speech in the way that the First Amendment putatively forbids. The constitutionally legitimate anti-corruption purpose was not, in the Court's view, reasonably pursued by this legislation, in contrast to such a statute restricting corporate giving to candidate elections. The constitutionality of limits on corporate contributions and expenditures to campaigns was later upheld. See *FEC* v. *National Right to Work Committee*, 459 US 197 (1982). Federal requirement that independent campaign expenditures be made out of segregated funds was held unconstitutional as applied to corporations more like voluntary political associations. See *FEC* v. *Massachusetts Citizens for Life*, 479 US 238 (1986). Later such a state requirement was held constitutional as applied to the Michigan Chamber of Commerce. See *Austin* v. *Michigan Chamber of Commerce*, 494 US 652 (1990).

[5] *Buckley*, 424 US at 48–9, citing, with approval, *New York Times Co.* v. *Sullivan*, 376 US 254 (1971), at 266.

that might require substantial support from a few donors before being able to muster sufficient general support from other donors so as not to be beholden to a few wealthy supporters. But this reasonable constitutional concern would be met by appropriate exemptions from the campaign financing law for such parties, who would thus be allowed and encouraged to establish their alternative perspectives and points of view. The restriction on expenditures does not diminish diversity in other electoral contexts. In fact, it requires that political support must be garnered from a broader and more diverse spectrum of the electorate, not from the much smaller groups of the wealthy and/or ideologically cohesive people who exercise a quite disproportionate power over electoral politics.

A second objection questions whether the fair regulation of electoral politics is, as the Court supposes, 'wholly foreign to the First Amendment'. Many constitutionally acceptable constraints on free speech activity restrict the speech of some in order thus to secure a fairer forum for free speech (for example, neutral time, place, and manner regulations, or the fairness doctrine applicable to certain media[6]). Related constitutional doctrines, like 'one person, one vote' as the standard to remedy malapportionment in the distribution of voting power, decisively rebuts the claim that the aspiration to equality is foreign to the First Amendment;[7] and the unconstitutionality of economic burdens on the right to vote bespeaks the legitimate weight of equality in the reasonable interpretation of the right to vote.[8] The confluence of such established constitutional principles suggests that the Court's simplistic aggregative conception fails to do justice to the fabric of relevant constitutional principles. Such doctrines suggest, if anything, that constitutional values of equality (integral to the rights of free speech and the vote) render unregulated electoral politics itself a distortion of background constitutional ideals.

The third objection concerns the Court's rejection of equalizing political power, which assumes that the First Amendment expresses a political theory hostile to such equalizing aims. In fact, however, the central values, guiding both religion clause and free speech jurisprudence (Chapter 2), are the primacy of equal respect for our highest-order moral powers of rationality and reasonableness. This moral sovereignty of the person over herself and her state is the background theory that rights of religious freedom and free speech, and much else, both preserve and express.[9] Consistent with equal respect of this background theory, such rights are thought of as equal rights, as aspects of the greatest equal liberty of each, with a like liberty of all. The right to vote, reasonably interpreted against this background, is the right to participate, as an equal, in the political life of the community in two relevant dimensions. First, each person

---

[6] See, e.g., *Red Lion Broadcasting Co.* v. *FCC*, 395 US 367 (1969).
[7] See *Baker* v. *Carr*, 369 US 186 (1962) (malapportionment of state legislature justiciable under the equal protection clause); *Reynolds* v. *Sims*, 377 US 533 (1964) (state legislature apportionment must weight voters equally, with roughly the same numbers of voters per representative).
[8] See *Harper* v. *Virginia Board of Elections*, 383 US 663 (1966) (poll tax is unconstitutional economic burden on vote); *Kramer* v. *Union Free School District No. 15*, 395 US 621 (1969) (right to vote in school district elections cannot be predicated, inter alia, on ownership of real property).
[9] For more extended defence of this claim, see Richards, n. 2 above.

has as equal right to be the judge of political contests. And secondly, each person has an equal right to participate in the process, including the political campaigns, leading up to exercise of the right to vote.

This second dimension of political equality is imperilled by allowing economic and associated inequalities, perhaps justified on independent grounds of greater merit and contribution, untrammelled expression in political campaigns. Economic and other inequalities, accorded for reasons relevant to the economic sphere alone, become, seductively, the measures of the respect accorded persons in violation of their status as equal citizens and participants in the political life of the nation; one's income becomes the measure of one's weight as a citizen. From the perspective of democratic constitutionalism, the idea that greater income or wealth as such is a criterion of one's political status as a citizen should be a disgusting deviation from the proper order of democratic equality. If permitted, if left regulated, this distortion of formal values of constitutional and political equality by economic inequality corrupts the internal ideals of equal respect that make democratic constitutionalism a defensible and legitimate form of government.[10]

For these reasons, attempts by the state to regulate electoral expenditures in the interest of equalizing political power should not, as the Supreme Court currently supposes, be regarded as antagonistic to the values of the First Amendment. On the contrary, the attempt to separate political from economic power, preserving the constitutionally compelled equality of the former from the inequalities of the latter, is required by the priority accorded equal respect for basic liberties of the person (including the right to vote) in a constitutional democracy. The diminution in speech activity from expenditure limits (if there is one) is not a content-biased restriction on speech (expressing preferring one topic of conversation or point of view over another) condemned by free speech jurisprudence.[11] It is directed not at the content of communications on grounds that are suspect, but at the reasonable regulation of the impact of economic resources on political power. Appropriate regulation of the impact of such resources is a wholly reasonable, indeed required, attempt to achieve in modern circumstances the underlying constitutional ideal of equal respect. This ideal is not met by levels of campaign contributions and expenditures and resulting political campaigns whose reality, instead of the free and equal exercise of the participatory political powers of a diverse people, displays the impact and interests of the economic power of the few in an unreasonably disproportionate political power and influence on politicians increasingly distracted by fundraising.[12] Such political power

[10] See, on this point, John Rawls, *A Theory of Justice* (Harvard University Press, Cambridge, Mass., 1971), at 221–8; 'The Basic Liberties and Their Priority', in S. McMurrin (ed), *The Tanner Lectures on Human Values* (Cambridge University Press, Cambridge, 1981), iii, 3–87, at 72–9.

[11] Cf. J. Skelly Wright, 'Politics and the Constitution: Is Money Speech?', 85 *Yale LJ* 1001 (1976) and 'Money and the Pollution of Politics: Is the First Amendment an Obstacle to Political Equality?', 82 *Colum. L Rev.* 609 (1982).

[12] See, on this point, Vincent Blasi, 'Free Speech and the Widening Gyre of Fund-Raising: Why Campaign Spending Limits May Not Violate the First Amendment After All,' 94 *Colum. L Rev.* 1281 (1994).

is not only unequal, it is unequal in a way and in an area that morally degrades the political sovereignty of one's equals under constitutional law. Limits on such expenditures advance the equal liberty that constitutional values require; they should be applied throughout American politics.[13] Both free speech and our common political life would be deliberatively responsive on fairer terms to the people, who as moral equals stand equal before the law and maintain their sovereignty over our common political life.

There is no tension between free speech and such equalizing aims in the political domain, as some of the most reflective legal thinkers on free speech today mistakenly suppose or once supposed.[14] Both aims are rooted in the same conception of equal respect, motivated by the same concerns about the equality central to the priority of free speech in American constitutional law. Indeed, from such a perspective (rooted in the argument for toleration), we may see *Buckley*, rather than the recent commercial speech cases,[15] as the free speech case that most clearly smacks of the discredited substantive economic due process of *Lochner* v. *New York*.[16] The blunder of *Lochner* was its holding the New York state's aim to equalize bargaining power between employers and employees in the baking industry was, in principle, constitutionally illegitimate. Today we properly recognize that such aims are consistent with a sound theory of distributive justice and with the theory of the Constitution. The essence of the blunder in *Buckley* is the blunder of *Lochner*: the holding that equalizing power is illegitimate. In fact, the mistake in *Buckley* is arguably more constitutionally egregious, for such equalizing of political power in electoral contexts is rooted in the egalitarian principles of the First Amendment itself. The spectre of *Lochner* still haunts American law; we will exorcize it only when we have in place better and more critical conceptions of our deepest ideals and thus are able to recognize the authentic corruptions of those ideals. In this area, political theory is not only a useful device of explanation and explication; it is a compelling moral need.

Both the coherence of American law and its background political theory require that political equality be acknowledged as a constitutionally legitimate aim in the context of the regulation of contributions and expenditures in political campaigns. Clarity on this important point of law and political theory renders the *Buckley*

---

[13] Cf. Paul G. Chevigny, 'The Paradox of Campaign Finance', 56 *NYU L Rev.* 206 (1981).

[14] See, e.g., Kathleen M. Sullivan, 'Political Money and Freedom of Speech', 30 *UC Davis L Rev.* 663 (1997); C. Edwin Baker, 'Scope of the First Amendment Freedom of Speech', 25 *UCLA L Rev.* 964 (1978); Martin H. Redish, 'The Value of Free Speech', 130 *U Pa. L Rev.* 591 (1982). Baker and Redish disagreed over the correctness of *First National Bank of Boston*, with Baker attacking and Redish defending it. But both accepted the legitimacy of *Buckley*. For an exchange between them, see Baker, 'Realizing Self-Realization: Corporate Political Expenditures and Redish's 'The Value of Free Speech', 130 *U Pa. L Rev.* 646 (1982); Redish, 'Self-Realization, Democracy, and Freedom of Expression: A Reply to Professor Baker', 130 *U Pa. L Rev.* 678 (1982). Both their theories, which are, I believe, implicitly rooted in the argument for toleration, failed properly to interpret how equal respect must shape questions of the legitimacy of state equalizing of free speech power. Prof. Baker has, more recently, changed his views on this matter. See C. Edwin Baker, 'Campaign Expenditures and Free Speech', 33 *Harvard Civil Rights–Civil Liberties Law Review* 1 (1998); I am grateful to Prof. Baker for bringing his change of views to my attention.

[15] For a defence of these cases, see Richards, n. 2 above, 209–15.

[16] *Buckley* v. *Valeo*, 424 US 1 (1976); *Lochner* v. *New York*, 198 US 45 (1905).

Court's emphasis on corruption, as (in contrast to equality) a constitutionally legitimate aim, much less defensible. The conventional form of clearly unacceptable political corruption, bribery, occurs when politicians exercise political power to enrich
themselves. But when the *quid pro quo* is remaining in political office longer (re-elec-
tion), democratic responsiveness to a political contribution is not necessarily a bad
thing, at least against the background of existing regulations of political campaigns
that have secured the constitutionally legitimate purpose of political equality. If political equality were thus secured, the weight placed on corruption by the *Buckley* Court
would appear much less democratically reasonable. Of course, there may be other
grounds for concern about the weight such contributions have on representative
democracy, including both heightening the power of interest groups on politics and
the role such contributions play in legitimating coercive demands by politicians for
contributions from citizens.[17] But both these reasons are not properly understood in
terms of the anti-corruption purposes improperly given weight by the *Buckley* Court.
Americans clearly need to reconsider this whole question fundamentally.

It is in an area of this sort that comparative public law, as I understand and practise it in this work, becomes a two-way street from which Americans have much to
learn (as well as to teach). In particular, Americans should study much more closely
than they do the alternative systems of campaign financing that now exist in so many
other constitutionally democratic countries.[18] Many nations, including Canada,
Germany, Israel, Italy, and Sweden, directly fund such campaigns.[19] Others, like
Great Britain, have a strict ceiling on the election spending of candidates.[20] Almost
all such nations, except the United States (and Mexico and Taiwan), give free time
for political broadcasting, and many forbid paid political broadcasts.[21] Americans
need to study and consider them all as alternative ways appropriately to regulate political campaigns in the interest of political equality. Even if political equality were constitutionally accepted in the United States as a legitimate state purpose in this domain
(as it should be), some of these alternatives might not be constitutional or otherwise
politically acceptable. But, as part of our fundamental rethinking of these issues,
Americans should study them all.

Such rethinking in the United States would be advanced by taking seriously the
argument of normative political theory of this book as the theory that best fits and
explains America's extraordinary constitutional scepticism of group-based harms as
grounds for the abridgment of speech in the domain of conviction. In particular, this
normative and interpretive argument defends the distinctive form of the American
principle of free speech as quite independent of the argument from democracy. If I
am right on this point, America's deepest contemporary commitments, as a matter of

---

[17] See, for consideration of all these points in depth, David A. Strauss, 'Corruption, Equality, and
Campaign Finance Reform', 94 *Colum. L Rev.* 1370 (1994).
[18] See, for an illuminating overview, Ruth Levush, Coordinator, *Campaign Financing of National
Elections in Foreign Countries* (Law Library of Congress, Washington, DC, April 1991).
[19] See *ibid.*, at 9–13, 39–62, 95–115, 147–51.   [20] See *ibid.*, at 63–74.
[21] See *ibid.*, at 14–15.

free speech principle, cannot be explained by the argument from democracy. Indeed, the uncritical dominance of this model, in thinking about the grounds for free speech, is very much at the root of the myopia that led to *Buckley.*

I have already discussed at some length how and why the argument from democracy cannot account for what I take to be perhaps the central role of free speech in our rights-based constitutionalism, namely, its empowerment on terms of principle of the legitimacy and integrity of the role the politics of identity has played and plays in the understanding and remedy of the constitutional evil of structural injustice in all its interlinked forms. The empowerment of such criticism is, in its nature (as a criticism of the deep cultural entrenchment of our most unspoken and even unspeakable evils), often conducted outside the dominant political consensus, indeed rejected as politically illegitimate subversive discourse. It extends to criticism of dehumanizing cultural stereotypes whose force depends on an uncritical privatization, warping the terms of both public and private life in all its broadly understood cultural domains. The politics of identity, understood in this way (as I have urged), is ethically transformative, aimed at issues of conscience and conviction. Many of its leading advocates in antebellum America were, as we have seen, accordingly hostile to ordinary Jacksonian majoritarian politics, precisely because in its nature it suppressed, indeed silenced the rights-based protest of the pervasive cultural terms of American moral slavery (including American racism and sexism). The contemporary American principle of free speech, understood in terms of the argument for toleration and the theory of structural injustice, explains and justifies, in a way that the argument from democracy cannot, the wholly legitimate role of free speech in making possible the legitimacy and integrity of such discourse.

The argument from democracy not only marginalizes such discourse, but its uncritical focus on political democracy ideologically undergirds a decision like *Buckley* v. *Valeo,* rendering invisible the harm such a decision inflicts on the integrity of American public law. *Buckley* thus affirmatively cites as its main authority a decision, *New York Times* v. *Sullivan,*[22] usually taken to establish the primacy of the argument from democracy as a theory of American public law.[23] That decision, which crucially supports the legitimate role of the anti-racist criticism at the heart of the Civil Rights Movement, does nothing of the sort, appealing, rather, to the alternative theory of free speech here defended. But the uncritical interpretation of this decision as an endorsement of the argument from democracy has its own dynamic, making possible the supposition of the Court in *Buckley* that restraints on political expenditures (interpreted as limits on political speech) must be subjected to the same demanding standards of constitutional scrutiny as the attempt, in *New York Times* v. *Sullivan,* to censor criticism of the structural injustice of American racism on illegitimate grounds.[24] But the

---

[22] See n. 5 above, and accompanying text.
[23] See, e.g., Cass R. Sunstein, *Democracy and the Problem of Free Speech* (Free Press, New York, 1993), at 133.
[24] For fuller discussion of the proper scope of libel laws consistent with free speech, see Richards, n. 2 above, 195–203.

attempt to censor from discourse rights-based protest of the terms of one's moral slavery has nothing in common with the quite different issues of *Buckley*, which address a wholly different set of concerns that do not implicate the proper understanding of the American principle of free speech, rooted in the argument for toleration and the theory of structural injustice. Indeed, if anything, a decision like *Buckley*, precisely because it allows fuller political expression to dominant interests, is in tension with the values free speech protects, namely, the empowerment of rights-based protest of the terms of moral slavery often ideologically invisible to the complacencies of majoritarian political common sense.

The theories of toleration and structural injustice offer compelling normative arguments of political theory for why it is the speech often dismissed as outside the governing democratic consensus (whether because it is subversive of the government or democratic values) which is most worthy of constitutional protection. Such consensus is often constructed on structural injustice, that is, on suppressing the persons and voices that most reasonably subject the dominant consensus to the criticism it requires. It is only when the principle of free speech is understood and defended on this sound basis that it empowers the legitimacy and integrity of the politics of identity in the reasonable understanding and remedy of the structural injustice of group and national identity whose political power has rested on the invisibility and unspeakability of such injustice.

These concerns are not implicated by the reasonable regulation of the financing of political campaigns in the interest of political equality. The principle of free speech has its scope, but also its limits. These limits include the reasonable regulation of economic resources, including their use in the exercise of achieving or advancing political power. The argument from democracy, as an argument for free speech, has deformed public understanding of these issues by confusing the moral freedom required in the domain of conviction (to achieve the ends of the theories of toleration and structural injustice) with partisan politics.

Any design of sensible policies in this area will, of course, face issues of line-drawing between aspects of politics thus subject to reasonable regulation and the domain of conviction that must always be constitutionally protected.[25] The observation that such lines may be difficult to draw should not, however, stop us from undertaking line-drawing if we are convinced, as we should be, that the risks to the principle of free speech and the threats to political equality have been, respectively, grotesquely overstated and understated in recent constitutional and political discourse in the United States.

Buckley is anomalous if seen, as it should be, in terms of the larger fabric of principles of American public law, whose principles (as we have seen) it conspicuously ignores and flouts. American judicial practice, which protects these principles (including much of the scope of protection of speech required by the theory here

---

[25] See, for an argument against campaign financing laws centring on this point, Sullivan, n. 14 above; see, for an attempt to draw lines sensitive to its reasonable force, C. Edwin Baker, 'Campaign Expenditures and Free Speech', 33 *Harvard Civil Rights–Civil Liberties Law Review* 1 (1998).

proposed), is conspicuously better than its theory (the argument from democracy). That theory cannot, as I have argued, explain, let alone justify much of current judicial understanding of the principle of free speech; and when it can justify it (*Buckley*), it is demonstrably wrong.

It bespeaks the depth of the problem that some critics of *Buckley*, as we have seen (Chapters 1–2), frame their criticism in terms of the argument from democracy. But their arguments make no sense as an interpretation of the argument from democracy, which, most plausibly interpreted, justifies *Buckley*. The argument from democracy interprets democracy as a procedure open and sensitive to the changing preferences of the electorate, whatever they are. Free speech expresses scepticism about the interposition of state judgements that distort the openness of this procedure to such preferences in ways that self-entrench the power of politicians. Within this framework, limitations on campaign expenditures self-entrench such power by thwarting preferences that might otherwise challenge or better challenge such power. It is all quite straightforward. The critics of *Buckley*, often hostile to current constitutional scepticism of group libel laws as well, rationalize this assortment of oddly mismatched views in terms of substantive principles of equality, in terms of which the argument for democracy must be understood. But building substantive normative principles into the very concept of democracy begs the hard constitutional questions, which turn, as I have argued, on the tension between substantive constitutional principles guaranteeing universal human rights to all persons and majoritarian democracy. It does not advance either understanding or evaluation of this tension to suppress it, particularly when it endorses positions (no free speech protection of group libel) that do not take seriously either substantive principles of human rights or the role of free speech in protecting them (Chapters 4–5).

We can do better, and the understanding of free speech, drawing on the argument for toleration and the theory of structural injustice, shows how. Free speech, on this view, is more closely linked normatively to effective guarantees of the inalienable human rights of all persons (as conditions for the legitimacy of any political power, including democratic political power) than it is to majoritarian political democracy itself. If free speech is understood and protected as this argument requires, it will render political democracy more, not less, legitimate, but not because it is more or less democratic but rather more democratically respectful of its foundational conditions of political legitimacy, respect for universal human rights on egalitarian terms of principle.

The principle of free speech, as I have explained and endorsed it in the argument of this book, is within its terms sceptical of state power (namely, censorious state judgements about the worth and value of conviction), but it is not sceptical of all forms of state power. As we have seen, regulations of both campaign contributions and expenditures do not violate its principle. Even reasonable regulations of intrinsically communicative media like radio and broadcasting (for example, requiring rights of access) would not, in my judgement, compromise the principle of free speech to the extent that they ensured broader access to dissenting speakers and points of view otherwise inaccessible to the public mind of the nation; but, the line should be drawn at state-imposed censorship (in the domain of conviction) of these and other media.[26]

My argument has linked understanding of the principle of free speech to what I have called the politics of identity. Drawing on both history and political theory, I have urged that we think of the principle of free speech as an interpretive legacy worth defending because of the role it plays and continues to play in the understanding and remedy of the structural injustices that most challenge the legitimacy of democratic constitutionalism. If one asks in conclusion yet again the question with which I began, why accord priority to speech among constitutionally protected interests?, we can now answer, on the cumulative basis of the argument of this book, because only protection of speech in the domain of conviction ensures respect for basic human rights in all their dimensions, including those rights most at threat from the structural injustices that have rendered them unspoken and even unspeakable. Free speech is the central human right it is in American constitutionalism because it is the foundation of liberal political culture understanding, as such culture does and must, the importance to progressive moral and political growth and change of maintaining the legitimacy and integrity of the politics of identity.

On the basis of an argument of normative political theory, I have generalized my argument to criticize the quite different interpretive views on this matter under other national and regional systems of law and public international law. In particular, I have criticized the appeal to group-based harms in these systems as an adequate ground for the abridgment of speech in the domain of conviction in various areas (group libel, obscenity, blasphemy). A normative argument of political theory can, I believe, have reasonable force for this purpose because the interpretive view under criticism bases itself on a normative view of the proper relationship between the human right of free speech and the right against unjust discrimination. The political theories of toleration and structural injustice, suitably interpreted, show that these human rights are structurally linked such that the abridgment of one abridges the other. The interpretive view of the relationship between these rights in these systems of law is, for this reason, normatively unjustified and interpretively incoherent. It is normatively unjustified because it rests on a trade-off between putatively separate rights that are not, in

---

[26] For fuller discussion of these and related points, see Richards, n. 2 above, 219–26. For recent judicial opinions outside the United States that acknowledge the force of this principle in the area of group libel, see *Jersild* v. *Denmark* (1995) 19 EHRR 1 (Ct.); *Meir Kahane* v. *the Broadcasting Authority*, 41(3) PD 225 (1987). Such concerns, for the role state censorship—ostensibly concerned with ensuring access of protesting voice—might play in impeding the free expression of such voice in its own terms, may underlie the Supreme Court's unanimous opinion in *Hurley* v. *Irish-American Gay, Lesbian and Bisexual Group of Boston (GLIB)*, 115 S Ct. 2338 (1995) (holding that a privately organized St Patrick's Day parade need not constitutionally include, against the organizers' will, a self-proclaimed gay contingent among its marchers).

fact, separate. It is incoherent because it claims reasonably to advance the right against unjust discrimination by sacrifice of the right in free speech when, in fact, it frustrates the protection of both rights.

The moral nerve of the problem with such laws (group libel, obscenity, blasphemy) is their invocation of group-based harms as the ground for abridgment of speech in what I have called the domain of conviction. The appeal of this view draws entirely on its ostensible concern with the constitutional evil I have called structural injustice, namely, a cultural pattern and practice that abridge the human rights of an entire class of persons on inadequate grounds of dehumanizing stereotypes of religion or race or gender or gendered sexuality. It is because we increasingly have come to understand that such grounds are used in service of such structural injustice that we condemn the role such stereotypes play in the distribution of the rights and benefits of political, economic, and social life. If we properly do so, why not also condemn, so the argument goes, the speech which uses and endorses such stereotypes? But the argument makes two normative mistakes. First, it draws and enforces (by state censorship) a line between good and bad speech and speakers in the domain of conviction that abridges the inalienable right to conscience, and thus abandons the normative standpoint of equal respect that alone renders the politics of identity legitimate. It is only against the background of a settled constitutional commitment to equal respect for conscience that the politics of identity can take up its stand, on the basis of the right to conscience, reasonably to confront the otherwise invisible patterns of structural injustice. Secondly, such state censorship compromises the integrity of the politics of identity, whose moral force depends on empowering persons, subject to a history of unjust subordination, to hear their own moral voice and to speak in that voice as morally independent persons, breaking the silence that had reduced them to the terms of a stereotype of race or gender empty of consciousness or moral agency. The imposition of state-endorsed stereotypes, as the measure of censorship in the domain of conviction, replicates and does not contest the underlying stereotypes that rationalize structural injustice. If the ostensible concern of such laws is thus to ameliorate the underlying structural injustice, they compound the problem by compromising the integrity of the politics of identity that is the decision procedure for both the understanding and remedy of structural injustice.

Structural injustice draws its pervasive cultural and political power from the ways in which such injustice has been rationalized in terms of alleged natural facts (for example, facts of race or gender), thus rendering invisible the cultural construction of unjust difference. Its invisibility has been constructed by the massive suppression of the voices and views of the persons afflicted by such injustice, thus making culturally possible the credibility of cultural stereotypes that dehumanize them. The denaturalization of such profound injustice *requires* the voice of a W. E. B. Du Bois (against American racism) or a Franz Boas (against European anti-Semitism and American racism) or a Betty Friedan (against American sexism) or a Walt Whitman (against homophobia). Such voices are the morally empowered and empowering voices that they have been, in the long struggle against structural injustice, because they fundamentally challenged the very dehumanized terms of the stereotypes that have afflicted them. The stereotypes, sustained by a silence and invisibility mistaken for facts of nature, was revealed as the unjust cultural construction that it is when a Du Bois or Boas or Friedan or Whitman (and the many other such voices before and after them) broke the silence in a voice empowered by the sense of oneself as a moral person, claiming one's basic human rights as a creative moral agent.

Our close study of the role moral voice has played in the struggle against structural injustice strengthens the case for an understanding of the scope of the principle of free speech that I have defended here (Chapters 3–5). This principle makes it the responsibility of each and every person to make one's own judgements in the domain of conviction morally independently of any censorship by the state based on its judgements of group-based harms, absent a clear and present danger of secular harms. This constitutional principle of personal responsibility limits the power of the state in the domain of conviction (though not of action), but, by virtue of its self-denying character, empowers moral voice in the way we have now studied in Du Bois, Boas, Friedan, Whitman, and so many others. Persons, thus empowered, find and hear their own moral voice, as persons, both in terms of the *grounds* and the *objects* of the exercise of free speech. The *grounds* of their so speaking are, of course, their basic human rights of conscience and speech, which empower every person to be a source and originator of claims thus grounded in basic human rights. Persons afflicted by a culture and history of structural injustice find and hear their own moral voice on the *grounds* of such rights and thus their very speaking in such terms contests and subverts the dehumanizing stereotypes of voicelessness and unspeakability that made possible the naturalization of injustice. The *objects*, in turn, of such speech must be the expression and exploration of their moral consciousness as persons against the hegemonic terms of their moral slavery that sought to render them as empty of such consciousness as rationalizing stereotypes of race or gender required them to be. Such protest naturally takes as one of its objects the affirmation of double consciousness, as we have seen in both Du Bois and Friedan (and earlier Sarah Grimke[27]), exploring both the consciousness shaped by such hegemonic stereotypes and the consciousness that develops and expands in protest of their injustice.

It is against this background that we may understand the role that empowering such voice, consistent with the principle of free speech as I have defended it, plays in the integrity of such voice in the protest of structural injustice. Individuals, empowered by the principle of free speech, protest the terms of structural injustice in a domain that the state cannot. The cultural and political power of structural injustice rests on the naturalization of its injustice in terms of natural facts that mask its cultural construction of unjust terms of difference. When Du Bois or Boas or Friedan or Whitman speaks in his or her rights-based voice against the structural injustice inflicted on him or her, both the *grounds* and *objects* of his or her protest resonate with

---

[27] On this point, see David A. J. Richards, *Women, Gays, and the Constitution: The Grounds for Feminism and Gay Rights in Culture and Law* (University of Chicago Press, Chicago, Ill., 1998), 100.

the moral voice of persons, hearing themselves as persons, and challenging in such terms the ways in which the cultural construction of structural injustice had masked itself by the appeal to natural facts. Such voice has thus importantly been culturally creative, forging a new conception of history and social theory (Du Bois), of cultural anthropology (Boas), of interpretive social theory (Friedan), and of poetry and prose (Whitman). Such cultural creativity enables the empowered voice of the speaker not only better to hear and understand its own moral voice, as such, but increasingly reasonably to be heard by others in the culture in that voice, thus challenging the hegemonic terms of longstanding patterns and practices of structural injustice. Such new forms of interpretive history and social and psychological theory afford more truthful narratives about the unjust cultural construction of structural injustice, including exploring the ways in which such injustice has been experienced and often creatively resisted by subjugated groups; the cultural diagnosis of racism or sexism thus made possible challenges the naturalization of injustice precisely by affording a space for the moral voices whose silencing had made such naturalization credible (for example, the important role played by Boasian interpretive social science in the American struggle against racism, Chapter 3). Correspondingly, linguistic experiments in various cultural forms (including novels, music, poetry, prose, and the like) forge an acoustic and acoustic space within which persons afflicted by structural injustice speak and hear their moral voice, breaking the silence of their dehumanization by the very terms of a new art (for example, Whitman's operatically sexual and musical voice of homosexual love, resonating in the later poetry of Kirkup and the plays of McNally and others) that challenge the unjust stereotypes of unspeakable and tone-deaf sexuality imposed on them.

The principle of free speech, as I have defended it here, crucially empowers such moral voice, precisely because, by its self-denying character, it correlatively denies such a power in the state. The principle of free speech, by making such protest each person's responsibility morally independent of the state, gives personal voice a moral authority it could not otherwise have. It is because such voice is personal (not based on the state's judgements of group-based harms) that it has the moral authority and integrity that it has in addressing the terms of structural injustice. The paternalism implicit in state censorship in the domain of conviction, even when ostensibly grounded in concerns for the respect due groups subject to unjust stigma, disempowers the voice and views that both demand and command respect on the only terms that may reasonably secure it as an aim of our public and private life. Such censorship, for this reason, defeats its aims.[28]

---

[28] Such concerns, for the role state censorship—ostensibly concerned with ensuring access of protesting voice—might play in impeding the free expression of such voice in its own terms, may underlie the Supreme Court's unanimous opinion in *Hurley* v. *Irish-American Gay, Lesbian and Bisexual Group of Boston (GLIB)*, 115 S Ct. 2338 (1995) (holding that a privately organized St Patrick's Day parade need not constitutionally include, against the organizers' will, a self-proclaimed gay contingent among its marchers).

To see this, I propose to generalize a point earlier made in my discussion of the importance of a protesting voice in the relatively recent human rights struggle against homophobia, where these issues are especially vivid (Chapter 3). There I argued that the most illuminating understanding of the distinctive character of choice of homosexual identity is to be drawn from the religious analogy, the right to choose gay and lesbian identity as a matter of conscience.

We understand such issues of conscience in terms of an inalienable right of liberty and the argument for toleration not because we choose our convictions any more than our beliefs in general, but because responsibility for our deepest convictions about value in living expresses the appropriate attitude of respect for the free moral powers of persons. Such responsibility empowers persons to live a life from reasonable conviction, exploring as much as organizing their experience of what gives enduring value to personal and ethical life. The right to liberty of conscience, in the terms protected by the argument for toleration, ensures the requisite moral independence rationally and reasonably to undertake and meet this responsibility free from the unjust imposition of sectarian views. The right to choose gay and lesbian identity is grounded on the right to conscience, thus understood, because only respect for this right ensures the required moral independence in taking responsibility, free of unjust sectarian views unsupported by compelling secular reasons, for convictions about homosexual love as deeply rooted in life experience and personality and the sense of enduring values in living as those about heterosexual love. It is in the nature of this kind of right that respect is accorded for our moral responsibility, as persons, for our reasonable convictions, whatever they are.

The case for gay rights thus appeals to the moral idea of responsibility for self central to the theory and practice of rights-based constitutional law and government.[29] The moral sense and role of this idea may be sharply drawn and appreciated by contrasting the idea to the picture of human life, as dictated by natural hierarchy, that it criticizes. Such natural hierarchy embeds human life in prescribed forms of status whose cultural and political force *depends* on the denial of the moral idea of responsibility for self. The connection between respect for human rights and the idea of responsibility for self may be clarified in terms of two ways in which values of human rights protest natural hierarchy. First, human rights ground self-originating claims that challenge the very terms of such hierarchy, in which one's role is externally dictated as exhaustive of meaning in living. Secondly, such claims of human rights also make possible reasonable criticism of the unjust political construction that has rendered such hierarchy ostensibly natural and uncontroversial. I have already discussed the force of such criticism in terms both of the argument for toleration and the theory of structural injustice. The theory of structural injustice thus is a criticism of certain ways in which unjust claims of natural hierarchy have been rationalized, for example, in terms of natural facts like race or gender. The criticism of such hierarchy,

---

[29] For extended defence of this view, see David A. J. Richards, *Foundations of American Constitutionalism* (Oxford University Press, New York, 1989).

as a naturalization of injustice, affirms the moral idea and value of responsibility for self, claiming one's reasonable moral powers against the stereotypical impositions of natural hierarchy that have blighted critical moral freedom.

The choice of gay and lesbian identity derives its moral sense and political and constitutional significance as the condition for exercising this kind of responsibility for self. That sense of responsibility ethically empowers thoughts, feelings, and convictions that challenge the naturalization of the structural injustice of homophobia, including the cultural meaning ascribed to one's homosexuality. Feelings need no longer be held in uncritical contempt nor regarded as an affliction, but interpreted as the basis for a confident and self-respecting sense of self, an identity, as a moral agent and person. Such a new interpretive attitude to self is made possible by and fosters moral powers to protest the structural injustice that had silenced such powers. The attempt thus to forge a sense of identity, not flawed by the repressive tradition of unspeakability, integrates one's understanding of sexual orientation with ethical convictions about the meaning and place of love and friendship, of intimacy and community, of justice in private and public life. Such integration insists on connection where cultural homophobia compelled isolation, making possible an interpretation of homoerotic sexual feeling and passion as a constructive moral resource, as Whitman urged,[30] for a more just understanding of the promise of democratic community on terms of principle. As I have suggested, such promise includes advances in moral and constitutional understandings from which all Americans will benefit, in particular, contesting the political enforcement of unjust gender roles in public and private life that stultify the just range of liberty and opportunity that should be available to all Americans.

I now propose a reasonable generalization of the idea of moral responsibility for self to include all the forms of protest of structural injustice examined in the course of the argument of this work. The empowered moral voice, that we examined in Du Bois and Boas and Friedan and Whitman and others, is the voice of moral responsibility for self against the unjust terms inflicted on the sense of self by entrenched patterns and practices of structural injustice. Protest in such a personal moral voice plays the role it does in the integrity of the struggle against structural injustice because its demand for and cultivation of moral consciousness exactly protests the dehumanizing stereotypes that masked, as a fact of nature, an invisibility and unspeakability made possible by the unjust cultural abridgment of basic human rights of conscience and speech. The censorious interference of state power in this domain, on the ground of group-based harms, worsens the problem it claims to solve because it asserts a paternalistic power in the state in the domain of conviction that the idea of moral responsibility for self repudiates and must repudiate. Such censorship, rather than contesting such stereotypes, replicates the underlying problem because it tries to remove from public discussion and debate exactly what such discussion and debate reasonably needs. The morally empowered voice, in contrast, forges a consciousness

---

[30] For development of this point, see Richards, n. 27 above, 297–310.

not only of the unjust weight of structural injustice but a consciousness of what is required to understand and remedy such injustice. A life lived from reasonable conviction becomes possible and new ethical forms of feeling and relationship are regarded with respect and, where appropriate, are the basis for love and all that means in a life well lived. To the extent much of the terms of structural injustice remain intact, one lives, as Du Bois and Friedan did, still under some of the terms of the unjust stereotype, but now increasingly understood as a cultural stereotype, an understanding that sustains a new consciousness and ways of life and relationships on self-respecting terms reasonably understood as just. Reasons of prudence and strategy may justify taking the terms of the dominant stereotype seriously, not least for reasons of a realistic sense of how one is being read and misread in reasonable efforts to contest its injustice. One moves, as it were, between two consciousnesses, but now with a creatively enlivened moral sense of freedom of consciousness, of reasons and thoughts and feelings rooted in responsibly living from conviction.

The principle of free speech, as I have defended it in this work, has played and continues to play the role it does in the understanding and remedy of structural injustice because its normative constitutional basis, the responsibility of each and every person in the domain of conviction, is the basis as well of the moral idea of responsibility for self that empowers the integrity of the politics of identity in the understanding and remedy of structural injustice. Our argument thus comes full circle: our normative proposal for the principle of free speech thus meets and matches our normative proposal for the understanding and remedy of structural injustice. Both meet at the moral axiom, responsibility for self in the domain of conviction. Both the right to free speech and the right against unjust discrimination must be defended and interpreted accordingly.

The sense of identity that emerges from the politics of identity must, in its nature, be contested and contestable as we see in the continuing debates among African-Americans, women, Jews, and homosexuals about how the terms of personal and ethical identity, forged against structural injustice, should be understood. There is an interpretive depth and complexity to all such disputes that resist any simplistic reduction to tribalizing slogans and rhetoric, let alone any reduction of them to the stereotypical terms (as a simple fact) that rationalized the injustice. Free speech plays the vital role it does when it fosters such complexity. What actuates such debates is resistance to any reductively stereotypical view of identity as a person of colour or woman or Jew or homosexual as an uninterpreted simple fact and a corresponding common sense of interpretive possibility and responsibility that the struggle for human rights against structural injustices, in all its forms, opens in terms of a new space for free moral imagination to explore. We can, in terms of that space, give a moral sense and interpretation to the idea of the legitimate invention of self. The invention of self is not always and everywhere a good thing; indeed, in some notorious cases, such invention (as by fascist demagogues appealing to the chauvinistic authenticity of national identity) has been at the heart of our twentieth century's moral heart of darkness. But the invention of self, as required in protesting the terms of structural injustice, is a humane moral need, indeed, as I understand it, an imperative of justice. It is that important fact about it (as an imperative of justice) that makes contemporary claims of identity, rooted in the politics of identity, at the core, not the periphery, of the most principled constitutional understanding of the inalienable human right of conscience and related rights. Persons thus remind us, in the voice of their recovered moral powers, of the deepest principles and values of respect for universal human rights of our constitutional traditions. We best respect those principles not when they are not at threat, but when they evidently are.

Nothing in this argument for the principle of free speech limits the legitimate state action outside its scope, in particular, in the domain of action, a point I have insisted on at several points. Indeed, it is very much the point of my argument, in contrast to other defences of free speech, to link the normative defence of its principle to the decision procedure that most reasonably advances the understanding and remedy of structural injustice in the domain of action. American experience under the principle of free speech I have defended supports this view; and any reasonable view of these matters must, in my judgement, come to terms with what this experience should mean for our understanding of the relationship between the basic human rights of free speech and against unjust discrimination. In particular, it is only through the moral empowerment of the politics of identity that Americans have come to some reasonable understanding of the entrenched culture and history of American racism, in particular, the role that institutions of racial segregation and anti-miscegenation laws played in the unjust subordination of persons of colour. The dimensions of structural injustice are, by their nature, often invisible and unspoken; and reasonable policies to understand and remedy such populist *assumptions* of ordinary life require opening the mind of the community to persons and issues usually ignored and sometimes held in irrational contempt. If we take the evils of structural injustice as seriously as we now constitutionally claim we do, we need more, not less, of the free discourse about these issues in the domain of conviction.

Taking free speech seriously in this way makes possible reasonable attention to the real sources of structural injustice. We will need to attend to the quality and nature of basic educational and job opportunity as well as higher education, all of which must be open more inclusively to the voices and views previously excluded and demeaned. Our conception of national citizenship must be rethought to render it less complicitous with the construction of structural injustice, as by endorsing unjust stereotypes of ethnicity or race or gender or sexual orientation as criteria for exercising the rights and responsibilities of citizenship (including political participation, service in the military, participation in the institutions of marriage and of religion). Traditional relationships between church and state must be re-examined in order to allow a just space for the voices and views of persons (Jews, women, homosexuals) often unjustly subordinated by a symbiotic relationship of religious and political power that corrupts both. The role that unjust abridgment of the right to intimate life plays in the dehumanization of persons must be more openly discussed, including the roots of anti-Semitism, racism, sexism, and homophobia in the abusive use of stereotypes of sexuality that dehumanize (Chapter 3). If we are to take such roots of structural injustice seriously, we will need to rethink quite fundamentally our racialized and gendered assumptions about the right to intimate life, including the right both to sexual love and to have and rear children. It is, in my judgement, an indication of how far we have yet to go that, in the United States, the very idea of same-sex marriage remains, in defiance of reason, an idea dismissed from the legitimate political agenda by almost all political leaders.

Free speech thus plays an indispensable role in advancing both the understanding and remedy of structural injustice, including the harms that are a just object of state action. I have defended the distinction between the domain of conviction and of action in terms of the quite different harms invoked to justify state power in each domain (Chapter 4). The group-based harms, alleged to justify the censorship of group libel or obscenity or blasphemy laws, inhere in evaluative disagreements about the interpretation of what speakers say and mean to say, and are harms that can be reasonably met by discourse and debate in the domain of conviction. The harms that justify laws that protect persons in their basic rights are not matters of disagreement in the domain of conviction, but attacks on basic human rights of personal and physical security. The domain of action marks the ample area in which the state has the responsibility to use its legal and political powers to render such rights secure.

This domain includes not only the power to protect minorities from actions and conspiracies that threaten such rights, but also the power and responsibility to protect such groups from unjust discrimination, including, as I have suggested, protecting basic rights and opportunities on fair terms. Forms of affirmative action play a reasonable constitutional role in the domain of action precisely because they take seriously the history and culture of structural injustice, giving appropriate weight to this culture of exclusion and marginalization in assuring a reasonable access on fair terms that rebuts and deconstructs the continuing power of this culture of dehumanization. If we are to advance public understanding of why such measures, broadly understood, are constitutionally necessary and proper, we will need more not less of the discourse of free speech that I have here defended against its critics.

The politics of identity, on the view I take of it, crucially plays a role in the denaturalization of structural injustice by advancing reasonable discourse about how the appeal to natural facts masks the cultural construction of such injustice. Such cultural construction includes not only the blatant exclusion of subordinated groups from basic rights and opportunities, but the ways in which the very terms of what counts as valued achievement or merit have often been unjustly coded in terms of unjust stereotypes like those of race or gender or sexual orientation. When we come reasonably to regard such terms of achievement or merit as themselves culturally constructed on unjust grounds, programmes of affirmative action may be more favourably assessed as ways of challenging the unjust terms of such valued performance, opening up access to such positions on more just terms. The politics of identity, because it empowers (as we have seen) such cultural analysis, renders a remedy like affirmative action altogether more understandable and reasonably justifiable.

A view of free speech that undercuts the legitimacy and integrity of such politics cor-relatively undercuts the reasonable appeal of such cultural analysis. Rather, the terms of structural injustice are fallaciously understood in terms of the earlier criticized view of suspect classification analysis in the United States, namely, as state endorsement of an immutable natural fact as the basis for distribution of rights and benefits (Chapter 3). It is exactly because this approach does not sufficiently address the naturalization of injustice that it often leads to ill-considered criticisms of affirmative action, because they ostensibly use such a natural fact for their ameliorative purposes. We can only begin to deal with this problem when the terms of the politics of identity are enlarged and deepened to render more reasonably perspicuous both the cultural terms of the construction of such injustice, and the remedial responsibility to rethink and reframe such a traditionally invisible culture of unjust marginalization and contempt.

Only such discourse reasonably exposes to public discussion and debate the depth of the culture and history of structural injustice, including its unjust impact not only on the groups unjustly subordinated, but often on other groups. American racism, for example, has not only treated unjustly people of colour, but, as I have argued, the non-visibly black immigrants to the United States who were themselves unjustly racialized in order to secure their allegiance to the unjust terms of American racism. The evil of sexism harms heterosexual women and gays and lesbians palpably, but it also unjustly imposes its irrationalist burdens on heterosexual men, whose lives are cramped to a narrow set of regimented sensitivities and responses that impoverish their lives.[31] The evils of various forms of structural injustice are structurally linked (Chapter 3), and thus the struggle against each such form of injustice requires that their common grounds be understood, resisting the scapegoating that is both morally corrupt and self-defeating. A discourse of free speech, as I understand and defend it here, opens to the public mind of the community such questions and issues, enlarg-ing our collective normative sense of how much we all stand to gain, as free and equal moral persons, by a life less hegemonically framed by the invisible assumptions of structural injustice. Such analysis renders programmes like affirmative action, that address some of the sources of structural injustice, more reasonably appealing, pre-cisely because it conceives such remedies not as a zero sum gain (from which a few gain and most lose), but as the reasonable terms for the remedy of a structural injus-tice that, on deeper understanding, harms people broadly.

THE PROMISE OF COMPARATIVE PUBLIC LAW

The Second World War may be regarded as a culminating cataclysm in defective con-stitutional institutions at the national, regional, and international levels. In its wake, governments at all these levels now claim to test the legitimacy of their institutions in

---

[31] See, for important reflections on this theme, James Gilligan, *Violence: Reflections on a National Epidemic* (Vintage, New York, 1996).

terms of their protection of basic human rights. My argument suggests a normative methodology, rooted in political theory, that makes possible a discourse of comparative public law that may be adequate to the challenge our generation faces in making the best sense we can of how these institutions should be interpreted, criticized, and developed.

There is renewed methodological interest in comparative public law in the United States but one still largely limited to whether formal categories of interpretation within American public law are or should be reasonably open to public law discourse outside the United States.[32] But the interest in comparative public law is not a matter of formal interpretive categories within a well-established system of law, nor does it arise in an aridly formalistic normative and historical vacuum. It has become sensible and increasingly normatively meaningful everywhere in the wake of the Second World War and the new directions in constitutional reconstruction to which it gave rise. The compelling interest of comparative public law is its invitation to deeper normative and interpretive discourse about the values of protection of basic human rights which systems of law at all levels increasingly acknowledge as the normative criteria for the legitimacy of constitutional argument. My argument has responded to this invitation by forging both a normative political theory of basic human rights and a critical and interpretive comparative theory of how these rights have been institutionalized both in the United States and other systems of law.

My approach has, I believe, the advantage not only of making clear the normative universality of free speech as a basic human right, but the universality of our common struggles, on the basis of free speech, against the entrenchment of structural injustice in the history and culture of all nations and peoples. What I have called the cataclysm of the Second World War was made possible by Hitler's morbidly successful mass politics of extreme religious intolerance and racism, organizing German nationality in a politics of imperialism and genocide that served these monstrous ends. We know, after Hitler, that political racism, as a means and end, is our moral heart of darkness. All peoples need better to understand how this could have happened and what it must mean for our normative understanding of constitutional institutions now dedicated to the values of universal human rights on which Hitler's racism self-consciously warred. A comparative public law, grounded in political theory, advances such understanding.

At various points, for example, my argument thus developed analogies between the development of racism in the United States and anti-Semitism in Germany in terms of how the abridgment of basic human rights in each culture importantly fostered the power that these evils have had over American and German politics; similarly, the argument explored at other points analogies in the construction of homophobia in the United States and Europe. Moreover, both the construction of and the resistance to structural injustice in various nations and peoples importantly influenced one

---

[32] See, for a recent example of this genre of argument, Mark Tushnet, 'The Possibilities of Comparative Constitutional Law', 108 *Yale LJ* 1225 (1999).

another. European and American racism rationalized imperialism and support of slavery; rights-based resistance in America and Europe led to the abolition of slavery and a growing sense of its roots in racism.[33] The horrors of German anti-Semitism were resisted and defeated by the Western allies in the Second World War. The development of serious anti-racist and related principles is now as much a European as an American undertaking, in the wake of the volcanic impact of the Second World War on American and certainly on European political theory and practice. The distinctive current form of American constitutional doctrine (for example, the unconstitutionality of group libel and related laws) developed in the United States only after the Second World War. It is important to see that these developments in the American law of free speech were structurally connected to greater understanding of its own racism, crystallized by its participation in that conflict; and that normative understanding has been deepened over time, by the impact of the politics of identity on our sense of basic human rights, in growing American constitutional understanding of the interlinked pattern of the structural injustice of racism, sexism, and homophobia and the need responsibly to address them (Chapter 3). Public law requires greater interpretive understanding of the moral dynamic underlying such historical developments, in place of the hermetic and ahistorical positivism which still dominates much academic discussion of these issues, both in America and abroad. The role of the politics of identity should be at centre stage in such discussions. These dissenting movements are, of course, now in play in many constitutional democracies, and American experience is thus continuous with that of many other nations. All people need, now more than ever, a discourse that enables them, as free people, to understand and explore these questions. Such a discourse of comparative religious intolerance, racism, sexism, and homophobia is one of the most appealing and promising avenues for investigation that the approach of this book makes possible.

The emphasis my normative argument has placed on the protection of the right to free speech must be understood against this background. On the admittedly provocative reading I give to the acceptance in Europe, as elsewhere, of the constitutional legitimacy of group libel and related laws, that acceptance suggests less rather than more readiness to understand and remedy the history and culture of structural injustice in European politics and politics elsewhere.[34] There is much more continuity between Europe before and after the Second World War than many Europeans want to believe.[35] The role of group libel and related laws in European politics suggests to

---

[33] See, on these points, David Brion Davis, *The Problem of Slavery in the Age of Revolution, 1770–1823* (Cornell University Press, Ithaca, NY, 1975); *The Problem of Slavery in Western Culture* (Cornell University Press, Ithaca, NY, 1967); *Slavery and Human Progress* (Oxford University Press, New York, 1984); on the American form of these struggles, see David A. J. Richards, *Conscience and the Constitution: History, Theory and Law of the Reconstruction Amendments* (Princeton University Press, Princeton, NJ, 1993).

[34] On Asian politics, see Amy L. Chua, 'Markets, Democracy, and Ethnicity: Toward a New Paradigm for Law and Development', 108 *Yale LJ* 1 (1998); on Africa, see Kwame Anthony Appiah, *In My Father's House: Africa in the Philosophy of Culture* (Oxford University Press, New York, 1992).

[35] See, on this point, Mark Mazower, *Dark Continent: Europe's Twentieth Century* (Knopf, New York, 1999).

an American a rather self-deceiving attempt at the denial of this continuity. It was in this spirit that the epigraph to this work quoted Lincoln's accusation of Stephen Douglas's attempt, in the name of democracy, to remove the question of slavery from American politics: 'Is it not a false statesmanship that undertakes to build up a system or policy upon the basis of caring nothing about *the very thing that every body does care the most about?*—a thing which all experience has shown we care a very great deal about?'[36] When a system of law like that of Germany or France cannot bear to hear that Germans or the French entertain convictions of Holocaust denial or of India that a bicultural artist has legitimate doubts about the Qur'an or of Britain that a gay poet believes the love of Christ embraces, in the meaning of his death, homosexual sex, we need to ask, as Lincoln did of Douglas, whether it is not 'a false statesmanship' thus, in the name of democracy, to repress the discourse of reasonable doubt about the issues that 'every body does care the most about'.

It is surely, in this connection, a remarkable feature of the contemporary defence of group libel and related laws that it takes the form of defending censorship as protecting the victims of structural injustice from being silenced.[37] This is, as we have seen, the very reverse of the truth of the matter. It is the principle of free speech, properly understood, that alone offers the required constitutional acoustics not only for hearing the previously silenced voices of groups afflicted by a history and culture of structural injustice, but for allowing persons in these groups to hear themselves as having a moral voice that challenges the terms of the unjust stereotypes that have traditionally dehumanized them. Such acoustics for both audience and speaker are inseparable. It is only when audiences are reasonably open to previously silenced voices and viewpoints that the persons, subject to such injustice, can hear themselves as having voices and views that resonate, at once, with themselves and with the larger audience they address. It is because the principle of free speech has the relationship that it does to the legitimacy and integrity of the politics of identity that it affords the appropriate acoustics for such voices. Such politics empowers persons afflicted by a history and culture that has naturalized structural injustice in terms of dehumanizing stereotypes of race or gender or gendered sexuality to speak in a voice, expressive of their moral powers as persons, that reasonably challenges such terms of their moral slavery in each of the domains we have now studied in depth (anti-Semitism, racism, sexism, and homophobia). In contrast, censorship in the domain of conviction, based on alleged harms to groups, enforces and does not contest the stereotypical rationalization of structural injustice. It perhaps exemplifies the continuing power of the paradox of intolerance (repressing doubts when they most reasonably require discussion and debate) that such censorship rationalizes its injustice in the very terms (silencing) that it rather conspicuously inflicts. To this extent, the very appeal of such

---

[36] Abraham Lincoln, in Robert W. Johannsen (ed.), *The Lincoln–Douglas Debates* (Oxford University Press, New York, 1965), at 315.

[37] See, e.g., Owen M. Fiss, *The Irony of Free Speech: Liberalism Divided* (Harvard University Press, Cambridge, Mass., 1993), at 16–17, 26; Frank I. Michelman, 'Conceptions of Democracy in American Constitutional Argument: The Case of Pornography Regulation', 56 *Tenn. L Rev.* 291, 295–6 (1989).

arguments for censorship at a certain time and place bespeaks the continuing power of traditional patterns of structural injustice, repressing exactly the voices and views that most reasonably raise and discuss reasonable doubts about the understanding and remedy of such injustice. To confront such structural injustice in our respective nations and traditions, we need not a censorship that legitimates denial and ignorance of who we are, but openly to hear all persons and views in the domain of conviction, the only legitimate and reliable decision procedure for frank understanding of how far we each have yet to go in the exercise of our moral freedom and the discharge of our moral responsibility, as persons, to accord equal respect for universal human rights under the rule of constitutional law.

An American, like the author of this book, may have at least some standing to voice such doubts to Europeans and others when his study of American racism, for example, increasingly traces the roots of such injustice to the forms of European racism that his ancestors experienced first hand in Europe before they emigrated to the United States. European-Americans, like myself, increasingly understand and evaluate their own experience in America experiencing and increasingly resisting its racism to the earlier resistance of their families to such racism in Europe.[38] It is painful for a Euro-American to face such questions, involving such fundamental criticisms both of American and European culture and history, but they are the questions that are, I am convinced, the ones that a proper understanding of free speech ethically empowers and requires us to raise. They make possible for Americans, as they do for others, at least the moral possibility of a new sense of nationalism, a liberal nationalism binding a people together by their mutual respect for basic human rights, a national identity no longer uncritically implicated with the patterns of structural injustice (hating the innocent outsider, the scapegoat of our unreasoning hatred) that are, as a basis for national union, our collective scandal and shame. Santayana, another Euro-American, spoke of alternative conceptions of nationalism in such terms:

A man who is just and reasonable must nowadays, so far as his imagination permits, share the patriotism of the rivals and enemies of his country,—a patriotism as inevitable and pathetic as his own. Nationality being an irrational accident, like sex or complexion, a man's allegiance to his country must be conditional, at least if he is a philosopher. His patriotism has to be subordinated to rational allegiance to such things as justice and humanity.[39]

Comparative public law, exploring the common threads within our multicultural traditions, may enable us to be more critical of both our American and our European and other backgrounds, and thus to forge a *political* consensus[40] that, as cosmopolitan citizens of an increasingly interdependent world, sustains a philosophical patriotism,

---

[38] See, on this point, David A. J. Richards, *Italian American: The Racializing of an Ethnic Identity* (New York University Press, New York, 1999).

[39] George Santayana, *Three Philosophical Poets: Lucretius, Dante, and Goethe* (Harvard University Press, Cambridge, Mass., 1947), at 85.

[40] On the relevance of the idea of an overlapping political consensus to liberal political philosophy and constitutionalism, see Samuel Freeman (ed.), *John Rawls: Collected Papers* (Harvard University Press, Cambridge, Mass., 1999), at 421–48.

in Santayana's sense, one that understands and deepens our shared humane values of freedom and reason, reflected in our growing commitment to human rights under the rule of constitutional law.

We need, now more than ever, a discourse of comparative public law not only about free speech, but about the religious intolerance, racism, sexism, and homophobia that have been at the centre of our political heart of darkness. If we are to understand and remedy the profound cultural roots of these evils, we must hear what we would prefer not to hear—that our valued sense of religious or ethnic or political identity may be tainted with unfathomable evil; and we must struggle to live, as moral persons, in the ethical truth of what such knowledge reasonably brings in our sense of the responsibilities of our moral freedom. No people is exempt from these problems, and our struggle must be, however rooted in our peculiar histories, to see our peculiarities under the aspect of an emerging cosmopolitan culture of human rights that is today more feasible than it has been since the end of the eighteenth century. This book will have served some purpose if it advances both the theory and practice of such a comparative public law not only of free speech, but of the right against discrimination in the domains of anti-Semitism, racism, sexism, and homophobia, which are the only real enemies of our common humanity.

My argument places, I realize, certain burdens on the politics of identity in the domain of conviction that some may not implausibly regard as unreasonable conditions for progressive change that critically addresses, as I insist, the cultural ravages of profound structural injustice. Does it not compound injustice to place such burdens on its victims? If one concedes that racism or sexism are great constitutional evils, why must the victims of such evils stand equal to the perpetrators of such evils in the domain of conviction and speech? As a French constitutional judge and public lawyer of great distinction remarked to me, how, in light of what France did to its Jews, can we now not stand with them by indicting advocates of Holocaust denial as criminals? But this understandable query assumes as true what my argument shows to be false, namely, that state protection of such victims at least in the domain of conviction advances either the understanding or remedy of the structural injustice that afflicts them. In fact, it does neither. It undercuts the legitimacy of the politics of identity, because it repudiates the standpoint of equal respect for the right to conscience on which the moral authority of such politics stands. It compromises the integrity of such politics because it does not require the impartial testing of its claims in the public forum, morally independent of the state, which renders its claims on that basis more freely accepted as reasonable. Such censorship, however well intentioned, for these reasons demonstrably renders structural injustice more intractable (worsening racism while inflicting anti-Semitism, or exacerbating sexism while worsening racism, or further entrenching homophobia and inflicting anti-Semitism, racism, and sexism as well). Above all, such censorship does not, as it claims, accord the equal respect due all persons, but rather disempowers the moral voice of those protesting from within the experience of structural injustice, the voice that reasonably demands and commands such respect. Such burdens of protest are thus reasonable because they alone address the injustice in the terms adequate to its understanding and remedy. In particular, such burdens bring benefits to those afflicted by such unjust stereotypes of subhumanity: they authenticate, in the very terms that one undertakes such protest, what is beyond price and the object of all struggles against dehumanizing injustice, one's claims of human dignity.

Bibliography

ABEL, RICHARD L., *Speaking Respect Respecting Speech* (University of Chicago Press, Chicago, Ill., 1998)

ABELOVE, HENRY, BARALE, MICHELE AINA, HALPERIN, DAVID M. (eds.), *The Lesbian and Gay Studies Reader* (Routledge, New York, 1993)

ABRAHAMSEN, DAVID, *The Mind and Death of a Genius* (Columbia University Press, New York, 1946)

ACKERMAN, BRUCE, 'Beyond *Carolene Products*', 98 *Harv. L Rev.* 713 (1985)

ACRON, ANNALISE, 'Case Comment and Note: Harm, Community Tolerance, and the Indecent: A Discussion of R. v. Mara', 36 *Alberta L Rev.* 258 (1997)

ADLER, AMY, 'What's Left?: Hate Speech, Pornography, and the Problem for Artistic Expression', 84 *Calif. L Rev.* 1499 (1996)

AHLSTROM, SYDNEY E., *A Religious History of the American People* (Yale University Press, New Haven, Conn., 1972)

ALLEN, DAVID S., and JENSEN, ROBERT (eds.), *Freeing the First Amendment: Critical Perspectives on Freedom of Expression* (New York University Press, New York, 1995)

ALTMAN, DENNIS, VANCE, CAROL, VICINUS, MARTHA, and WEEKS, JEFFREY, *Homosexuality, Which Homosexuality?: International Conference on Gay and Lesbian Studies* (GMP Publishers, London, 1989)

AMSTERDAM, ANTHONY G., 'Thurgood Marshall's Image of the Blue-Eyed Child in *Brown*', 68 *NYU L Rev.* 226 (1993)

AN-NA'IM, ABDULLAHI AHMED, *Toward an Islamic Reformation: Civil Liberties, Human Rights, and International Law* (Syracuse University Press, Syracuse, NY, 1990)

APPIAH, KWAME ANTHONY, *In My Father's House: Africa in the Philosophy of Culture* (Oxford University Press, New York, 1992)

APPLEBOME, PETER, 'Ideas & Trends; Blasphemy? Again? Somebody's Praying for a Hit', *New York Times*, 18 October 1998, sec. 4–4

AQUINAS, THOMAS, *On the Truth of the Catholic Faith: Summa Contra Gentiles* (trans. Vernon Bourke, Image, New York, 1956)

ARENDT, HANNAH, *The Origins of Totalitarianism* (Harcourt Brace Jovanovich, New York, 1973)

ASSOCIATED PRESS, 'Judge Overturns Ban on Film', *New York Times*, 11 September 1988, sec. 1, 34

AUGUSTINE, *The City of God* (trans. Henry Bettenson, Penguin, Harmondsworth, 1972)

BACON, MARGARET HOPE, *Mothers of Feminism: The Story of Quaker Women in America* (Harper & Row, San Francisco, Cal., 1989)

BAILEY, DERRICK SHERWIN, *Homosexuality and the Western Christian Tradition* (originally published 1955) (Archon Books, Hamden, Conn., 1975)

BAILEY, J. MICHAEL, and PILLARD, RICHARD C., 'A Genetic Study of Male Sexual Orientation', 48 *Archives Gen. Psychiatry* 1089 (1991)

BAKER, C. EDWIN, 'Scope of the First Amendment Freedom of Speech', 25 *UCLA L Rev.* 964 (1978)

—— 'Realizing Self-Realization: Corporate Political Expenditures' and Redish's 'The Value of Free Speech', 130 *U Pa. L Rev.* 646 (1982)

BAKER, C. EDWIN, *Human Liberty and Freedom of Speech* (Oxford University Press, New York, 1989)

—— 'Campaign Expenditures and Free Speech', 33 *Harvard Civil Rights–Civil Liberties Law Review* 1 (1998)

BALDWIN, JAMES, *No Name in the Street* (Dell, New York, 1972)

—— *The Price of the Ticket: Collected Non-fiction, 1948–1985* (St. Martin's, New York, 1985)

BARENDT, ERIC, *Freedom of Speech* (Clarendon Press, Oxford, 1985)

BARKAN, ELAZAR, *The Retreat of Scientific Racism: Changing Concepts of Race in Britain and the United States Between the World Wars* (Cambridge University Press, Cambridge, 1992)

BARKER-BENFIELD, G. J., *The Horrors of the Half-Known Life: Male Attitudes Toward Women and Sexuality in Nineteenth-Century America* (Harper & Row, New York, 1976)

BAWER, BRUCE, *A Place at the Table: The Gay Individual in American Society* (Poseidon Press, New York, 1993)

—— *Beyond Queer: Challenging Gay Left Orthodoxy* (Free Press, New York, 1996)

BAYER, RONALD, *Homosexuality and American Psychiatry: The Politics of Diagnosis* (Basic Books, New York, 1981)

BEATTIE, JAMES, *Elements of Moral Science* (Scholars' Facsimiles & Reprints, Delmar, NY, 1976)

—— *An Essay on the Nature and Immutability of Truth* (Garland Publishing, Inc. New York, 1983)

BEAUVOIR, SIMONE DE, *The Second Sex* (trans. H. M. Parshley, first published in English, 1953) (Vintage, New York, 1974)

BELL, ALAN P., WEINBERG, MARTIN S., and HAMMERSMITH, SUE K., *Sexual Preference* (Simon & Schuster, New York, 1978)

BENDERSKY, JOSEPH W., *Carl Schmitt: Theorist for the Reich* (Princeton University Press, Princeton, NJ, 1983)

BENEDICT, RUTH, *Race: Science and Politics* (The Viking Press, New York, 1945)

BENITO, ELIZABETH ODIO, *Elimination of All Forms of Intolerance and Discrimination Based on Religion or Belief* (United Nations, New York, 1989)

BERGER, JOHN, *Ways of Seeing* (Penguin, London, 1972)

BERGER, MAURICE, *White Lies: Race and the Myths of Whiteness* (Farrar, Straus, Giroux, New York, 1999)

BERNSTEIN, ALAN E., *The Formation of Hell: Death and Retribution in the Ancient and Early Christian Worlds* (Cornell University Press, Ithaca, NY, 1993)

BLACKSTONE, WILLIAM, *Commentaries on the Laws of England*, 4 vols. (1768–69, reprint, University of Chicago Press, Chicago, Ill., 1979)

BLASI, VINCENT, 'The Pathological Perspective and the First Amendment', 85 *Colum. L Rev.* 449 (1985)

—— 'Free Speech and the Widening Gyre of Fund-Raising: Why Campaign Spending Limits May Not Violate the First Amendment After All', 94 *Colum. L Rev.* 1281 (1994)

BLEYS, RUDI C., *The Geography of Perversion: Male-to-Male Sexual Behaviour Outside the West and the Ethnographic Imagination, 1750–1918* (New York University Press, New York, 1995)

BLUMENTHAL, RALPH, 'Canceled Play May Be Staged', *New York Times*, 28 May 1998, E–1

BLUMSTEIN, PHILIP, and SCHWARTZ, PEPPER, *American Couples* (William Morrow, New York, 1983)

Boas, Franz, *The Mind of Primitive Man* (rev. edn., 1911; Greenwood Press, Westport, Conn., 1983)

Bork, Robert, 'Neutral Principles and Some First Amendment Problems', 47 *Indiana LJ* 1 (1971)

Boswell, John, *Christianity, Social Tolerance, and Homosexuality* (University of Chicago Press, Chicago, Ill., 1980)

—— *Same-Sex Unions in Premodern Europe* (Villard Books, New York, 1994)

Bourdieu, Pierre, *The Political Ontology of Martin Heidegger* (trans. Peter Collier, Polity Press, Cambridge, 1991)

Bower, Tom, *The Pledge Betrayed: America and Britain and the Denazification of Postwar Germany* (Doubleday, Garden City, NY, 1982)

Boyd, Julian P. (ed.), *The Papers of Thomas Jefferson, 1777–1779* (Princeton University Press, Princeton NJ, 1950), ii

Branch, Taylor, *Parting the Waters: Martin Luther King and the Civil Rights Movement, 1954–63* (Papermac, London, 1990)

Brantley, Ben, 'Nice Young Man and Disciples Appeal for Tolerance', *New York Times*, 14 October 1998, E–1

Braude, Ann, *Radical Spirits: Spiritualism and Women's Rights in Nineteenth-Century America* (Beacon Press, Boston, Mass., 1995)

Bray, Alan, *Homosexuality in Renaissance England* (Gay Men's Press, London, 1982)

Brod, Harry (ed.), *The Making of Masculinities: The New Men's Studies* (Routledge, New York, 1987)

Brodkin, Karen, *How Jews Became White Folks and What That Says about Race in America* (Rutgers University Press, New Brunswick, 1998)

Brooten, Bernadette J., *Love Between Women: Early Christian Responses to Female Homoeroticism* (University of Chicago Press, Chicago, Ill., 1996)

Brown, Peter, *The Body and Society: Men, Women, and Sexual Renunciation in Early Christianity* (Columbia University Press, New York, 1988)

Brubaker, Rogers, *Citizenship and Nationhood in France and Germany* (Harvard University Press, Cambridge, Mass., 1992)

Bull, Chris, and Gallagher, John, *Perfect Enemies: The Religious Right, the Gay Movement, and the Politics of the 1990's* (Crown Publishers, New York, 1996)

Bullock, Alan, *Hitler: A Study in Tyranny* (rev. edn., Harper & Row, New York, 1962)

Burstyn, Varda (ed.), *Women Against Censorship* (Douglas & McIntrye, Vancouver, 1985)

Bushnell, Horace, *Women's Suffrage: The Reform against Nature* (Charles Scribner and Co., New York, 1869)

Calhoun, Emily, 'The Thirteenth and Fourteenth Amendments: Constitutional Authority for Federal Legislation Against Private Sex Discrimination', 61 *Minn. L Rev.* 313 (1977)

Campbell, Tom, and Sadurski, Wojciech, *Freedom of Communication* (Dartmouth, Aldershot, 1994)

Campion, Nardi Reeder, *Ann the Word: The Life of Mother Ann Lee, Founder of the Shakers* (Little, Brown, Boston, Mass., 1976)

Canby, Vincent, 'Battered and Broker, So That She May Rise', *New York Times*, 18 October 1998, sec. 2–9

Cantarella, Eva, *Bisexuality in the Ancient World* (trans. Cormac O'Cuilleanain, Yale University Press, New Haven, Conn., 1992)

CARNES, MARK C., and GRIFFEN, CLYDE (eds.), *Meanings for Manhood: Constructions of Masculinity in Victorian America* (University of Chicago Press, Chicago, Ill., 1990)

CARPENTER, EDWARD, *The Intermediate Sex: A Study of Human Evolution and Transfiguration* (Mitchell Kennerley, New York, 1912)

CASE, MARY ANN C., 'Disaggregating Gender from Sex and Sexual Orientation: The Effeminate Man in the Law and Feminist Jurisprudence', 105 *Yale LJ* 90 (1995)

CASH, W. J., *The Mind of the South* (Vintage Books, New York, 1941)

CASSIRER, ERNST, *The Question of Jean-Jacques Rousseau* (trans. Peter Gay, Yale University Press, New Haven, Conn., 1989)

CERVANTES, FERNANDO, *The Devil in the New World: The Impact of Diabolism in New Spain* (Yale University Press, New Haven, Conn., 1994)

CHAFE, WILLIAM H., *The Paradox of Change: American Women in the 20th Century* (Oxford University Press, New York, 1991)

—— *Women and Equality: Changing Patterns in American Culture* (Oxford University Press, New York, 1977)

CHAMBERLAIN, HOUSTON STEWART, *The Foundations of the Nineteenth Century* (trans. John Lees, John Lane, London, 1911), 2 vols.

CHASE, ANTHONY, ' "Pakistan or the Cemetery": Muslim Minority Rights in Contemporary India', 16 *BC Third World LJ* 35 (1966)

—— 'Legal Guardians: Islamic Law, International Law, Human Rights Law, and the Salman Rushdie Affair', 11 *Am. UJ Int'l L & Pol'y* 375 (1996)

CHAUNCEY, GEORGE, *Gay New York: Gender, Urban Culture, and the Making of the Gay Male World 1890–1940* (BasicBooks, New York, 1994)

CHESLER, ELLEN, *Woman of Valor: Margaret Sanger and the Birth Control Movement in America* (Anchor, New York, 1992)

CHEVIGNY, PAUL G., 'The Paradox of Campaign Finance', 56 *NYU L Rev.* 206 (1981)

CHEYETTE, BRYAN (ed.), *Between 'Race' and Culture: Representations of 'the Jew' in English and American Literature* (Stanford University Press, Stanford, Cal., 1996)

CHUA, AMY L., 'Markets, Democracy, and Ethnicity: Toward a New Paradigm for Law and Development', 108 *Yale LJ* 1 (1998)

CHURCHILL, WAINWRIGHT, *Homosexual Behaviour Among Males* (Hawthorn, New York, 1967)

CLENDINNEN, INGA, *Reading the Holocaust* (Cambridge University Press, Cambridge, 1999)

COBB, THOMAS R. R., *An Inquiry into the Law of Negro Slavery in the United States of America* (1858; reprint, Negro Universities Press, New York, 1968)

COHEN, JANE MASLOW, 'Regimes of Private Tyranny: What Do They Mean to Morality and for the Criminal Law?', 57 *U Pitt. L Rev.* 757 (1996)

COHEN, ROGER, 'Germany Makes Citizenship Easier for Foreigners to Get', *New York Times*, 22 May 1999, A–3

COHEN-ALMAGOR, RAPHAEL, *The Boundaries of Liberty and Tolerance: The Struggle Against Kahanism in Israel* (University Press of Florida, Gainesville, Flo., 1994)

COLIVER, SANDRA (ed.), *Striking a Balance: Hate Speech, Freedom of Expression and Non-discrimination* (Article 19, International Centre against Censorship, London, and Human Rights Centre, University of Essex, 1992)

CONNELL, R. W., *Masculinities* (University of California Press, Berkeley, Cal., 1995)

COOKE, JACOB E. (ed.), *The Federalist* (Wesleyan University Press, Middletown, Conn., 1961)

COOPER, ANNA JULIA, *A Voice from the South* (1892, reprinted and ed. by Mary Helen Washington, Oxford University Press, New York, 1988)

CRIMP, DOUGLAS, *Cultural Analysis/Cultural Activism* (The MIT Press, Cambridge, Mass., 1988)

CUMPER, PETER, 'Religious Human Rights in the World Today: A Report on the 1994 Atlanta Conference: Legal perspectives on Religious Human Rights Today: Religious Human Rights in the United Kingdom', 10 *Emory Int'l L Rev.* 115 (1996)

CURRIE, DAVID P., *The Constitutional of the Federal Republic of Germany* (University of Chicago Press, Chicago, Ill., 1994)

DAHL, ROBERT A., *Democracy and Its Critics* (Yale University Press, New Haven, Conn., 1989)

DAVIS, DAVID BRION, *The Problem of Slavery in Western Culture* (Cornell University Press, Ithaca, NY, 1967)

—— *The Problem of Slavery in the Age of Revolution, 1770–1823* (Cornell University Press, Ithaca, NY, 1975)

—— *Slavery and Human Progress* (Oxford University Press, New York, 1984)

DAVIS, DENNIS, CHEADLE, HALTON, HAYSOM, NICHOLAS, *Fundamental Rights in the Constitution* (Juta and Co., Kenwyn, 1997)

DAVIS, F. JAMES, *Who Is Black?: One Nation's Definition* (Pennsylvania State University Press, University Park, Penn., 1991)

DEBERG, BETTY A., *Ungodly Women: Gender and the First Wave of American Fundamentalism* (Fortress Press, Minneapolis, Min., 1990)

DEGLER, CARL N., *At Odds: Women and the Family in America from the Revolution to the Present* (Oxford University Press, New York, 1980)

—— *In Search of Human Nature: The Decline and Revival of Darwinism in American Social Thought* (Oxford University Press, New York, 1991)

DELGADO, RICHARD, and STEFANCIC, JEAN, *Critical White Studies: Looking Behind the Mirror* (Temple University Press, Philadelphia, Penn., 1997)

—— —— *Must We Defend the Nazis: Hate Speech, Pornography, and the New First Amendment* (New York University Press, New York, 1997)

D'EMILIO, JOHN, *Sexual Politics, Sexual Communities: The Making of a Homosexual Minority in the United States, 1940–1970* (University of Chicago Press, Chicago, Ill., 1983)

—— and FREEDMAN, ESTELLE B., *Intimate Matters: A History of Sexuality in America* (Harper & Row, New York, 1988)

DESROCHE, HENRI, *The American Shakers: From Neo-Christianity to Presocialism* (trans. John K. Savacool, University of Massachusetts Press, Amherst, Mass., 1971)

DIJKSTRA, BRAM, *Idols of Perversity: Fantasies of Feminine Evil in Fine-de-Siecle Culture* (Oxford University Press, New York, 1986)

DOLLIMORE, JONATHAN, *Sexual Dissidence: Augustine to Wilde, Freud to Foucault* (Clarendon Press, Oxford, 1991)

DOUGLAS, ANN, *Terrible Honesty: Mongrel Manhattan in the 1920s* (Farrar, Straus and Giroux, New York, 1995)

DOVER, KENNETH J., *Greek Popular Morality in the Time of Plato and Aristotle* (Basil Blackwell, Oxford, 1974)

—— *Greek Homosexuality* (Duckworth, London, 1978)

—— *The Greeks and Their Legacy* (Blackwell, Oxford, 1988)

DREYFUS, HUBERT L., *Being-in-the-World: A Commentary on Heidegger's Being and Time, Division I* (The MIT Press, Cambridge, Mass., 1991)

DRINNON, RICHARD, *Rebel in Paradise: A Biography of Emma Goldman* (University of Chicago Press, Chicago, Ill., 1961)

—— and DRINNON, ANNA MARIA, *Nowhere at Home: Letters from Exile of Emma Goldman and Alexander Berkman* (Schocken, New York, 1975)

DUBERMAN, MARTIN BAUML, VICINUS, MARTHA, and CHAUNCEY, GEORGE (eds.), *Hidden from History: Reclaiming the Gay and Lesbian Past* (New American Books, New York, 1989)

DU BOIS, W. E. B., *Black Reconstruction in America, 1860–1880* (1935, Atheneum, New York, 1969)

DUDZIAK, MARY L., 'Desegregation as a Cold War Imperative', 41 *Stan. L Rev.* 41 (1988)

DUGGAN, LISA, and HUNTER, NAN D., *Sex, Sexual Dissent, and Political Culture* (Routledge, New York, 1995)

DWORKIN, RONALD, *Law's Empire* (Harvard University Press, Cambridge, Mass., 1986)

—— *Life's Dominion: An Argument about Abortion, Euthanasia, and Individual Freedom* (Knopf, New York, 1993)

—— *Freedom's Law: The Moral Reading of the American Constitution* (Harvard University Press, Cambridge, Mass., 1996)

DYER, RICHARD, *White* (Routledge, London, 1997)

DYNES, WAYNE R. (ed.), *Encyclopedia of Homosexuality* (Garland Publishing, Inc., New York, 1990), i

EHRENREICH, BARBARA, HESS, ELIZABETH, and JACOBS, GLORIA, *Remaking Love: The Feminization of Sex* (Anchor, New York, 1986)

EIBL-EIBESFELDT, IRENAUS, *Love and Hate: The Natural History of Behaviour Patterns* (trans. Geoffrey Strachan, Holt, Rinehart, and Winston, New York, 1971)

ELLIOT, JONATHAN (ed.), *Debates on the Federal Constitution* (Printed for the editor, Washington, DC, 1836), iv

—— (ed.), *The Debates in the Several State Conventions on the Adoption of the Federal Constitution*, vols. 2 and 3 (Printed for the editor, Washington, DC, 1836)

ELLISON, RALPH, *Invisible Man* (Vintage, New York, 1989)

ELY, JOHN HART, *Democracy and Distrust: A Theory of Judicial Review* (Harvard University Press, Cambridge, Mass., 1980)

ESTLUND, DAVID M., and NUSSBAUM, MARTHA C., *Sex, Preference, and Family: Essays on Law and Nature* (Oxford University Press, New York, 1997)

EVANS, SARA, *Personal Politics: The Roots of Women's Liberation in the Civil Rights Movement and the New Left* (Vintage, New York, 1980)

FADERMAN, LILLIAN, *Surpassing the Love of Men* (William Morrow, New York, 1981)

—— *Odd Girls and Twilight Lovers: A History of Lesbian Life in Twentieth-Century America* (Columbia University Press, New York, 1991)

—— (ed.), *Chloe Plus Olivia: An Anthology of Lesbian Literature from the Seventeenth Century to the Present* (Viking, New York, 1994)

FALUDI, SUSAN, *Backlash: The Undeclared War Against American Women* (Doubleday, New York, 1991)

FANON, FRANTZ, *Black Skin, White Masks* (trans. Charles Lam Markmann, Grove Weidenfeld, New York, 1967)

FARBER, DANIEL A., and SHERRY, SUZANNA, *Beyond All Reason: The Radical Assault on Truth in American Law* (Oxford University Press, New York, 1997)

FARIAS, VICTOR, *Heidegger and Nazism* (Temple University Press, Philadelphia, Penn., 1989)

FARRIOR, STEPHANIE, 'Molding the Matrix: The Historical and Theoretical Foundations of International Law Concerning Hate Speech', 14 *Berkeley J of International Law* 3, 65–8 (1996)

FAUST, DREW GILPIN (ed.), *The Ideology of Slavery: Proslavery Thought in the Antebellum South, 1830–1860* (Louisiana State University Press, Baton Rouge, La., 1981)

FICINO, MARSILIO, *Commentary on Plato's Symposium* (trans. and introduction, Sears Reynolds Jayne, University of Missouri, Columbia, Miss., 1944)

FINNIS, JOHN, *Natural Law and Natural Rights* (Clarendon Press, Oxford, 1980)

FIRESTONE, SHULAMITH, *The Dialectic of Sex: The Case for Feminist Revolution* (originally published, 1970) (Woman's Press, London, 1988)

FISH, STANLEY, *There's No Such Thing as Free Speech and It's a Good Thing, Too* (Oxford University Press, New York, 1994)

FISS, OWEN M., *Liberalism Divided: Freedom of Speech and the Many Uses of State Power* (Westview Press, Boulder, Colo. 1996)

—— *The Irony of Free Speech* (Harvard University Press, Cambridge, Mass., 1996)

FITZGIBBON, CONSTANTINE, *Denazification* (W. W. Norton, New York, 1969)

FLAGG, BARBARA J., *Was Blind But Now I See: White Race Consciousness and the Law* (New York University Press, New York, 1998)

FONER, PHILIP S. (ed.), *The Life and Writings of Frederick Douglass* (International Publishers, New York, 1975), ii

FORD, CLELLAN S., and BEACH, FRANK A., *Patterns of Sexual Behaviour* (Harper & Row, New York, 1951)

FOSTER, LAWRENCE, *Women, Family, and Utopia: Communal Experiments of the Shakers, the Oneida Community, and the Mormons* (Syracuse University Press, Syracuse, NY, 1991)

FOUCAULT, MICHEL, *The History of Sexuality* (trans. Robert Hurley, Pantheon, New York, 1978), i

FOUT, JOHN C. (ed.), *Forbidden History: The State, Society, and the Regulation of Sexuality in Modern Europe* (University of Chicago Press, Chicago, Ill., 1992)

FOX-GENOVESE, ELIZABETH, *Feminism Without Illusions: A Critique of Individualism* (University of North Carolina Press, Chapel Hill, NC, 1991)

—— *'Feminism Is Not the Story of My Life': How Today's Feminist Elite Has Lost Touch with the Real Concerns of Women* (Doubleday, New York, 1996)

FRANKE, KATHERINE M., 'What's Wrong With Sexual Harassment?', 49 *Stan. L Rev.* 691 (1997)

—— 'The Central Mistake of Sex Discrimination Law: The Dissagregation of Sex from Gender', 144 *U Penn. L Rev.* 1 (1995)

FRANKENBERG, RUTH, *The Social Construction of Whiteness: White Women, Race Matters* (University of Minnesota Press, Minneapolis, Min., 1993)

FRANKLIN, DANIEL P., and BAUN, MICHAEL J. (eds.), *Political Culture and Constitutionalism: a Comparative Approach* (M. E. Sharpe, Armonk, NY, 1995)

FRANKLIN, JOHN HOPE, *The Militant South, 1800–1861* (Harvard University Press, Belknap Press, Cambridge, Mass., 1956)

FREDRICKSON, GEORGE M., *The Black Image in the White Mind: The Debate on Afro-American Character and Destiny, 1817–1914* (Wesleyan University Press, Middletown, Conn., 1971)

FREEDMAN, MONROE H., and FREEDMAN, ERIC M. (eds.), *Group Defamation and Freedom of Speech: The Relationship Between Language and Violence* (Greenwood Press, Westport, Conn., 1995)

FREEMAN, JO, *The Politics of Women's Liberation: A Case Study of an Emerging Social Movement and Its Relation to the Policy Process* (Longman, New York, 1975)

FREEMAN, SAMUEL (ed.), *John Rawls: Collected Papers* (Harvard University Press, Cambridge, Mass., 1999)

FRENCH, MARILYN, *The War Against Women* (Penguin, London, 1992)

FRIEDAN, BETTY, *The Feminine Mystique* (originally published, 1963) (Penguin, London, 1982)

FURET, FRANÇOIS, *The Passing of an Illusion: The Idea of Communism in the Twentieth Century* (trans. Deborah Furet, University of Chicago Press, Chicago, Ill., 1999)

GATES, JR., HENRY LOUIS, GRIFFIN, ANTHONY P., LIVELY, DONALD E., POST, ROBERT C., RUBENSTEIN, WILLIAM B., and STROSSEN, NADINE, *Speaking of Race, Speaking of Sex: Hate Speech, Civil Rights, and Civil Liberties* (New York University Press, New York, 1994)

GENOVESE, EUGENE D., *Roll, Jordan, Roll: The World the Slaves Made* (Vintage Books, New York, 1974)

GEORGE, ROBERT P., *Making Men Moral: Civil Liberties and Public Morality* (Clarendon Press, Oxford, 1993)

GERARD, KENT, and HEKMA, GERT, *The Pursuit of Sodomy: Male Homosexuality in Renaissance and Enlightenment Europe* (Harrington Park Press, New York, 1989)

GIDDENS, ANTHONY, *The Transformation of Intimacy: Sexuality, Love, and Eroticism in Modern Societies* (Polity, Cambridge, 1992)

GIDDINGS, PAULA, *When and Where I Enter . . . : The Impact of Black Women on Race and Sex in America* (William Morrow, New York, 1984)

GILFOYLE, TIMOTHY J., *City of Eros: New York City, Prostitution, and the Commercialization of Sex, 1790–1920* (W. W. Norton, New York, 1992)

GILLIGAN, JAMES, *Violence: Reflections on a National Epidemic* (Vintage, New York, 1996)

GILMAN, CHARLOTTE PERKINS, 'Dr. Weininger's "Sex and Character"', in *The Critic*, vol. XLVIII, no. 5 (May, 1906), 387–417

GILMAN, SANDER L., *Difference and Pathology: Stereotypes of Sexuality, Race, and Madness* (Cornell University Press, Ithaca, NY, 1985)

—— *Jewish Self-Hatred: Anti-Semitism and the Hidden Language of the Jews* (Johns Hopkins University Press, Baltimore, Md., 1986)

—— *Disease and Representation: Images of Illness from Madness to AIDS* (Cornell University Press, Ithaca, NY, 1988)

—— *Freud, Race, and Gender* (Princeton University Press, Princeton, NJ, 1993)

GILMORE, DAVID D., *Manhood in the Making: Cultural Concepts of Masculinity* (Yale University Press, New Haven. Conn. 1990)

GOFFEN, RONA, *Titian's Women* (Yale University Press, New Haven, Conn., 1997)

GOLDIN, CLAUDIA, *Understanding the Gender Gap: An Economic History of American Women* (Oxford University Press, New York, 1990)

GOLDMAN, EMMA, *Anarchism and Other Essays* (ed. by Richard Drinnon, Dover, New York, 1969)

—— *The Traffic in Women and Other Essays on Feminism* (Times Change Press, New York, 1970)

GOLDSTEIN, ANNE B., 'Reasoning About Homosexuality: A Commentary on Janet Halley's "Reasoning About Sodomy: Act and Identity In and After *Bowers v. Hardwick*"', 79 *Va. L Rev.* 1781 (1993)

—— 'History, Homosexuality, and Political Values: Searching for the Hidden Determinants of *Bowers v. Hardwick*', 97 *Yale LJ* 1073 (1988)

GOSSETT, THOMAS F., *Race: The History of an Idea in America* (Schocken Books, New York, 1965)

GOULD, STEPHEN J., *The Mismeasure of Man* (W. W. Norton, New York, 1981)

GRABER, MARK A., *Transforming Free Speech: The Ambiguous Legacy of Civil Libertarianism* (University of California Press, Berkeley, Cal., 1991)

GRANT, JACQUELYN, *White Women's Christ and Black Women's Jesus: Feminist Christology and Womanist Response* (Scholars Press, Atlanta, Ga., 1989)

GRANT, MADISON, *The Passing of the Great Race or The Racial Basis of European History* (Charles Scribner's Sons, New York, 1919)

GREELEY, REVD. ANDREW, 'Blasphemy or Artistry?', *New York Times*, 14 August 1988, sec. 2–1

GREEN, PETER, *Classical Bearings: Interpreting Ancient History and Culture* (Thames and Hudson, New York, 1989)

GREEN, RICHARD, *Sexual Science and the Law* (Harvard University Press, Cambridge, Mass., 1992)

GREENAWALT, KENT, *Speech, Crime, and the Uses of Language* (Oxford University Press, New York, 1989)

—— *Fighting Words: Individuals, Communities, and Liberties of Speech* (Princeton University Press, Princeton, NJ, 1995)

GREENBERG, JACK, *Crusaders in the Courts: How a Dedicated Band of Lawyers Fought for the Civil Rights Revolution* (BasicBooks, New York, 1994)

GREENBERG, KENNETH S., *Masters and Statesman: The Political Culture of American Slavery* (The Johns Hopkins University Press, Baltimore, Md., 1985)

GREENFELD, LIAH, *Nationalism: Five Roads to Modernity* (Harvard University Press, Cambridge, Mass., 1992)

GREENSPAN, LOUIS, and LEVITT, CYRIL (eds.), *Under the Shadow of Weimar: Democracy, Law, and Racial Incitement in Six Countries* (Praeger, Westport, Conn., 1993)

GROSS, LARRY, *Contested Closets: The Politics and Ethics of Outing* (University of Minnesota Press, Minneapolis, Minn., 1993)

GUTMAN, HERBERT G., *The Black Family in Slavery and Freedom, 1750–1925* (Vintage Books, New York, 1976)

HAKSAR, VINIT, *Equality, Liberty, and Perfectionism* (Oxford University Press, Oxford, 1979)

HALLEY, JANET E., 'Reasoning About Sodomy: Act and Identity In and After *Bowers v. Hardwick*', 79 *Va. L Rev.* 1721 (1993)

—— 'Sexual Orientation and the Politics of Biology: A Critique of the Argument from Immutability', 46 *Stan. L Rev.* 503 (1994)

HALPERIN, DAVID M., *One Hundred Years of Homosexuality: And Other Essays on Greek Love* (Routledge, New York, 1990)

—— WINKLER, JOHN J., and ZEITLIN, FROMA I. (eds.), *Before Sexuality: The Construction of Erotic Experience in the Ancient Greek World* (Princeton University Press, Princeton, NJ, 1990)

HAMANN, BRIGITTE, *Hitler's Vienna: a Dictatorship's Apprenticeship* (trans. Thomas Thornton, Oxford University Press, New York, 1999)

HAMER, DEAN H., HU, STELLA, MAGNUSON, VICTORIA, HU, NAN, and PATTATUCCI, ANGELA M. L., 'A Linkage between DNA Markers on the X Chromosome and Male Sexual Orientation', *Science*, 16 July 1993

HAMILTON, EDITH, and CAIRNS, HUNTINGTON (eds.), *The Collected Dialogues of Plato* (Pantheon, New York, 1961)

HARROWITZ, NANCY A. and HYAMS, BARBARA (eds.), *Jews and Gender: Responses to Otto Weininger* (Temple University Press, Philadelphia, Pa., 1996)

HEINRICHS, TERRY, 'Censorship as Free Speech! Free Expression Values and the Logic of Silencing in R. v. Keegstra', 36 *Alberta L Rev.* 835 (1998)

HENKIN, LOUIS, 'US Ratification of the Human Rights Conventions: The Ghost of Senator Bricker', 89 *AJIL* 341 (1995)

HENRY, SHERRYE, *The Deep Divide: Why American Women Resist Equality* (Macmillan, New York, 1994)

HERF, JEFFREY, *Divided Memory: The Nazi Past in the Two Germanys* (Harvard University Press, Cambridge, Mass., 1997)

HERMAN, DIDI, *The Anti-gay Agenda: Orthodox Vision and the Christian Right* (University of Chicago Press, Chicago, Ill., 1997)

HERTZBERG, ARTHUR, *The French Enlightenment and the Jews* (Columbia University Press, New York, 1990)

HILBERG, RAUL, *The Destruction of the European Jews* (Holmes & Meier, New York, 1985), 3 vols

HIRSCH, MARIANNE, and KELLER, EVELYN FOX, *Conflicts in Feminism* (Routledge, New York, 1990)

HODGE, WILLIAM C., 'Incitement to Racial Hatred in New Zealand' (1981) 30 *Int'l & Comparative Law Quarterly* 918

HOLE, JUDITH, and LEVINE, ELLEN, *Rebirth of Feminism* (Quadrangle, New York, 1971)

HOLMES, OLIVER WENDELL, 'The Path of the Law', 10 *Harv. L Rev.* 457 (1897)

HONORÉ, TONY, *Sex Law* (Duckworth, London, 1978)

HOOKS, BELL, *Ain't I a Woman: Black Women and Feminism* (South End Press, Boston, Mass., 1981)

—— *Feminist Theory: From Margin to Center* (South End Press, Boston, Mass., 1984)

HUGGINS, NATHAN (ed.), *W. E. B. Du Bois* (1896, Library of America, New York, 1986)

HUME, DAVID, *Essays Moral Political and Literary* (Liberty Classics, Indianapolis, Ind., 1987)

HUMEZ, JEAN M., *Mother's First-Born Daughters: Early Shaker Writings on Women and Religion* (Indiana University Press, Bloomington, Ind., 1993)

HUNTER, NAN D., 'Life After *Hardwick*', 27 *Harv. Civ Rts.–Civ. Lib. L Rev.* 531 (1992)

HUTCHESON, FRANCIS, *A System of Moral Philosophy* (1755, Augustus M. Kelley, New York, 1968)

HUTCHINSON, GEORGE, *The Harlem Renaissance in Black and White* (Harvard University Press, Cambridge, Mass., 1995)

IGNATIEV, NOEL, *How the Irish Became White* (Routledge, New York, 1995)

JACOBS, HARRIET A., *Incidents in the Life of a Slave Girl Written by Herself* (ed. Jean Fagan Yellin, Harvard University Press, Cambridge, Mass., 1987)

JACOBSON, MATTHEW FRYE, *Whiteness of a Different Color: European Immigrants and the Alchemy of Race* (Harvard University Press, Cambridge, Mass., 1998)

JAMES, HENRY, *Collected Travel Writings: Great Britain and America* (Library of America, New York, 1993)

JANIS, MARK W., and KAY, RICHARD S., *European Human Rights Law* (University of Connecticut Law School Foundation Press, Hartford, Conn., 1990)

JEFFERSON, THOMAS, *Notes on the State of Virginia* (ed. William Peden, University of North Carolina Press, Chapel Hill, NC, 1955)

JOHANNSEN, ROBERT W. (ed.), *The Lincoln–Douglas Debates* (Oxford University Press, New York, 1965)

JONES, THOMAS DAVID, *Human Rights: Group Defamation, Freedom of Expression and the Law of Nations* (Martinus Nijhoff Publishers, The Hague, 1998)

JORDAN, MARK D., *The Invention of Sodomy in Christian Theology* (University of Chicago Press, Chicago, Ill., 1997)

JUNKER, DETLEF, BOEMEKE, MANFRED F., and MICUNEK, JANINE (eds.), *Cornerstone of Democracy: The West German Grundgesetz, 1949–1989* (German Historical Institute, Washington, DC, 1995)

KALVEN, JR., HARRY, *The Negro and the First Amendment* (University of Chicago Press: Chicago, Ill., 1965)

—— *A Worthy Tradition: Freedom of Speech in America* (Harper & Row, New York, 1988)

KARST, KENNETH I., 'Equality as a Central Principle of the First Amendment', 43 *U. Chi. L Rev.* 20 (1975)

KATZ, JACOB, *From Destruction to Destruction: Anti-Semitism, 1700–1933* (Harvard University Press, Cambridge, Mass., 1980)

KAZANTZAKIS, NIKOS, *The Last Temptation of Christ* (trans. P. A. Bien, Simon & Schuster, New York, 1988)

KERN, LOUIS J., *An Ordered Love: Sex Roles and Sexuality in Victorian Utopias—the Shakers, the Mormons, and the Oneida Community* (University of North Carolina Press, Chapel Hill, NC, 1981)

KERSHAW, IAN, *Hitler 1889–1936: Hubris* (W. W. Norton, New York, 1998)

KIMMEL, MICHAEL, *Manhood in America: A Cultural History* (Free Press, New York, 1996)

KIRKUP, JAMES, 'The Love that Dares to Speak Its Name', *Gay News*, June 1976, at 26

KLINEBERG, OTTO, *Race Differences* (Harper & Brothers, New York, 1935)

KOMMERS, DONALD P., *The Constitutional Jurisprudence of the Federal Republic of Germany* (2nd edn., Duke University Press, Durham, NC, 1997)

KOPPELMAN, ANDREW, 'The Miscegenation Analogy: Sodomy Laws as Sex Discrimination', 98 *Yale LJ* 145 (1988)

—— *Anti-discrimination Law and Social Equality* (Yale University Press, New Haven, Conn., 1996)

KRAFFT-EBING, RICHARD VON, *Psychopathia Sexualis* (first published in German, 1886) (trans. Franklin S. Klaf, Bell Publishing Co., New York, 1965)

KRETZMER, DAVID, 'Free Speech and Racism', 8 *Cardozo L Rev.* 445 (1987)

—— 'Racial Incitement in Israel' (1992) 22, *Israel Yearbook on Human Rights* 243–59

KYMLICKA, WILL, *Liberalism, Community, and Culture* (Clarendon Press, Oxford, 1989)

LAFRANCHI, HOWARD, 'In Conservative Chile, What You See Isn't What you Get', *The Christian Science Monitor*, 29 November 1996, International Section, 7

LANGMUIR, GAVIN I., *History, Religion, and Anti-semitism* (University of California Press, Berkeley and Los Angeles, Cal., 1990)

LAQUEUR, THOMAS, *Making Sex: Body and Gender from the Greeks to Freud* (Harvard University Press, Cambridge, Mass., 1990)

LASSON, KENNETH, 'Racism in Great Britain: Drawing the Line on Free Speech', 7 *Boston College Third World LJ* 161 (1987)

LAW, SYLVIA A., 'Homosexuality and the Social Meaning of Gender', [1988] *Wisc. L Rev.* 187

LAYCOCK, DOUGLAS, 'Free Exercise and the Religious Freedom Restoration Act', 62 *Ford. L Rev.* 883 (1994)

LEDERMAN, ELIEZER, and TABORY, MALA, 'Criminalization of Racial Incitement in Israel', 24 *Stanford J of International Law* 55 (1988)

LEEMING, DAVID, *James Baldwin* (Knopf, New York, 1994)

Legal Instruments to Combat Racism and Xenophobia (Commission of the European Communities, Brussels, 1992)

LERNER, MICHAEL, *The Socialism of Fools: Anti-Semitism on the Left* (Tikkun Books, Oakland, Cal., 1992)

LERNER, NATAN, *The U.N. Convention on the Elimination of all Forms of Racial Discrimination* (Sijthoff & Noordhoff International Publishers, Alphen aan den Rijn, 1980)

—— *Group Rights and Discrimination in International Law* (Martinus Nijhoff Publishers, Dordrecht, 1991)

LESTER, ANTHONY, and BINDMAN, GEOFFREY, *Race and Law in Great Britain* (Harvard University Press, Cambridge, Mass., 1972)

LeVAY, SIMON, 'A Difference in Hypothalamic Structure Between Heterosexual and Homosexual Men', *Science*, 30 August 1991

LEVUSH, RUTH, Coordinator, *Campaign Financing of National Elections in Foreign Countries* (Law Library of Congress, Washington, DC, April 1991)

LEVY, LEONARD W., *Jefferson and Civil Liberties: The Darker Side* (Quadrangle, New York, 1973)

—— *Treason Against God: A History of the Offense of Blasphemy* (Schocken Books, New York, 1981)

—— *Blasphemy: Verbal Offense Against the Sacred, From Moses to Salman Rushdie* (Alfred A. Knopf, New York, 1993)

LEWES, KENNETH, *The Psychoanalytic Theory of Male Homosexuality* (Simon and Schuster, New York, 1988)

LEWIS, ANTHONY, *Make No Law: The Sullivan Case and the First Amendment* (Random House, New York, 1991)

LEWIS, DAVID LEVERING, *W. E. B. Du Bois: Biography of a Race, 1868–1919* (Henry Holt, New York, 1993)

LINDQVIST, SVEN, *'Exterminate All the Brutes'* (trans. Joan Tate, The New Press, New York, 1996)

LIPSTADT, DEBORAH, *Denying the Holocaust: The Growing Assault on Truth and Memory* (Plume, New York, 1994)

LOFGREN, CHARLES A., *The Plessy Case* (Oxford University Press, New York, 1987)

'London Cool to "Temptation"', *New York Times*, 10 September 1988, sec. 1–16

LOPEZ, IAN F. HANEY, *White By Law: The Legal Construction of Race* (New York University Press, New York, 1996)

LORCA, FEDERICO GARCIA, *Poet in New York* (trans. Greg Simon and Steven White, Noonday Press, New York, 1998)

LOUX, ANDREA, 'Idols and Icons: Catharine MacKinnon and Freedom of Expression in North America', 6 *Feminist Legal Studies* 85 (1998)

LURYI, YURI, and LYUBECHANSKY, ALEXANDER, 'Soviet/Russian Legislation Against National or Racial Hatred and Discrimination', *Review of Central and East European Law*, vol. 20, no. 2, 217–31 (1994)

LYOTARD, JEAN-FRANÇOIS, *Heidegger and 'the Jews'* (trans. Andreas Michel and Mark Roberts, University of Minnesota Press, Minneapolis, Minn., 1990)

McGLEN, NANCY E., and O'CONNOR, KAREN, *Women's Rights: The Struggle for Equality in the Nineteenth and Twentieth Centuries* (Praeger, New York, 1983)

MacKinnon, Catharine A., *Sexual Harassment of Working Women* (Yale University Press, New Haven, Conn., 1979)

—— *Feminism Unmodified: Discourses on Life and Law* (Harvard University Press, Cambridge, Mass., 1987)

—— *Toward a Feminist Theory of the State* (Harvard University Press, Cambridge, Mass., 1989)

—— *Only Words* (Harvard University Press, Cambridge, Mass., 1993)

McNally, Terrence, *Corpus Christi* (Grove Press, New York, 1998)

McNeil, Genna Rae, *Groundwork: Charles Hamilton Houston and the Struggle for Civil Rights* (University of Pennsylvania Press, Philadelphia, Penn., 1983)

Mansbridge, Jane J., *Why We Lost the ERA* (University of Chicago Press, Chicago, Ill., 1986)

Markesinis, Basil S. (ed.), *Law Making, Law Finding and Law Shaping: The Diverse Influences*, The Clifford Chance Lectures Volume 2 (Oxford University Press, Oxford, 1997)

Massey, Calvin R., 'Hate Speech, Cultural Diversity, and the Foundational Paradigms of Free Expression', 40 *UCLA L Rev.* 103 (1992)

Massey, Douglas S., and Denton, Nancy A., *American Apartheid: Segregation and the Making of the Underclass* (Harvard University Press, Cambridge, Mass., 1993)

Mathews, Donald G., and Sherron De Hart, Jane, *Sex, Gender, and the Politics of ERA: A State and the Nation* (Oxford University Press, New York, 1990)

Matsuda, Mari J., Lawrence, Charles R. III, Delgado, Richard, and Williams Crenshaw, Kimberlè, *Words That Wound: Critical Race Theory, Assaultive Speech, and the First Amendment* (Westview Press, Boulder, Colo., 1993)

Matthews, Glenna, *'Just a Housewife' The Rise and Fall of Domesticity in America* (Oxford University Press, New York, 1987)

May, Elaine Tyler, *Barren in the Promised Land: Childless Americans and the Pursuit of Happiness* (BasicBooks, New York, 1995)

Mazower, Mark, *Dark Continent: Europe's Twentieth Century* (Knopf, New York, 1999)

Meiklejohn, Alexander, *Political Freedom* (Oxford University Press, New York, 1965)

Meron, Theodor, 'The Meaning and Reach of the International Convention on the Elimination of All Forms of Racial Discrimination', 79 *American J of Int'l Law* 283 (1985)

Michaelis, Meir, *Mussolini and the Jews: German–Italian relations and the Jewish Question in Italy, 1922–1945* (Clarendon Press, Oxford, 1978)

Michelman, Frank I., 'Conceptions of Democracy in American Constitutional Argument: The Case of Pornography Regulation', 56 *Tenn. L Rev.* 291 (1989)

Mill, John Stuart, *On Liberty* (ed. Alburey Castell, Appleton-Century-Crofts, New York, 1947)

—— *Utilitarianism* (ed. Oskar Piest, Library of Liberal Arts, Indianapolis, Ind., 1957)

Miller, Stuart, 'Lady Birdwood's Failing Memory Brings Early End to Racism Trial', *Guardian*, 20 January 1998, 6

Millett, Kate, *Sexual Politics* (Avon, New York, 1969)

Moeller, Robert G. (ed.), *West Germany under Construction: Politics, Society, and Culture in the Adenauer Era* (University of Michigan Press, Ann Arbor, Mich., 1997)

Money, John, *Gay, Straight, and In-Between: The Sexology of Erotic Orientation* (Oxford University Press, New York, 1988)

—— and Ehrhardt, Anke A., *Man & Woman, Boy & Girl* (Johns Hopkins University Press, Baltimore, Md., 1972)

—— Hampson, J. G., and Hampson, J. L., 'An Evidence of Some Basic Sexual Concepts: The Evidence of Human Hermaphroditism', 97 *Bull. Johns Hopkins Hosp.* 301 (1955)

MONK, RAY, *Ludwig Wittgenstein: The Duty of Genius* (Free Press, New York, 1990)

MORRISON, TONI, *Playing in the Dark: Whiteness and the Literary Imagination* (Vintage Books New York, 1993)

MOSSE, GEORGE L., *Nationalism and Sexuality: Middle-Class Morality and Sexual Norms in Modern Europe* (University of Wisconsin Press, Madison, Wis., 1985)

—— *The Image of Man: The Creation of Modern Masculinity* (Oxford University Press, New York, 1996)

MURPHY, TIMOTHY F., *Gay Science: The Ethics of Sexual Orientation Research* (Columbia University Press, New York, 1997)

MYRDAL, GUNNAR, *An American Dilemma: The Negro Problem and Modern Democracy*, 2 vols. (1944, Pantheon Books, New York, 1972)

NEISSER, ERIC, 'Hate Speech in the New South Africa: Constitutional Considerations for a Land Recovering from Decades of Racial Repression', 3 *DCLJ of Int'l L & Prac.* 335 (1994)

NETANYAHU, B., *The Origins of the Inquisition in Fifteenth Century Spain* (Random House, New York, 1995)

NOTE, 'Jones v. Mayer: The Thirteenth Amendment and the Federal Anti-Discrimination Laws', 69 *Colum. L Rev.* 1019 (1969)

NOTE, 'The "New" Thirteenth Amendment: A Preliminary Analysis', 82 *Harv. L Rev.* 1294 (1969)

OKIN, SUSAN MOLLER, *Justice, Gender, and the Family* (BasicBooks, New York, 1989)

OLSEN, FRANCES, 'Statutory Rape: A Feminist Critique of Rights Analysis', 63 *Tex. L Rev.* 387 (1984)

PAGDEN, ANTHONY, *The Fall of Natural Man: The American Indian and the Origins of Comparative Ethnology* (Cambridge University Press, Cambridge, 1982)

PAGELS, ELAINE, *The Origin of Satan* (Random House, New York, 1996)

PARKER, ANDREW, RUSSO, MARY, SOMMER, DORIS, and YAEGER, PATRICIA (eds)., *Nationalisms and Sexualities* (Routledge, New York, 1992)

PELLAUER, MARY D., *Toward a Tradition of Feminist Theology: The Religious Social Thought of Elizabeth Cady Stanton, Susan B. Anthony, and Anna Howard Shaw* (Carlson Publishing Inc., Brooklyn, NY, 1991)

PERCY III, WILLIAM ARMSTRONG, *Pederasty and Pedagogy in Archaic Greece* (University of Illinois Press, Urbana, Ill., 1996)

PERRY, MICHAEL J., 'Modern Equal Protection: A Conceptualization and Appraisal', 79 *Colum. L Rev.* 1023 (1979)

PEUKERT, DETLEV J., *The Weimar Republic: The Crisis of Classical Modernity* (trans. Richard Deveson, Hill and Wang, New York, 1987)

PHARR, SUZANNE, *Homophobia: A Weapon of Sexism* (Chardon Press, Inverness, Cal., 1988)

PIPES, DANIEL, *The Rushdie Affair: The Novel, the Ayatollah, and the West* (A Birch Lane Press Book, New York, 1990)

PLATO, *Gorgias* (trans. Walter Hamilton, Penguin, Harmondsworth, 1973)

POLIAKOV, LEON, *The Aryan Myth: A History of Racist and Nationalist Ideas in Europe* (trans. Edmund Howard, Sussex University Press, London, 1971)

—— *The History of Anti-Semitism* (trans. Miriam Kochan, Vanguard Press, New York, 1975), iii

POST, ROBERT C., 'Cultural Heterogeneity and Law: Pornography, Blasphemy, and the First Amendment', 76 *Calif. L Rev.* 297 (1988)

—— 'Free Speech and Religious, Racial, and Sexual Harassment: Racist Speech, Democracy, and the First Amendment', 32 *Wm. and Mary L Rev.* 267 (1991)

—— (ed.), *Censorship and Silencing: Practices of Cultural Regulation* (The Getty Research Institute, Los Angeles, Cal., 1998)

PRICE, KENNETH M., *Whitman and Tradition: The Poet in His Century* (Yale University Press, New Haven, Conn., 1990)

PROCTER-SMITH, MARJORIE, *Women in Shaker Community and Worship: A Feminist Analysis of the Uses of Religious Symbolism* (Edwin Mellen Press, Lewiston, NY, 1985)

PULZER, PETER, *The Rise of Political Anti-Semitism in Germany and Austria* (Harvard University Press, Cambridge, Mass., 1988)

QUINT, PETER E., 'Free Speech and Private Law in German Constitutional Theory', 48 *Md. L Rev.* 247 (1989)

—— *The Imperfect Union: Constitutional Structures of German Unification* (Princeton University Press, Princeton, NJ, 1997)

QUISTGAARD, BETTINA, 'Pornography, Harm, and Censorship: A Feminist (Re)vision of the Right to Freedom of Expression', 52 *U of Toronto Faculty of Law Review* 132 (1993)

RABBAN, DAVID M., *Free Speech in Its Forgotten Years* (Cambridge University Press, Cambridge, 1997)

RAWLS, JOHN, *A Theory of Justice* (Harvard University Press, Cambridge, Mass., 1971)

—— 'The Basic Liberties and Their Priority', *The Tanner Lectures on Human Values* (ed. S. McMurrin, Cambridge University Press, Cambridge, 1981), iii, 3–87

RAZ, JOSEPH, *The Morality of Freedom* (Clarendon Press, Oxford, 1986)

RECHETOV, YURI, 'Incitement of National Enmity in the Context of International Law, Foreign and Soviet Practice' (1992) 22 *Israel Yearbook on Human Rights* 155–68

REDISH, MARTIN H., 'Self-Realization, Democracy, and Freedom of Expression: A Reply to Professor Baker', 130 *U Pa. L Rev.* 678 (1982)

—— 'The Value of Free Speech.', 130 *U Pa. L Rev.* 591 (1982)

REED, JR., ADOLPH L., *W. E. B. Du Bois and American Political Thought: Fabianism and the Color Line* (Oxford University Press, New York, 1997)

REITZ, JEFFREY G., 'Less Racial Discrimination in Canada, or Simply Less Racial Conflict?: Implications of Comparisons with Britain', 14 *Canadian Public Policy* 424 (1988)

REYNOLDS, DAVID, *Walt Whitman's America* (Knopf, New York, 1995)

RICHARDS, DAVID A. J., *A Theory of Reasons for Action* (Clarendon Press, Oxford, 1971)

—— 'Free Speech and Obscenity Law: Toward a Moral Theory of the First Amendment', 123 *U Penn. L Rev.* 45 (1974)

—— 'Unnatural Acts and the Constitutional Right to Privacy: A Moral Theory', 45 *Ford. L Rev.* 1281 (1977)

—— 'Sexual Autonomy and the Constitutional Right to Privacy: A Case Study in Human Rights and the Unwritten Constitution', 30 *Hastings LJ* 957 (1979)

—— 'Commercial Sex and the Rights of the Person: A Moral Argument for the Decriminalization of Prostitution', 127 *U Penn. L Rev.* 1195 (1979)

—— *Sex, Drugs, Death, and the Law: An Essay on Human Rights and Overcriminalization* (Rowman and Littlefield, Totowa, NJ, 1982)

—— *Toleration and the Constitution* (Oxford University Press, New York, 1986)

—— 'Constitutional Legitimacy and Constitutional Privacy', 61 *NYU L Rev.* 800 (1986)

—— 'Kantian Ethics and the Harm Principle: A Reply to John Finnis', 87 *Colum. L Rev.* 547 (1987)

—— *Foundations of American Constitutionalism* (Oxford University Press, New York, 1989)

RICHARDS, DAVID A. J., *Conscience and the Constitution: History, Theory, and Law of the Reconstruction Amendments* (Princeton University Press, Princeton, NJ, 1993)

—— 'Perfectionist Moral Theory, the Criminal Law, and the Liberal State', 13 *Criminal Justice Ethics* 93 (1994)

—— 'Public Reason and Abolitionist Dissent', 69 *Chicago-Kent L Rev.* 787 (1994)

—— *Women, Gays, and the Constitution: The Grounds for Feminism and Gay Rights in Culture and Law* (University of Chicago Press, Chicago, Ill., 1998)

—— *Italian American: The Racializing of an Ethnic Identity* (New York University Press, New York, 1999)

—— *Identity and the Case for Gay Rights: Race, Gender, Religion as Analogies* (University of Chicago Press, Chicago, Ill., in press)

RICHARDSON, III, HENRY J., '"Failed States", Self-Determination, and Preventive Diplomacy: Colonialist Nostalgia and Democratic Expectations', 10 *Temp. Int'l Comp. LJ* 1 (1996)

RIESMAN, DAVID, 'Democracy and Defamation: Control of Group Libel', 42 *Colum. L Rev.* 727 (1942); 'Democracy and Defamation: Fair Game and Fair Comment I', 42 *Colum. L Rev.* 1085 (1942); 'Democracy and Defamation: Fair Game and Fair Comment II', 42 *Colum. L Rev.* 1282 (1942)

RILEY, PATRICK, *Kant's Political Philosophy* (Rowman & Littlefield, Totowa, NJ, 1983)

ROCKE, MICHAEL, *Forbidden Friendship: Homosexuality and Male Culture in Renaissance Florence* (Oxford University Press, New York, 1996)

ROEDIGER, DAVID R., *The Wages of Whiteness: Race and the Making of the American Working Class* (Verso, New York, 1991)

ROSE, KENNETH D., *American Women and the Repeal of Prohibition* (New York University Press, New York, 1996)

ROSENBERG, ROSALIND, *Beyond Separate Spheres: Intellectual Roots of Modern Feminism* (Yale University Press, New Haven, Conn., 1982)

ROTELLO, GABRIEL, *Sexual Ecology: AIDS and the Destiny of Gay Men* (Dutton, New York, 1997)

ROTH, STEPHEN J., 'Curbing Racial Incitement in Britain: Four Times Tried—Still Without Success' (1992) 22 *Israel Yearbook on Human Rights* 193–228

RUDDICK, SARA, *Maternal Thinking: Towards a Politics of Peace* (Beacon Press, Boston, Mass., 1989)

RUGGIERO, GUIDO, *The Boundaries of Eros: Sex Crime and Sexuality in Renaissance Venice* (Oxford University Press, New York, 1985)

RUSE, MICHAEL, *Homosexuality* (Basil Blackwell, Oxford, 1988)

RUSHDIE, SALMAN, *Satanic Verses* (Henry Holt and Company, New York, 1988)

SACERDOTI, GIORGIO, 'Italian Legislation and Case Law on Racial and Religious Hatred and Group Libel: International Aspects' (1992) 22 *Israel Yearbook on Human Rights* 229–42

SADURSKI, WOJCIECH, 'On "Seeing Speech Through an Equality Lens": A Critique of Egalitarian Arguments for Suppression of Hate Speech and Pornography' (1996) 16 *Oxford Journal of Legal Studies* 713–23

SAJO, ANDRAS, 'Hate Speech for Hostile Hungarians', *East European Constitutional Law*, vol. 3, no. 2, spring 1994, at 82–7

SANGER, MARGARET, *Woman and the New Race* (first published, 1920) (Maxwell Reprint Company, Elmsford, NY, 1969)

SANTAYANA, GEORGE, *Three Philosophical Poets: Lucretius, Dante, and Goethe* (Harvard University Press, Cambridge. Mass., 1947)

SCAMMELL, MICHAEL, 'Film; Why Not Let the Show Go On, Then Rebut It?', *New York Times*, 20 September 1998, sec. 2–27

SCHMITT, CARL, *The Concept of the Political* (trans. George Schwab Rutgers University Press, New Brunswick, NJ, 1976)

—— *Political Theology* (trans. George Schwab, Harvard University Press, Cambridge, Mass., 1985)

—— *The Crisis of Parliamentary Democracy* (trans. Ellen Kennedy, MIT Press, Cambridge, Mass., 1985)

—— *Political Romanticism* (trans. Guy Oakes, The MIT Press, Cambridge, Mass., 1986)

SCHOPENHAUER, ARTHUR, *Essays and Aphorisms* (trans. R. J. Hollindale, Penguin, Harmondsworth, 1970)

SCHULHOFER, STEPHEN J. *Unwanted Sex: The Culture of Intimidation and the Failure of Law* (Harvard University Press, Cambridge, Mass., 1998)

SCHWEITZER, CARL-CHRISTOPH, KARSTEN, DETLEV, SPENCER, ROBERT, COLE, R. TAYLOR, KOMMERS, DONALD, and NICHOLLS, ANTHONY, *Politics and Government in Germany, 1944–1994* (Berghahn Books, Providence, RI, 1995)

SELIGMAN, EDWIN R. A. (ed.), *Encyclopaedia of the Social Sciences* (Macmillan, New York, 1937), vii

SEN, AMARTYA, and WILLIAMS, BERNARD (eds.), *Utilitarianism and Beyond* (Cambridge University Press, Cambridge, 1982)

SERED, SUSAN STARR, *Priestess, Mother, Sacred Sister: Religions Dominated by Women* (Oxford University Press, New York, 1994)

SHAW, BRENT D., 'A Groom of One's Own?', *New Republic*, 18 and 25 July 1994, at 33–41

SHERMAN, JEFFREY G., 'Love Speech: The Social Utility of Pornography', 47 *Stan. L Rev.* 661 (1995)

SHIFFRIN, STEVEN H., *The First Amendment, Democracy, and Romance* (Harvard University Press, Cambridge, Mass., 1990)

SHOWALTER, ELAINE, *Sexual Anarchy: Gender and Culture in the Fin De Siecle* (St. Martin's Press, New York, 1993)

SLOSS, DAVID, 'The Domestication of International Human Rights: Non-Self-Executing Declarations and Human Rights Treaties', 24 *Yale J. Int'l L* 129 (1999)

SMITH, DENIS MACK, *Mussolini* (Vintage, New York, 1983)

SMITH, JEFFERY A., *Printers and Press Freedom: The Ideology of Early American Journalism* (Oxford University Press, New York, 1988)

SMITH, ROGERS M., *Civic Ideals: Conflicting Visions of Citizenship in U.S. History* (Yale University Press, New Haven, Conn., 1997)

SMITH-ROSENBERG, CARROLL, *Disorderly Conduct: Visions of Gender in Victorian America* (Knopf, New York, 1985)

SNITOW, ANNE, STANSELL CHRISTINE, and THOMPSON, SHARON (eds.), *Powers of Desire* (Monthly Review Press, New York, 1983)

SOLLORS, WERNER, *Beyond Ethnicity: Consent and Descent in American Culture* (Oxford University Press, New York, 1986)

SOUTHERN, DAVID W., *Gunnar Myrdal and Black–White Relations: The Use and Abuse of an American Dilemma, 1944–1969* (Louisiana State University Press, Baton Rouge, La., 1987)

STAMPP, KENNETH M., *The Peculiar Institution* (Vintage, New York, 1956)

STANTON, WILLIAM, *The Leopard's Spots: Scientific Attitudes toward Race in America, 1815–59* (University of Chicago Press, Chicago, Ill., 1960)

STEAKLEY, JAMES D., *The Homosexual Emancipation Movement in Germany* (Arno Press, New York, 1975)

STEIN, ERIC, 'History Against Free Speech: The New German Law Against the "Auschwitz"— and Other—"Lies" ', 85 *Mich. L Rev.* 277 (1986)

STEIN, STEPHEN J., *The Shaker Experience in America* (Yale University Press, New Haven, Conn., 1992)

STEINBERG, JONATHAN, *All or Nothing The Axis and the Holocaust, 1941–1943* (Routledge, London, 1990)

STEINBERG, LEO, *The Sexuality of Christ in Renaissance Art and in Modern Oblivion* (University of Chicago Press, Chicago, Ill., 1996)

STIMPSON, CATHARINE R., and PERSON, ETHEL SPECTOR, *Women: Sex and Sexuality* (University of Chicago Press, Chicago, Ill., 1980)

STOCKING, JR., GEORGE W., *Race, Culture, and Evolution: Essays in the History of Anthropology* (The Free Press, New York, 1968)

——(ed.), *A Franz Boas Reader: The Shaping of American Anthropology, 1883–1911* (University of Chicago Press, Chicago, Ill., 1974)

STRACHEY, JAMES (ed.), *Standard Edition of the Complete Psychological Works of Sigmund Freud* (Hogarth Press, London, 1959–64), ix, xxi, xxiii

STRAUSS, DAVID A., 'Persuasion, Autonomy, and Freedom of Expression', 91 *Colum. L Rev.* 334 (1991)

—— 'Corruption, Equality, and Campaign Finance Reform', 94 *Colum. L Rev.* 1370 (1994)

STROSSEN, NADINE, *Defending Pornography: Free Speech, Sex, and the Fight for Women's Rights* (Scribner, New York, 1995)

SULLIVAN, ANDREW, *Virtually Normal: An Argument About Homosexuality* (Knopf, New York, 1995)

SULLIVAN, KATHLEEN M., 'Political Money and Freedom of Speech', 30 *UC Davis L Rev.* 663 (1997)

SUNDQUIST, ERIC J., *To Wake the Nations: Race in the Making of American Literature* (Harvard University Press, Belknap Press, Cambridge, Mass., 1993)

SUNSTEIN, CASS R., *Democracy and the Problem of Free Speech* (Free Press, New York:, 1993)

TABORY, MALA, 'Legislation against Incitement to Racism in Israel' (1987) 17 *Israel Yearbook on Human Rights* 270–99

—— and ZVI, M., 'Racial Prejudice and Incitement to Hatred Against Jews in the USSR: Legal and Political Aspects' (1992) 22 *Israel Yearbook on Human Rights* 169–91

TAHZIB, BAHIYYIH G., *Freedom of Religion or Belief: Ensuring Effective International Legal Protection* (Martinus Nijhoff Publishers, The Hague, 1996)

TAL, URIEL, *Christians and Jews in Germany* (trans. Noah Jonathan Jacobs, Cornell University Press, Ithaca, NY, 1975)

TAMIR, YAEL, *Liberal Nationalism* (Princeton University Press, Princeton, NJ, 1993)

TAVRIS, CAROL, *The Mismeasure of Woman* (Simon & Schuster, New York, 1992)

TEN, C. L., *Mill on Liberty* (Clarendon Press, Oxford, 1980)

TENBROEK, JACOBUS, 'Thirteenth Amendment to the Constitution of the United States: Consummation to Abolition and Key to the Fourteenth Amendment', 39 *Calif. L Rev.* 171 (1951)

—— *Equal under Law* (Collier, New York, 1969)

THOMAS, KENDALL, 'The Eclipse of Reason: A Rhetorical Reading of *Bowers v. Hardwick*', 79 *Va. L Rev.* 1805 (1993)

TORGOVNICK, MARIANNA DE MARCO, *Crossing Ocean Parkway* (University of Chicago Press, Chicago, Ill., 1996)

TREXLER, RICHARD C., *Sex and Conquest: Gendered Violence, Political Order, and the European Conquest of the Americas* (Cornell University Press, Ithaca, NY, 1995)

TRIPP, C. A., *The Homosexual Matrix* (McGraw-Hill, New York, 1975)

TROUBRIDGE, UNA, LADY, *The Life and Death of Radclyffe Hall* (Hammond, London, 1961)

TRUMBACH, RANDOLPH, 'The Original and Development of the Modern Lesbian Role in the Western Gender System: Northwestern Europe and the United States, 1750–1990' (1994) 20 *Historical Reflections* 288–320

—— *Sex and the Gender Revolution: Volume One Heterosexuality and the Third Gender in Enlightenment London* (University of Chicago Press, Chicago, Ill., 1998)

TUSHNET, MARK V., *The NAACP's Legal Strategy against Segregated Education, 1925–1950* (University of North Carolina Press, Chapel Hill, NC, 1967)

—— *Making Civil Rights Law: Thurgood Marshall and the Supreme Court, 1956–1961* (Oxford University Press, New York, 1994)

—— 'The Possibilities of Comparative Constitutional Law', 108 *Yale LJ* 1225 (1999)

TUSSMAN, JOSEPH, and TENBROEK, JACOBUS, 'The Equal Protection of the Laws', 37 *Calif. L Rev.* 341 (1949)

US DEPARTMENT of STATE, Chile Country Report on Human Rights Practices for 1996, Department of State Human Rights Country Reports (Government Printing Office, Washington, DC, February 1997), at 9–11

VANCE, CAROLE S. (ed.), *Pleasure and Danger: Exploring Female Sexuality* (Routledge & Kegan Paul, Boston, Mass., 1984)

VAUGHAN, ALDEN T., *Roots of American Racism: Essays on the Colonial Experience* (Oxford University Press, New York, 1995)

VLASTOS, GREGORY, *Platonic Studies* (Princeton University Press, Princeton, NJ, 1973)

WALTERS, RONALD G., *The Anti-slavery Appeal: American Abolitionism after 1830* (W. W. Norton, New York, 1978)

WASHINGTON, JAMES MELVIN (ed.), *A Testament of Hope: The Essential Writings of Martin Luther King, Jr.* (1963, Harper & Row, New York, 1986)

WEEKS, JEFFREY, *Sex, Politics, and Society: The Regulation of Sexuality since 1800* (2nd edn., Longman, London, 1989)

—— *Coming Out: Homosexual Politics in Britain from the Nineteenth Century to the Present* (rev. edn., Quartet Books, London, 1990)

WEININGER, OTTO, *Sex and Character* (William Heinemann, London, 1907)

WEISBERG, RICHARD, *Vichy Law and the Holocaust in France* (New York University Press, New York, 1996)

WELD, THEODORE, *American Slavery as It Is* (1839, Arno Press and The New York Times, New York, 1968)

WEST, DONALD J., *Homosexuality* (Aldine, Chicago, Ill., 1968)

WHARTON, EDITH, *The Uncollected Critical Writings* (ed. Frederick Wegener, Princeton University Press, Princeton, NJ, 1996)

WILLIAMS, WALTER L., *The Spirit and the Flesh: Sexual Diversity in American Indian Culture* (Beacon Press, Boston, Mass., 1986)

WINTEMUTE, ROBERT, *Sexual Orientation and Human Rights: The United States Constitution, the European Convention, and The Canadian Charter* (Clarendon Press, Oxford, 1995)

WITHERSPOON, JOHN, *Lectures of Moral Philosophy* (ed. Jack Scott, Associated University Presses, East Brunswick, NJ, 1982)

WOLFE, ALAN, *One Nation, After All* (Viking, New York, 1998)

WOLFFE, W. J., 'Values in Conflict: Incitement to Racial Hatred and the Public Order Act 1986' [1987] *Public Law* 85

WOLIN, RICHARD, *The Politics of Being: The Political Thought of Martin Heidegger* (Columbia University Press, New York, 1990)

WOLLSTONECRAFT, MARY, *A Vindication of the Rights of Woman*, in *The Works of Mary Wollstonecraft* (ed. Janet Todd and Marilyn Butler, 1790, New York University Press, New York, 1989), v, 65–266

WOOLF, VIRGINIA, *A Room of One's Own* (Harcourt, Brace, New York, 1929)

WRIGHT, J. SKELLY, 'Politics and the Constitution: Is Money Speech?', 85 *Yale LJ* 1001 (1976)

—— 'Money and the Pollution of Politics: Is the First Amendment an Obstacle to Political Equality?', 82 *Colum. L Rev.* 609 (1982)

WRIGHT, RICHARD, *Black Boy* (Perennial Classics, New York, 1998)

YOUNG-BRUEHL, ELISABETH, *The Anatomy of Prejudices* (Harvard University Press, Cambridge, Mass., 1996)

ZUCCOTTI, SUSAN, *The Italians and the Holocaust: Persecution, Rescue, Survival* (Basic Books, New York, 1987)

Index

abortion:
    moral arguments for prohibition 86–7
Addams, Jane 68
Adenauer, Konrad:
    and anti-Semitism 158
Americanization:
    and cultural racism 137–8
anti-discrimination laws 147–8
anti-miscegenation laws:
    and racism 56
    struggle against 87–8
anti-Semitism 53–4

Baker, C. Edwin 21
Baker, Ella 64–5
Baldwin, James:
    and homophobia 117
    on racism 57–8
Beattie, James:
    on race 49–50
Beecher, Catherine 67
Benedict, Ruth 63
    on race 52
Blackstone, William:
    on homosexuality 219
blasphemy laws 209–28
Boas, Franz:
    on race 51, 53–4
Brennan, Justice:
    opinion in *Frontiero* v. *Richardson* 71
Britain:
    public order law 171–5

Canada:
    group libel 167–71
    obscenity laws 199–201
Carmichael, Stokely:
    sexism 66
Chamberlain, Houston:
    racist theory 53
Chauncey, George:
    on homosexuality 222–3
Clay, Lucius D.:
    on anti-Semitism 157
comparative public law 229–54
    promise of 248–54
contraception:
    right to 81
Convention on the Elimination of all Forms of
    Racial Discrimination 176–80
Cooper, Anna 65

Debs, Eugene 16, 27
Douglas, Stephen:
    on popular sovereignty 131
Douglass, Frederick:
    on Irish immigrants 139–40
    on slavery 48
Du Bois, W. E. B. 70
    on racism 43–4, 48, 51, 57
Ely, John Hart:
    on democracy 18
Equal Employment Opportunities Commission
    68
European Court of Human Rights 165–6
    and group identity 165–6
Evans, Sara:
    on sexism 64

feminism:
    second wave 60–1
Ficino, Marsilio:
    on homophobia 115–16
Finnis, John:
    on moral evils 18
Firestone, Shulamith 67
France:
    Holocaust denial 161–5
free speech:
    abolitionist understanding 132
    American judicially enforceable principles 2
    and anti-discrimination principles 7–8
    Canada 2–3
    'clear and present danger test' 144–5
    comparative constitutionalism 12–13
    and constitutional theory 13–14
    defensible principles 6
    and democracy 6–7
    European Convention on Human Rights 3
    Germany 3
    group libel and related laws 10–11
    and harm 143–4
    hate speech 5
    and Hitler's Germany 11–12
    and human rights guarantees 8–9
    interpretive history 1
    judicial review 1
    normative priority 14–15
    political theory 1
    and powers of government 7
    priority accorded 14
    and race discrimination 4–5
    South Africa 3–4

free speech (*cont.*):
  and structural injustice 9
  and US States 9–10
  written constitutions 1
Friedan, Betty:
  The Feminine Mystique 61–2, 63

Gay News 214–17
gay rights 38–9, 76–105
  anti-Semitism analogy 94
  case for 92–3, 110–11, 120–5
  and obscenity laws 187–9
  political opposition to 93
  and religion 95–6
  religious analogy 93–4
  and sexism 80–1
gender identity, *see* homophobia
Germany:
  anti-Semitism 150–60
  Basic Law 156
  constitutional theory 30–1, 32–3
  group libel 30–1, 157
  Holocaust denial 161–5
Ginsberg, Judge:
  on single-sex education 185–6
Goldman, Emma:
  on homosexuality 189–90
  and obscenity laws 186
Grant, Madison:
  racist theory 53
Greenawalt, Kent 21
Griffiths, Martha 67–8
Grimke sisters 64–5, 70
group libel:
  aim of laws 143
  constitutional objection to 148–9
  nature of laws 134–5

Hamilton, Alexander:
  on right to marriage 82
Hayden, Casey:
  on sexism 66
Heidegger, Martin:
  moral nihilism 154
Henry, Patrick:
  on right to marriage 82
Holocaust denial:
  France 161–5
  Germany 161–5
homophobia 76–105, 181–228.
  background of anti-homosexuality laws 87
  comparable cultural background of moral
    slavery 102–3, 104–5
  constitutional evil of 76–105
  cultural tradition 100–1
  and dehumanization 112, 113
  and family life 119–20

feminist backlash 121
free speech as remedy for structural injustice
  181–228
gender identity 77 *et seq.*
  modernist 118
  moral arguments 98–9
  privatization of homosexuality 119
  and right to choose gay and lesbian identity
    122–3
  and right to conscience 89–90
  role of human sexuality 114–15
  and segregation 88–9
  and structural injustice 107–8
  theory of double consciousness 111
  vulnerability of gay and lesbian identity
    109–10
  see also gay rights
Honoré, Tony:
  on homosexuality 92
Hume, David:
  on race 49
Hutcheson, Francis:
  on right to marriage 82

identity:
  idea of 106
intimate life:
  right to 81–2
Israel:
  racial incitement 175–6

Jackson, Andrew:
  and free speech 128
Jacobs, Harriet:
  on racism 56
  on sexism 59
  on slavery 141
Jefferson, Thomas:
  Virginia Bill for Religious Freedom 24

Khomeini, Ayatollah 211–12
King, Martin Luther 48–9
King, Mary:
  on sexism 66
Klineberg, Otto:
  on race 52
Krafft-Ebing, Richard von:
  on homosexuality 191

limits of principle of free speech 230–9
Lincoln, Abraham:
  on constitutional morality 131
Lorca, Federico Garcia:
  on homosexuality 187–8
Lueger, Karl:
  anti-Semitism 166

McNally, Terrence:
  Corpus Christi 224–5
Madison, James:
  on free speech 24–5, 26
Mahoney, Kathleen E.:
  on pornography 204
Marshall, Thurgood:
  on racism 55–6
Mead, Margaret 63–4
Meron, Theodore:
  on contextual differences 177–8
Mill, John Stuart 16–17
Millett, Kate:
  on sexism 67
moral slavery:
  structural injustice 129–30
Myrdal, Gunnar:
  on race 52
  on sexism 63

National Organization for Women 68
Nazism:
  and human rights 155

obscenity laws 182–209
  American constitutional debate over 198–9
  and anti-Semitism 193–4
  and Canadian Supreme Court 199–201
  function of 186
  and gay rights 187–9
  pornographic images 202–3
  and psychiatry 195–6
  and rights-based feminism 183–4
  and segregation 184–5

Parker, Theodore:
  abolitionist feminism 62
Parks, Rosa 64
perfectionist models 17–22
  democracy, argument from 18–22
  and democratic constitutionalism 21–2
  restrictions on campaign expenditures 19
Plato:
  on homosexuality 97
public international law 176–80
public order law:
  Britain 171–5

Rabban, David:
  on obscenity laws 197
racism 36–59, 126–80
  American perspective 127–50
  anti-miscegenation laws 56
  constitutional evil of 36–59
  cultural definition 41–2
  and differential rewards 41
  ethical identity 39

free speech as remedy for structural injustice 126–80
  interpretive status of race 42–3
  Montesquieu on 49
  political powerlessness, theory of 37, 39–40
  and religious intolerance 42
  and right to conscience 44–5
  rights-based analogy with sexism 69–70
  and Second World War 54–5
  and sexual orientation 37
  suspect classification analysis 40–1
religious intolerance:
  and racism 42
religious persecution:
  history of 45–7
religious toleration 22–3
  development of 45–7
Robinson, Jo Ann 64
Rushdie, Salman 211–14

Sanger, Bill 81
Sanger, Margaret 81
Scarman, Lord:
  on blasphemy 216–17
Schmitt, Carl 159–60
  constitutional theory 152–5
scope of principle of free speech 239–48
Second World War:
  and racism 54–5
sexism:
  constitutional evil of 59–76
  and cultural tradition 76
  free speech as remedy for structural injustice 181–228
  and gay rights 80–1
  judicial elaboration of anti-sexist principles 75
  and moral slavery 71–2
  rights-based analogy with racism 69–70
  rights-based feminism 65–6
sexual orientation:
  and racism 37
slavery:
  and right to intimate life 83–4
Stanton, Elizabeth:
  abolitionist feminism 62
stereotypes:
  political power of enforcement of 106–7
structural injustice:
  theory of 36–125
  rationalization of 105–25
Student Non-Violent Coordinating Committee 64–5, 66

toleration:
  argument for 16–35, 36–125
toleration model 22–35
  Alien and Sedition Act 1798 25

toleration model *(cont.)*:
   and constitutional principle 34–5
   constitutional priority of free speech 27
   reasonable limits on scope of protection of free
      speech 28
   and scepticism 31–2
   and state intolerance 28–9
Trumbach, Randolph:
   on gender 221
Truth, Sojourner:
   on racism and sexism 112–13

utilitarian models 16–17

Venice:
   homosexuality in 219–20

Weimar Republic, *see* Germany
Weininger, Otto:
   on homosexuality 191–3, 194–5
Wells-Barnett, Ida:
   on racism 56
   on sexism 59
Wendell Holmes, Oliver 16
Whitman, Walt:
   on homosexuality 96, 187–8
Willard, Frances 67, 68
   on sexism 59
Witherspoon, John:
   on right to marriage 82
Wright, Richard:
   on racism 141–2